KV-029-754

EVERYMAN'S LIBRARY

Founded 1906 by J. M. Dent (d. 1926)
Edited by Ernest Rhys (d. 1946)

REFERENCE

THESAURUS OF ENGLISH WORDS AND PHRASES BY PETER ROGET · REVISED BY ANDREW BOYLE AND CHARLES LEE IN 2 VOLS.   VOL. 1

THESAURUS OF ENGLISH WORDS AND PHRASES

VOLUME ONE

PETER ROGET

LONDON: J. M. DENT & SONS LTD.
NEW YORK: E. P. DUTTON & CO. INC.

This book is copyright. It may not be
reproduced whole or in part by any method
without written permission.   Application
should be made to the publishers:

J. M. DENT & SONS LTD..
Aldine House · Bedford St. · London

Made in Great Britain
by
The Temple Press · Letchworth · Herts.
First published 1852
First published in this edition 1912
Revised and reset 1925
Further revised 1930
Last reprinted 1948

W 97/22 m

EDITORIAL NOTE

In the revision of this book I have added most of the terms made necessary by modern science. I have added, too, many foreign phrases ,and have tried to improve the Index in various ways. Where anything has become obsolete I have left it out, but I have done this very sparingly. Most of the errors I have corrected, but in such a work as this many must pass by unnoticed.

A. B.

August 1912.

NOTE TO THE 1925 EDITION

In this new revision of Roget's *Thesaurus* an attempt has been made to incorporate the many and great changes that our vocabulary has undergone since the work was first published. All obsolete words (some amusing curiosities excepted) have been removed; spellings have been modernised, naturalised words deprived of the stigma of italics, and new words and new meanings of old ones added, to the number of several thousands. In accordance with the original plan, colloquialisms and slang expressions have been freely admitted. The index has been revised, corrected and greatly augmented. Roget's system of classification, though bearing in places the marks of its early nineteenth-century origin, is still sound and serviceable, and, except for a few minor alterations, has been left unchanged.

C. L.

NOTE TO THE 1930 EDITION

In this edition a number of new words and phrases have been added, and the index has undergone a further revision.

C. L.

BIBLIOGRAPHY OF WORKS BY PETER MARK ROGET

Tentamen Physicum de Chemicæ Affinitatis Legibus, 1798; an introductory Lecture on Human and Comparative Physiology, 1826; wrote
four treatises on Electricity, Galvanism, Magnetism, Electro-Magnetism
for the Library of Useful Knowledge, 1832; Animal and Vegetable
Physiology considered with reference to Natural Theology, 2 vols., for
Bridgewater Treatises, 1834; re-issued, 1839; with additions and emenda-
tions, 1840, 1862; Physiology and Phrenology (reprinted from 7th edition
Encyclopædia Britannica), 1838; The Economic Chess-board, 1846;
Thesaurus of English Words and Phrases, 1852; 2nd edition, enlarged,
1853; 3rd edition, enlarged and improved, 1855; 4th edition, enlarged
and improved, 1856; 5th edition, enlarged, 1857; 6th, 1857; an edition
enlarged by his son, John Lewis Roget, 1879; later editions, 1888, 1896,
1899, 1901, 1904.

INTRODUCTION

THE present work is intended to supply, with respect to the English language, a desideratum hitherto unsupplied in any language; namely, a collection of the words it contains and of the idiomatic combinations peculiar to it, arranged, not in alphabetical order, as they are in a dictionary, but according to the *ideas* which they express.[1] The purpose of an ordinary dictionary is simply to explain the meaning of words; and the problem of which it professes to furnish the solution may be stated thus: The word being given, to find its signification, or the idea it is intended to convey. The object aimed at in the present undertaking is exactly the converse of this; namely, the idea being given, to find the word, or words, by which that idea may be most fitly and aptly expressed. For this purpose, the words and phrases of the language are here classed, not according to their sound or their orthography, but strictly according to their *signification*.

The communication of our thoughts by means of language, whether spoken or written, like every other object of mental exertion, constitutes a peculiar art, which, like other arts, cannot be acquired in any perfection but by long and continued practice. Some, indeed, there are, more highly gifted than others with a facility of expression, and naturally endowed with the power of eloquence; but to none is it at all times an easy process to embody in exact and appropriate language the various trains of ideas that are passing through the mind, or to depict in their true colours and proportions the diversified and nicer shades of feeling which accompany them. To those who are unpractised in the art of composition, or unused to extempore speaking, these difficulties present themselves in their most formidable aspect. However distinct may be our views, however vivid our conceptions, or however fervent our emotions, we cannot but be often conscious that the phraseology we have at our command is inadequate to do them justice. We seek in vain the words we need, and strive ineffectually to devise forms of

[1] See note on p. 16.

I

expression which shall faithfully portray our thoughts and sentiments. The appropriate terms, notwithstanding our utmost efforts, cannot be conjured up at will. Like "spirits from the vasty deep," they come not when we call; and we are driven to the employment of a set of words and phrases either too general or too limited, too strong or too feeble, which suit not the occasion, which hit not the mark we aim at; and the result of our prolonged exertion is a style at once laboured and obscure, vapid and redundant, or vitiated by the still graver faults of affectation or ambiguity.

It is to those who are thus painfully groping their way and struggling with the difficulties of composition, that this work professes to hold out a helping hand. The assistance it gives is that of furnishing on every topic a copious store of words and phrases, adapted to express all the recognisable shades and modifications of the general idea under which those words and phrases are arranged. The inquirer can readily select, out of the ample collection spread out before his eyes in the following pages, those expressions which are best suited to his purpose, and which might not have occurred to him without such assistance. In order to make this selection, he scarcely ever need engage in any elaborate or critical study of the subtle distinctions existing between synonymous terms; for if the materials set before him be sufficiently abundant, an instinctive tact will rarely fail to lead him to the proper choice. Even while glancing over the columns of this work, his eye may chance to light upon a particular term, which may save the cost of a clumsy paraphrase, or spare the labour of a tortuous circumlocution. Some felicitous turn of expression thus introduced will frequently open to the mind of the reader a whole vista of collateral ideas, which could not, without an extended and obtrusive episode, have been unfolded to his view; and often will the judicious insertion of a happy epithet, like a beam of sunshine in a landscape, illumine and adorn the subject which touches it, imparting new grace, and giving life and spirit to the picture.

Every workman in the exercise of his art should be provided with proper implements. For the fabrication of complicated and curious pieces of mechanism, the artisan requires a corresponding assortment of various tools and instruments. For giving proper effect to the fictions of the drama, the actor should have at his disposal a well-furnished wardrobe, supplying the costumes best suited to the personages he is to represent. For the perfect delineation of the beauties of nature, the painter should have within reach of his pencil every variety and combination of hues and tints. Now the writer, as well as the orator, employs for the accomplishment of his purposes the instrumentality of words; it is in words that he clothes his thoughts; it is by means of words that he depicts his feelings. It is therefore essential to his success that he be provided with a copious vocabulary, and that he possess an entire command of all the resources and appliances of his language. To the acquisition of this power no procedure appears more directly conducive than the study of a methodised system such as that now offered to his use.

The utility of the present work will be appreciated more especially by those who are engaged in the arduous process of translating into English a work written in another language. Simple as the operation may appear, on a superficial view, of rendering into English each of its sentences, the task of transfusing, with perfect exactness, the sense of the original, preserving at the same time the style and character of its composition, and reflecting with fidelity the mind and the spirit of the author, is a task of extreme difficulty. The cultivation of this useful department of literature was in ancient times strongly recommended both by Cicero and by Quintilian as essential to the formation of a good writer and accomplished orator. Regarded simply as a mental exercise, the practice of translation is the best training for the attainment of that mastery of language and felicity of diction which are the sources of the highest oratory and are requisite for the possession of a graceful and persuasive eloquence. By rendering ourselves the faithful interpreters of the thoughts and feelings of others, we are rewarded with the acquisition of greater readiness and facility in correctly expressing our own; as he who has best learned to execute the orders of a commander becomes himself best qualified to command.

In the earliest periods of civilisation, translations have been the agents for propagating knowledge from nation to nation, and the value of their labours has been inestimable; but, in the present age, when so many different languages have become the depositories of the vast treasures of literature and of science which have been accumulating for centuries, the utility of accurate translations has greatly increased, and it has become a more important object to attain perfection in the art.

The use of language is not confined to its being the medium

through which we communicate our ideas to one another; it fulfils a no less important function as an *instrument of thought*, not being merely its vehicle, but giving it wings for flight. Metaphysicians are agreed that scarcely any of our intellectual operations could be carried on to any considerable extent without the agency of words. None but those who are conversant with the philosophy of mental phenomena can be aware of the immense influence that is exercised by language in promoting the development of our ideas, in fixing them in the mind, and detaining them for steady contemplation. In every process of reasoning, language enters as an essential element. Words are the instruments by which we form all our abstractions, by which we fashion and embody our ideas, and by which we are enabled to glide along a series of premises and conclusions with a rapidity so great as to leave in the memory no trace of the successive steps of the process; and we remain unconscious how much we owe to this potent auxiliary of the reasoning faculty. It is on this ground, also, that the present work founds a claim to utility. The review of a catalogue of words of analogous signification will often suggest by association other trains of thought, which, presenting the subject under new and varied aspects, will vastly expand the sphere of our mental vision. Amidst the many objects thus brought within the range of our contemplation, some striking similitude or appropriate image, some excursive flight or brilliant conception, may flash on the mind, giving point and force to our arguments, awakening a responsive chord in the imagination or sensibility of the reader, and procuring for our reasonings a more ready access both to his understanding and to his heart.

It is of the utmost consequence that strict accuracy should regulate our use of language, and that every one should acquire the power and the habit of expressing his thoughts with perspicuity and correctness. Few, indeed, can appreciate the real extent and importance of that influence which language has always exercised on human affairs, or can be aware how often these are determined by causes much slighter than are apparent to a superficial observer. False logic, disguised under specious phraseology, too often gains the assent of the unthinking multitude, disseminating far and wide the seeds of prejudice and error. Truisms pass current, and wear the semblance of profound wisdom, when dressed up in the tinsel garb of antithetical phrases, or set off by an imposing pomp of paradox. By a confused jargon of involved and mystical sentences, the imagination is easily inveigled into a transcendental region of clouds, and the understanding beguiled into the belief that it is acquiring knowledge and approaching truth. A misapplied or misapprehended term is sufficient to give rise to fierce and interminable disputes: a misnomer has turned the tide of popular opinion; a verbal sophism has decided a party question; an artful watchword, thrown among combustible materials, has kindled the flames of deadly warfare, and changed the destiny of an empire.

In constructing the following system of classification of the ideas which are expressible by language, my chief aim has been to obtain the greatest amount of practical utility. I have accordingly adopted such principles of arrangement as appeared to me to be the simplest and most natural, and which would not require, either for their comprehension or application, any disciplined acumen, or depth of metaphysical or antiquarian lore. Eschewing all needless refinements and subtleties, I have taken as my guide the more obvious characters of the ideas for which expressions were to be tabulated, arranging them under such classes and categories as reflection and experience had taught me would conduct the inquirer most readily and quickly to the object of his search. Commencing with the ideas expressing mere abstract relations, I proceed to those which relate to the phenomena of the material world, and lastly to those in which the mind is concerned, and which comprehend intellect, volition, and feeling; thus establishing six primary Classes of Categories.

1. The first of these classes comprehends ideas derived from the more general and ABSTRACT RELATIONS among things, such as *Existence, Resemblance, Quantity, Order, Number, Time, Power*.

2. The second class refers to SPACE and its various relations, including *Motion*, or change of place.

3. The third class includes all ideas that relate to the MATERIAL WORLD; namely, the *Properties of Matter*, such as *Solidity, Fluidity, Heat, Sound, Light,* and the *Phenomena* they present, as well as the simple *Perceptions* to which they give rise.

4. The fourth class embraces all ideas of phenomena relating to the INTELLECT and its operations; comprising the *Acquisition*, the *Retention*, and the *Communication of Ideas*.

5. The fifth class includes the ideas derived from the exercise of VOLITION; embracing the phenomena and results of our *Voluntary and Active Powers*; such as *Choice, Intention, Utility, Action, Antagonism, Authority, Compact, Property*, etc.

6. The sixth and last class comprehends all ideas derived from the operation of our SENTIENT AND MORAL POWERS; including our *Feelings, Emotions, Passions*, and *Moral and Religious Sentiments*.[1]

The further subdivisions and minuter details will be best understood from an inspection of the Tabular Synopsis of Categories prefixed to the work, in which are specified the several *topics* or *heads of signification*, under which the words have been arranged. By the aid of this table, the reader will, with a little practice, readily discover the place which the particular topic he is in search of occupies in the series; and on turning to the page in the body of the work which contains it, he will find the group of expressions he requires, out of which he may cull those that are most appropriate to his purpose. For the convenience of reference, I have designated each separate group or heading by a particular number; so that if, during the search, any doubt or difficulty should occur, recourse may be had to the copious alphabetical index of words in the second volume, which will at once indicate the number of the required group.[2]

The object I have proposed to myself in this work would have been but imperfectly attained if I had confined myself to a mere catalogue of words, and had omitted the numerous phrases and forms of expression, composed of several words, which are of such frequent use as to entitle them to rank among the con-

---

[1] It must necessarily happen in every system of classification framed with this view, that ideas and expressions arranged under one class must include also ideas relating to another class; for the operations of the *Intellect* generally involve also those of the *Will*, and *vice versa*; and our *Affections* and *Emotions*, in like manner, generally imply the agency both of the *Intellect* and the *Will*. All that can be effected, therefore, is to arrange the words according to the principal or dominant idea they convey. *Teaching*, for example, although a Voluntary act, relates primarily to the Communication of Ideas, and is accordingly placed at No. 537, under Class IV. Division II. On the other hand, *Choice, Conduct, Skill*, etc., although implying the co-operation of Voluntary with Intellectual acts, relate principally to the former, and are therefore arranged under Class V.

[2] It often happens that the same word admits of various applications, or may be used in different senses. In consulting the Index the reader will be guided to the number of the heading under which that word, in each particular acceptation, will be found, by means of *supplementary words*, printed in italics; which words, however, are not to be understood as explaining the meaning of the word to which they are annexed, but only assisting in the required reference. I have also, for shortness' sake, generally omitted words immediately derived from the primary one inserted, which sufficiently represents the whole group of correlative words referable to the same heading. Thus the number affixed to *Beauty* applies to all its derivatives, such as *Beautiful, Beauteous, Beautify, Beautifulness, Beautifully*, etc., the insertion of which was therefore needless.

stituent parts of the language.[1] Very few of these verbal combinations, so essential to the knowledge of our native tongue, and so profusely abounding in its daily use, are to be met with in ordinary dictionaries. These phrases and forms of expression I have endeavoured diligently to collect and to insert in their proper places, under the general ideas they are designed to convey. Some of these conventional forms, indeed, partake of the nature of proverbial expressions; but actual proverbs, as such, being wholly of a didactic character, do not come within the scope of the present work; and the reader must therefore not expect to find them here inserted.

For the purpose of exhibiting with greater distinctness the relations between words expressing opposite and correlative ideas, I have, whenever the subject admitted of such an arrangement, placed them in two parallel columns in the same page, so that each group of expressions may be readily contrasted with those which occupy the adjacent column, and constitute their antitheses. By carrying the eye from the one to the other, the inquirer may often discover forms of expression of which he may avail himself advantageously to diversify and infuse vigour into his phraseology. Rhetoricians, indeed, are well aware of the power derived from the skilful introduction of antitheses in giving point to an argument, and imparting force and brilliancy to the diction. A too frequent and indiscreet employment of this figure of rhetoric may, it is true, give rise to a vicious and affected style; but it is unreasonable to condemn indiscriminately the occasional and moderate use of a practice on account of its possible abuse.

The study of correlative terms existing in a particular language may often throw valuable light on the manners and customs of the nations using it. Thus, Hume has drawn important inferences with regard to the state of society among the ancient Romans, from certain deficiencies which he remarked in the Latin language.[2]

[1] For example: To take time by the forelock,—to turn over a new leaf,—to show the white feather,—to have a finger in the pie,—to let the cat out of the bag,—to take care of number one,—to kill two birds with one stone, etc., etc.

[2] "It is an universal observation," he remarks, "which we may form upon language, that where two related parts of a whole bear any proportion to each other, in numbers, rank, or consideration, there are always correlative terms invented which answer to both the parts and express their mutual relation. If they bear no proportion to each other, the term is only invented for the less, and marks its distinction from the whole. Thus, *man* and *woman*, *master* and *servant*, *father* and *son*, *prince* and *subject*, *stranger* and *citizen*, are correlative terms. But the words *sea-*

In many cases, two ideas, which are completely opposed to each other, admit of an intermediate or neutral idea, equidistant from both: all these being expressible by corresponding definite terms. Thus, in the following examples, the words in the first and third columns, which express opposite ideas, admit of the intermediate terms contained in the middle column having a neutral sense with reference to the former:

Identity,	*Difference,*	*Contrariety.*
Beginning,	*Middle,*	*End.*
Past,	*Present,*	*Future.*

In other cases, the intermediate word is simply the negative to each of two opposite positions; as, for example—

Convexity,	*Flatness,*	*Concavity.*
Desire,	*Indifference,*	*Aversion.*

Sometimes the intermediate word is properly the standard with which each of the extremes is compared; as in the case of

Insufficiency,   *Sufficiency,*   *Redundance ;*

for here the middle term, *Sufficiency,* is equally opposed, on the one hand to *Insufficiency,* and on the other to *Redundance.*

These forms of correlative expressions would suggest the use of triple, instead of double, columns for tabulating this threefold order of words; but the practical inconvenience attending such an arrangement would probably overbalance its advantages.

It often happens that the same word has several correlative terms, according to the different relations in which it is con-

---

man, carpenter, smith, tailor, etc., have no correspondent terms which express those who are no seamen, no carpenters, etc. Languages differ very much with regard to the particular words where this distinction obtains; and may thence afford very strong inferences concerning the manners and customs of different nations. The military government of the Roman emperors had exalted the soldiery so high, that they balanced all the other orders of the state: hence *miles* and *paganus* became relative terms; a thing, till then, unknown to ancient, and still so to modern languages."—"The term for a slave, born and bred in the family, was *verna.* As *servus* was the name of the genus, and *verna* of the species without any correlative, this forms a strong presumption that the latter were by far the least numerous: and from the same principles I infer that if the number of slaves brought by the Romans from foreign countries had not extremely exceeded those which were bred at home, *verna* would have had a correlative, which would have expressed the former species of slaves. But these, it would seem, composed the main body of the ancient slaves, and the latter were but a few exceptions."—HUME, *Essay on the Populousness of Ancient Nations.*

The warlike propensity of the same nation may in a like manner be inferred from the use of the word *hostis* to denote both a *foreigner* and an *enemy.*

sidered. Thus, to the word *Giving* are opposed both *Receiving* and *Taking*; the former correlation having reference to the *persons* concerned in the transfer, while the latter relates to the *mode* of transfer. *Old* has for opposite both *New* and *Young*, according as it is applied to *things* or to *living beings*. *Attack* and *Defence* are correlative terms; as are also *Attack* and *Resistance*. *Resistance*, again, has for its other correlative *Submission*. *Truth in the abstract* is opposed to *Error*; but the opposite of *Truth communicated* is *Falsehood*. *Acquisition* is contrasted both with *Deprivation* and with *Loss*. *Refusal* is the counterpart both of *Offer* and of *Consent*. *Disuse* and *Misuse* may either of them be considered as the correlative of *Use*. *Teaching*, with reference to what is taught, is opposed to *Misteaching*; but with reference to the act itself, its proper reciprocal is *Learning*.

Words contrasted in form do not always bear the same contrast in their meaning. The word *Malefactor*, for example, would, from its derivation, appear to be exactly the opposite of *Benefactor*; but the ideas attached to these two words are far from being directly opposed; for while the latter expresses one who confers a benefit, the former denotes one who has violated the laws.

Independently of the immediate practical uses derivable from the arrangement of words in double columns, many considerations, interesting in a philosophical point of view, are presented by the study of correlative expressions. It will be found, on strict examination, that there seldom exists an exact opposition between two words which may at first sight appear to be the counterparts of one another; for, in general, the one will be found to possess in reality more force or extent of meaning than the other with which it is contrasted. The correlative term sometimes assumes the form of a mere negative, although it is really endowed with a considerable positive force. Thus *Disrespect* is not merely the absence of *Respect*; its signification trenches on the opposite idea, namely, *Contempt*. In like manner, *Untruth* is not merely the negative of *Truth*; it involves a degree of *Falsehood*. *Irreligion*, which is properly *the want of Religion*, is understood as being nearly synonymous with *Impiety*. For these reasons, the reader must not expect that all the words which stand side by side in the two columns shall be the precise correlatives of each other; for the nature of the subject, as well as the imperfections of language, renders it impossible always to preserve such an exactness of correlation.

There exist comparatively few words of a general character to which no correlative term, either of negation or of opposition, can be assigned, and which therefore require no corresponding second column. The correlative idea, especially that which constitutes a sense negative to the primary one, may, indeed, be formed or conceived; but, from its occurring rarely, no word has been framed to represent it; for in language, as in other matters, the supply fails when there is no probability of a demand. Occasionally we find this deficiency provided for by the contrivance of prefixing the syllable *non*; as, for instance, the negatives of *existence, performance, payment*, etc., are expressed by the compound words, *non-existence, non-performance, non-payment*, etc. Functions of a similar kind are performed by the prefixes *dis-*,[1] *anti-, contra-, mis-, in-*, and *un*.[2] With respect to all these, and especially the last, great latitude is allowed according to the necessities of the case; a latitude which is limited only by the taste and discretion of the author.

On the other hand, it is hardly possible to find two words having in all respects the same meaning, and being therefore interchangeable; that is, admitted of being employed indiscriminately, the one or the other, in all their applications. The investigation of the distinctions to be drawn between words apparently synonymous forms a separate branch of inquiry which I have not presumed here to enter upon; for the subject has already occupied the attention of much abler critics than myself, and its complete exhaustion would require the devotion of a whole life. The purpose of this work, it must be borne in mind, is not to explain the signification of words, but simply to classify and arrange them according to the sense in which they are now used, and which I presume to be already known to the reader. I enter into no inquiry into the changes of meaning they may have undergone in the course of time.[3] I am content to accept them at the value of their present currency,

---

[1] The word *disannul*, however, had the same meaning as *annul*.

[2] In the case of adjectives, the addition to a substantive of the terminal syllable *less*, gives it a negative meaning: as *taste, tasteless*: *care, careless*; *hope, hopeless*; *friend, friendless*; *fault, faultless*, etc.

[3] Such changes are innumerable; for instance, the words *tyrant, parasite, sophist, churl, knave, villain*, anciently conveyed no opprobrious meaning. *Impertinent* merely expressed *irrelative*; and implied neither *rudeness* nor *intrusion*, as it does at present. *Indifferent* originally meant *impartial*; *extravagant* was simply *digressive*; and *to prevent* was properly to *precede* and *assist*. The old translations of the Scriptures furnish many striking examples of the alterations which time has brought in the signification of words. Much curious information on this subject is contained in Trench's *Lectures on the Study of Words*.

and have no concern with their etymologies, or with the history of their transformations; far less do I venture to thrid the mazes of the vast labyrinth into which I should be led by any attempt at a general discrimination of synonyms. The difficulties I have had to contend with have already been sufficiently great without this addition to my labours.

The most cursory glance over the pages of a dictionary will show that a great number of words are used in various senses, sometimes distinguished by slight shades of difference, but often diverging widely from their primary signification, and even, in some cases, bearing to it no perceptible relation. It may even happen that the very same word has two significations quite opposite to one another. This is the case with the verb *to cleave*, which means *to adhere tenaciously*, and also *to separate by a blow*. *To propugn* sometimes expresses *to attack*; at other times, *to defend*. *To ravel* means both *to entangle* and *to disentangle*. The alphabetical index at the end of this work sufficiently shows the multiplicity of uses to which, by the elasticity of language, the meaning of words has been stretched so as to adapt them to a great variety of modified significations in subservience to the nicer shades of thought which, under peculiarity of circumstances, require corresponding expression. Words thus admitting of different meanings have therefore to be arranged under each of the respective heads corresponding to these various acceptations. There are many words, again, which express ideas compounded of two elementary ideas belonging to different classes. It is therefore necessary to place these words respectively under each of the generic heads to which they relate. The necessity of these repetitions is increased by the circumstance that ideas included under one class are often connected by relations of the same kind as the ideas which belong to another class. Thus we find the same relations of *order* and of *quantity* existing among the ideas of *Time* as well as those of *Space*. Sequence in the one is denoted by the same terms as sequence in the other; and the measures of time also express the measures of space. The cause and the effect are often designated by the same word. The word *Sound*, for instance, denotes both the impression made upon the ear by sonorous vibrations, and also the vibrations themselves, which are the cause or source of that impression. *Mixture* is used for the act of mixing, as well as for the product of that operation. *Taste* and *Smell* express both the sensations and the qualities of material bodies giving rise to them. *Thought* is the act of thinking; but the same word denotes also the idea resulting from that act. *Judgment* is the act of deciding, and also the decision come to. *Purchase* is the acquisition of a thing by payment, as well as the thing itself so acquired. *Speech* is both the act of speaking and the words spoken; and so on with regard to an endless multiplicity of words. Mind is essentially distinct from Matter; and yet, in all languages, the attributes of the one are metaphorically transferred to those of the other. Matter, in all its forms, is endowed by the figurative genius of every language with the functions which pertain to intellect; and we perpetually talk of its phenomena and of its powers as if they resulted from the voluntary influence of one body on another, acting and reacting, impelling and being impelled, controlling and being controlled, as if animated by spontaneous energies and guided by specific intentions. On the other hand, expressions of which the primary signification refers exclusively to the properties and actions of matter are metaphorically applied to the phenomena of thought and volition, and even to the feelings and passions of the soul; and in speaking of a *ray of hope*, a *shade of doubt*, a *flight of fancy*, a *flash of wit*, the *warmth of emotion*, or the *ebullitions of anger*, we are scarcely conscious that we are employing metaphors which have this material origin.

As a general rule, I have deemed it incumbent on me to place words and phrases which appertain more especially to one head also under the other heads to which they have a relation, whenever it appeared to me that this repetition would suit the convenience of the inquirer, and spare him the trouble of turning to other parts of the work; for I have always preferred to subject myself to the imputation of redundance, rather than incur the reproach of insufficiency.[1] When, however, the divergence ofthe associated from the primary idea is sufficiently marked, I have contented myself with making a reference to the place where the modified signification will be found. But in

---

[1] Frequent repetitions of the same series of expressions, accordingly, will be met with under various headings. For example, the word *Relinquishment*, with its synonyms, occurs as a heading at No. 624, where it applies to *intention*, and also at No. 782, where it refers to *property*. The word *Chance* has two significations, distinct from one another: the one implying the *absence of an assignable* cause; in which case it comes under the category of the relation of Causation, and occupies the No. 156: the other, the *absence of design*, in which latter sense it ranks under the operations of the Will, and has assigned to it the place No. 621. I have, in like manner, distinguished *Sensibility, Pleasure, Pain, Taste*, etc., according as they relate to *Physical* or to *Moral Affections*; the former being found at Nos. 375, 377, 378, 390, etc., and the latter at Nos. 822, 827, 828, 850, etc.

order to prevent needless extension, I have, in general, omitted *conjugate words* [1] which are so obviously derivable from those that are given in the same place, that the reader may safely be left to form them for himself. This is the case with adverbs derived from adjectives by the simple addition of the terminal syllable *-ly*; such as *closely, carefully, safely*, etc., from *close, careful, safe*, etc., and also with adjectives or participles immediately derived from the verbs which are already given. In all such cases, an "etc." indicates that reference is understood to be made to these roots. I have observed the same rule in compiling the index; retaining only the primary or more simple word, and omitting the conjugate words obviously derived from them. Thus I assume the word *short* as the representative of its immediate derivatives *shortness, shorten, shortening, shortened, shorter, shortly*, which would have had the same references, and which the reader can readily supply.

The same verb is frequently used indiscriminately either in the active or transitive, or in the neuter or intransitive sense. In these cases I have generally not thought it worth while to increase the bulk of the work by the needless repetition of that word; for the reader, whom I suppose to understand the use of the words, must also be presumed to be competent to apply them correctly.

There are a multitude of words of a specific character, which although they properly occupy places in the columns of a dictionary, yet, having no relation to general ideas, do not come within the scope of this compilation, and are consequently omitted. The names of objects in Natural History, and technical terms belonging exclusively to Science or to Art, or relating to particular operations, and of which the signification is restricted to those specific objects, come under this category. Exceptions must, however, be made in favour of such words as admit of metaphorical application to general subjects with which custom has associated them, and of which they may be cited as being typical or illustrative. Thus, the word *Lion* will find a place under the head of *Courage*, of which it is regarded as the type. *Anchor*, being emblematic of *Hope*, is introduced among the words expressing that emotion; and, in like manner, *butterfly* and *weathercock*, which are suggestive of fickleness, are included in the category of *Irresolution*.

[1] By "*conjugate* or *paronymous* words is meant, correctly speaking, different parts of speech from the same root, which exactly correspond in point of meaning."—*A Selection of English Synonyms*, edited by Archbishop Whately.

With regard to the admission of many words and expressions which the classical reader might be disposed to condemn as vulgarisms, or which he, perhaps, might stigmatise as pertaining rather to the slang than to the legitimate language of the day, I would beg to observe that, having due regard to the uses to which this work was to be adapted, I did not feel myself justified in excluding them solely on that ground, if they possessed an acknowledged currency in general intercourse. It is obvious that, with respect to degrees of conventionality, I could not have attempted to draw any strict lines of demarcation; and far less could I have presumed to erect any absolute standard of purity. My object, be it remembered, is not to regulate the use of words, but simply to supply and to suggest such as may be wanted on occasion, leaving the proper selection entirely to the discretion and taste of the employer. If a novelist or a dramatist, for example, proposed to delineate some vulgar personage, he would wish to have the power of putting into the mouth of the speaker expressions that would accord with his character; just as the actor, to revert to a former comparison, who had to personate a peasant, would choose for his attire the most homely garb, and would have just reason to complain if the theatrical wardrobe furnished him with no suitable costume.

Words which have, in process of time, become obsolete, are of course rejected from this collection. On the other hand, I have admitted a considerable number of words and phrases borrowed from other languages, chiefly the French and Latin, some of which may be considered as already naturalised; while others, though avowedly foreign, are frequently introduced in English composition, particularly in familiar style, on account of their being peculiarly expressive, and because we have no corresponding words of equal force in our own language.[1] The rapid advances which are being made in scientific knowledge, and consequent improvement in all the arts of life, and the extension of those arts and sciences to so many new purposes and objects, create a continual demand for the formation of new terms to express new agencies, new wants, and new combinations. Such terms, from being at first merely technical, are rendered, by more general use, familiar to the multitude, and having a well-defined acceptation, are eventually incorporated into the language, which they contribute to enlarge and to enrich. *Neologies* of this kind are perfectly legitimate, and highly advantageous; and they necessarily introduce those

[1] All these words and phrases are printed in italics.

gradual and progressive changes which every language is destined to undergo.[1] Some modern writers, however, have indulged in a habit of arbitrarily fabricating new words and a new-fangled phraseology without any necessity, and with manifest injury to the purity of the language. This vicious practice, the offspring of indolence or conceit, implies an ignorance or neglect of the riches in which the English language already abounds, and which would have supplied them with words of recognised legitimacy, conveying precisely the same meaning as those they so recklessly coin in the illegal mint of their own fancy.

A work constructed on the plan of classification I have proposed might, if ably executed, be of great value in tending to limit the fluctuations to which language has always been subject, by establishing an authoritative standard for its regulation. Future historians, philologists, and lexicographers, when investigating the period when new words were introduced, or discussing the import given at the present time to the old, might find their labours lightened by being enabled to appeal to such a standard, instead of having to search for data among the scattered writings of the age. Nor would its utility be confined to a single language; for the principles of its construction are universally applicable to all languages, whether living or dead. On the same plan of classification there might be formed a French, a German, a Latin, or a Greek Thesaurus, possessing, in their respective spheres, the same advantages as those of the English model. Still more useful would be a conjunction of these methodised compilations in two languages, the French and the English, for instance; the columns of each being placed in parallel juxtaposition. No means yet devised would so greatly facilitate the acquisition of the one language by those who are acquainted with the other: none would afford such ample assistance to the translator in either language; and none would supply such ready and effectual means of instituting an accurate comparison between them, and of fairly appreciating their respective merits and defects. In a still higher degree

[1] Thus in framing the present classification I have frequently felt the want of substantive terms corresponding to abstract qualities or ideas denoted by certain adjectives, and have been often tempted to invent words that might express these abstractions; but I have yielded to this temptation only in the four following instances: having framed from the adjectives *irrelative, amorphous, sinistral,* and *gaseous* the abstract nouns *irrelation, amorphism, sinistrality,* and *gaseity.* I have ventured also to introduce the adjective *intersocial* to express the active voluntary relations between man and man.

would all those advantages be combined and multiplied in a *Polyglot Lexicon* constructed on this system.

Metaphysicians engaged in the more profound investigation of the Philosophy of Language will be materially assisted by having the ground thus prepared for them in a previous analysis and classification of our ideas; for such classification of ideas is the true basis on which words, which are their symbols, should be classified.[1] It is by such analysis alone that we can arrive at a clear perception of the relation which these symbols bear to their corresponding ideas, or can obtain a correct knowledge of the elements which enter into the formation of compound ideas, and of the exclusions by which we arrive at the abstractions so perpetually resorted to in the process of reasoning, and in the communication of our thoughts.

Lastly, such analyses alone can determine the principles on

---

[1] The principle by which I have been guided in framing my verbal classification is the same as that which is employed in the various departments of natural history. Thus the sectional divisions I have formed correspond to natural families in botany and zoology, and the filiation of words presents a network analogous to the natural filiation of plants or animals.

The following are the only publications that have come to my knowledge in which any attempt has been made to construct a systematic arrangement of Ideas with a view to their expression. The earliest of these, supposed to be at least nine hundred years old, is the AMERA CÓSHA, or *Vocabulary of the Sanscrit Language*, by Amera Sinha, of which an English translation, by the late Henry T. Colebrooke, was printed at Serampoor in the year 1808. The classification of words is there, as might be expected, exceedingly imperfect and confused, especially in all that relates to abstract Ideas or mental operations. This will be apparent from the very title of the first section, which comprehends "*Heaven, Gods, Demons, Fire, Air, Velocity, Eternity, Much*"; while *Sin, Virtue, Happiness, Destiny, Cause, Nature, Intellect, Reasoning, Knowledge, Senses, Tastes, Odours, Colours*, are all included and jumbled together in the fourth section. A more logical order, however, pervades the sections relating to natural objects, such as *Seas, Earth, Towns, Plants*, and *Animals*, which form separate classes; exhibiting a remarkable effort at analysis at so remote a period of Indian literature.

The well-known work of Bishop Wilkins, entitled *An Essay towards a Real Character and a Philosophical Language*, published in 1668, had for its object the formation of a system of symbols which might serve as a universal language. It professed to be founded on a "scheme of analysis of the things or notions to which names were to be assigned"; but notwithstanding the immense labour and ingenuity expended in the construction of this system, it was soon found to be far too abstruse and recondite for practical application.

In the year 1797 there appeared in Paris an anonymous work, entitled *Pasigraphie, ou Premiers Éléments du nouvel Art-Science d'écrire et d'imprimer une langue de manière à être lu et entendu dans toute autre langue sans traduction*, of which an edition in German was also published. It contains a great number of tabular schemes of categories, all of which appear to be excessively arbitrary and artificial, and extremely difficult of application, as well as of apprehension.

which a strictly *Philosophical Language* might be constructed. The probable result of the construction of such a language would be its eventual adoption by every civilised nation; thus realising that splendid aspiration of philanthropists—the establishment of a Universal Language. However Utopian such a project may appear to the present generation, and however abortive may have been the former endeavours of Bishop Wilkins and others to realise it,[1] its accomplishment is surely not beset with greater difficulties than have impeded the progress to many other beneficial objects which in former times appeared to be no less visionary, and which yet were successfully achieved, in later ages, by the continued and persevering exertions of the human intellect. Is there at the present day, then, any ground for despair that, at some future stage of that higher civilisation to which we trust the world is gradually tending, some new and bolder effort of genius towards the solution of this great problem may be crowned with success, and compass an object of such vast and paramount utility? Nothing, indeed, would conduce more directly to bring about a golden age of union and harmony among the several nations and races of mankind than the removal of that barrier to the interchange of thought and mutual good understanding between man and man which is now interposed by the diversity of their respective languages.

[1] "The languages," observes Horne Tooke, "which are commonly used throughout the world, are much more simple and easy, convenient and philosophical, than Wilkins's scheme for a *real character*; or than any other scheme that has been at any other time imagined or proposed for the purpose."—Ἔπεα Πτερόεντα, p. 125.

PLAN OF CLASSIFICATION

TABULAR SYNOPSIS OF CATEGORIES

CLASS I. ABSTRACT RELATIONS

I. EXISTENCE

1°. ABSTRACT	.	1. Existence.	2. Inexistence.
2°. CONCRETE	.	3. Substantiality.	4. Unsubstantiality
3°. FORMAL	.	*Internal.*	*External.*
		5. Intrinsicality.	6. Extrinsicality.
4°. MODAL	.	*Absolute.*	*Relative.*
		7. State.	8. Circumstance.

II. RELATION

1°. ABSOLUTE	.	9. Relation.	10. Irrelation.
		11. Consanguinity.	
		12. Reciprocality.	
		13. Identity.	14. Contrariety.
			15. Difference.
2°. CONTINUOUS	.	16. Uniformity.	
		17. Similarity.	18. Dissimilarity.
3°. PARTIAL	.	19. Imitation.	20. { Non-imitation. Variation.
		21. Copy.	22. Prototype.
4°. GENERAL	.	23. Agreement.	24. Disagreement.

III. QUANTITY

		Absolute.	*Relative.*
1°. SIMPLE	.	25. Quantity.	26. Degree.
		27. Equality.	28. Inequality.
		29. Mean.	
		30. Compensation.	
		By comparison with a Standard.	
2°. COMPARATIVE		31. Greatness.	32. Smallness.
		By comparison with a similar Object.	
		33. Superiority.	34. Inferiority.
		Changes in Quantity.	
		35. Increase.	36. Decrease.
		37. Addition.	38. { Non-addition. Subduction.
		39. Adjunct.	40. Remainder.
3°. CONJUNCTIVE		41. Mixture.	42. Simpleness.
		43. Junction.	44. Disjunction.
		45. Vinculum.	
		46. Coherence.	47. Incoherence.
		48. Combination.	49. Decomposition.

4°. CONCRETE	50. Whole.	51. Part.
	52. Completeness.	53. Incompleteness.
	54. Composition.	55. Exclusion.
	56. Component.	57. Extraneousness.

IV. ORDER

1°. GENERAL	58. Order.	59. Disorder.
	60. Arrangement.	61. Derangement.
2°. CONSECUTIVE	62. Precedence.	63. Sequence.
	64. Precursor.	65. Sequel.
	66. Beginning.	67. End.
	68. Middle.	
	69. Continuity.	70. Discontinuity.
	71. Term.	
3°. COLLECTIVE	72. Assemblage.	73. { Non-assemblage. Dispersion. }
	74. Focus.	
4°. DISTRIBUTIVE	75. Class.	
	76. Inclusion.	77. Exclusion.
	78. Generality.	79. Speciality.
5°. CATEGORICAL	80. Rule.	81. Multiformity.
	82. Conformity.	83. Unconformity.

V. NUMBER

1°. ABSTRACT	84. Number.	
	85. Numeration.	
	86. List.	
2°. DETERMINATE	87. Unity.	88. Accompaniment.
	89. Duality.	
	90. Duplication.	91. Bisection.
	92. Triality.	
	93. Triplication.	94. Trisection.
	95. Quaternity.	
	96. Quadruplication.	97. Quadrisection.
	98. Five, &c.	99. Quinquesection,&c.
3°. INDETER- MINATE	100. Plurality.	101. Zero.
	102. Multitude.	103. Fewness.
	104. Repetition.	
	105. Infinity.	

VI. TIME

1°. ABSOLUTE	106. Duration.	107. Neverness.
	Definite.	*Indefinite.*
	108. Period.	109. Course.
	110. Diuturnity.	111. Transientness.
	112. Perpetuity.	113. Instantaneity.
	114. Chronometry.	115. Anachronism.

2°. RELATIVE—

to Succession .
- 116. Priority.
- 117. Posteriority.
- 118. Present time.
- 119. Different time.
- 120. Synchronism.
- 121. Futurity.
- 122. Preterition.

to a Period .
- 123. Newness.
- 124. Oldness.
- 125. Morning.
- 126. Evening.
- 127. Youth.
- 128. Age.
- 129. Infant.
- 130. Veteran.
- 131. Adolescence.

to an Effect or Purpose
- 132. Earliness.
- 133. Lateness.
- 134. Opportunity.
- 135. Intempestivity.

3°. RECURRENT .
- 136. Frequency.
- 137. Infrequency.
- 138. Periodicity.
- 139. Irregularity

VII. CHANGE

1°. SIMPLE .
- 140. Change.
- 141. Cessation.
- 142. Permanence.
- 143. Continuance.
- 144. Conversion.
- 145. Reversion.
- 146. Revolution.
- 147. Substitution.
- 148. Interchange.

2°. COMPLEX .
- 149. Mutability.
- 150. Immutability.
- *Present.*
- *Future.*
- 151. Eventuality.
- 152. Destiny.

VIII. CAUSATION

1°. CONSTANCY OF SEQUENCE
- 153. { *Constant Antecedent.* Cause. }
- 154. { *Constant Sequent.* Effect. }
- 155. { *Assignment of Cause.* Attribution. }
- 156. { *Absence of Assignment.* Chance. }

2°. CONNECTION BETWEEN CAUSE AND EFFECT
- 157. Power.
- 158. Impotence.

Degrees of Power.
- 159. Strength.
- 160. Weakness.

3°. POWER IN OPERATION
- 161. Production.
- 162. Destruction.
- 163. Reproduction.
- 164. Producer.
- 165. Destroyer.
- 166. Paternity.
- 167. Posterity.
- 168. Productiveness.
- 169. Unproductiveness.
- 170. Agency.
- 171. Energy.
- 172. Inertness.
- 173. Violence.
- 174. Moderation.

4°. INDIRECT POWER
- 175. Influence.
- 176. Tendency.
- 177. Liability.

5°. COMBINATIONS OF CAUSES
- 178. Concurrence.
- 179. Counteraction.

CLASS II. SPACE

I. SPACE IN GENERAL

1°. ABSTRACT SPACE	180. *Indefinite.* Space.	181.	*Definite.* Region.
		182.	*Limited.* Place.
2°. RELATIVE SPACE	183. Situation. 184. Location.	185. Displacement.	
3°. EXISTENCE IN SPACE	186. Presence. 188. Inhabitant. 190. Contents.	187. Absence. 189. Abode. 191. Receptacle.	

II. DIMENSIONS

1°. GENERAL	192. Size. 194. Expansion. 196. Distance. 198. Interval.	193. Littleness. 195. Contraction. 197. Nearness. 199. Contiguity.	
2°. LINEAR	200. Length. 202. Breadth. Thickness. 204. Layer. 206. Height. 208. Depth. 210. Summit. 212. Verticality. 214. Pendency. 216. Parallelism. 218. Inversion.	201. Shortness. 203. Narrowness. Thinness. 205. Filament. 207. Lowness. 209. Shallowness. 211. Base. 213. Horizontality. 215. Support. 217. Obliquity. 219. Crossing.	
3°. CENTRICAL—			
General	220. Exteriority. 222. Covering. 225. Investment. 227. Circumjacence. 229. Outline. 230. Edge. 231. Circumscription. 232. Enclosure. 233. Limit.	221. Interiority. 223. Centrality. 224. Lining. 226. Divestment. 228. Interjacence.	
Special	234. Front. 236. Laterality. 238. Dextrality.	235. Rear. 237. Antiposition. 239. Sinistrality.	

III. FORM

1°. GENERAL	240. Form. 242. Symmetry.	241. Amorphism. 243. Distortion.	

2°. SPECIAL .

- 244. Angularity.
- 245. Curvature.   246. Straightness.
- 247. Circularity.   248. Convolution.
- 249. Rotundity.

3°. SUPERFICIAL .

- 250. Convexity.   251. Flatness.
-                      252. Concavity.
- 253. Sharpness.   254. Bluntness.
- 255. Smoothness.   256. Roughness.
- 257. Notch.
- 258. Fold.
- 259. Furrow.
- 260. Opening.   261. Closure.
- 262. Perforator.   263. Stopper.

IV. MOTION

1°. MOTION IN GENERAL

- 264. Motion.   265. Quiescence.
- 266. Journey.   267. Navigation.
- 268. Traveller.   269. Mariner.
- 270. Transference.
- 271. Carrier.
- 272. Vehicle.   273. Ship.

2°. DEGREES OF MOTION

- 274. Velocity.   275. Slowness.

3°. CONJOINED WITH FORCE

- 276. Impulse.   277. Recoil.

4°. WITH REFERENCE TO DIRECTION

- 278. Direction.   279. Deviation.
- 280. Percession.   281. Sequence.
- 282. Progression.   283. Regression.
- 284. Propulsion.   285. Traction.
- 286. Approach.   287. Recession.
- 288. Attraction.   289. Repulsion.
- 290. Convergence.   291. Divergence.
- 292. Arrival.   293. Departure.
- 294. Ingress.   295. Egress.
- 296. Reception.   297. Ejection.
- 298. Food.   299. Excretion.
- 298a. Tobacco.
- 300. Insertion.   301. Extraction.
- 303. Passage.
- 303. Transcursion.   304. Shortcoming.
- 305. Ascent.   306. Descent.
- 307. Elevation.   308. Depression.
- 309. Leap.   310. Plunge.
- 311. Circuition.
- 312. Rotation.   313. Evolution.
- 314. Oscillation.
- 315. Agitation.

CLASS III. MATTER

I. MATTER IN GENERAL

316. Materiality.	317. Immateriality.
318. World.	
319. Gravity.	320. Levity.

II. INORGANIC MATTER

	321. Density.	322. Rarity.
	323. Hardness.	324. Softness.
	325. Elasticity.	326. Inelasticity.
1°. SOLIDS	327. Tenacity.	328. Brittleness.
	329. Texture.	
	330. Pulverulence.	
	331. Friction.	332. Lubrication.
2°. FLUIDS— 1. *In General*	333. { Fluidity. / Liquidity. }	334. Gaseity.
	335. Liquefaction.	336. Vaporisation.
	337. Water.	338. Air.
	339. Moisture.	340. Dryness.
2. *Specific*	341. Ocean.	342. Land.
	343. { Gulf. / Lake. }	344. Plain.
	345. Marsh.	346. Island.
	347. Stream.	
3. *In Motion*	348. River.	349. Wind.
	350. Conduit.	351. Air-pipe.
3°. IMPERFECT FLUIDS	352. Semiliquidity.	353. Bubble.
	354. Pulpiness.	355. Unctuousness.
		356. Oil.

III. ORGANIC MATTER

1°. VITALITY—	357. Organisation.	358. Inorganisation.
	359. Life.	360. Death.
In General		361. Killing.
		362. Corpse.
		363. Interment.
	364. Animality.	365. Vegetability.
	366. Animal.	367. Plant.
Special	368. Zoology.	369. Botany.
	370. Cicuration.	371. Agriculture.
	372. Mankind.	
	373. Man.	374. Woman.
2°. SENSATION—		
(1) *General*	375. Sensibility.	376. Insensibility.
	377. Pleasure.	378. Pain.
(2) *Special*— 1. *Touch.*	379. Touch.	
	380. { Perceptions of Touch. }	381. Numbness.

2. *Heat* .
- 382. Heat.
- 383. Cold.
- 384. Calefaction.
- 385. Frigefaction.
- 386. Furnace.
- 387. Refrigeratory.
- 388. Fuel.
- 389. Thermometer.

3. *Taste* .
- 390. Taste.
- 391. Insipidity.
- 392. Pungency.
- 393. Condiment.
- 394. Savouriness.
- 395. Unsavouriness.
- 396. Sweetness.
- 397. Sourness.

4. *Odour* .
- 398. Odour.
- 399. Inodorousness.
- 400. Fragrance.
- 401. Fetor.

5. *Sound* .
1. *Sound in General.*
- 402. Sound.
- 403. Silence.
- 404. Loudness.
- 405. Faintness.
2. *Specific Sounds.*
- 406. Snap.
- 407. Roll.
- 408. Resonance.
- 409. Sibilation.
- 410. Stridor.
- 411. Cry.
- 412. Ululation.
3. *Musical Sounds.*
- 413. Harmony.
- 414. Discord.
- 415. Music.
- 416. Musician.
- 417. Musical Instruments.
4. *Perception of Sound.*
- 418. Hearing.
- 419. Deafness.

6. *Light* .
1. *Light in General.*
- 420. Light.
- 421. Darkness.
- 422. Dimness.
- 423. Luminary.
- 424. Shade.
- 425. Transparency.
- 426. Opacity,
- 427. Semi-transparency.
2. *Specific Light.*
- 428. Colour.
- 429. Achromatism.
- 430. Whiteness.
- 431. Blackness.
- 432. Grey.
- 433. Brown.
- 434. Redness.
- 435. Greenness.
- 436. Yellowness.
- 437. Purple.
- 438. Blueness.
- 439. Orange.
- 440. Variegation.
3. *Perceptions of Light.*
- 441. Vision.
- 442. Blindness.
- 443. Dimsightedness.
- 444. Spectator.
- 445. Optical Instruments.
- 446. Visibility.
- 447. Invisibility.
- 448. Appearance.
- 449. Disappearance.

CLASS IV. INTELLECT

DIVISION I. FORMATION OF IDEAS

DIVISION II. COMMUNICATION OF IDEAS

I. NATURE OF IDEAS COMMUNICATED

516. Meaning.	517. Unmeaningness.
518. Intelligibility.	519. Unintelligibility.
520. Equivocalness.	
521. Metaphor.	
522. Interpretation.	523. Misinterpretation.
524. Interpreter.	

II. MODES OF COMMUNICATION

525. Manifestation.	526. Latency.
527. Information.	528. Concealment.
529. Disclosure.	530. Ambush.
531. Publication.	
532. News.	533. Secret.
534. Messenger.	
535. Affirmation.	536. Negation.
537. Teaching.	538. Misteaching.
	539. Learning.
540. Teacher.	541. Learner.
542. School.	
543. Veracity.	544. Falsehood.
	545. Deception.
	546. Untruth.
547. Dupe.	548. Deceiver.
	549. Exaggeration.

III. MEANS OF COMMUNICATION—

1°. *Natural Means*

550. Indication.	
551. Record.	552. Obliteration.
553. Recorder.	
554. Representation.	555. Misrepresentation.
556. Painting.	
557. Sculpture.	
558. Engraving.	
559. Artist.	

2°. *Conventional Means*—

1. *Language generally*

560. Language.	
561. Letter.	
562. Word.	563. Neology.
564. Nomenclature.	565. Misnomer.
566. Phrase.	
567. Grammar.	568. Solecism.
569. Style.	

Qualities of Style.

570. Perspicuity.	571. Obscurity.
572. Conciseness.	573. Diffuseness.
574. Vigour.	575. Feebleness.
576. Plainness.	577. Ornament.
578. Elegance.	579. Inelegance.

2. *Spoken Language*	580. Voice.	581. Aphony.
	582. Speech.	583. Stammering.
	584. Loquacity.	585. Taciturnity.
	586. Allocution.	587. Response.
	588. Interlocution.	589. Soliloquy.
3. *Written Language*	590. Writing.	591. Printing.
	592. Correspondence.	593. Book.
	594. Description.	
	595. Dissertation.	
	596. Compendium.	
	597. Poetry.	598. Prose.
	599. The Drama.	

CLASS V. VOLITION

DIVISION I. INDIVIDUAL VOLITION

I. VOLITION IN GENERAL—

	600. Will.	601. Necessity.
	602. Willingness.	603. Unwillingness.
	604. Resolution.	605. Irresolution.
1°. *Acts*	606. Obstinacy.	607. Tergiversation.
		608. Caprice.
	609. Choice.	610. Rejection.
	611. Predetermination.	612. Impulse.
	613. Habit.	614. Desuetude.
2°. *Causes*	615. Motive.	616. Dissuasion.
	617. Plea.	
3°. *Objects*	618. Good.	619. Evil.

II. PROSPECTIVE VOLITION—

	620. Intention.	621. Chance.
	622. Pursuit.	623. Avoidance.
		624. Relinquishment.
1°. *Conceptional*	625. Business.	
	626. Plan.	
	627. Method.	
	628. Mid-course.	629. Circuit.
	630. Requirement.	

1. *Actual Subservience.*

	631. Instrumentality.	
	632. Means.	
	633. Instrument.	
2°. *Subservience to Ends*	634. Substitute.	
	635. Materials.	
	636. Store.	
	637. Provision.	638. Waste.
	639. Sufficiency.	640. Insufficiency.
	641. Redundance.	

2. *Degree of Subservience.*

642. Importance.	643. Unimportance.
644. Utility.	645. Inutility.
646. Expedience.	647. Inexpedience.
648. Goodness.	649. Badness.
650. Perfection.	651. Imperfection.
652. Cleanness.	653. Uncleanness.
654. Health.	655. Disease.
656. Salubrity.	657. Insalubrity.
658. Improvement.	659. Deterioration.
660. Restoration.	661. Relapse.
662. Remedy.	663. Bane.

2°. *Subservience to Ends*—contd.

3. *Contingent Subservience.*

664. Safety.	665. Danger.
666. Refuge.	667. Pitfall.
668. Warning.	
669. Alarm.	
670. Preservation.	
671. Escape.	
672. Deliverance.	

3°. *Precursory Measures.*

673. Preparation.	674. Non-preparation.
675. Essay.	
676. Undertaking.	
677. Use.	678. Disuse.
	679. Misuse.

III. ACTION—

1°. *Simple.*

680. Action.	681. Inaction.
682. Activity.	683. Inactivity.
684. Haste.	685. Leisure.
686. Exertion.	687. Repose.
688. Fatigue.	689. Refreshment.
690. Agent.	
691. Workshop.	

2°. *Complex.*

692. Conduct.	
693. Direction.	
694. Director.	
695. Advice.	
696. Council.	
697. Precept.	
698. Skill.	699. Unskilfulness.
700. Proficient.	701. Bungler.
702. Cunning.	703. Artlessness.

IV. ANTAGONISM—

1°. *Conditional.*   704. Difficulty.   705. Facility.

2°. *Active* . .

706. Hindrance.   707. Aid.
708. Opposition.   709. Co-operation.
710. Opponent.   711. Auxiliary.
712. Party.
713. Discord.   714. Concord.
715. Defiance.
716. Attack.   717. Defence.
718. Retaliation.   719. Resistance.
720. Contention.   721. Peace.
722. Warfare.   723. Pacification.
724. Mediation.
725. Submission.
726. Combatant.   726a. Non-combatant.
727. Arms.
728. Arena.

V. RESULTS OF ACTION

729. Completion.   730. Non-completion.
731. Success.   732. Failure.
733. Trophy.
734. Prosperity.   735. Adversity.
736. Mediocrity.

DIVISION II. INTERSOCIAL VOLITION

I. GENERAL . .

737. Authority.   738. Laxity.
739. Severity.   740. Lenity.
741. Command.
742. Disobedience.   743. Obedience.
744. Compulsion.
745. Master.   746. Servant.
747. Sceptre.
748. Freedom.   749. Subjection.
750. Liberation.   751. Restraint.
    752. Prison.
753. Keeper.   754. Prisoner.
755. Commission.   756. Abrogation.
    757. Resignation.
758. Consignee.
759. Deputy.

II. SPECIAL . .

760. Permission.   761. Prohibition.
762. Consent.
763. Offer.   764. Refusal.
765. Request.   766. Deprecation.
767. Petitioner.

CLASS VI. AFFECTIONS

I. AFFECTIONS GENERALLY

II. PERSONAL

1°. PASSIVE		
827. Pleasure.		828. Pain.
829. Pleasurableness.		830. Painfulness.
831. Content.		832. Discontent.
		833. Regret.
834. Relief.		835. Aggravation.
836. Cheerfulness.		837. Dejection.
838. Rejoicing.		839. Lamentation.
840. Amusement.		841. Weariness.
842. Wit.		843. Dullness.
844. Humorist.		

2°. DISCRIMINATIVE		
845. Beauty.		846. Ugliness.
847. Ornament.		848. Blemish.
		849. Simplicity.
850. Taste.		851. Vulgarity.
852. Fashion.		853. Ridiculousness.
		854. Fop.
		855. Affectation.
		856. Ridicule.
		857. Laughing-stock.

3°. PROSPECTIVE		
858. Hope.		859. Hopelessness.
860. Fear.		
861. Courage.		862. Cowardice.
863. Rashness.		864. Caution.
865. Desire.		866. Indifference.
		867. Dislike.
		868. Fastidiousness.
		869. Satiety.

4°. CONTEMPLATIVE		
870. Wonder.		871. Expectance.
872. Prodigy.		

5°. EXTRINSIC		
873. Repute.		874. Disrepute.
875. Nobility.		876. Commonality.
877. Title.		
878. Pride.		879. Humility.
880. Vanity.		881. Modesty.
882. Ostentation.		
883. Celebration.		
884. Boasting.		
885. Insolence.		886. Servility.
887. Blusterer.		

III. SYMPATHETIC

1°. SOCIAL

888. Friendship.	889. Enmity.
890. Friend.	891. Enemy.
892. Sociality.	893. Seclusion.
894. Courtesy.	895. Discourtesy.
896. Congratulation.	
897. Love.	898. Hate.
899. Favourite.	
	900. Resentment.
	901. Irascibility.
902. Endearment.	
903. Marriage.	904. Celibacy.
	905. Divorce.

2°. DIFFUSIVE

906. Benevolence.	907. Malevolence.
	908. Malediction.
	909. Threat.
910. Philanthropy.	911. Misanthropy.
912. Benefactor.	913. Evil-doer.

3°. SPECIAL

914. Pity.	
915. Condolence.	

4°. RETROSPECTIVE

916. Gratitude.	917. Ingratitude.
918. Forgiveness.	919. Revenge.
	920. Jealousy.
	921. Envy.

IV. MORAL

1°. OBLIGATIONS

922. Right.	923. Wrong.
924. Dueness.	925. Undueness.
926. Duty.	927. Exemption.

2°. SENTIMENTS

928. Respect.	929. Disrespect.
	930. Contempt.
931. Approbation.	932. Disapprobation.
933. Flattery.	934. Detraction.
935. Flatterer.	936. Detractor.
937. Vindication.	938. Accusation.

3°. CONDITIONS

939. Probity.	940. Improbity.
	941. Knave.
942. Disinterestedness.	943. Selfishness.
944. Virtue.	945. Vice.
946. Innocence.	947. Guilt.
948. Saint.	949. Sinner.
950. Penitence.	951. Impenitence.
952. Atonement.	

4°. PRACTICE

953. Temperance.	954. Intemperance.
955. Asceticism.	
956. Fasting.	957. Gluttony.
958. Sobriety.	959. Drunkenness.
960. Purity.	961. Impurity.
	962. Libertine.

963. Legality.
965. Jurisprudence.
966. Tribunal.
967. Judge.
968. Lawyer.
5°. INSTITUTIONS 969. Lawsuit.
970. Acquittal.

973. Reward.

964. Illegality.

971. Condemnation.
972. Punishment.
974. Penalty.
975. Scourge.

V. RELIGIOUS

1°. SUPERHUMAN
BEINGS AND
OBJECTS

976. Deity.
977. Angel.
979. Jupiter.
981. Heaven.

978. Satan.
980. Demon.
982. Hell.

2°. DOCTRINES .

983. Theology.
985. Revelation.

984. Heterodoxy.
986. Pseudo-revelation.

3°. SENTIMENTS .

987. Piety.

988. Irreligion.
989. Impiety.

4°. ACTS . .

990. Worship.

991. Idolatry.
992. Occult Arts.
993. Spell.
994. Sorcerer.

5°. INSTITUTIONS

995. Churchdom.
996. Clergy.
998. Rite.
999. Canonicals.
1000. Temple.

997. Laity.

THESAURUS OF ENGLISH WORDS AND PHRASES

CLASS I

WORDS EXPRESSING ABSTRACT RELATIONS

SECTION I.—EXISTENCE

1°. BEING IN THE ABSTRACT

1. EXISTENCE (*Substantives*), being, entity, ens, subsistence, co-existence (120).

Reality, actuality, positiveness, absoluteness, fact, truth, etc. (494); actualisation.

Science of existence: Ontology.

Existence in space, 186.

(*Phrases*). The sober reality; hard fact; matter of fact; the whole truth.

(*Verbs*). To be, to exist, have being, subsist, live, breathe, stand, obtain, occur, prevail, be so, find itself, take place, consist in, lie in.

To come into existence, arise, come out, emerge, come forth, appear (448).

To bring into existence, produce, bring forth, discover, etc. (161), objectify.

(*Adjectives*). Existing, being, subsisting, subsistent, in being, in existence, extant, living, breathing, obtaining, prevailing, prevalent, current.

Real, actual, positive, absolute, substantial, substantive, self-ex-

2. INEXISTENCE (*Substantives*), non-existence, nonentity, *nihil*, nil, non-subsistence, non-existence, nullity, vacuity (4), negativeness, absence (187), removal (185).

Annihilation, abeyance, extinction, *see* Destruction (162) and Disappearance (449); Absence (187); nirvana.

Philosophy of non-existence: Nihilism.

(*Phrases*). No such thing; daydream; *fata Morgana* ; mirage; Mrs. Harris; "men in buckram."

(*Verbs*). Not to be, not to exist, etc.

(*Phrases*). To have no being; to have no existence; to be null and void.

To cease to be, pass away, perish, vanish, fade away, dissolve, melt away, disappear (449), to be annihilated, extinct, etc., to die (360), to die out.

(*Phrases*). To be no more; "to leave not a rack behind"; "disappear into thin air"; to be brought out of existence.

(*Adjectives*). Inexistent, non-

35

isting, self-existent; undestroyed, tangible, not ideal, not imagined, not supposititious, not potential, virtual, effective, unideal, true, mere, objective.

(*Adverbs, etc.*). Actually, really, absolutely, positively, etc., in fact, *de facto, ipso facto, in esse.*

(*Phrase*). *In posse.*

existent, non-existing, etc., negative, blank, absent.

Unreal, potential, virtual, baseless, unsubstantial (4), imaginary, ideal, vain, fanciful, unpractical, shadowy, supposititious.

Unborn, uncreated, unbegotten.

Annihilated, destroyed, extinct, gone, lost, perished, melted, dissolved, faded, exhausted, vanished, missing, disappeared, departed, defunct (360).

(*Adverbs*). Negatively, virtually, etc.

(*Phrase*). *In nubibus.*

2°. Being in the Concrete

3. Substantiality (*Substantives*), hypostasis, person, thing, being, something, existence, entity, body, physique, substance, object, article, creature, matter, material, stuff (316), substratum, *plenum*, protoplasm.

Totality of existences, *see* World (318).

(*Phrase*). Something or other.

(*Adjectives*). Substantive, substantial, hearty, bodily, tangible, corporal, corporeal, material, objective, hypostatic.

(*Adverbs*). Substantially, etc., essentially.

4. Unsubstantiality (*Substantives*), insubstantiality, nothingness, nihility, nothing, naught, *nihil*, nil, zero, cipher, nonentity, nobody, *see* 187.

(*Phrases*). Nothing at all; nothing whatever; nothing on earth; nothing under the sun.

A desert.

A shadow, phantom, phantasm, phantasmagoria, dream, mockery, air, thin air, idle dream, idle talk, *ignis fatuus*, mirage.

Void, vacuum, vacuity, vacancy, voidness, vacuousness, inanity, emptiness, hollowness, blank, chasm, gap, hiatus (198); empty space.

(*Adjectives*). Unsubstantial, immaterial, void, vacant, vacuous, blank, null, inane, idle, hollow, airy, visionary, *see* 515.

3°. Formal Existence

Internal Conditions

5. Intrinsicality (*Substantives*), inbeing, immanence, inherence, inhesion, essence; essentiality, subjectiveness, subjectivity, essential part, soul, quintessence, quiddity, gist, pith, core, backbone, marrow; incarnation.

External Conditions

6. Extrinsicality (*Substantives*), extraneousness, objectiveness, objectivity, accident, superficiality, incident.

(*Adjectives*). Derived from without, objective, extrinsic, extrinsical, extraneous, modal,

Nature, constitution, character, quality (157), crasis, temperament, temper, manner, spirit, habit, humour, grain, endowment, capacity, capability, moods, declensions, features, aspects, specialities, peculiarities (79), particularities, idiosyncrasy, idiocrasy, diagnostics.

adventitious, adscititious, incidental, accidental, non-essential, *see* 220.

Implanted, engrafted.

(*Adverb*). Extrinsically, etc.

(*Verb Phrase*). To be in the blood.

(*Adjectives*). Derived from within, subjective, intrinsic, intrinsical, inherent, essential, natural, internal, inborn, innate, inbred, engrained, inherited, immanent, indwelling, congenital, connate, hereditary, instinctive, indigenous.

(*Phrases*). In the grain; in the blood; bred in the bone.

Characteristic, peculiar, qualitative, special, diagnostic (79), invariable.

(*Adverbs*). Intrinsically, subjectively, at bottom, at the core.

(*Phrase*). Rotten at the core.

4°. Modal Existence

Absolute	Relative

Absolute

7. STATE (*Substantives*), condition, category, class, kind, estate, case, constitution, habitude, diathesis, mood, pickle, plight, temper, morale.

Frame, fabric, structure, texture, contexture (329), conformation, organism.

Mode, modality, schesis, form, shape, figure, cut, cast, mould, stamp, set, fit, tone, tenor, trim, turn, guise, fashion, aspect, complexion, style, manner, character, kind, get-up, *format, genre*.

(*Verbs*). To be in a state, to be in condition, to be on a footing, etc.

To fare, have, possess, enjoy, etc., a state, condition, etc.

To bring into a state, etc. (144).

(*Adjectives*). Conditional, modal, formal, structural, organic, textual.

(*Phrases*). As the matter

Relative

8. CIRCUMSTANCE (*Substantives*), situation, phase, position, posture, attitude, place, point, terms, fare, régime, footing, standing, status, predicament, contingency, occasion, juncture, conjuncture, emergency, exigence, exigency, crisis, pinch, pass, push, plight.

(*Adjectives*). Circumstantial; given, conditional, provisional, critical, contingent, incidental (6, 151), circumstanced, placed.

(*Verb Phrases*). To bow before the storm; take things as they are; cut one's coat according to the cloth.

(*Adverbs*). In or under the circumstances, conditions, etc.; thus, in such a case, contingency, etc., accordingly, being so, such being the case; since, sith, seeing that, as matters stand, as things go.

Conditionally, provided, if, an

stands; as things are; such being the case.

(*Adverb*). Conditionally, etc.

if, if so, if so be, if it be so, if it so prove, or turn out, or happen; in the event of, provisionally, unless, without.

(*Phrases*). According to circumstances; as it may happen, or turn out; as the case may be; *pro re nata*; according as the wind blows; rain or shine; sink or swim; at all events; *ceteris paribus*.

SECTION II.—RELATION

1°. ABSOLUTE RELATION

9. RELATION (*Substantives*), bearing, reference, standing, concern, cognation, correlation, analogy, affinity, homology, alliance, homogeneity, association, approximation, filiation, affiliation, etc. (166), interest, habitude; relativity.

Relevancy, pertinency, fitness, etc. (646 and 23).

Aspect, point of view, comparison (464); ratio, proportion.

Link, tie (45), homologue.

(*Verbs*). To be related, have a relation, etc., to relate to, refer to, have reference to, bear upon, regard, concern, touch, affect, have to do with, pertain to, belong to, appertain to, answer to, interest.

To bring into relation with, connect, affiliate, link (43), bring near (197), homologise; to bring to bear upon.

(*Adjectives*). Relative, correlative, cognate, relating to, relative to, relevant, in relation with, referable to, pertinent (*see* 23), germane, belonging to, pat, to the point, apposite, to the purpose, apropos, *ad rem, in loco*, just the thing, quite the thing; pertaining to, appertaining to,

10. Want or absence of relation.

IRRELATION (*Substantives*), disconnection, dissociation, disassociation, misrelation, independence, isolation (44), multifariousness, disproportion; incommensurability, irrelevancy; heterogeneity, irreconcilableness (24), impertinence.

(*Verbs*). To have no relation with, or to, to have nothing to do with, not to concern, etc., not to admit of comparison.

To isolate, separate, detach, disconnect, segregate (44).

(*Adjectives*). Irrelative, irrespective, unrelated, without reference, etc., to, arbitrary, episodic, remote, far-fetched, out of place, out of tune (414), inharmonious, malapropos, irrelevant, foreign to, alien, impertinent, extraneous to, strange to, stranger to, independent, incidental, outlandish, exotic, unallied, unconnected, disconnected, unconcerned, adrift, isolated, insular.

Not comparable, incommensurable, inapplicable (24), irreconcilable, heterogeneous (83), unconformable.

appurtenant, affiliated, allied, related, implicated, connected. associated, bound up with, homological, homologous.

Approximate, approximative, approximating, proportional, proportionate, proportionable, allusive, comparable (23), like, similar (17).

(*Adverbs*). Relatively, thereof, as to, about, connecting, concerning, touching, anent, as relates to, with relation to, relating to, as respects, with respect to, in respect of, respecting, as regards, with regard to, regarding, in the matter of, with reference to, according to, while speaking of, apropos of, in connection with, inasmuch as, whereas, in consideration of, in point of, as far as, on the part of, on the score of, *quoad hoc, in re*; pertinently, etc.

In various ways, in all manner of ways, in all respects, everyway, under the head, category, class, etc., of (75).

(*Phrases*). Foreign to the purpose; nothing to the purpose; having nothing to do with; beside the question; neither here nor there; beside the mark; *à propos des bottes*; brought in by the head and shoulders.

(*Adverbs*). Parenthetically, by the way, by the by, *obiter dicta*, *en passant*, incidentally.

---

11. Relations of kindred.

CONSANGUINITY (*Substantives*), relationship, kindred, blood, parentage, filiation, affiliation, lineage, agnation, connection, alliance, family connection, family tie, nepotism, *see* Paternity (166).

A kinsman, kinsfolk, kith and kin, relation, relative, one's people, clan, connection, sib, cousin, brother, sister, father, mother, uncle, aunt, nephew, niece, step-father, etc., first, second cousin, grandor great-grandfather, etc., great-uncle, etc., a near relation, a bloodrelation, a distant relation or relative, congener, collateral.

Family, fraternity, sisterhood, brotherhood, parentage, cousinhood, etc.; race, stock, generation, sept, etc.

(*Verbs*). To be related, to have or claim relationship with.

(*Adjectives*). Related, akin, consanguineous, congeneric, family, allied, collateral, sib, agnate, agnatic, fraternal, of the same blood, nearly or closely related, remotely or distantly related.

(*Phrase*). Blood is thicker than water.

12. Double relation.

RECIPROCALNESS (*Substantives*), reciprocity, mutuality, correlation, correlativeness, interdependence, interchange, interaction, reciprocation, etc. (148), alternation (149), barter (794).

(*Verbs*). To reciprocate, alternate, interchange, interact, exchange, counterchange, interdepend.

(*Adjectives*). Reciprocal, mutual, correlative, alternate, alternative; interchangeable, interdependent, international.

(*Phrases*). *Mutatis mutandis*; each other; *vice versa*; change and change about.

13. IDENTITY (*Substantives*), sameness, oneness, coincidence, coalescence, convertibility; selfness, self, ego, oneself, number one; identification, monotony.

(*Verbs*). To be identical, to be the same, etc., to coincide, to coalesce.

To render the same.

To recognise the identity of: to identify, to recognise, *see* to compare (464).

(*Adjectives*). Identical, identic, same, self, selfsame, very same, no other, ilk, one and the same, unaltered, coincident, coinciding, coessential, coalescing, coalescent, indistinguishable, equivalent, equipollent, convertible, much the same.

(*Adverbs*). All one, all the same, identically, likewise.

(*Phrases*). *Semper idem; toujours la même chose; alter ego;* the very thing; just the thing; the actual thing; *hic est quod petis.*

14. Non-coincidence.

CONTRARIETY (*Substantives*), contrast, foil, antithesis, contradiction, opposition, oppositeness, antagonism (179, 708), distinction (15).

Inversion, reversion (218).

The opposite, the reverse, inverse, converse, the antipodes (237), counterpart.

(*Phrases*). The reverse of the medal; the other side of the shield; the tables being turned.

(*Verbs*). To be contrary, etc., to contrast with, contradict, contravene, oppose, negate, antagonise, invert, reverse, turn the tables, to militate against.

(*Adjectives*). Contrary, opposite, counter, converse, reverse, opposed, antipodean, antagonistic, opposing, inconsistent, contradictory, contrarious, negative.

(*Phrases*). Differing *toto cœlo;* diametrically opposite; as black to white; light to darkness; fire to water; worlds apart.

(*Adverbs*). Contrarily, contrariously, contrariwise, *per contra*, oppositely, *vice versa*, on the contrary, *tout au contraire*, quite the contrary, no such thing.

---

15. DIFFERENCE (*Substantives*), variance, variation, variety, diversity, modification, allotropy, shade of difference, nuance; deviation, divergence, divarication (291), disagreement (24).

Distinction, contradistinction, differentiation, discrimination (465); a nice or a fine or a subtle distinction.

(*Verbs*). To be different, etc., to differ, vary, mismatch, contrast, differ *toto cœlo.*

To render different, etc., to vary, change, modify, varify, diversify, etc. (140).

To distinguish, differentiate, severalise (465), split hairs, discriminate.

(*Adjectives*). Different, differing, disparate, heterogeneous, heteromorphic, allotropic, varying, distinguishable, discriminative, varied, modified, diversified, deviating, diverging, devious, disagreeing (24), various, divers, all manner of, multifarious, multiform, etc. (81), variegated (440), diacritical.

Other, another, not the same, quite another thing, a *tertium quid.* Unmatched, widely apart, changed (140), something else.

(*Phrases*). As different as chalk is from cheese; this, that, or the other; another pair of shoes.

(*Adverbs*). Differently, variously, otherwise.

2°. CONTINUOUS RELATION

16. UNIFORMITY (*Substantives*), homogeneity, homogeneousness, consistency, conformity (82), homology, accordance; *see* Agreement (23) and Regularity (58); monotony, constancy.

Absence, or want of uniformity, *see* 83.

———

(*Verbs*). To be uniform, etc., to accord with, to harmonise with, to hang together, to go together.

To become uniform, to conform with, to fall in with, to follow suit.

To render uniform, to assimilate, level, smooth, etc. (255).

(*Adjectives*). Uniform, homogeneous, homologous, of a piece, of a kind, consistent, connatural, monotonous, constant.

(*Adverbs*). Uniformly, uniformly with, conformably, consistently with, in unison with, in harmony with, in conformity with, according to (23).

Regularly, at regular intervals, invariably, constantly, always.

(*Phrases*). *Ab uno disce omnes ; noscitur a sociis.*

3°. PARTIAL RELATION

17. SIMILARITY (*Substantives*), resemblance, likeness, similitude, affinity, semblance, approximation, parallelism (216), analogy, brotherhood, family likeness; alliteration, assonance, repetition (104), reproduction.

An analogue, copy (21), the like, facsimile, match, double, pendant, fellow, pair, mate, twin, *alter ego*, parallel, counterpart, brother, sister; simile, metaphor (521), resemblance, imitation (19).

(*Phrases*). One's second self; *Arcades ambo*; birds of a feather; *et hoc genus omne*; a chip of the old block; the very moral of.

(*Verbs*). To be similar, like, resembling, etc., to resemble, bear resemblance, favour, approximate, parallel, match, imitate, take after (19), represent,

18. DISSIMILARITY (*Substantives*), unlikeness, dissimilitude, diversity; novelty (123), originality (515), disparity.

(*Verbs*). To be unlike, etc., to vary (20).

To render unlike, to diversify, vary, etc.

(*Phrase*). To strike out something new.

(*Adjectives*). Dissimilar, unlike, disparate, of a different kind, class, etc. (75); diversified, novel, new (123), unmatched, unique.

(*Phrases*). Nothing of the kind; far from it; cast in a different mould; as like a dock as a daisy; "very like a whale"; as different as chalk is from cheese.

———

simulate, personate, savour of, have a flavour of, favour, feature.

To render similar, assimilate, approximate, reproduce, bring near, copy, plagiarise.

(*Adjectives*). Similar, like, alike, resembling, twin, analogous, analogical, parallel, allied to, of a piece, such as, connatural, congener, matching, conformable, on all fours with.

Near, something like, such-like, mock, pseudo, simulating, representing, approximating, a show of, a kind of, a sort of.

Exact, accurate, true, faithful, close, speaking, life-like, breathing.

(*Phrases*). True to nature; to the life; the very image; the picture of; for all the world like; as like as two peas; *comme deux gouttes d'eau*; as like as it can stare; *ab uno disce omnes*; *instar omnium*; birds of a feather; *noscitur a sociis*; cast in the same mould; a chip of the old block; like father, like son.

(*Adverbs*). As if, so to speak, as it were, *quasi*, as if it were, just as, after, in the fashion or manner of, *à la*.

---

19. IMITATION (*Substantives*), assimilation, copying, transcription, transcribing, following, repetition (104), duplication, reduplication, quotation, reproduction.

Mockery, mocking, mimicry, echoing, simulation, counterfeiting, plagiarism, forgery, fake, fakement, acting, personation, impersonation, representation, parody, paraphrase, travesty, burlesque, semblance, mimesis.

Result of imitation: *see* Copy (21).

Instrument of imitation: camera, gramophone, phonograph, mimeograph, dictograph diagraph, pantograph, etc.

Photography, etc.

An imitator, mimic, impersonator, echo, cuckoo, parrot, ape, monkey, mocking-bird.

Plagiary, plagiarist, forger, photographer.

(*Phrase*). *O imitatores, servum pecus.*

20. NON-IMITATION (*Substantives*), originality, novelty.

(*Adjectives*). Unimitated, uncopied, unmatched, unparalleled, inimitable, unique, original, novel.

(*Verb*). To originate.

VARIATION (*Substantives*), alteration, modification, *see* Difference (15), Change (140), Deviation (279), Divergence (291); moods and tenses.

(*Verbs*). To vary, modify, change, alter, diversify, etc. (140).

(*Phrase*). To steer clear of.

(*Adjectives*). Varied, modified, diversified, etc.

(*Adverbs*). Variously, in all manner of ways.

(*Verbs*). To imitate, copy, plagiarise, forge, fake, reproduce, photograph, repeat (104), echo, re-echo, transcribe, match, parallel, emulate, do like, take off, hit off, reflect, model after (554), to be fashionable.

(*Phrase*). To take or catch a likeness.

To mock, mimic, ape, simulate, personate, impersonate (554), act, represent, adumbrate, counterfeit, parody, travesty, caricature, burlesque.

(*Phrases*). To take after; follow or tread in the steps of, or in the footsteps of; take a leaf out of another's book; model after; strike in with; follow suit; to walk in the shoes of; to go with the stream; to be in the fashion.

(*Adjectives*). Imitated, copied, matched, repeated, paralleled, mimic, parodied, etc., modelled after, moulded on, paraphrastic, imitative, mimetic, slavish, mechanical, second-hand, second-rate, imitable.

(*Adverbs*). Literally, verbatim, *literatim, sic, totidem verbis,* so to speak, in so many words, word for word, *mot à mot* (562).

21. Result of imitation.	22. Thing copied.
COPY (*Substantives*), facsimile, counterpart, effigies, effigy, form, likeness, similitude, semblance, reflex, portrait, photograph (556), enlargement, miniature, study, cast, ectype, autotype, electrotype, imitation, replica, representation, adumbration.	PROTOTYPE (*Substantives*), original, model, pattern, standard, type, scale, scantling, archetype, protoplast, antitype, module, exemplar, example, ensample, paradigm, fugleman, lay figure.
Duplicate, transcript, repetition (104), réchauffé, reflection, shadow, record (phonograph).	Text, copy, design, key-note. Mould, matrix, last, plasm, proplasm, mint, negative.
(*Phrases*). A second edition; a twice-told tale; a chip of the old block; like father, like son.	(*Verbs*). To set a copy, to set an example.

Rough copy, fair copy, carbon copy, rough cast, *ébauche,* draft or draught, proof, *brouillon,* protoplast, reprint.

Counterfeit, parody, caricature, burlesque, travesty, paraphrase, forgery.

4°. GENERAL RELATION

23. AGREEMENT (*Substantives*),	24. DISAGREEMENT (*Substantives*),
accord, accordance, unison, uniformity, harmony, union, concord, concert, concordance (714), cognation, conformity, consonance, consentaneousness, consensus, consistency, congruity, congruence, congeniality, correspondence, parallelism.	discord, discordance, dissonance, disharmony, dissidence, discrepancy, unconformity, disconformity, nonconformity, incongruity, incongruence, *mésalliance,* discongruity, jarring, clashing, jostling (713), inconsistency, inconsonance, disparity, disproportion, disproportionateness, variance, jar, misfit.
Fitness, pertinence, suitableness, adaptation, meetness, patness, relevancy, aptitude, coap-	(*Phrase*). *Concordia discors.*

tation, propriety, apposition, appositeness, reconcilableness, applicability, applicableness, admissibility, commensurability, compatibility, adaptability.

Adaptation, adjustment, graduation, accommodation, reconciliation, reconcilement, concurrence, concord, co-operation.

(*Verbs*). To be accordant, to agree, accord, correspond, tally, respond, harmonise, match, suit, fit, hit, fall in with, chime in with, quadrate with, square with, cancel with, comport with, assimilate, unite with, *see* 714.

(*Phrase*). To fit like a glove.

To render accordant, to fit, suit, adapt, match, accommodate, adjust, reconcile, fadge, dovetail, dress, square, regulate, accord, comport, graduate, gradate, grade.

(*Adjectives*). Agreeing, accordant, concordant, consonant, congruous, consentaneous, consentient, corresponding, correspondent, congenial, harmonising, harmonious with, tallying with, conformable with, in accordance with, in harmony with, in unison with, in keeping with, squaring with, quadrating with, falling in with, of a piece, consistent with, compatible, reconcilable with, commensurate.

Apt, apposite, pertinent, germane, relating to, pat, bearing upon (9), applicable, relevant, fit, fitting, suitable, happy, proper, meet, appropriate, suiting, befitting, seasonable, sortable, deft, accommodating, topical.

(*Phrases*). *In loco* ; *en rapport*; *ad rem*; *nemine discrepante*; *rem acu tetigisti*; whom the cap may fit; at home; to the point; apropos; to the purpose; in one's (proper) element; just the thing; the very thing; quite the thing.

Unfitness, repugnance, unsuitableness, unsuitability, unaptness, ineptitude, inaptness, impropriety, inapplicability, inadmissibility, irreconcilableness, irreconcilability, incommensurability, inconcinnity, incompatibility, inadaptability, interference, intrusion, *see* Irrelation (10).

(*Verbs*). To disagree, belie, clash, jar, oppose (708), interfere, jostle (713), intrude.

(*Phrases*). To have no business there; to drag or lug in head and shoulders.

(*Adjectives*). Disagreeing, discordant, discrepant, jarring, clashing, repugnant, incompatible, irreconcilable, intransigent, inconsistent with, unconformable, incongruous, disproportionate, disproportioned, unproportioned, inharmonious, inconsonant, mismatched, misjoined, misjudged, unconsonant, unconformable, incommensurable, incommensurate, divergent (291).

Unapt, inappropriate, improper, unsuited, unsuitable, inapt, inapposite, inapplicable, irrelevant, not pertinent, impertinent, malapropos, ill-timed, intrusive, clumsy, unfit, unfitting, unbefitting, unbecoming, forced, unseasonable, far-fetched, inadmissible, uncongenial, ill-assorted, ill-sorted, repugnant to, unaccommodating, irreducible.

(*Phrases*). Out of season; out of character; out of keeping; out of tune; out of place; out of one's element; at odds; a fish out of water; on all fours; neither here nor there; beside the mark; "*humano capite cervicem pictor equinam jungere*"; "compact of jars."

(*Adverbs*). At variance with, in defiance of, in contempt of, in spite of, despite.

SECTION III.—QUANTITY

1°. SIMPLE QUANTITY

25. Absolute quantity.

QUANTITY (*Substantives*), magnitude (192), amplitude, size, mass, amount, *quantum*, measure, substance.

Science of quantity: Mathematics.

Definite or finite quantity: handful, mouthful, etc., stock, batch, lot.

(*Adjective*). Quantitative.

(*Phrase*). To the tune of.

---

26. Relative quantity.

DEGREE (*Substantives*), grade, extent, measure, ratio, stint, standard, height, pitch, reach, amplitude, magnitude, water, range, scope, gradation, shade, tenor, compass, sphere, rank, standing, rate, way, sort.

Point, mark, stage, step, position, peg; term (71), gradation, degree.

Intensity, might, fullness, strength, *see* Conversion (144) and Limit (233).

(*Adjectives*). Comparative, gradual, shading off.

(*Adverbs*). By degrees, gradually, *gradatim*, inasmuch, *pro tanto*, however, howsoever, step by step, rung by rung, bit by bit, little by little, by inches, inch by inch, by slow degrees, by little and little.

2°. COMPARATIVE QUANTITY

27. Sameness of quantity or degree.

EQUALITY (*Substantives*), parity, co-extension, evenness, equipoise, level, balance, equivalence, equipollence, equilibrium, poise, equiponderance, par, quits, tie.

Equalisation, equation, equilibration, co-ordination, adjustment, symmetry.

A drawn game or battle, a dead heat, a draw.

A match, peer, compeer, equal, mate, fellow, brother, etc. (17), a make-weight.

(*Verbs*). To be equal, etc., to equal, match, come up to, keep pace with; come to, amount to, balance, cope with.

(*Phrases*). To be or lie on a level with, to come to the same thing.

---

28. Difference of quantity or degree.

INEQUALITY (*Substantives*), disparity, imparity, odds, handicap, bisque, difference (15), unevenness.

Preponderance, preponderation, inclination of the balance, advantage, prevalence, partiality.

Superiority (33), a casting weight.

Shortcoming, *see* 304.

(*Verbs*). To be unequal, etc., to preponderate, outweigh, outbalance, overbalance, prevail, countervail, predominate, overmatch, outmatch, *see* 33.

(*Phrases*). To have or give the advantage; to turn the scale; to kick the beam; to topple over.

To fall short of, to want (304), not to come up to.

(*Adjectives*). Unequal, uneven,

To render equal, equalise, level, balance, equate, trim, dress, adjust, poise, square; to readjust, equipoise, equilibrate, set against.

(*Phrases*). To strike a balance; to establish or restore equality; to stretch on the bed of Procrustes; to cry quits.

(*Adjectives*). Equal, even, quit, level, coequal, co-ordinate, equivalent, tantamount, convertible, equipollent, equiponderant, equiponderous, square.

disparate, partial, unbalanced, overbalanced, top-heavy, lopsided, preponderating, outweighing, prevailing.

(*Phrases*). More than a match for; above par; below par; *haud passibus æquis*.

(*Phrases*). On a par with; on a level with; much of a muchness; as broad as long; as good as; pretty well; up to the mark; up to the scratch; six of one and half a dozen of the other; tarred with the same brush; diamond cut diamond.

Rendered equal, made equal, equalised, equated, drawn, poised, levelled, balanced, symmetrical, trimmed, dressed.

(*Adverbs*). *Pari passu*, equally, symmetrically, *ad eundem*, *ceteris paribus*, practically, to all intents and purposes, neck and neck.

29. MEAN (*Substantives*), medium, intermedium, compromise, average, balance, middle (68), *via media*, *juste milieu*.

Neutrality, middle course, shuffling.

(*Phrases*). The golden mean; the average man; the man in the street.

(*Verbs*). To compromise, pair off, cancel.

(*Phrases*). To sit on the fence; split the difference; strike a balance; take the average; reduce to a mean; to take a safe course.

(*Adjectives*). Mean, intermediate, middle, average, ordinary (82), neutral.

(*Adverb Phrases*). On an average; in the long run; half-way; taking the one with the other; taking all things together; taking all in all; one year with another; *communibus annis*.

30. COMPENSATION (*Substantives*), equation, indemnification, neutralisation, counteraction.

(*Phrases*). Measure for measure; tit for tat.

A set-off, offset, makeweight, casting-weight, counterpoise, amends, equivalent, a *quid pro quo*. See Counteraction (179), Recoil (277), Atonement (952).

(*Verbs*). To compensate, make up for, indemnify, countervail, counterpoise, balance, compromise, outbalance, overbalance, counterbalance, set off, hedge, redeem, neutralise (*see* 27), cover.

(*Phrases*). To make good; split the difference; fill up; make amends.

(*Adjectives*). Compensating, compensatory, countervailing, etc., equipollent (27).

(*Phrase*). In the opposite scale.

(Adverbs). However, yet, but, still, all the same, nevertheless, none the less, notwithstanding, on the other hand, *en revanche, per contra.*

(Phrases). As broad as it's long; 'tis an ill wind that blows nobody any good.

Quantity by Comparison with a Standard

31. GREATNESS *(Substantives),* largeness, magnitude, size (192), fullness, vastness, immensity, enormity, infinity (105), intensity (26), importance (642), strength.

A large quantity, deal, power, world, mass, heap (72), pile, sight, peck, bushel, load, heap, stack, cart-load, waggon-load, truck-load, ship-load, cargo, lot, flood or spring-tide, abundance (639), wholesale, store (636).

The greater part, *see* 50.

(Verbs). To be great, etc., run high, soar, tower, transcend, rise, carry to a great height, etc. (305).

(Phrases). To know no bounds; to break the record.

(Adjectives). Great, gross, large, considerable, big, ample, above par, huge, full, saturated, plenary, deep, signal, extensive, sound, passing, goodly, famous, heavy, precious, mighty (157), arch, sad, piteous, arrant, red-hot, downright, utter, uttermost, cross, lamentable, consummate, rank, thorough-paced, thorough-going, sovereign, unparalleled, matchless, unapproached, extraordinary, intense, extreme, pronounced, unsurpassed, unsurpassable.

Vast, immense, enormous, towering, inordinate, severe, excessive, monstrous, shocking, extravagant, exorbitant, outrageous, glaring, preposterous, egregious, overgrown, stupendous, monumental, prodigious, astonishing, surprising (870), in-

32. SMALLNESS *(Substantives),* littleness, minuteness (193), tenuity, scantness, scantiness, slenderness, meanness, mediocrity, insignificance (643), paucity.

A small quantity, modicum, atom, particle, molecule, corpuscle, jot, iota, dot, speck, scintilla, spark, ace, *minutiæ,* thought, idea, *soupçon,* whit, tittle, shade, shadow, touch, cast, taste, grain, scruple, spice, sprinkling, drop, dash, smack, scantling, dole, scrap, mite, slip, bit, morsel, crumb, paring, shaving, trifle, thimbleful, spoonful, cupful, mouthful, handful, fistful, *see* 51.

Finiteness, a finite quantity.

(Phrases). The shadow of a shade; a drop in a bucket or in the ocean.

(Verbs). To be small, etc., to run low, diminish, shrink, decrease, etc., *see* 195.

(Phrases). To lie in a nutshell; to pass muster.

(Adjectives). Small, little, scant, inconsiderable, diminutive, minute (193), tiny, minikin, puny, petty, sorry, miserable, shabby, wretched, paltry (643), weak (640), slender, feeble, faint, slight, scrappy, fiddling, trivial, scanty, light, trifling, moderate, low, mean, tender, mediocre, passable, passing, light, sparing.

Below par, below the mark, under the mark, at low ebb, imperfect, unfinished, partial (651), inappreciable, evanescent, infinitesimal, atomic, homœopathic.

credible, marvellous, transcendent, incomparable, tremendous, amazing, phenomenal, superhuman, Titanic, immoderate.

Indefinite, boundless, unbounded, unlimited, incalculable, illimitable, immeasurable, infinite, unapproachable, unutterable, unspeakable, inexpressible, beyond expression, swingeing, unconscionable, fabulous, uncommon, unusual (83).

Undiminished, unrestricted, unabated, unreduced, unmitigated, unredeemed, untempered.

Absolute, positive, stark, decided, staring, unequivocal, serious, grave, essential, perfect, finished, completed, abundant (639).

(*Adverbs*). *In a great degree :* much, muckle, well, considerably, largely, grossly, greatly, very, very much, a deal, not a little, pretty, pretty well, enough, richly, to a large extent, to a great extent, ever so, mainly, ever so much, on a large scale, insomuch, all lengths, wholesale, in a great measure.

In a positive degree : truly (494), positively, verily, really, indeed, actually, in fact, fairly, assuredly, decidedly, surely, clearly, obviously, unequivocally, purely, absolutely, seriously, essentially, fundamentally, radically, downright, in grain, altogether, entirely, completely.

In a comparative degree : comparatively, *pro tanto*, as good as, to say the least, above all, most, of all things, pre-eminently.

In a complete degree : altogether, quite, entirely, wholly, totally, *in toto*, *toto cœlo*, utterly, thoroughly, out and out, completely, outright, out and away, every respect, *sous tous les rapports*,

Mere, simple, sheer, stark, bare.

(*Adverbs*). *In a small degree :* on a small scale, to a small extent, something, somewhat, next to nothing, little, inconsiderably, slightly, so-so, minutely, faintly, feebly, lightly, imperfectly, perceptibly, moderately, scantily, shabbily, miserably, wretchedly, sparingly, tolerably, passably, weakly, pretty well, well enough, slenderly, modestly.

In a limited degree : in a certain degree, to a certain degree or extent, partially, in part, some, somewhat, rather, in some degree, in some measure, something, simply, purely, merely, in a manner, at the most, at least, at the least, at most, ever so little, thus far, *pro tanto*, next to nothing.

(*Phrases*). As little as may be; *tant soit peu*; to say the least; in ever so small a degree.

Almost, nearly, well-nigh, all but, short of, not quite, *peu s'en faut*, near the mark.

(*Phrases*). Within an ace of; on the brink of; next door to; a close shave.

In an uncertain degree : about, thereabouts, scarcely, hardly, barely, somewhere about, nearly, more or less, *à peu près*, there or thereabouts.

In no degree : noways, nowise, nohow, in no wise, by no means, not in the least, not at all, not a bit, not a bit of it, not a whit, not a jot, in no respect, by no manner of means, on no account, at no hand.

————

fairly, clean, to the full, in all respects, on all

accounts, nicely, perfectly, fully, amply, richly, wholesale, abundantly, consummately, widely, as . . . as . . . can be, every inch, *à fond, de fond, en comble,* far and wide, over head and ears, to the backbone, through and through, *ne plus ultra.*

In a greater degree : even, yea, *a fortiori,* still more.

In a high degree: highly, deeply, strongly, mighty, mightily, powerfully (157), with a witness, with a vengeance, profoundly, superlatively, ultra, in the extreme, extremely, exceedingly, excessively, consumedly, sorely, intensely, exquisitely, acutely, soundly, vastly, hugely, immensely, enormously, stupendously, passing, surpassing, supremely, beyond measure, immoderately, monstrously, inordinately, over head and ears, extraordinarily, exorbitantly, indefinitely, immeasurably, unspeakably, inexpressibly, ineffably, unutterably, incalculably, infinitely, unsurpassably.

In a marked degree : particularly, remarkably, singularly, uncommonly, unusually, peculiarly, notably, *par excellence,* signally, famously, egregiously, prominently, glaringly, emphatically, κατ' ἐξοχήν, strangely, wonderfully, amazingly, surprisingly, astonishingly, prodigiously, monstrously, incredibly, inconceivably, marvellously, awfully, stupendously.

In a violent degree : violently, severely, furiously, desperately, tremendously, outrageously, extravagantly, confoundedly, deucedly, devilishly, diabolically, with a vengeance, *à outrance. See* 173.

In a painful degree : sadly, grievously, woefully, wretchedly, piteously, sorely, lamentably, shockingly, frightfully, dreadfully, fearfully, terribly, horribly.

Quantity by Comparison with a Similar Object

33. SUPERIORITY (*Substantives*), majority, supremacy, primacy, advantage, excess (641), prevalence, pre-eminence, championship.

Maximum, acme, climax, zenith, summit, utmost height, record, culminating point (210), the height of, lion's share, Benjamin's mess, overweight.

(*Phrases*). The *ne plus ultra ; summum genus ; summum bonum.*

(*Verbs*). To be superior, etc.; exceed, surpass, excel, eclipse, top, over-top, o'ertop, cap, beat, cut out, outclass, over-ride, outherod, kick the beam, outbalance,

34. INFERIORITY (*Substantives*), minority, subordination, shortcoming (304); deficiency, minimum.

(*Verbs*). To be less, inferior, etc., to fall or come short of, not to pass (304).

To become smaller, to render smaller (195); to subordinate.

(*Phrases*). To be thrown into the shade; to hide its diminished head.

(*Adjectives*). Inferior, deficient, smaller, minor, less, lesser, lower, sub, subordinate, subaltern, second-rate, second-best, amateurish.

overbalance, overweigh, overshadow, outdo; render larger,
magnify (194).

(*Phrases*). To have the advantage of; have the pull of; turn
the scale; beat hollow; take the
shine out of; throw into the
shade; to be a cut above.

(*Adjectives*). Superior, greater,
major, higher, surpassing, exceeding, excelling, passing, ultra,
vaulting, transcending, un-
equalled, unparalleled, without
parallel, *sans pareil*.

Least, smallest, minutest, etc.,
lowest.

(*Phrases*). Weighed in the
balance and found wanting; not
fit to hold a candle to.

(*Adverbs*). Less, under or below the mark, below par, at
the bottom of the scale, at a low
ebb, short of, at a disadvantage.

———

Supreme, greatest, utmost, paramount, pre-eminent, sovereign, culminating, superlative, topmost, top-hole, highest,
first-rate, champion, A1, the last word, the limit.

(*Phrases*). *Facile princeps* ; *nulli secundus* ; *primus inter
pares* ; a Triton among the minnows.

(*Adverbs*). Beyond, more, over and above the mark, above
par, over and above, at the top of the scale, at its height.

In a superior degree : eminently, pre-eminently, egregiously,
prominently, superlatively, supremely, above all, principally,
especially, particularly, peculiarly, *par excellence, a fortiori,
nil ultra.*

Changes in Quantity

35. INCREASE (*Substantives*),
augmentation, enlargement, extension, dilatation (*see* 194), increment, accretion, development,
growth, swell, swelling, expansion, aggrandisement, aggrava-
tion, rise, exacerbation, spread,
diffusion (73), flood-tide; accession.

(*Verbs*). To increase, augment,
enlarge, amplify, extend, dilate,
swell, wax, expand, grow, stretch,
shoot up, rise, run up, sprout,
advance, spread, gather head, aggrandise, add, superadd, raise,
heighten, strengthen, greaten,
exalt, enhance, magnify, redouble, aggravate, exaggerate,
exasperate, exacerbate.

(*Phrases*). To add fuel to the
flame; to pour oil on the flames.

36. NON-INCREASE.

DECREASE (*Substantives*), diminution, depreciation, lessening,
reduction, abatement, bating,
declension, falling off, dwindling,
contraction (195), shrinking, attenuation, extenuation, abridgment, curtailment (201), coarctation, narrowing.

Subsidence, wane, ebb, decrement.

(*Verbs*). To decrease, diminish,
lessen, dwindle, decay, shrink,
contract, shrivel, fall off, fall
away, waste, wear, wane, ebb,
decline, wear off, run low, grow
downward.

To abridge, reduce, curtail, cut
down, pare down, cut short,
dock, etc. (201), bate, abate,
extenuate, lower, weaken, dwarf;

(*Adjectives*). Increased, augmented, enlarged, etc., undiminished; cumulative.

(*Adverb*). *Crescendo.*

———

to mitigate, etc. (174), to throw in the shade.

(*Phrase*). To hide its diminished head.

(*Adjectives*). Decreased, diminished, lessened, etc., shorn, short by, decreasing, on the wane.

(*Adverbs*). *Diminuendo, decrescendo.*

3°. CONJUNCTIVE QUANTITY

37. ADDITION (*Substantives*), introduction, superinduction, annexation, superposition, superaddition, subjunction, supervention, accession, superfetation, corollary, reinforcement, supplement, accompaniment (88), sprinkling.

(*Verbs*). To add, annex, affix, superadd, supplement, subjoin, superpose, throw in, clap on, tack to, append, tag, engraft, saddle on, saddle with, sprinkle, superinduce, introduce, work in; to extra-illustrate, grangerise.

To become added, to accrue, advene, supervene.

(*Phrase*). To swell the ranks of.

(*Adjectives*). Added, annexed, etc., additional, supplementary, suppletory, subjunctive, adscititious, additive, accessory, cumulative, extra.

(*Adverbs*). In addition, more, *plus*, extra.

And, also, likewise, too, furthermore, item, and also, and eke, else, besides, to boot, etcetera, and so forth, into the bargain, *cum multis aliis*, over and above, moreover.

With, together with, withal, along with, including, inclusive, as well as, not to mention, to say nothing of; conjointly (43).

38. NON-ADDITION.

SUBDUCTION (*Substantives*), subtraction, deduction, deducement, retrenchment, removal, elimination, ablation, purgation, curtailment, etc. (36), garbling, mutilation, truncation, abscission, excision, amputation, detruncation, sublation, castration, *see* 789, apocope.

(*Verbs*). To subduct, exclude, deduct, subtract, abscind, retrench, remove, withdraw, bate, detract, deduce, take away, deprive of, curtail, etc. (36), garble, truncate, mutilate, eviscerate, exenterate, detruncate, castrate, spay, geld, purge, amputate, cut off, excise, cut out, dock, lop, prune, pare, dress, clip, thin, shear, decimate, abrade (330).

(*Adjectives*). Subtracted, deducted, etc., subtractive.

(*Adverbs*). In deduction, etc., less, *minus*, without, except, excepting, with the exception of, but for, barring, save, exclusive of, save and except (83).

———

39. Thing added.

ADJUNCT (*Substantives*), additament, addition, affix, appendage, suffix, augment, increment,

40. Thing remaining.

REMAINDER (*Substantives*), residue, remains, remnant, the rest, relics, leavings, heel-tap, odds

augmentation, acessory, item, garnish, sauce, supplement, extra, bonus (810), adjective, addendum, complement, corollary, continuation, reinforcement, pendant, apanage.

Sequel, postscript, codicil, envoy, rider, heel-piece, tag, tab, skirt, flap, lappet, trappings, tail, tail - piece (67), queue, train, suite, cortège, accompaniment (88).

(*Phrase*). More last words.

––––––

and ends, cheese-parings, candle-ends, off-scourings, orts.

Residuum, *caput mortuum*, dregs, refuse, scum, recrement (*see* 653), ashes, dross, cinders, slag, sediment, silt, alluvium, stubble; slough, exuviæ, result, educt.

Surplus, overplus, surplusage, superfluity, excess (641), balance, complement, fag - end, wreck, wreckage, ruins, skeleton.

(*Verbs*). To remain, be left, be left behind, exceed, survive.

(*Adjectives*). Remaining, left, left behind, residual, exuvial, residuary, sedimentary, outstanding, net, cast off, odd, unconsumed, surviving, outlying.

Superfluous, over and above, exceeding, redundant, supernumerary.

41. Forming a whole without coherence.

MIXTURE (*Substantives*), admixture, commixture, commixtion, intermixture, alloyage, marriage, miscegenation.

Impregnation, infusion, infiltration, diffusion, suffusion, interspersion, transfusion, seasoning, sprinkling, interlarding, interpolation, interposition (228), intrusion; adulteration, sophistication.

Thing mixed: a touch, spice, tinge, tincture, dash, smack, sprinkling, seasoning, infusion, etc., *soupçon*, shade, bit, portion, dose.

Compound resulting from mixture: alloy, amalgam, magma, *mélange*, half and half, hybrid, *tertium quid*, miscellany, medley, pastiche, *pasticcio*, patchwork,

42. Freedom from mixture.

SIMPLENESS (*Substantives*), singleness, purity, clearness, homogeneity.

Purification (652), elimination, sifting, winnowing.

(*Verbs*). To render simple, simplify, sift, winnow, eliminate; to separate, disjoin (44).

To purify (652).

(*Adjectives*). Simple, uniform, of a piece, homogeneous, single, pure, clear, sheer, blank, neat, elementary; unmixed, unmingled, untinged, unblended, uncombined, uncompounded, undecomposed, unadulterated, unsophisticated.

Free from, exempt from.

(*Phrase*). Pure and simple.

––––––

odds and ends; farrago, jumble (59), mess, salad, sauce, hash, hodge-podge (hotch-potch, or hotchpot), mash, mishmash, job lot, omnium gatherum, gallimaufry, *olla podrida*, olio, salmagundi, *pot-pourri*, Noah's ark, cauldron, marquetry, mosaic (440), complex.

(*Phrases*). A mingled yarn; a scratch team.

(*Verbs*). To mix, commix, immix, intermix, associate, mingle, commingle, intermingle, bemingle, interlard, intersperse, interpose, interpolate (228); shuffle together, hash up, huddle together, deal, pound together, stir up, knead, brew, jumble (59); impregnate with.

To be mixed, to get among, to be entangled with.

To instil, imbue, infuse, infiltrate, dash, tinge, tincture, season, sprinkle, besprinkle, suffuse, transfuse, attemper, medicate, blend, alloy, amalgamate, compound (48), adulterate, sophisticate, cross, intercross, interbreed, interblend.

(*Adjectives*). Mixed, mingled, intermixed, etc., promiscuous; complex, composite, mixed up with, half-and-half, linsey-woolsey, cross, hybrid, half-caste, Eurasian, mulatto (83), quadroon, octoroon, sambo, mongrel, heterogeneous; miscible.

43. JUNCTION (*Substantives*), joining, union, connection, connecting, conjunction, conjugation, annexion, annexation, annexment, attachment, compagination, astriction, alligation, colligation, fastening, linking, coupling, matrimony (903), grafting; infibulation, inosculation, symphysis, anastomosis, association (72), concatenation, communication, approach (197).

Joint, join, juncture, pivot, hinge, suture, articulation, commissure, miûre, seam, stitch, meeting, reunion, mortise, scar, cicatrix.

Closeness, firmness, tightness, compactness, attachment, communication.

(*Verbs*). To join, conjoin, unite, connect, associate, put together, embody, re-embody, hold together, lump together, pack, fix together, attach, affix, saddle on, fasten, bind, secure, make fast, clench (or clinch), catch, tie, pinion, strap, sew, lace, string, stitch, tack, knit, tat, crochet, knot, button, buckle, hitch, lash, truss, bandage, braid, splice, swathe, gird, tether, picket, harness, inspan, bridge over.

44. DISJUNCTION (*Substantives*), disconnection, disunity, disunion, disassociation, disengagement, abstractedness, isolation, insularity, oasis, separateness, severalness, severality.

Separation, parting, detachment, divorce, sejunction, seposition, segregation, insulation, diduction, discerption, elision, cæsura, division, subdivision, break, fracture, rupture, dismemberment, disintegration, dislocation, luxation, severance, disseverance, severing, fission, scission, rescission, abscission, laceration, dilaceration, wrenching, disruption, avulsion, divulsion, tearing asunder, section, cutting, resection, cleavage, fissure, breach, rent, split, crack, slit, tear, rip, dispersion (73), incision, dissection, vivisection, anatomy.

Anatomist, prosector.

(*Verbs*). To be disjoined, separated, etc., to come off, fall off, fall to pieces.

To disjoin, disconnect, disunite, part, dispart, detach, separate, space, space out, cut off, rescind, segregate, insulate, dissociate, isolate, disengage, set apart, liberate, loose, set free,

Chain, enchain, shackle, pinion, manacle, handcuff, lock, latch, belay, brace, hook, clap together, leash, couple, link, yoke, bracket, hang together, pin, nail, bolt, hasp, clasp, clamp, screw, rivet, impact, wedge, rabbet, mortise, mitre, jam, dovetail, enchase, engraft, interlink, inosculate, entwine, interlace, intertwine, intertwist, interweave, interlock.

To be joined, etc., to hang or hold together.

(*Adjectives*). Joined, conjoined, coupled, etc., bound up together, conjunct, corporate, compact.

(*Phrase*). Rolled into one.

Firm, fast, close, tight, taut, secure, set, fixed, impacted, jammed, locked, etc., intervolved, intertwined, inseparable, indissoluble, inseverable, untearable.

(*Adverbs*). Conjointly, jointly, etc.

With, along with, together with, in conjunction with.

Fast, firmly, closely, etc.

———

unloose, unfasten, untie, unbind, disband, unfix, unlace, unclasp, undo, unbuckle, unchain, unfetter, untack, unharness, ungird, unpack, unbolt, unlatch, unlock, unlink, uncouple, unpin, unclinch, unscrew, unhook, unrivet, untwist, unshackle, unyoke, unknit, unsolder, ravel, unravel, disentangle, unpick, unglue, switch off, shut off.

Sunder, divide, subdivide, sever, dissever, abscind, cut, scissor, incide, incise, snip, nib, cleave, rive, slit, split, split in twain, splinter, chip, crack, snap, rend, break or tear asunder, shiver, crunch, chop, cut up, rip up, hack, hew, slash, whittle, haggle, hackle, discind, tear, lacerate, mangle, mince, gash, hash, knap.

Dissect, cut up, carve, castrate, detruncate, anatomise; take, pull, or pick to pieces; unseam, tear to tatters, tear piecemeal, divellicate, disintegrate; dismember, disbranch, dislocate, disjoint, mince, break up, crunch, gride, comminute (330), vivisect.

(*Adjectives*). Disjoined, disconnected, etc., snippety, disjointed, multipartite, abstract, disjunctive, isolated, insular, separate, discrete, apart, asunder, loose, free, liberated, disengaged, unattached, unannexed, distinct, unassociated, adrift, straggling, dispersed, disbanded, segregated.

Cut off, rescinded, etc., rift, reft.

Capable of being cut, scissile; fissile; discerptible.

(*Adverbs*). Separately, etc., one by one, severally, apiece, apart, adrift, asunder; in the abstract, abstractedly.

45. Connecting medium.

VINCULUM (*Substantives*), link, connective, conjunction, copula, intermedium, hyphen, bridge, stepping-stone, isthmus, span.

Bond, filament, fibre (205), hair, cordage, cord, thread, string, packthread, twine, twist, whipcord, tape, ferret, raffia, line, ribbon, riband, rope, cable, hawser, halyard, guy, guy-rope, wire, chain.

Fastening, tie, ligament, ligature, strap, tackle, rigging, traces, harness, yoke, band, tire, brace, bandage, roller, fillet, thong, braid, girder, girth, cestus, garter, halter, noose, lasso, lariat, surcingle, knot, running-knot, slip-knot, reef-knot, sailor's knot, granny-knot, etc.

Pin, corking-pin, safety-pin, nail, brad, tack, skewer, staple, clamp, vice, bracket, cramp, screw, button, buckle, brooch, clasp, hasp, hinge, hank, catch, latch, latchet, tag, hook, tooth, hook and eye, lock, locket, holdfast, padlock, rivet, grappling-iron, stake, post, gyve, shackle, etc. (752), clip.

Cement, glue, gum, paste, size, solder, lute, putty, birdlime, mortar, stucco, plaster, grout.

46. COHERENCE (*Substantives*), cohesion, adherence, adhesion, accretion, concretion, agglutination, conglutination, aggregation, consolidation, set, cementation, soldering, welding, grouting.

Sticking, clinging, adhesiveness, stickiness, gumminess, gummosity, glutinosity, cohesiveness, density (321), inseparability, inseparableness, tenaciousness, tenacity.

Clot, concrete, cake, lump, solid, conglomerate (321).

(*Verbs*). To cohere, adhere, stick, cling, cleave, hold, take hold of, hold fast, hug, grow or hang together, twine round.

To concrete, curdle, cake.

(*Phrases*). To stick like a leech; to stick like wax; to cling like ivy, like a bur, like a limpet.

47. Want of adhesion, non-adhesion, immiscibility.

INCOHERENCE (*Substantives*), looseness, laxity, slackness, relaxation, freedom, disjunction.

(*Phrases*). A rope of sand; *disjecta membra*.

(*Verbs*). To loosen, make loose, slacken, relax, unglue, unsolder, etc., detach, untwist, unravel, unroll, etc. (44, 313).

To comminute (330).

(*Adjectives*). Incoherent, immiscible, detached, non-adhesive, loose, slack, lax, relaxed, baggy.

Segregated, flapping, streaming, dishevelled, unincorporated, unconsolidated, uncombined, etc., like grains of sand.

To glue, agglutinate, conglutinate, consolidate, solidify (321), cement, lute, paste, gum, grout, stick, solder, weld.

(*Adjectives*). Cohesive, adhesive, cohering, tenacious, etc., sticky, glutinous, gluey, gummy, viscous (352), agglutinatory.

United, unseparated, sessile, inseparable, infrangible (321).

---

48. COMBINATION (*Substantives*), union, unification, synthesis, incorporation, amalgamation, coalescence, crasis, fusion, synthesis, conflation, absorption, blending, centralisation.

Compound, composition, amalgam, impregnation.

(*Verbs*). To combine, unite, unify, incorporate, amalgamate, synthesise, embody, unify, re-embody, blend, merge, fuse, absorb, melt into one, consoli-

49. DECOMPOSITION (*Substantives*), disjunction, analysis, resolution, dissolution, catalysis, corruption (653).

(*Verbs*). To decompose, disembody, analyse, decompound, resolve, take to pieces, separate into its elements, dissect, unravel, etc., break up.

(*Adjectives*). Decomposed, etc., catalytic, analytic, analytical, corrupted, dissolved.

date, coalesce, centralise; to impregnate, to put together, to lump together.

(*Adjectives*). Combined, etc., coalescent, synthetic, synthetical, impregnated with, engrained.

4°. CONCRETE QUANTITY

50. WHOLE (*Substantives*), totality, integrity, entireness, entirety, *ensemble*, collectiveness, individuality, unity (87), indivisibility, indiscerptibility, indissolubility; integration.

All, the whole, total, aggregate, integer, gross, amount, sum, sum total, *tout ensemble*, upshot, alpha and omega, root and branch, head and shoulders, neck and heels, trunk, hull, skeleton, hulk, lump, heap (72).

The principal part, bulk, mass, tissue, staple, body, compages, the main, the greater part, major part, essential part, best part, any part, aught, marrow, soul of, pith, nucleus (642).

(*Phrases*). Lion's share; Benjamin's mess.

(*Verbs*). To form or constitute a whole, to integrate, embody, aggregate, amass (72), to amount to, come to.

(*Adjectives*). Whole, total, integral, entire, one, unbroken, uncut, undivided, seamless, individual, unsevered, unclipped, uncropped, unshorn. undiminished, undemolished, undissolved, unbruised, undestroyed, indivisible, indissoluble, indissolvable, indiscerptible.

Wholesale, sweeping.

(*Adverbs*). Wholly, altogether, totally, entirely, all, all in all, as a whole, wholesale, in the mass, *en masse*, in the lump, on the whole, *in toto*, in the gross, *in extenso*, in the bulk, to the full, throughout, every inch.

51. PART (*Substantives*), portion, item, division, subdivision, section, chapter, verse, sector, segment, fraction, fragment, frustum, detachment, piece, bit, scrap, whit, aught, morsel, mouthful, scantling, cantle, cantlet, slip, crumb, fritter, rag, tag, shred, shive, tatter, splinter, snatch, flitter, cut, cutting, snip, snippet, snick, collop, slice, chip, chipping, shiver, sliver, matchwood, spillikin, smithereens, driblet, clipping, paring, shaving, *débris*, odds and ends, oddments, sundries, detritus, scale, lamina, shadow, flotsam and jetsam, pickings.

Part and parcel, share, instalment, contingent, dividend, dose, particular, article, chapter, clause, count, paragraph.

Member, limb, lobe, lobule, arm, branch, scion, bough, joint, link, ramification (256), twig, bush, spray, sprig, offshoot, leaf, leaflet, stump, stub, torso.

(*Verbs*). To part, divide, subdivide, break, etc. (44); to partition, parcel out, portion, apportion (786); to ramify, branch, branch out.

(*Adjectives*). Part, fractional, fragmentary, scrappy, lobular, sectional, aliquot, divided, multifid, partitioned, etc., isomeric.

(*Adverbs*). Partly, in part, partially, piecemeal, in detail, part by part, by driblets, bit by bit, by inches, inch by inch, foot by foot, drop by drop, in lots.

(*Phrases*). The long and short of it; nearly or almost all; head and shoulders; neck and heels; in the long run; in the main; neck and crop; from end to end; from beginning to end; from first to last; from head to foot; from top to toe; fore and aft; from alpha to omega; the whole boiling.

52. COMPLETENESS (*Substantives*), entirety, fullness, completion (729), perfection (650), solidity, stop-gap, makeweight, padding, filling up, integration, absoluteness, sufficiency.

Complement, supplement (39).

(*Verbs*). To be complete, etc., suffice (639).

To render complete or whole, to complete, exhaust, perfect, finish, make up, fill up, make good, piece out, eke out.

(*Phrases*). To give the last finish; to supply deficiencies; to go the whole length; to go the whole hog; to ring the changes; to thrash out.

(*Adjectives*). Complete, entire, absolute, perfect, full, plenary, solid, undivided, with all its parts, supplementary, adscititious, thorough, exhaustive, searching.

(*Adverbs*). Completely; entirely, to the full, outright, thoroughly (*see* 31), *in toto, toto cœlo*, in all respects, etc.

(*Phrases*). *De fond en comble; à fond; ne plus ultra*; from first to last; from beginning to end; *ab ovo usque ad mala; à outrance*.

53. INCOMPLETENESS (*Substantives*), deficiency, defectiveness, unreadiness, defalcation, failure, imperfection (651), hollowness, patchiness.

Part wanting, omission, defect, deficit, ullage, *caret*, hiatus (198).

(*Verbs*). To be incomplete, etc., to fail, fall short (304).

To dock, lop, mutilate, garble, truncate, castrate (38).

(*Adjectives*). Incomplete, imperfect, defective, deficient, wanting, failing, short by, hollow, meagre, insufficient, half-baked, scrappy, patchy.

Mutilated, garbled, docked, lopped, truncate, castrated.

(*Phrase*). *Cetera desunt.*

54. COMPOSITION (*Substantives*), constitution, constituency, crasis.

Inclusion, admission, comprehension, reception.

Inclusion in a class (76).

(*Verbs*). To be composed of, to consist of, be made of, formed of, made up of, be resolved into.

To contain, include, hold, comprehend, take in, admit, embrace, involve, implicate.

To compose, constitute, form, make, make up, fill up, build up, put together, embody.

55. EXCLUSION (*Substantives*), non-admission, omission, exception, rejection, proscription, repudiation, exile, banishment, excommunication.

Separation, segregation, seposition.

Exclusion from a class (77).

(*Verbs*). To be excluded from, etc., to be out of it.

To exclude, shut out, bar, leave out, omit, garble, reject, repudiate, neglect, blackball; lay, put, or set apart or aside; segregate, pass over, throw overboard,

To enter into the composition of, to be or form part of (51), to merge in, be merged in.

(*Adjectives*). Comprehending, containing, including, comprising, etc.

Component, constituent, formative, forming, constituting, composing, etc., entering into, being or forming part of, etc., belonging to, appertaining to, inclusive.

---

56. COMPONENT (*Substantives*), component part, integral part, element, constituent, ingredient, member, limb (51), part and parcel, contents (190), appurtenance.

slur over, neglect (460), excommunicate, banish, expatriate, ostracise, relegate, send down (297), rule out.

To eliminate, weed, winnow, bar, separate (44), strike off.

(*Adjectives*). Excluding, omitting, etc., exclusive.

Excluded, omitted, etc., unrecounted, inadmissible.

(*Adverbs*). Exclusive of, barring, etc., excepting.

57. EXTRANEOUSNESS (*Substantives*), foreign body, alien, stranger, intruder, outsider, interloper, foreigner, *novus homo*, a new-comer, a new chum, a Johnny Newcome, a tenderfoot.

(*Adjectives*). Extraneous, foreign, alien, interloping.

(*Adverbs*). Abroad, in foreign parts, overseas.

SECTION IV.—ORDER

1°. ORDER IN GENERAL

58. ORDER (*Substantives*), regularity, orderliness, uniformity, even tenor, symmetry.

(*Phrase*). *Lucidus ordo.*

Gradation, progression, pedigree, line, descent, subordination, course, array, routine.

Method, disposition, arrangement, system, economy, discipline, plan.

Rank, station, hierarchy, place, status, stand, scale, step, stage, period, term (71), footing; rank and file.

(*Verbs*). To be, or become in order, to form, form fours, fall in, arrange itself, place itself, range itself, fall into its place, fall into rank.

59. Absence, or want of Order, etc.

DISORDER (*Substantives*), irregularity, asymmetry, anomaly, confusion, confusedness, disarray, jumble, huddle, litter, lumber, farrago, mess, muddle, mix-up, upset, hodge-podge, huggermugger, anarchy, anarchism, imbroglio, chaos, *tohu-bohu*, omnium gatherum (41), *disjecta membra*.

Complexedness, complexity, complication, intricacy, intricateness, implication, perplexity, involution, ravelling, entanglement, knot, coil, skein, sleave, Gordian knot.

(*Phrase*). Wheels within wheels.

(*Adjectives*). Orderly, regular, in order, arranged, etc. (60), in its proper place, tidy, shipshape, *en règle*, well regulated, methodical, business-like, uniform, symmetrical, systematic, unconfused, undisturbed. u n t a n g l e d, unruffled, unravelled, still, etc. (265).

(*Phrase*). In apple-pie order.

(*Adverbs*). Systematically, etc., in turn, in its turn.

Step by step, by regular steps, gradations, stages, periods, or intervals, periodically (138).

At stated periods (138), *gradatim, seriatim*.

———

Turmoil, *mêlée*, tumult, ferment, stew, fermentation, pudder, pother, riot, rumpus, scramble, fracas, vortex, whirlpool, maelstrom, hurly-burly, bear-garden, Babel, Saturnalia, pandemonium.

Tumultuousness, riotousness, inquietude (173).

(*Phrases*). *Rudis indigestaque moles*; confusion worse confounded; most admired disorder; *concordia discors*; hell broke loose.

A pretty kettle of fish; all the fat in the fire; *le diable à quatre*; the devil to pay.

Derangement (61), inversion of order.

Topsy - turvy (218), hocus-pocus.

(*Phrases*). The cart before the horse; *hysteron proteron*.

(*Verbs*). To be out of order, irregular, disorderly, etc., to ferment, misplace.

To put out of order (61).

(*Phrases*). To fish in troubled waters; to make hay of.

(*Adjectives*). Disorderly, orderless, out of order, misplaced, out of place, deranged, disarranged (61), irregular, desultory, anomalous, untidy, tousled, straggling, unarranged, immethodical, unsymmetrical, unsystematic, unmethodical, undigested, unsorted, unclassified, unclassed, asymmetrical.

Disjointed, out of joint, out of gear, confused, tangled, involved, fumbled, inextricable, irreducible.

Mixed, scattered, promiscuous, indiscriminate, casual.

Tumultuous, turbulent, riotous, troublous, tumultuary (173), rough-and-tumble.

(*Adverbs*). Irregularly, etc., by fits and snatches, pell-mell; higgledy - piggledy; at sixes and sevens; helter - skelter; harum-scarum, in a ferment, at cross purposes; *à bâtons rompus*; anyhow.

60. Reduction to Order.

ARRANGEMENT (*Substantives*), disposal, disposition, collocation, allocation, distribution, sorting, assortment, allotment, apportionment, marshalling, alinement, taxis, taxonomy, gradation, organisation, ordination.

61. Subversion of Order, bringing into disorder.

DERANGEMENT (*Substantives*), disarrangement, misarrangement, displacement, misplacement, discomposure, disturbance, bedevilment, disorganisation, perturbation, shuffling, rumpling, em-

Analysis, sifting, classification.

Result of arrangement: digest, synopsis, analysis, *syntagma*, table, register (551).

Instrument for sorting: sieve, riddle, screen (260).

(*Verbs*). To order, reduce to order, bring into order, introduce order into.

To arrange, dispose, place, form; to put, set, place, etc., in order; to set out, collocate, pack, marshal, range, aline (or align), rank, group, parcel out, allot, distribute, assort, sort, sift, riddle.

(*Phrases*). To put or set to rights; to assign places to.

To class, classify, file, string, tabulate, register, take stock.

To methodise, digest, regulate, grade, gradate, graduate, organise, settle, fix, rearrange.

To unravel (246), disentangle, ravel, card, disembroil.

(*Adjectives*). Arranged, methodical, etc. (*see* 58), embattled, in battle array.

broilment, corrugation (258), inversion (218), jumble, muddle.

(*Verbs*). To derange, disarrange, misplace, mislay, discompose, disorder, embroil, unsettle, disturb, confuse, perturb, jumble, tumble, huddle, shuffle, muddle, toss, hustle, fumble, riot; misarrange, bring, put, or throw into disorder, trouble, confusion, etc., break the ranks, upset.

To unhinge, put out of joint, turn over, invert; turn topsyturvy; turn inside out (218), bedevil, throw out of gear.

To complicate, involve, perplex, tangle, entangle, ravel, ruffle, tousle, rumple, dishevel, litter, scatter, make a mess of, monkey with, make hay of.

(*Adjectives*). Deranged, etc., *see* 59.

Irreducible.

2°. Consecutive Order

62. Precedence (*Substantives*), coming before, antecedence, priority, anteriority, antecedency, the *pas*, the lead.

Superiority (33), precession (280).

(*Verbs*). To precede, come before, lead, introduce, usher in.

(*Phrases*). To have the *pas*; to take the lead; to get the start; set the fashion; to get before.

To place before; to prefix, affix, premise, prelude, preface, prologise.

To prepare (673).

(*Adjectives*). Preceding, precedent, antecedent, anterior, prior, previous, before, ahead of, leading.

63. Sequence (*Substantives*) coming after, consecution, succession, posteriority, secondariness.

Runner-up.

(*Phrase*). *Proxime accessit.*

Continuation, order of succession, successiveness.

Subordination, inferiority (34).

Alternation (138).

(*Verbs*). To succeed, come after, follow, come next, ensue, come on, tread close upon; to alternate.

(*Phrases*). To be in the wake or trail of; to tread on the heels of; to step into the shoes of; to play second fiddle to.

To place after, to suffix, append.

Former, foregoing; coming or going before; precursory, precursive, prevenient, preliminary, prefatory, introductory, prelusive, prelusory, proemial, preparatory, preambulatory.

(*Adverbs*). In advance, ahead, etc., in front of, before, in the van, *see* 234.

(*Adjectives*). Succeeding, coming after, following, subsequent, ensuing, sequent, sequacious, consequent, next; consecutive; alternate (138).

Latter, posterior.

(*Adverbs*). After, subsequently, since, behind, in the wake of, in the train of, at the tail of, in the rear of, *see* 235.

64. PRECURSOR (*Substantives*), antecedent, predecessor, fore-runner, pioneer, outrider, avant-courier, leader, bell-wether, harbinger.

Prelude, preamble, preface, foreword, prologue, *avant-propos*, protasis, prolusion, *preludium*, proem, prolepsis, prolegomena, prefix, introduction, note, advertisement, frontispiece, ground-work (673).

(*Adjectives*). See 62.

65. SEQUEL (*Substantives*), after-part, aftermath, suffix, successor, tail, queue, train, wake, trail, rear, retinue, suite, appendix (39), postscript, epilogue, excursus, after-piece, after-thought, second thoughts, codicil, continuation, sequela, apodosis.

(*Phrases*). More last words; to be continued.

66. BEGINNING (*Substantives*), commencement, opening, outset, incipience, inception, inchoation, initiative, overture, exordium, inauguration, onset, brunt, alpha.

Origin, source, rise, birth, infancy, bud, embryo, rudiment, *incunabula*, start, cradle, starting-point, starting-post, *see* Departure (293).

Van, vanguard, title-page, heading, front (234), fore-part, head (210).

Dawn, morning (125).

Opening, entrance, entry, inlet, orifice, porch, portal, portico, gateway, door, gate, postern, wicket, threshold, vestibule, mouth, *fauces*, chops, chaps, lips.

(*Phrase*). The rising of the curtain.

(*Verbs*). To begin, commence, inchoate, rise, arise, originate, initiate, open, dawn, set in, take

67. END (*Substantives*), close, termination, desinence, conclusion, finish, finis, finale, period, term, terminus, last, omega, extreme, extremity, butt-end, fag-end, stub, tail, nib, after-part, rear (235), colophon, coda, tail-piece, tag, *cul-de-lampe*, peroration, swan-song, *bonne-bouche*.

Completion (729), winding-up, *dénouement*, catastrophe, consummation, finishing stroke, death-blow, *coup de grâce*, upshot, issue, fate, doom, Day of Judgment, doomsday.

(*Phrases*). The *ne plus ultra*; the fall of the curtain; the turning point; "*le commencement de la fin.*"

(*Verbs*). To end, close, finish, expire, terminate, conclude; come or draw to an end, close or stop; to pass away; to give out, peter out; to run its course; to say one's say, perorate, be through with.

its rise, enter upon, set out (293), recommence, to undertake (676).

To usher in, to lead off, lead the way, take the lead or the initiative; head, stand at the head, stand first; broach, set on foot, set a-going, set abroach, set up, institute, launch, strike up.

(*Phrases*). To make a beginning; break ground; set the ball in motion; take the initiative; break the ice; fire away; open the ball; tee off; pipe up.

(*Adjectives*). Beginning, commencing, arising, initial, initiatory, initiative, incipient, proemial, inaugural, inchoate, inchoative, embryonic, primigenial, aboriginal, rudimental, nascent, natal, opening, dawning, entering.

First, foremost, leading, heading, maiden (*e.g.* maiden speech).

Begun, commenced, etc.

To come last, bring up the rear.

To bring to an end, close, etc., to put a period, etc., to; to make an end of; to close, finish, seal, etc., to wind up, complete, achieve (729), crown, determine.

(*Phrases*). To cut the matter short; to shut up shop.

(*Adjectives*). Ending, closing, etc., final, terminal, desistive, definitive, crowning.

Last, ultimate, penultimate, antepenultimate, hindermost, rear, caudal, conterminal, conterminous.

Ended, closed, terminated, etc.

Unbegun, fresh, uncommenced.

(*Adverbs*). Once for all; finally, for good, for good and all.

(*Adverbs*). At, or in the beginning; first, in the first place, *imprimis*, first and foremost, *in limine*, in the bud, in embryo.

From the beginning, *ab initio*; *ab ovo*; *ab incunabulis*.

---

68. MIDDLE (*Substantives*), mean, medium, happy medium, *via media*, middle term, centre (223), *mezzo termine*, *juste milieu*, half-way house, nave, navel, omphalos, nucleus.

Equidistance, midst, equator, diaphragm, midriff; bisection (91). Intervenience, interjacence, intervention (228), mid-course (628).

(*Adjectives*). Middle, medial, median, mean, mid, middlemost, midmost, mediate, intermediate (29), intervenient, interjacent (228), central (222), equidistant, embosomed, merged.

Mediterranean, equatorial.

(*Adverbs*). In the middle, amid, amidst, midway, amidships, midships, half-way.

(*Phrases*). In the thick of; *in mediis rebus*.

---

69. Uninterrupted sequence.

CONTINUITY (*Substantives*), consecution, succession, suite, progression, series, train, chain, catenation, concatenation, scale, gradation, course, procession, column, retinue, cortège, cavalcade, rank and file, line of battle,

70. Interrupted sequence.

DISCONTINUITY (*Substantives*), interruption, pause, period, interregnum, break, interval, cut, gap, fracture, chasm, hiatus (198), cæsura, parenthesis, rhapsody, anacoluthon.

Intermission, alternation, *see*

array, pedigree, genealogy, lineage, race.

File, queue, echelon, line, row, range, tier, string, thread, team, tandem, suite, colonnade.

(*Verbs*). To follow in a series, etc.; to form a series, etc.; to fall in.

To arrange in a series, to marshal, etc. (60); to string together, file, thread, graduate, tabulate.

(*Adjectives*). Continuous, sequent, consecutive, progressive, serial, successive, continued, uninterrupted, unbroken, entire, linear, in a line, in a row, etc., gradual, unintermitting (110).

(*Adverbs*). Continuously, consecutively, etc., *seriatim*; in a line, in a string, in a row, series, etc., in succession, etc., running, gradually, step by step; uninterruptedly, at a stretch, at one go.

(*Phrase*). In Indian file.

Periodicity (138); a broken thread, broken melody.

(*Verbs*). To be discontinuous, etc.; to alternate, intermit.

To discontinue, pause, interrupt, break, interpose (228); to break in upon, disconnect (44); to break or snap the thread.

(*Adjectives*). Discontinuous, inconsecutive, broken, interrupted, desultory, *décousu*, disconnected, unconnected, rhapsodical, spasmodic, sporadic, scattered.

Alternate, every other, intermitting, alternating (138).

(*Phrase*). Few and far between.

(*Adverbs*). At intervals, by snatches, *per saltum*, by fits and starts, *longo intervallo*.

71. TERM (*Substantives*), rank, station, stage, step, rung (of a ladder), degree (26), remove, grade, link, place, point, *pas*, period, pitch, stand, standing, footing, range.

(*Verbs*). To hold, occupy, find, fall into a place, station.

3°. COLLECTIVE ORDER

72. ASSEMBLAGE (*Substantives*), collection, dozen, collocation, levy, gathering, ingathering, muster, round-up, colligation, contesseration, *attroupement*, association, concourse, conflux, meeting, assembly, congregation, levee, club, reunion, soirée, conversazione, accumulation, cumulation, array, mobilisation.

Congress, convocation, convention, *comitium*, committee, quorum, conclave, synod, caucus, conventicle, *posse*, *posse comitatus*, eisteddfod, mass-meeting.

73. NON-ASSEMBLAGE.

DISPERSION (*Substantives*), scattering, dissemination, diffusion, dissipation, spreading, casting, distribution, apportionment, sprinkling, respersion, circumfusion, interspersion, divergence (291), demobilisation.

Odds and ends, waifs and strays, flotsam and jetsam.

(*Verbs*). To disperse, scatter, sow, disseminate, diffuse, shed, spread, overspread, dispense, disband, distribute, dispel, cast forth; strew, bestrew, sprinkle,

Miscellany, museum, *collectanea*, menagerie, Noah's ark, encyclopædia, portfolio, a drag-net.

A multitude (102), crowd, throng, rabble, mob, press, crush, *cohue*, horde, posse, body, tribe, crew, gang, knot, band, party, swarm, shoal, bevy, galaxy, covey, flock, herd, drove, corps, troop, troupe, squad, squadron, phalanx, platoon, company, regiment, battalion, legion, host, army, myrmidons. Store, *see* 636.

Clan, brotherhood, fraternity, sisterhood, party (712).

Volley, shower, storm, cloud, etc.

issue, deal out, utter, resperse, intersperse, set abroach, circumfuse; to decentralise, demobilise.

(*Phrases*). To turn adrift; to scatter to the winds; to sow broadcast; to spread like wild-fire.

(*Adjectives*). Unassembled, uncollected, dispersed, scattered, diffused, sparse, spread, dispread, widespread, sporadic, cast, broadcast, etc., adrift, dishevelled, streaming, etc.

(*Adverbs*). *Sparsim*, here and there, *passim*.

———

Group, cluster, Pleiades, clump, set, batch, pencil, lot, pack, budget, assortment, bunch, parcel, packet, package, bundle, fascicle, fascicule, *fasciculus*, faggot, wisp, truss, tuft, rosette, shock, rick, fardel, stack, sheaf, stook.

Accumulation, congeries, heap, hoard, lump, pile, *rouleau*, tissue, mass, pyramid, bale, drift, snow-ball, acervation, cumulation, glomeration, agglomeration, conglobation, conglomeration, conglomerate, coacervation, aggregation, concentration, congestion, Pelion upon Ossa, *spicilegium*, omnium gatherum. *See* Convergence (290).

Collector, tax-gatherer, whip, whipper-in.

(*Verbs*). To assemble, collect, muster, meet, unite, cluster, flock, herd, crowd, throng, associate, congregate, conglomerate, congest, rendezvous, resort, flock together, get together, reassemble.

To bring, get or gather together, collect, draw together, group, convene, convoke, convocate, collocate, colligate, round up, scrape together, rake up, dredge, bring into a focus, amass, accumulate, heap up, pile, pack, do up, stack, truss, pack together, congest, acervate, agglomerate, garner up, lump together, make a parcel of; to centralise; to mobilise.

(*Phrases*). To heap Pelion upon Ossa; to collect in a drag-net.

(*Adjectives*). Assembled, collected, etc., undispersed, met together, closely packed, dense, crowded, huddled together, teeming, swarming, populous.

(*Phrase*). Packed like sardines.

74. Place of meeting.

Focus (*Substantives*), point of convergence, corradiation, rendezvous, headquarters, club, centre (222), gathering-place, meeting-place, trysting-place, resort, museum, repository, depot (636). Home.

4°. Distributive Order

75. CLASS (*Substantives*), division, category, *categorema*, predicament, head, order, section, department, province.

Kind, sort, genus, species, family, race, tribe, caste, sept, clan, *gens*, phratry, breed, kith, sect, set, assortment, feather, suit, range, run.

Gender, sex, kin, kidney, manner, description, denomination, designation, predicament, character, stamp, stuff, *genre*.

(*Adjectives*). Generic, racial, tribal, etc.

(*Verbs*). To class, etc., *see* 60.

76. INCLUSION (*Substantives*), comprehension under a class, reference to a class, subsumption.

Inclusion in a compound (54).

Inclusion, admission, reception.

(*Verbs*). To be included in, to come under, to fall under, to range under; to belong, or pertain to, appertain; to range with, to merge in, to be of.

To include, comprise, comprehend, contain, admit, embrace, enumerate among, reckon among, reckon with, number among, refer to, place under, class with or among, arrange under or with, subsume.

To take into account.

(*Adjectives*). Including, etc., inclusive, congener, congeneric, congenerous, *et hoc genus omne*, etcetera, etc.

Included, merged, etc.

(*Phrase*). Birds of a feather.

77. EXCLUSION from a class (*Substantives*),[1] rejection, etc., proscription, nobody.

Exclusion from a compound (55).

(*Verbs*). To be excluded from etc.; to exclude, proscribe, etc., to set apart.

(*Phrase*). To shut the door upon.

(*Adjectives*). Exclusive, excluding, etc.

———

78. GENERALITY (*Substantives*), universality, catholicism, catholicity.

Every, every man, everyone, everybody, all, all hands, to a man.

(*Phrases*). The world and his wife; "All people that on earth do dwell."

Miscellaneousness, miscellany, encyclopædia, generalisation, prevalence, drag-net.

79. SPECIALITY (*Substantives*), *specialité*, particularity, individuality, peculiarity, individuality, personality, *propria persona*, characteristic, mannerism, idiosyncrasy, trick, specificness, specificity, singularity (83), thisness.

Version, reading (522).

Particulars, details, items, counts.

(*Phrases*). *Argumentum ad hominem*; local colour.

———

[1] The same set of words are used to express *Exclusion from a class* and *Exclusion from a compound*. Reference is therefore here made to the former at 55. This identity does not occur with regard to *Inclusion*, which therefore required to be made a separate heading.

(*Verbs*). To be general, common, or prevalent, to prevail.

To render general, to generalise.

(*Adjectives*). General, generic, collective, comprehensive, encyclopædic, sweeping, radical, universal, world-wide, cosmopolitan, catholic, common, œcumenical, transcendental, prevalent, prevailing, all-pervading, all-inclusive.

Unspecified, impersonal.

(*Adverbs*). Whatever, whatsoever, generally, universally, on the whole, for the most part.

———

I, myself, self, I myself, *moi qui vous parle*.

(*Verbs*). To specify, particularise, individualise, realise, specialise, designate, determine.

(*Phrases*). To descend to particulars; to enter into detail.

(*Adjectives*). Special, particular, individual, specific, proper, personal, private, respective, definite, determinate, especial, certain, esoteric, endemic, partial, party, peculiar, characteristic, typical, unique, diagnostic, exclusive, *sui generis*, singular, exceptional (83). This, that, yonder, yon, such and such.

(*Adverbs*). Specially, specifically, etc., in particular, respectively, personally, individually, *in propria persona, ad hominem.*

Each, apiece, one by one, severally, seriatim, *videlicet*, viz., to wit.

5°. ORDER AS REGARDS CATEGORIES

80. RULE (*Substantives*), regularity, uniformity, constancy, standard, model, nature, principle, the order of things, routine, prevalence, practice, usage, custom, use, habit (613), regulation, convention, *convenances*.

Form, formula, law, canon, principle, key-note, catchword.

Type, pattern, precedent, paradigm, the normal, natural, ordinary or model state or condition, norm.

(*Phrases*). A standing dish; the Procrustean law; laws of the Medes and Persians.

———

82. CONFORMITY (*Substantives*), conformance, observance, naturalisation, harmony.

Example, instance, specimen, sample, ensample, exemplar,

81. MULTIFORMITY (*Substantives*), variety, diversity, multifariousness, allotropy.

(*Adjectives*). Multiform, polymorphic, multifold, manifold, multifarious, multigenerous, omnifarious, heterogeneous, motley, epicene, indiscriminate, desultory, irregular, diversified, allotropic.

(*Phrases*). *Et hoc genus omne*; of all sorts and kinds; and what not? *de omnibus rebus et quibusdam aliis.*

———

83. UNCONFORMITY (*Substantives*), informality, arbitrariness, abnormity, abnormality, anomaly, anomalousness, lawlessness, peculiarity, exclusiveness,

exemplification, illustration, case in point, quotation, the rule.

(*Phrases*). The order of the day; the common or ordinary run of things (*see* 23); matter of course; "familiar matter of to-day."

(*Verbs*). To conform to rule, be regular, to be orthodox, etc., to follow, observe, go by, bend to, obey rules, to be guided or regulated by, be wont, etc. (613), to chime in with, to be in harmony with, follow suit; to standardise, naturalise.

(*Phrases*). *Hurler avec les loups*; to do in Rome as the Romans do; to swim with the stream.

To exemplify, illustrate, cite, quote, put a case, produce an instance, etc., to set an example.

(*Phrase*). To keep one in countenance.

(*Adjectives*). Conformable to rule, regular, uniform, constant, steady, according to rule, *selon les règles, de règle, en règle, de rigueur*, normal, well regulated, formal, canonical, orthodox, conventional, strict, rigid, positive, uncompromising, *see* 23.

Ordinary, natural, usual, common, wonted, accustomed, habitual, household, average, everyday, current, rife, prevailing, prevalent, established, received, acknowledged, typical, accepted, recognised, representative, hackneyed, well - known, familiar, vernacular, commonplace, trite, banal, cut and dried, naturalised, orderly, stereotyped, *cliché*.

Exemplary, illustrative, in point, of daily or every-day occurrence, in the order of things.

(*Phrases*). Regular as clockwork; being in the order of the day.

(*Adverbs*). Conformably, by rule, regularly, etc., agreeably to.

infraction, breach, violation, etc., of law or rule, eccentricity, aberration, irregularity, unevenness, variety, singularity, oddity, oddness, exemption, salvo.

Exception, nondescript, a character, nonesuch, monster, monstrosity, prodigy (872), *lusus naturæ, rara avis*, freak, curiosity, queer fish, half-caste, half-breed, cross-breed, *métis*, mongrel, hybrid, mule, mulatto (41), *tertium quid*, hermaphrodite, sport.

Phœnix, chimera, hydra, sphinx, minotaur, griffin, centaur, hippocentaur, hippogriff, tragelaph, kraken, dragon, seaserpent, mermaid, unicorn, etc.

(*Phrases*). Out of one's element; a fish out of water; neither one nor another; neither fish, flesh, nor fowl, nor good red herring; a law to oneself.

(*Verbs*). To be unconformable to rule, to be exceptional; to stretch a point.

(*Phrases*). To have no business there; to beggar description.

(*Adjectives*). Unconformable, exceptional, abnormal, anomalous, anomalistic, out of order, out of place, misplaced, irregular, uneven, arbitrary, informal, aberrant, stray, peculiar, exclusive, unnatural, eccentric, unconventional, Bohemian.

Unusual, unaccustomed, unwonted, uncommon, rare, singular, unique, curious, odd, extraordinary, strange, *outré*, out of the way, egregious, out of the ordinary, unheard of, queer, quaint, old-fashioned, nondescript, undescribed, unexampled, *sui generis*, unprecedented, unparalleled, unfamiliar, fantastic, new-fangled, grotesque, bizarre, weird, eerie, outlandish, exotic, preternatural, unexampled, un-

Usually, generally, ordinarily, commonly, for the most part, as usual, *ad instar*, *instar omnium*, *more solito*, *more suo*, *pro more*.

Of course, as a matter of course, *pro forma*.

Always, uniformly, invariably, without exception, never otherwise.

For example, *par exemple*, for instance, *exempli gratia*, *inter alia*, to wit, namely, *videlicet*, that is to say.

(*Phrases*). *Ab uno disce omnes*; *cela va sans dire*; birds of a feather; *noscitur a sociis*.

representative, uncanny, denaturalised.

Heterogeneous, heteroclite, amorphous, out of the pale of, mongrel, amphibious, epicene, half-blood, hybrid (41), androgynous, betwixt and between.

(*Phrases*). Unlike what the world ever saw; without a parallel; "none but himself could be his parallel"; fallen from the clouds; caviar to the general.

(*Adverbs*). Except, unless, save, barring, beside, without, but for, save and except, let alone, to say nothing of.

However, yet, but, unusually, etc.

(*Phrases*). Never was seen, or heard, or known the like.

SECTION V.—NUMBER

1°. NUMBER IN THE ABSTRACT

84. NUMBER (*Substantives*), symbol, numeral, figure, cípher, digit, integer, counter, a round number, notation, a formula; series.

Sum, difference, complement, product, factorial, multiplicand, multiplier, multiplicator, coefficient, multiple, least common multiple, greatest common multiple, dividend, divisor, factor, highest common factor, quotient, sub-multiple, fraction, numerator, denominator, decimal, circulating decimal, recurring decimal, repetend, common measure, aliquot part, reciprocal, prime number; permutation, combination, election.

Ratio, proportion, progression (arithmetical, geometrical, harmonical), percentage.

Power, root, exponent, index, function, logarithm, antilogarithm; differential, integral, fluxion, fluent.

(*Adjectives*). Numeral, complementary, divisible, aliquot, reciprocal, prime, fractional, decimal, factorial, etc., fractional, mixed, incommensurable.

Proportional, exponential, logarithmic, logometric, differential, fluxional, integral.

Positive, negative, rational, irrational, surd, radical, real, imaginary, impossible.

85. NUMERATION (*Substantives*), numbering, counting, tale, telling, tally, calling over, recension, enumeration, summation, reckoning, computation, supputation, ciphering, calculation, calculus, algorism, rhabdology.

Arithmetic, analysis, algebra, fluxions, differential and integral calculus.

Statistics: dead reckoning, muster, poll, census, capitation, roll-call, muster-roll, account, score, recapitulation, demography.

Operations: addition, subtraction, multiplication, division, reduction, involution, evolution, practice, approximation, interpolation, differentiation, integration.

Instruments: abacus, logometer, ready-reckoner, sliding-rule, tallies, Napier's bones, tabulator, tot, cash-register, etc.

(*Verbs*). To number, count, tell, tally, call over, take an account of, enumerate, muster, poll, run over, recite, recapitulate; sum, sum up, tell off, score, cipher, compute, calculate, reckon, estimate, figure up, tot up; add, subtract, etc., to amount to.

Check, prove, demonstrate, balance, audit, overhaul, take stock.

(*Adjectives*). Numerical, arithmetical, logarithmic, numeral, analytic, algebraic, statistical, computable, calculable, commensurable, incommensurate.

(*Phrase*). According to Cocker.

86. List (*Substantives*), catalogue, inventory, schedule, register, record (551), account, registry, syllabus, roll, terrier, tally, file, muster-roll, roster, bead-roll, panel, calendar, index, table, book, ledger, day-book, synopsis, *catalogue raisonné*, bibliography, contents, invoice, bill of lading, bill of fare, menu, red book, peerage, baronetage, *Almanach de Gotha*, *cadastre*, prospectus, programme, directory, gazetteer, who's who.

Registration, etc. (551).

2°. Determinate Number

87. Unity (*Substantives*), unification, oneness, individuality, singleness, solitariness, solitude, isolation, abstraction; monism.

One, unit, ace.

Someone, somebody, no other, none else, an individual; monist.

(*Verbs*). To be alone, etc.; to isolate, insulate, set apart; to unify.

(*Adjectives*). One, sole, single, individual, apart, alone, lone, isolated, solitary, lonely, lonesome, desolate, dreary, insular, insulated, disparate, discrete, detached; monistic.

88. Accompaniment (*Substantives*), coexistence, concomitance, company, association, companionship, partnership, collaboration, copartnership, coefficiency.

Concomitant, accessory (39), coefficient, companion, attendant, fellow, associate, consort, spouse, colleague, collaborator, partner, copartner, satellite, escort, hanger-on, parasite, shadow; travelling tutor, chaperon, duenna.

(*Verbs*). To accompany, chaperon, coexist, attend, be asso-

Unaccompanied, unattended, *solus*, single-handed, singular, odd, unique, unrepeated, azygous.

Inseverable, irresolvable, indiscerptible, compact.

(*Adverbs*). Singly, etc., alone, by itself, *per se*, only, apart, in the singular number, in the abstract, one by one.

One and a half, *sesqui-*.

(*Phrase*). "His soul was like a star and dwelt apart."

ciated with, collaborate with, hang on, shadow, wait on, to join, tie together.

(*Phrase*). To go hand in hand with.

(*Adjectives*). Accompanying, coexisting, attending, etc., concomitant, fellow, twin, joint, associated with, accessory.

(*Adverbs*). With, withal, together with, along with, in company with, collectively, hand in hand, together, in a body, cheek by jowl, etc.; therewith, herewith, moreover, besides, also, and (37), not to mention.

---

89. DUALITY (*Substantives*), dualism, duplicity, doubleness, biformity; polarity.

Two, deuce, couple, brace, pair, twins, Siamese twins, Castor and Pollux, Damon and Pythias, fellows, gemini, yoke, conjugation, twosome; dualist.

(*Verbs*). To unite in pairs, to pair, pair off, couple, bracket, yoke.

(*Adjectives*). Two, twain, dual, binary, dualistic, duplex, twofold, bifold, biform, bifarious, duplicate, dyadic, binomial, twin, *tête-à-tête*, *bifrons*, Janus-headed, bilateral, bicentric, bifocal.

Coupled, bracketed, paired, etc., conjugate.

Both, the one and the other.

---

90. DUPLICATION (*Substantives*), doubling, gemination, reduplication, ingemination, repetition, iteration (104), renewal.

(*Verbs*). To double, redouble, geminate, reduplicate, repeat, iterate, re-echo, renew.

(*Adjectives*). Doubled, redoubled, etc.

Biform, bifarious or bifold, bifacial, duplex, duplicate, ingeminate.

(*Adverbs*). Twice, once more, over again, *da capo*, *bis*, *encore*, anew, as much again, twofold (104, 136).

Secondly, in the second place, again.

91. Division into two parts.

BISECTION (*Substantives*), bipartition, dichotomy, halving, dimidiation, bifurcation, forking, branching, ramification, divarication, splitting, cleaving.

Fork, prong, fold, branch.

Half, moiety, semi-, demi-, hemi-.

(*Verbs*). To bisect, halve, divide, split, cut in two, cleave, dimidiate, dichotomise.

(*Phrases*). To go halves; split the difference.

To separate, fork, bifurcate, branch out, ramify.

(*Adjectives*). Bisected, halved, divided, etc., bipartite, bicuspid, bifurcated, bifid, bifurcate, cloven, cleft, split, etc.

92. TRIALITY (*Substantives*), trinity.[1]

Three, triad, triplet, trey, trio, trinomial, leash, threesome, trefoil, triquetra.

Third power, cube.

(*Adjectives*). Three, triform, trinal, trinomial, tertiary, triquetrous.

93. TRIPLICATION (*Substantives*). triplicity, trebleness, trine.

(*Verbs*). To treble, triple, triplicate, cube.

(*Adjectives*). Treble, triple, tern, ternary, ternate, triplicate, trigeminal, threefold, third.

(*Adverbs*). Three times, thrice, threefold, in the third place, thirdly.

94. Division into three parts. TRISECTION (*Substantives*), tripartition, trichotomy; third part, third.

(*Verbs*). To trisect, divide into three parts, take the cube root.

(*Adjectives*). Trifid, trisected, tripartite, trichotomous, trisulcate, triform.

95. QUATERNITY (*Substantives*), four, tetrad, quartet, quaternion, foursome, square, quadrature, quarter.

(*Verbs*). To reduce to a square, to square.

(*Adjectives*). Four, quaternary, quaternal, quadratic, quartile, tetractic, tetra-.

96. QUADRUPLICATION.

(*Verbs*). To multiply by four, quadruplicate, biquadrate.

(*Adjectives*). Fourfold, quadruple, quadruplicate, fourth.

(*Adverbs*). Four times, in the fourth place, fourthly, to the fourth degree.

97. Division into four parts. QUADRISECTION (*Substantives*), quadripartition, quartering, a fourth, a quarter.

(*Verbs*). To quarter, to divide into four parts, etc.

(*Adjectives*). Quartered, etc., quadrifid, quadripartite.

98. FIVE (*Substantives*), cinque, cinqfoil, quint, quincunx, quintet.

(*Adjectives*). Five, quinary, quintuple, fivefold, fifth.

SIX, half-a-dozen, sextet.

(*Adjectives*). Senary, sextuple, sixfold, sixth.

SEVEN, heptad, septet.

EIGHT, octad, octet, ogdoad.

(*Adjectives*). Octuple, eightfold.

TEN, a decade.

(*Adjectives*). Decimal, denary, decuple, tenth.

TWELVE, a dozen.

(*Adjective*). Duodenary.

99. QUINQUESECTION, etc.

(*Adjectives*). Quinquefid, quinquarticular, quinquepartite.

Sexpartite.

Octofid.

DECIMATION.

(*Verb*). To decimate.

(*Adjectives*). Decimal, tenth, tithe.

DUODECIMAL, twelfth.

---

[1] *Trinity* is hardly ever used except in a theological sense (976).

THIRTEEN, a long dozen, a baker's dozen.

TWENTY, a score.

FORTY, twoscore.

FIFTY, twoscore and ten.

SIXTY, threescore.   Sexagesimal, sexagenary.

SEVENTY, threescore and ten.

EIGHTY, fourscore.

NINETY, fourscore and ten.

HUNDRED, centenary, heca-   HUNDREDTH, centesimal.
tomb, century. One hundred
and forty-four, a gross.

(*Verb*). To centuriate.

(*Adjectives*). Centuple, centu-
plicate, centennial, centenary.
centurial.

THOUSAND, chiliad.   Millesimal, etc.

MYRIAD, lac, crore.

MILLION, billion, trillion, etc.   ———

(*Adjectives*). Thirteenth, twen-
tieth, vigesimal, thirtieth, etc.

3°. INDETERMINATE NUMBER

100. More than one.

PLURALITY (*Substantives*), a
number, a certain number, a
round number.

(*Adjectives*). Plural, more than
one, upwards of, some, a few, one
or two, two or three, certain,
someone, somebody.

(*Adverb*). Etcetera.

101. ZERO (*Substantives*), nothing (4), naught, cipher, a solitude,
a desert.

(*Adjectives*). None, not one,
not any, *nemo*, nobody, not a
soul.

102. MULTITUDE (*Substantives*), numerousness, numerosity,
numerality, multiplicity, majority, profusion, legion, host, a
great or large number, numbers,
array, sight, army, sea, galaxy,
populousness (72), a hundred,
thousand, myriad, million, etc.

A shoal, swarm, draught, bevy,
flock, herd, drove, flight, covey,
hive, brood, litter, teem, fry,
nest, crowd, etc. (72).

Increase of number, multiplication.

103. FEWNESS (*Substantives*),
paucity, a small number, minority, handful, scantiness, rareness,
rarity, thinness.

Diminution of number, reduction, weeding, elimination, thin-
ning.

(*Verbs*). To be few, etc.

To render few, reduce,
diminish the number, weed, weed
out, prick off, eliminate, thin,
thin out, decimate.

(*Adjectives*). Few, scanty, rare,
sparse, thinly scattered, hardly

(*Verbs*). To be numerous, etc., to swarm, teem, crowd, come thick upon, outnumber, multiply, to people.

(*Phrase*). To swarm like locusts or bees.

(*Adjectives*). Many, several, sundry, divers, various, a great many, very many, full many, ever so many, no end, numerous, profuse, manifold, multiplied, multitudinous, multiple, multinomial, endless (105), teeming, populous, peopled.

Frequent, repeated, reiterated, outnumbering, thick, crowding, crowded, thick-coming, many more.

(*Phrases*). Thick as hops; thick as hail; thick as leaves in Vallombrosa; plentiful as blackberries; *cum multis aliis*; in profusion; and what not? and Heaven knows what; numerous as the stars in the firmament; as the sands on the sea-shore; as the hairs on the head; their name is "Legion."

or scarcely any, reduced, thinned, weeded, etc., unrepeated.

(*Phrases*). Few and far between; *rari nantes in gurgite vasto*.

---

104. REPETITION (*Substantives*), iteration, reiteration, harping, recurrence (136), recrudescence, tautology, monotony, cuckoo-note, chimes, repetend, echo, burden of a song, refrain, renewal, rehearsal, rechauffé, rehash. *See* 19.

Cuckoo, mocking-bird, mimic, imitator, parrot.

Periodicity (138), frequency (136).

(*Verbs*). To repeat, iterate, reiterate (535), renew, reproduce, echo, re-echo, drum, rehearse, redouble, recrudesce, reappear, hammer.

(*Phrases*). Do or say over again; ring the changes on; to harp on the same string; to din or drum in the ear; to conjugate in all its moods, tenses, and inflexions; to begin again, recommence.

(*Adjectives*). Repeated (136), repetitional, repetitionary, repetitive, recurrent, recurring, reiterated, renewed, ever-recurring, thick-coming, monotonous, harping, mocking, chiming, aforesaid.

(*Phrases*). Regular as clockwork; "*Ecce iterum Crispinus*"; *crambe repetita*.

(*Adverbs*). Repeatedly, often (136), again, anew, over again, afresh, ding-dong, ditto, *encore, de novo, da capo. See* Twice (90).

(*Phrases*). *Toties quoties*; again and again; in quick succession; over and over again; ever and anon; time after time; year after year; times out of number; *usque ad nauseam*.

105. INFINITY (*Substantives*), infinitude.

(*Adjectives*). Infinite, numberless, innumerable, countless, sumless, untold, unnumbered, unsummed, incalculable, unlimited, limitless, illimitable, immeasurable, unmeasured, measureless, unbounded, boundless, endless, interminable, unfathomable, exhaustless, termless, indefinite, without number, without limit, unending.

(*Adverbs*). Infinitely, etc., without measure, limit, etc., *ad infinitum*, world without end.

SECTION VI.—TIME

1°. ABSOLUTE TIME

106. DURATION (*Substantives*), period, term, space, span, spell, season, era, decade, century, chiliad, æon.

Intermediate time, while, interval, interim, pendency, intervention, intermission, interregnum, interlude, *intermezzo, entr'acte*, intermittence, respite (265).

Long duration (110).

(*Verbs*). To continue, last, endure, remain, to take, take up, fill or occupy time, to persist, to intervene.

To pass, pass away, spend, employ, while away or consume time, waste time.

(*Adjectives*). Continuing, lasting, enduring, remaining, persistent, perpetual, permanent (150).

(*Adverbs*). While, whilst, so long as, during, or pending, till, until, up to, during the time or interval, the whole time, or period, all the time or while, in the long run, all along, throughout, from beginning to end, from alpha to omega.

(*Phrases*). *Ab ovo usque ad mala*; from first to last.

Pending, meantime, meanwhile, in the meantime, in the interim, *ad interim, pendente lite*, from day to day, *de die in diem*, for a time, for a season, for good, yet, up to this time.

107. NEVERNESS[1] (*Substantives*), absence of time, no time. Short duration (111).

(*Adverbs*). Never, ne'er, at no time, on no occasion, at no period, nevermore, *sine die, dies non*.

(*Phrases*). On Tib's eve; on the Greek Calends; "at the coming of the Coquecigrues"; "jam every other day."

———

108. Definite duration, or portion of time.

PERIOD (*Substantives*), second, minute, hour, day, week, month, quarter, year, leap-year, lustrum, quinquennium, decade, lifetime, generation, lunation, light-year.

Century, age, millennium, *annus magnus, annus mirabilis*.

(*Adjectives*). Hourly, horary; daily, diurnal, quotidian; weekly, hebdomadal, menstrual, monthly, annual, secular, centennial, bicentennial, etc., bissextile, seasonal.

109. Indefinite duration.

COURSE (*Substantives*), progress, process, succession, lapse, flow, flux, stream, tract, current, tide, march, step, flight, etc., of time.

(*Phrases*). The scythe of time; the glass of time.

Indefinite time, aorist.

(*Verbs*). To elapse, lapse, flow, run, proceed, roll on, advance, pass, slide, press on, flit, fly, slip, glide.

(*Adjectives*). Elapsing, passing, etc., aoristic.

---

[1] A term introduced by Bishop Wilkins.

(*Adverbs*). From day to day, day in, day out; *de die in diem*, from hour to hour, etc., then, till, until, up to.

Once upon a time; Anno Domini, A.D.; Before Christ, B.C.

108A. CONTINGENT DURATION.
During pleasure, during good behaviour, *quamdiu se bene gesserit.*

110. Long duration.

DIUTURNITY (*Substantives*), a long time, an age, a century, an eternity.

(*Phrases*). *Temporis longinquitas*; a month of Sundays.

Durableness, durability, persistence, lastingness, continuance, permanence (150), longevity, survival.

Distance of time, protraction, extension or prolongation of time (133).

(*Verbs*). To last, endure, stand, etc.; abide, tarry, protract, prolong, outlast, outlive, survive; spin out, draw out, eke out, linger, loiter, lounge (275), wait.

(*Adjectives*). Durable, of long duration, permanent, enduring, chronic, intransient, intransitive, intransmutable, lasting, abiding, persistent; livelong, longeval, long-lived, diuturnal, evergreen, perennial, unintermitting, unremitting, *see* 112.

Protracted, prolonged, spun out, long-winded, surviving, etc.

(*Adverbs*). Long, a long time, permanently.

(*Phrases*). As the day is long; all the day long; all the year round; the livelong day; *sine die*; for good; for many a long day.

(*Adverbs*). In course of time, in due time or season; in process of time; in the fullness of time.

(*Phrases*). *Truditur dies die; "fugaces labuntur anni."*

111. Short duration.

TRANSIENTNESS (*Substantives*), transitoriness, impermanence, evanescence, transitiveness, fugitiveness, fugacity, fugaciousness, caducity, mortality, span, shortness, brevity.

(*Phrases*). A nine days' wonder; one's days being numbered.

Quickness, promptness (132), suddennness, abruptness.

Interregnum.

A *coup de main*, bubble, Mayfly.

(*Verbs*). To be transient, etc., to flit, pass away, fly, gallop, vanish, intromit.

(*Adjectives*). Transitory, transient, transitive, passing, impermanent, evanescent, fleeting, fugacious, fugitive, flitting, vanishing, shifting, flying, temporary, provisional, provisory, rough and ready, temporal, cursory, galloping, short-lived, ephemeral, deciduous, meteoric.

Brief, sudden, quick, prompt, brisk, abrupt, extemporaneous, summary, hasty, precipitate.

(*Adverbs*). Temporarily, etc., *pro tempore, in transitu,* extempore.

In a short time, soon, at once, awhile, anon, by and by, briefly, presently, apace, eftsoons, straight, straightway, quickly, speedily, promptly, presto, slapdash, directly, immediately, incontinently, forthwith, *à vue d'œil.*

Suddenly, *per saltum,* at one jump.

(*Phrases*). At short notice; the time being up; before the ink is dry; here to-day and gone to-morrow (149); *non semper erit œstas; "eheu, fugaces labuntur anni!"* "As for man, his days are as grass."

112. PERPETUITY (*Substantives*), eternity, everness,[1] aye, sempiternity, immortality, athanasy, everlastingness, perpetuation.

(*Verbs*). To last or endure for ever, to have no end; to eternise, perpetuate.

(*Adjectives*). Perpetual, eternal, everlasting, sempiternal, coeternal; endless, unending, ceaseless, incessant, unceasing, interminable, having no end, unfading, evergreen, never-fading, amaranthine, ageless, deathless, immortal, undying, never-dying, imperishable, indestructible.

(*Phrase*). Stretching to the crack of doom.

(*Adverbs*). Always, ever, evermore, aye, for ever, for aye, for evermore, still, perpetually, eternally, etc., in all ages, from age to age, every day.

(*Phrases*). For ever and a day; *esto perpetua;* for ever and ever; world without end; time without end; *in secula seculorum;* to the end of time; till Doomsday; "*rusticus exspectat dum defluat amnis.*"

113. Point of time.

INSTANTANEITY (*Substantives*), instantaneousness, moment, instant, second, minute, twinkling, trice, flash, breath, span, jiffy, flash of lightning, stroke of time, epoch, the twinkling of an eye, suddennness, *see* 111.

(*Verbs*). To twinkle, flash, to be instantaneous, etc.

(*Adjectives*). Instantaneous, sudden, momentary, extempore.

(*Phrases*). Quick as thought; quick as lightning.

(*Adverbs*). Instantly, momentarily, *subito,* presto, instanter, suddenly, slap-dash, in a moment, in an instant, in a second, in no time, in a trice, in a twinkling, at one jump, in a breath, extempore, *per saltum,* in a crack, out of hand.

(*Phrases*). Before one can say "Jack Robinson"; between the cup and the lip; on the spur of the moment; on the spot; on the instant; in less than no time; no sooner said than done.

---

114. Estimation, measurement, and record of time.

CHRONOMETRY (*Substantives*), chronology, horology, horometry, registry, date, epoch, style.

Almanac, calendar, ephemeris, chronicle, annals, register, journal, diary, chronogram, time-book.

Instruments for the measurement of time: clock, watch,

115. False estimate of time.

ANACHRONISM (*Substantives*), prolepsis, metachronism, prochronism, parachronism, anticipation.

(*Verbs*). To misdate, antedate, postdate, overdate, anticipate.

(*Adjectives*). Misdated, etc., undated, overdue, postdated, antedated.

[1] Bishop Wilkins.

stop-watch, chronograph, chronometer, sextant, timepiece, dial, sun-dial, horologe, pendulum, hour-glass, clepsydra.

Chronographer, chronologer, chronologist, annalist.

(Verbs). To fix or mark the time, date, register, etc., to bear date, to measure time, to beat time, to mark time, to time.

(Adjectives). Chronological, chronometrical, chronogrammatical, etc., o'clock.

Disregard, neglect, or oblivion of time.

(Phrases). To take no note of time; to prophesy after the event.

2°. RELATIVE TIME

1. Time with reference to Succession

116. PRIORITY (Substantives), antecedence, anteriority, precedence, pre-existence.

Precursor, predecessor, prelude, forerunner, etc. (64), harbinger, dawn, introduction, prodrome, antecedent.

(Verbs). To precede, come before, pre-exist, prelude, usher in, dawn, forerun, announce, etc. (511), foretell, anticipate.

(Phrases). To be beforehand; to steal a march upon.

(Adjectives). Prior, previous, preceding, precedent, anterior, antecedent, pre-existing, former, foregoing, aforesaid, prehistoric, antediluvian, pre-Adamite.

Precursory, prelusive, prelusory, proemial, introductory, prefatory, prodromal, prodromic.

117. POSTERIORITY (Substantives), succession, sequence, subsequence, supervention, sequel, successor (65).

(Verbs). To follow, come or go after, succeed, supervene.

(Phrases). To tread on the heels of.

(Adjectives). Subsequent, posterior, following, after, later, succeeding, post-glacial, postdiluvial, postdiluvian, puisné, posthumous, postprandial.

(Adverbs). Subsequently, after, afterwards, since, later, later on, at a subsequent or later period, next, in the sequel, close upon, thereafter, thereupon, whereupon, upon which, eftsoons.

(Adverbs). Before, prior to, previously, anteriorly, antecedently, aforetime, ere, ere now, erewhile, before now, already, yet, beforehand.

(Phrase). Before the flood.

118. THE PRESENT TIME (Substantives), the existing time, the time being, the present moment, juncture, the nonce, crisis, epoch, day, hour.

Age, time of life.

(Verb). To strike while the iron is hot.

119. Time different from the present.

DIFFERENT TIME (Substantives), other time.

Indefinite time, aorist.

(Adjective). Aoristic.

(Adverbs). At that time, moment, etc., then, at which time,

(*Adjectives*). Present, actual, instant, current, existing, that is.

(*Adverbs*). At this time, moment, etc., now, at present, at this time of day, at the present time, day, etc., to-day, nowadays, already, even now, but now, just now, upon which.

(*Phrases*). For the time being; for the nonce; *pro hac vice*; on the nail; on the spot; on the spur of the moment; while the iron is hot; now or never.

etc., on that occasion, upon, in those days.

When, whenever, whensoever, upon which, on which occasions, at another or a different time, etc., otherwhile, otherwhiles, at various times, ever and anon.

(*Phrases*). Once upon a time; one day.

———

120. SYNCHRONISM (*Substantives*), synchronisation, coexistence, coincidence, simultaneousness, coevality, contemporaneousness, contemporaneity, concurrence, concomitance.

Having equal times, isochronism.

A contemporary, coeval.

(*Verbs*). To coexist, concur, accompany, synchronise.

(*Adjectives*). Synchronous, synchronal, synchronistic, simultaneous, coexisting, coincident, concomitant, concurrent, coeval, coetaneous, contemporary, contemporaneous, coeternal, isochronous.

(*Adverbs*). At the same time, simultaneously, etc., together, during the same time, etc., in the interim, in the same breath, *pari passu*, meantime, meanwhile (106), while, whilst.

121. Prospective time.

FUTURITY (*Substantives*), the future, futurition, the approaching time, hereafter, the time to come, after time, after age, the coming time, the morrow, after days, hours, years, etc., after life, millennium, doomsday, the day of judgment, the crack of doom.

The approach of time, the process of time, advent, time drawing on, the womb of time.

Prospection, anticipation, prospect, perspective, expectation (507), horizon, outlook, heritage, heirs, posterity, descendants, heir apparent, heir presumptive.

Future existence, future state, post-existence, after-life, beyond.

(*Verbs*). To look forward, anticipate, have in prospect, keep in view, wait (133), expect.

122. Retrospective time.

PRETERITION (*Substantives*), the past, past time, *status quo*, days of yore, time gone by, former times, old times, the olden time, ancient times, antiquity, antiqueness, lang syne, time immemorial, prehistory.

(*Phrases*). The good old times; time out of mind; the rust of antiquity.

Archæology, palæology, palæography, archaism, retrospection, retrospect, looking back.

Archæologist, palæographer, palæologist.

Ancestry (166), pre-existence.

(*Verbs*). To pass, lapse, go by, elapse, run out, expire, blow over, to look back, cast the eyes back, retrospect, trace back.

(*Adjectives*). Past, gone, gone

(*Phrases*). Lie in wait for; bide one's time; to wait impatiently; kick one's heels; dance attendance.

To impend, hang over, lie over, approach, await, threaten, overhang, draw near, prepare.

(*Phrases*). To be in the wind; to loom in the future.

(*Adjectives*). Future, to come, coming, going to happen, approaching, impending, instant, at hand, about to be or happen, next, hanging, awaiting, forthcoming, near, near at hand, imminent, threatening, brewing, preparing, in store, eventual, ulterior, in view, in prospect, prospective, in perspective, in the horizon, in the wind, on the cards, that will be, overhanging.

Unborn, in embryo, in the womb of time.

(*Phrase*). All in good time.

(*Adverbs*). Prospectively, hereafter, by and by, some fine day, one of these days, anon, in future, to-morrow, in course of time, in process of time, sooner or later, *proximo*, *paulo post futurum*, in after time.

(*Phrase*). In the dim vista of the future.

by, over, bygone, foregone, pristine, prehistoric, quondam, lapsed, preterlapsed, expired, late, *ci-devant*, run out, blown over, that has been.

Former, foregoing, late, last, latter, recent, overnight, preterperfect, preterpluperfect, forgotten, irrecoverable, out of date.

Looking back, retrospective, retroactive, *ex post facto*.

Pre-existing, pre-existent.

(*Adverbs*). Formerly, of old, erst, whilom, erewhile, before now, time was, ago, over, in the olden time, anciently, in days of yore, long since, retrospectively, ere now, before now, till now, once, once upon a time, hitherto, heretofore, *ultimo*.

The other day, yesterday, just now, recently, lately, of late, latterly.

Long ago, a long while or time ago, some time ago.

(*Phrases*). Once upon a time; from time immemorial; in the memory of man; time out of mind.

Already, yet, at length, at last.

————

On the eve of, soon, ere long, at hand, near at hand, on the point of, *in articulo*, beforehand, against the time.

After a time, from this time, henceforth, henceforwards, thence, thenceforth, thenceforward, whereupon, upon which.

2. *Time with reference to a particular Period*

123. NEWNESS (*Substantives*), novelty, recentness, recency, modernity, freshness, greenness, immaturity, rawness.

Innovation, renovation, renewal.

Nouveau riche, *parvenu*, upstart, mushroom.

(*Adjectives*). New, novel, re-

124. OLDNESS (*Substantives*), age, antiquity, primitiveness, maturity, decline, decay, obsolescence; seniority, first-born, eldest, doyen, eldership, primogeniture.

(*Adjectives*). Old, ancient, antique, after-age, antiquated, out of date, of long standing, time-

cent, fresh, green, evergreen, raw, immature, untrodden, late, modern, neoteric, new-born, nascent, new-fashioned, up-to-date, new-fangled, vernal, renovated, virgin.

(*Phrases*). Fresh as a rose; fresh as a daisy; fresh as paint; brand-new; spick and span.

(*Adverbs*). Newly, recently, etc., afresh, anew.

honoured, venerable, primitive, diluvian, antediluvian, palæolithic, neolithic, primeval, primordial, prime, pre-Adamite, prehistoric, *laudator temporis acti*, antemundane, archaic.

Immemorial, inveterate, rooted, mediæval.

Senior, elder, eldest, oldest, first-born (128).

Obsolete, obsolescent, out of date, stale, time-worn, faded, decayed, effete, declining, etc., crumbling, decrepit (128), *passé*.

(*Phrases*). Nothing new under the sun; old as the hills; old as Methuselah; old as Adam; *nihil sub sole novi*; having had its day; before the Flood; time out of mind; *ancien régime*.

125. MORNING (*Substantives*), morn, morrow, forenoon, prime, dawn, daybreak, peep of day, break of day, aurora, first blush of the morning, prime of the morning, twilight, crepuscule, sunrise, cockcrow.

Noon, midday, noontide, meridian, noonday, prime, spring, summer.

(*Adjectives*). Matutinal, auroral, vernal, heliacal.

126. EVENING (*Substantives*), eve, e'en, decline of day, fall of day, eventide, nightfall, curfew, dusk, twilight, gloaming, eleventh hour, sunset, afternoon, going down of the sun, midnight; autumn, winter, the fall.

(*Phrases*). The witching time of night; the dead of night; blind-man's holiday.

(*Adjectives*). Nocturnal, vespertine, autumnal.

127. YOUTH (*Substantives*), infancy, babyhood, boyhood, juvenility, childhood, youthhood, juniority, juvenescence, adolescence (131), minority, nonage, teens, tender age, bloom, heyday, boyishness, girlishness.

Cradle, nursery, leading strings, pupilage, pupilship, puberty.

(*Phrases*). Prime or flower of life; the rising generation; salad days.

(*Adjectives*). Young, youthful, juvenile, sappy, beardless, under age, in one's teens, boyish, girlish, junior, younger.

(*Phrase*). *In statu pupillari.*

128. AGE (*Substantives*), old age, senility, senescence, oldness, years, anility, grey hairs, climacteric, decrepitude, hoary age, caducity, crow's-feet, superannuation, dotage, vale of years, seniority, green old age, eldership, elders.

(*Phrases*). The vale of years; decline of life; the sere and yellow leaf; wane of life; second childhood.

(*Adjectives*). Aged, old, elderly, senile, matronly, anile, in years, ripe, mellow, grey, grey-headed, hoary, hoar, venerable, time-worn, declining, antiquated, *passé*, rusty, effete, decrepit, superannuated.

(Phrases). With one foot in the grave; marked with crow's feet; advanced in life, or in years; stricken in years; no chicken,
   Patriarchal, ancestral, primitive, pre-Adamite, ante-diluvian, diluvian.
   Older, elder, senior.
   Eldest, oldest, first-born, bantling, firstling.

129. INFANT *(Substantives)*, babe, baby, nursling, suckling.
   Child, bairn, little one, brat, kid, chit, urchin, bantling, bratling, papoose, elf, piccaninny.
   Youth, boy, lad, stripling, youngster, younker, gossoon, nipper, whipster, whippersnapper, school-boy, hobbardehoy, hobbledehoy, cadet, minor.
   Scion, sapling, seedling, tendril, mushroom, nestling, chicken, larva, chrysalis, tadpole, whelp, cub, pullet, fry, fœtus, calf, colt, filly, pup, puppy, foal, kitten.
   Girl, lass, lassie, wench, miss, flapper, damsel, maid, maiden, virgin.
   (Adjectives). Infantine, infantile, puerile, boyish, girlish, childish, baby, babyish, unfledged, new-fledged, kittenish, callow.
   (Phrases). In leading-strings; at the breast; in arms; in one's teens; tied to mother's apron-strings.

130. VETERAN *(Substantives)*, old man, seer, patriarch, grey-beard, gaffer, grandsire, grandam, matron, crone, beldam, sexagenarian, octogenarian, centenarian, oldster.
   Pre - Adamite,   Methuselah, Nestor.
   Elders, forefathers, forbears, fathers, ancestors, ancestry.

_____

131. ADOLESCENCE *(Substantives)*, puberty, majority, adultness, maturity, ripeness, manhood, virility.
   (Phrases). Prime of life; man's estate; flower of age; meridian of life; years of discretion; *toga virilis*.
   A man, adult (373), a woman, matron (374), *parti*; ephebe.
   (Adjectives). Adolescent, of age, out of one's teens, grown up, mature, middle-aged, manly, virile, adult.
   Womanly, matronly, nubile, marriageable.

3. *Time with reference to an Effect or Purpose*

132. EARLINESS *(Substantives)*, timeliness, punctuality, readiness, promptness, promptitude, expedition, quickness, haste, acceleration, hastening, hurry, bustle, precipitation, anticipation, precociousness, precocity.
   (Phrase). A stitch in time saves nine.

133. LATENESS *(Substantives)*, tardiness, slowness, delay, cunctation, procrastination, deferring, postponement, dilatoriness, adjournment, shelving, prorogation.
   (Phrase). Fabian tactics.
   Protraction, prolongation, leeway.
   (Phrase). An afternoon man.

Suddenness, abruptness (111).

(*Verbs*). To be early, to be in time, etc., to keep time.

To anticipate, forestall, book, bespeak, reserve.

To expedite, hasten, haste, quicken, press, dispatch, accelerate, precipitate, hurry, bustle.

(*Phrases*). To take time by the forelock; to steal a march upon; to be beforehand with; to be pressed for time.

(*Adjectives*). Early, prime, timely, punctual, matutinal, forward, ready, quick, expeditious, precipitate, summary, prompt, premature, precocious, prevenient, anticipatory.

Sudden, abrupt, unexpected (508), subitaneous, extempore.

(*Adverbs*). Early, soon, anon, betimes, rath, apace, eft, eftsoons, in time, ere long, presently, shortly, punctually, to the minute.

(*Phrases*). In good time; in pudding-time; at sunrise; with the lark; extempore.

Beforehand, prematurely, before one's time, in anticipation.

Suddenly, abruptly, at once, instanter.

(*Phrases*). On the point of; at short notice; on the spur of the moment; all at once; before you can say "knife."

(*Verbs*). To be late, etc., tarry, wait, stay, bide, take time, dally, dawdle, linger, loiter, bide one's time, shuffle, *see* 275, 683.

To stand over, lie over.

To put off, defer, delay, leave over, suspend, shift off, stave off, postpone, adjourn, carry over, shelve, procrastinate, prolong, protract, draw out, hang up, prorogue.

(*Phrases*). To tide it over; to drive to the last; to let the matter stand over.

(*Adjectives*). Late, tardy, slow, behindhand, posthumous, backward, unpunctual, procrastinatory, belated, out-of-date.

Delayed, etc., suspended, in abeyance.

(*Adverbs*). Late, after time, too late, *sine die*, behind time.

At length, at last, backward, at sunset.

Slowly, leisurely, deliberately.

(*Phrases*). *Nonum prematur in annum*; a day after the fair; at the eleventh hour; after death, the doctor.

---

134. OCCASION (*Substantives*), opportunity, chance, opening, room, suitable or proper time or season, high time, opportuneness, tempestivity, seasonableness, crisis, turn, juncture, conjuncture.

(*Phrases*). Golden opportunity; the nick of time; *mollia tempora*; well-timed opportunity; a stitch in time.

Spare time, leisure, holiday

135. INTEMPESTIVITY (*Substantives*), unsuitable time, improper time, unseasonableness, inopportuneness, evil hour, *contretemps*.

(*Verbs*). To be ill-timed, etc., to mistime, intrude.

To lose, omit, let slip, let go, neglect, pretermit, allow, or suffer the opportunity or occasion to pass, slip, go by, escape, lapse; to lose time, to fritter away time (683).

(685), spare moments, hours, etc., time on one's hands.

(*Verbs*). To take the opportunity, to temporise, to time well, to improve the opportunity.

To use, make use of, employ, profit by, avail oneself of, lay hold of, embrace, catch, seize, snatch, clutch, pounce upon, grasp, etc., the opportunity.

To give, offer, present, afford, etc., the opportunity.

To spend or consume time.

(*Phrases*). To turn the occasion to account; to seize the occasion; to strike the iron while it is hot; to make hay while the sun shines; *carpe diem*; to take the tide at the flood; to furnish a handle for.

(*Phrase*). To let slip through the fingers.

(*Adjectives*). Ill-timed, untimely, intrusive, mistimed, unseasonable, out of season, unpunctual, inopportune, intrusive, too late (133), malapropos, unlucky, inauspicious, unpropitious, unfortunate, unfavourable, unsuited, unsuitable.

(*Adverb*). Inopportunely, etc.

(*Phrases*). As ill luck would have it; in evil hour; after meat, mustard; after death, the physician; *en mala hora*; out of date; the day before (or after) the fair.

———

(*Adjectives*). Opportune, timely, well-timed, timeful, seasonable, happy, lucky, fortunate, favourable, propitious, auspicious, critical.

(*Adverbs*). Opportunely, etc., on the spot, in proper or due time or season, high time, for the nonce.

(*Phrases*). In the nick of time; in pudding-time; in the fullness of time; between the cup and the lip; on the spur of the moment (612); now or never; at the eleventh hour.

By the way, by the by, *en passant*, *à propos*, *pro re nata*; *pro hac vice*; *par parenthèse*.

(*Phrases*). *Non semper erit æstas* ; time and tide wait for no man.

3°. RECURRENT TIME

136. FREQUENCY (*Substantives*), oftness, recurrence, repetition (104), recrudescence, reiteration, iteration, run, reappearance, renewal, *ritornello, ritournelle*, burden.

(*Verbs*). To recur, revert, return, repeat, reiterate, reappear, renew, reword.

(*Adjectives*). Frequent, common, not rare, repeated, reiterated, thick-coming, recurring, recurrent, incessant, everlasting, etc., rife.

(*Adverbs*). Often, oft, oft-times,

137. INFREQUENCY (*Substantives*), rareness, rarity, variety, seldomness.

(*Verb*). To be rare, etc.

(*Adjectives*). Infrequent, rare, unfrequent, uncommon.

(*Adverbs*). Seldom, rarely, scarcely, hardly, scarcely ever, ever, hardly ever, not often, unfrequently.

Once, once for all, once in a way, *pro hac vice*.

(*Phrases*). Once in a blue moon; angels' visits.

———

not unfrequently, frequently, oftentimes, many times, several times, repeatedly.

(*Phrases*). A number of times; many a time; full many a time; many a time and oft; times out of number.

Again, anew, afresh, *de novo*, ditto, over again, *da capo*, again and again, over and over, ever and anon, many times over, time after time, time and again, repeatedly (104).

Perpetually, continually, constantly, incessantly, everlastingly, without ceasing.

Sometimes, occasionally, at times, now and then, now and again, from time to time, at intervals, between whiles, once in a while, there are times when, etc., *toties quoties*.

Most often, for the most part, generally, usually, commonly, most frequently, as often as not.

138. REGULARITY of recurrence, punctuality.

PERIODICITY (*Substantives*), intermittence, beat, pulse, pulsation, rhythm, alternation, pulsation, bout, round, revolution, rotation, turn.

Anniversary, centenary, bicentenary, tercentenary, etc.

Regularity of return, rota, cycle, period, stated time, routine.

(*Phrase*). The swing of the pendulum.

139. IRREGULARITY of recurrence, uncertainty, etc.

(*Adjectives*). Irregular, uncertain, unpunctual, capricious, desultory, unrhythmic, unrhythmical, fitful, flickering, casual.

(*Adverbs*). Irregularly, etc., by fits, by snatches, by starts, by catches, skippingly, by skips, now and then, occasionally, *per saltum, à batons rompus*.

————

(*Verbs*). To recur in regular order or succession, to come round, return, revolve, alternate, come in its turn, beat, pulsate, intermit; to regularise.

(*Adjectives*). Periodic, periodical, recurrent, cyclical, revolving, intermittent, remittent, alternate, alternating, rhythmic, rhythmical, steady, punctual.

Diurnal, quotidian, annual, biennial, etc.

(*Phrase*). Regular as clockwork.

(*Adverbs*). Periodically, at regular intervals, at stated times, at fixed periods, punctually, *de die in diem*, from day to day.

By turns, in turn, in rotation, alternately, off and on, ride and tie.

In turns or shifts.

SECTION VII.—CHANGE

1°. SIMPLE CHANGE

140. Difference at different times.

CHANGE (*Substantives*), alteration, mutation, permutation, variation, modification, modulation, mood, qualification, innovation, metastasis, metabolism, deviation, turn, inversion, reversion, reversal, eversion, subversion (162), *bouleversement*, upset, organic change, revolution (146), transit, transition.

Transformation, transmutation, transfiguration, metamorphosis, transmigration, transubstantiation, transmogrification, metempsychosis, avatar.

Vicissitude, flux, unrest (149).

(*Phrase*). The wheel of fortune.

(*Verbs*). To change, alter, vary, modify, modulate, diversify, qualify, tamper with, edit, turn, shift, veer, tack, chop, shuffle, swerve, warp, deviate, turn aside, turn topsy-turvy, upset, invert, reverse, introvert, subvert, evert, turn inside out.

Form, fashion, mould, model, vamp, warp, work a change, superinduce, resume, disturb (61), innovate, reform, remodel, refound, new-model, modernise, revolutionise.

Transform, transume, transmute, transfigure, transmogrify, metamorphose, to ring the changes, pass to, leap to, transfer.

(*Phrases*). *Nous avons changé tout cela*; to take a turn; turn over a new leaf; to turn the corner.

(*Adjectives*). Changed, altered, new-fangled, warped, etc.; metamorphic, metabolic, metastatic.

(*Adverbs*). *Mutatis mutandis; quantum mutatus! tempora mutantur.*

142. Absence of change, *see* Stability (150), Quiescence (265).

PERMANENCE (*Substantives*), persistence, endurance, *status quo*; maintenance, preservation, conservation, rest, sleep, stability, establishment, conservatism, truce, suspension, settledness (265), perdurability.

(*Phrases*). The law of the Medes and Persians; *laudator temporis acti.*

(*Verbs*). To remain, stay, stop, tarry, hold, last, endure, continue, bide, abide, aby, maintain, keep, hold on, stand, subsist, live, stand still, outlive, survive.

To let alone, let be.

(*Phrases*). To keep one's footing; to take root; to stand fast.

(*Adjectives*). Persisting, etc., unchanged, unmodified, unrenewed, unaltered, fixed, settled, unvaried, intact, persistent, stagnant, rooted, monotonous, unreversed, conservative, unprogressive, undestroyed, unrepealed, unsuppressed, unfailing, stationary (265), stereotyped, perdurable.

(*Adverbs*). *In statu quo*, for good, finally, at a stand, at a standstill, *uti possidetis*.

(*Phrases*). *J'y suis, j'y reste; plus cela change, plus cela est la même chose; esto perpetua.*

141. Change from action to rest.

CESSATION (*Substantives*), discontinuance, desistance, quiescence.

Intermission, remission, suspension, interruption, suspense, stop, stoppage, pause, rest, lull, breathing-space, respite, truce, drop, interregnum, abeyance.

Comma, colon, semicolon, period, etc.

(*Verbs*). To discontinue, cease, desist, break off, leave off, hold, stop, pause, rest, drop, lay aside, give up, have done with, give over, shut down, knock-off, relinquish (624), surcease.

(*Phrases*). To shut up shop; to stay one's hand.

To come to a stand, or standstill, suspend, cut short, cast off, go out, be at an end; intromit, interrupt, suspend, intermit, remit; put an end or stop to.

143. CONTINUANCE in action (*Substantives*), continuation, perseverance, repetition (104), persistence, run.

(*Verbs*). To continue, persist, go on, keep on, abide, keep, pursue, hold on, run on, follow on, carry on, keep up, uphold, hold up, persevere, keep it up, peg away, maintain, maintain one's ground, harp upon, repeat (104), take root.

(*Phrases*). To let be; to keep going; keep the ball rolling; let sleeping dogs lie; *stare super antiquas vias*; *quieta non movere*; *nolumus mutari leges Angliæ*.

(*Adjectives*). Continual, continuous, continuing, etc., uninterrupted, inconvertible, unintermitting, unreversed, unstopped, unrevoked, unvaried, unshifting.

___

To pass away, go off, pass off, blow over, die away, wear away, wear off (122).

(*Phrase*). Pass away like a shadow or cloud.

(*Interjections*). Hold! hold on! stop! enough! avast! *basta !* have done! a truce to! stop it! drop it! cheese it! chuck it!

144. Gradual change to something different.

CONVERSION (*Substantives*), reduction, transmutation, resolution, assimilation; chemistry, alchemy; growth, lapse, progress, becoming.

Passage, transit, transition, transmigration, flux, shifting, sliding, running into, etc.; phase, conjugations; convertibility.

Laboratory, alembic, etc. (691).

(*Verbs*). To be converted into; to become, to wax, come to, turn to, assume the form of, pass into, slide into, glide into, lapse, shift, run into, fall into, merge into, melt, grow, grow into, open into, resolve itself into, settle into, mature, mellow; assume the form, shape, state, nature, character, etc., of; illapse.

To convert into, make, render, form, mould, reduce, resolve into; transume (140), fashion, model, remodel, reorganise, shape, modify; assimilate to; reduce to, bring to; refound, re-form, reshape.

(*Adjectives*). Converted into, become, etc., convertible.

(*Adverbs*). Gradually, *gradatim*, by degrees, step by step, by inches, inch by inch, by little and little, by slow degrees, consecutively, *seriatim*, *in transitu*.

145. REVERSION (*Substantives*), return, reconversion, relapse, reaction, recoil, rebound, ricochet, revulsion, alternation (138), inversion.

Reinstatement, re-establishment, etc. (660).

(*Phrases*). The turning-point; the turn of the tide; *status quo ante bellum*; undoing the work of Penelope.

(*Verbs*). To revert, return to, relapse, recoil, rebound, react; to restore, etc. (660), to undo, unmake.

(*Phrase*). To turn the tables (719).

(*Adjectives*). Reverting, etc., restored, etc., placed *in statu quo*, revulsive, reactionary.

(*Adverb*). *Uti possidetis.*

(*Interjection*). As you were!

146. Sudden or violent change.

REVOLUTION (*Substantives*), counter-revolution, transilience, jump, leap, plunge, jerk, start, spasm, convulsion, throe, storm, earthquake, catastrophe, cataclysm (173).

Legerdemain, conjuration, sleight of hand, hocus-pocus, harlequinade, witchcraft, etc. (992).

A revolutionary, revolutionist; the red flag.

(*Verbs*). To revolutionise, remodel.

(*Adverbs*). Root and branch; before you can say "Jack Robinson."

147. Change of one thing for another.

SUBSTITUTION (*Substantives*), commutation, enallage, metonymy, supplanting, synecdoche, antonomasia.

(*Phrase*). Borrowing of or robbing Peter to pay Paul.

Thing substituted: substitute (634), succedaneum, makeshift, locum-tenens, representative, proxy; deputy (759), vice, double, dummy, changeling, stop-gap, jury-mast, palimpsest, metaphor (521).

(*Verbs*). To substitute, commute, supplant, change for, supersede, take over from.

To give place to; to replace.

(*Phrases*). To serve as a substitute, etc.; to do duty for; to stand in the shoes of; to take the place of; to change hands (783).

(*Adjectives*). Substituted, etc., vicarious, subdititious.

(*Adverbs*). Instead, in place of, in lieu of, in the room of, *mutato nomine*; *mutatis mutandis.*

148. Double and mutual change.

INTERCHANGE (*Substantives*), exchange, commutation, reciprocation, transposition, permutation, shuffling, castling (at chess), hocus-pocus, interchangeableness.

Reciprocity (12), retaliation (719), barter (794).

(*Phrase*). A *quid pro quo.*

(*Verbs*). To interchange, exchange, bandy, transpose, shuffle, change hands, swap, permute, reciprocate, commute, counterchange.

(*Phrases*). To play at puss in the corner; to give and take; you scratch my back and I'll scratch yours.

(*Adjectives*). Interchanged, etc., reciprocal, mutual, commutative, interchangeable, intercurrent.

(*Phrases*). A Roland for an Oliver; tit for tat; *vice versa.*

(*Adverbs*). In exchange.

2°. Complex Changes

149. MUTABILITY (*Substantives*), changeableness, inconstancy, variableness, mobility, instability, unsteadiness, vacillation, unrest, restlessness, slipperiness, impermanence, fragility, fluctuation, vicissitude, alternation, vibration, oscillation (314), flux, ebbing and flowing, ebbs and flows, ups and downs, fidgets, fugitiveness, disquiet, disquietude.

A Proteus, chameleon, quicksilver, weathercock, a harlequin.

(*Phrases*). April showers; the wheel of fortune; the Cynthia of the minute.

Alternation, subalternation.

(*Verbs*). To fluctuate, vary, waver, flounder, vibrate, flicker, flitter, shift, shuffle, shake, totter, tremble, ebb and flow, turn and turn about, change and change about.

To fade, pass away like a cloud, shadow, or dream.

(*Adjectives*). Mutable, changeable, variable, ever-changing, inconstant, impermanent, unsteady, unstable, protean, proteiform, unfixed, fluctuating, vacillating, shifting, versatile, restless, erratic, unsettled, mobile, fickle, wavering, flickering, flitting, flittering, fluttering, oscillating, vibratory, vagrant, wayward, desultory, afloat, alternating, plastic, disquiet, alterable, casual, unballasted.

(*Phrase*). Subject to alteration.

Frail, tottering, shaking, shaky, trembling, fugitive, ephemeral, transient (111), fading, fragile, deciduous, slippery, unsettled, irresolute (605), rocky, groggy.

150. IMMUTABILITY (*Substantives*), stability, unchangeableness, constancy, permanence, persistence (106), invariableness, durability, steadiness (604), immobility, fixedness, stableness, settledness, stabiliment, firmness, stiffness, anchylosis, solidity, aplomb, ballast, incommutability, insusceptibility, irrevocableness.

(*Phrases*). The law of the Medes and Persians; *nolumus leges Angliæ mutari*.

Rock, pillar, tower, foundation.

(*Verbs*). To be permanent, etc. (265), to stand, remain.

To settle, establish, stablish, fix, set, stabilitate, retain, keep, hold, make sure, nail, clinch, rivet, fasten (43), settle down, set on its legs.

(*Adjectives*). Immutable, incommutable, unchangeable, unaltered, unalterable, not to be changed, constant, permanent, invariable, undeviating, stable, durable (265), perennial (110), valid.

Fixed, steadfast, firm, fast, steady, confirmed, immovable, irremovable, rooted, stablished, established, inconvertible, stereotyped, indeclinable, settled, etc., stationary, stagnant.

Moored, at anchor, on a rock, firmly seated, established, etc.

Indefeasible, irretrievable, intransmutable, irresoluble, irrevocable, irreversible, inextinguishable, irreducible, indissoluble, indissolvable, indestructible, undying, imperishable, indelible, indeciduous, insusceptible of change.

(*Phrases*). *J'y suis, j'y reste*;

(*Phrases*). *Tempora mutantur, et nos mutamur in illis*; changeable as the moon, as a weather-cock; *sic transit gloria mundi*; here to-day and gone to-morrow.

qualis ab incepto; firm as a rock; when the Ethiopian changes his skin.

Present events

151. EVENTUALITY (*Substantives*), event, occurrence, incident, affair, transaction, proceeding, fact, matter of fact, phenomenon, advent.

Business, concern, circumstance, particular, casualty, accident, adventure, passage, crisis, episode, pass, emergency, contingency, consequence.

The world, life, things, doings, course of things, the course, tide, stream, current, run, etc., of events.

(*Phrases*). Stirring events; the ups and downs of life; the chapter of accidents; the cast of the die (156).

(*Verbs*). To happen, occur, take place, take effect, come, come of, become of, come about, come off, pass, come to pass, fall, fall out, run, be on foot, fall in, befall, betide, bechance, befortune, turn out, go off, prove, eventuate, draw on, turn up, cast up, supervene, survene, issue, arrive, ensue, arise, spring, start, come into existence.

Pass off, wear off, blow over.

To experience, meet with, go through, pass through, endure (821), suffer, fare.

(*Adjectives*). Happening, occurring, etc., current, incidental, eventful, stirring, bustling.

(*Phrase*). The plot thickening.

(*Adverbs*). Eventually, in the event of, on foot, on the *tapis*, as it may happen, happen what may, at all events, sink or swim, come what may.

(*Phrases*). In the course of things; in the long run; as the tree falls; as the cat jumps; as the world goes.

Future events

152. DESTINY (*Substantives*), fatality, fate, doom, destination, lot, fortune, star, planet, preordination, predestination, fatalism, inevitableness, kismet, *see* Futurity (121), and Necessity (601).

(*Phrases*). The decrees of fate; the wheel of fortune.

(*Verbs*). To impend, hang over, overhang, be in store, await, come on, approach, stare one in the face, foreordain, preordain, predestine, doom, must be.

(*Adjectives*). About to happen, impending, coming, etc., inevitable, ineluctable, inexorable, fated, doomed, devoted.

(*Adverbs*). Necessarily, *ex necessitate rei*.

(*Phrases*). What must be, must; *che sarà sarà*; "It is written"; the die is cast; the Rubicon is crossed; *jacta est alea*.

SECTION VIII.—CAUSATION

1°. CONSTANCY OF SEQUENCE IN EVENTS

153. Constant antecedent.

CAUSE (*Substantives*), origin, source, principle, element, occasioner, prime mover, *primum mobile*, spring, mainspring, agent, seed, leaven, groundwork, fountain, well, fount, fountain-head, spring-head, parent (166), *fons et origo, raison d'être*.

Pivot, hinge, turning-point, key, lever.

Final cause, ground, reason, the reason why, the why and the wherefore, rationale, occasion, derivation, provenance.

Rudiment, germ, embryo, mushroom, bud, root, *radix*, radical, etymon, nucleus, seed, ovum, stem, stock, trunk, taproot.

Nest, cradle, womb, *nidus*, birthplace, hot-bed, forcing-bed.

Causality, origination, causation, production (161), ætiology.

Theories of causation: Creationism; Evolution, Lamarckism, Darwinism, Spencerism, Orthogenesis, etc.

(*Phrases*). Behind the scenes; *le dessous des cartes*.

(*Verbs*). To be the cause of, to originate, germinate, give origin to, cause, occasion, give rise to, kindle, suscitate, bring on, bring to pass, give occasion to, produce,

154. Constant sequent.

EFFECT (*Substantives*), consequence, product, result, resultant, resultance, upshot, issue, end (67), fruit, crop, aftermath, harvest, development, outgrowth, karma.

Production, produce, work, performance, creature, creation, offshoot, fabric, first-fruits, firstlings, output, *dénouement*, derivation, heredity, evolution (161).

(*Verbs*). To be the effect, work, fruit, result, etc., of, to be owing to, originate in or from, rise from, to take its rise from, arise, spring, proceed, evolve, come of, emanate, come, grow, bud, sprout, issue, flow, result, follow, accrue, etc., from; come to; to come out of, be derived from, be caused by, depend upon, hinge upon, turn upon, result from, to be dependent upon, hang upon; to pan out.

(*Adjectives*). Owing to, resulting from, through, etc., all along of, hereditary, genetic, derivative.

(*Adverbs*). Of course, consequently, necessarily, eventually.

(*Phrases. Cela va sans dire*; thereby hangs a tale.

---

bring about, found, lay the foundation of, lie at the root of, procure, draw down, induce, realise, evoke, entail, develop, evolve, operate (*see* 161), to elicit.

To conduce, contribute, tend to (176).

(*Phrases*). To have a hand in; to have a finger in the pie; *see* Produce (161); to open the door to; to be at the bottom of; to sow the seeds of.

(*Adjectives*). Caused, occasioned, etc., causal, original,

primary, primordial, having a common origin, connate, radical, embryonic, embryotic, *in ovo*, in embryo.

Evolutionary, Darwinian, etc; ætiological.

155. Assignment of cause.

ATTRIBUTION (*Substantives*), theory, ætiology, ascription, reference to, rationale, accounting for, palætiology,[1] imputation, derivation from, filiation, genealogy, pedigree, paternity, maternity (166).

(*Verbs*). To attribute, ascribe, impute, refer to, derive from, lay to, point to, charge on, ground on, invest with, assign as cause, trace to, father upon, account for, theorise, ground, etc.

(*Phrases*). To put the saddle on the right horse; point out the reason of; lay to the door of; tell how it comes.

(*Adjectives*). Attributable, imputable, ascribable, referable, owing to, derivable from, etc.,

Putative, attributed, imputed, etc.

(*Adverbs*). Hence, thence, therefore, because, from that cause, for that reason, on that account, owing to, thanks to, forasmuch as, whence, *propter hoc*, wherefore, since, inasmuch as.

Why? wherefore? whence? how comes it? how is it? how happens it? how does it happen?

In some way, somehow, somehow or other, in some such way.

---

156. Absence of assignable cause.

CHANCE[2] (*Substantives*), indetermination, accident, fortune, hazard, hap, haphazard, chance-medley, random, lot, fate (152), casualty, contingency, adventure, venture, pot-luck, treasure trove, hit.

A lottery, toss-up, game of chance, *sortes*, *rouge et noir*, heads or tails, etc, sweepstake.

(*Phrases*). The turn or hazard of the die or cards; the chapter of accidents; a cast or throw of the dice.

Possibility, contingency, odds, long odds, a near shave, close run, bare chance.

(*Verbs*). To chance, hap, to fall to one's lot, to be one's fate, etc. (152); to light upon.

To game, gamble, cast lots, raffle, play for.

(*Phrases*). To take one's chance; toss up for; stand the hazard of the die, *see* 621.

(*Adjectives*). Casual, fortuitous, random, accidental, adventitious, causeless, incidental, contingent, uncaused, undetermined, indeterminate, suppositional, possible (470), aleatory.

(*Adverbs*). By chance, by accident, perchance, peradventure, perhaps, maybe, mayhap, haply, possibly.

Casually, etc., at random, at a venture, as it may be, as it may chance, as it may turn up, as it may happen, as chance, luck, fortune, etc., would have it.

(*Phrases*). *Jacta est alea*; the die is cast; the Rubicon is crossed.

---

[1] Whewell, *Indications of a Creator*.

[2] The word *Chance* has two distinct meanings; the first, the absence of assignable *cause*, as above; and the second, the absence of *design*: for the latter, *see* 621.

2°. Connection between Cause and Effect

157. Power (*Substantives*), potentiality, potency, prepotency, prepollence, puissance, might, force, energy, metal, dint, right hand, ascendancy, sway, control, almightiness, ability, ableness, competency, efficiency, effectiveness, efficacy, efficaciousness, validity, cogency, enablement; agency (170), causality (153), influence (175), voluntary power (737).

Capability, capacity, faculty, quality, attribute, endowment, virtue, gift, property.

Pressure, high pressure.

(*Verbs*). To be powerful, etc., to exercise power, sway, etc., to constrain.

To be the property, virtue, attribute, etc., of; to belong to, pertain to, to appertain to, to lie or be in one's power.

To give or confer power, to empower, enable, invest, endue, endow, arm, etc., *see* Strengthen (159).

To gain power, to take root.

(*Adjectives*). Productive, prolific, powerful, potent, puissant, potential, capable, able, cogent, valid, effective, effectual, efficient, efficacious, adequate, competent.

Forcible, energetic, vigorous, vivid, sturdy, rousing, all-powerful, resistless, irresistible, inextinguishable, sovereign, invincible, unconquerable, indomitable.

(*Adverbs*). Powerfully, etc., by virtue of, in full force.

158. Impotence (*Substantives*), inability, disability, disablement, impuissance, imbecility, inaptitude, incapacity, incapability, invalidity, inefficacy, inefficiency, inefficaciousness, ineffectualness, disqualification, helplessness, incompetence.

Tele imbellum; *sine ictu*; *brutum fulmen*; blank cartridge.

(*Verbs*). To be impotent, powerless, etc.

To render powerless, etc., to deprive of power, disable, disenable, incapacitate, disqualify, invalidate, nullify, deaden, cripple, cramp, paralyse, muzzle, hamstring, bowl over.

(*Phrases*). Clip the wings of; spike the guns; put *hors de combat*; break the neck of; break the back; put a spoke in one's wheel; *see* Weaken (160).

(*Adjectives*). Powerless, impotent, unable, incapable, incompetent, inadequate, unequal to, inefficient, inefficacious, inept, ineffectual, ineffective, inoperative, nugatory, incapacitated, imbecile, disqualified, disabled, armless, disarmed, unarmed, weaponless, defenceless; unnerved, paralysed, disjointed, nerveless, adynamic, unendowed.

(*Phrases*). Laid on the shelf, laid on one's back; *hors de combat*; not having a leg to stand on.

---

159. Degree of power.

Strength (*Substantives*), energy (171), vigour, vitality, force, main force, physical force, brute

160. Weakness (*Substantives*), feebleness, debility, atony, relaxation, helplessness, languor, slackness, enervation, nervous-

force, spring, elasticity, tone, tension, tonicity.

Stoutness, sturdiness, lustiness, lustihood, stamina, nerve, muscle, thews and sinews, backbone, pith, pithiness.

Adamant, steel, iron, oak, heart of oak.

An athlete, an Atlas, a Hercules, an Antæus, a Sampson, Cyclops, Goliath.

A giant refreshed, a tower of strength.

Strengthening, invigoration, bracing, recruital, recruitment, refreshment, refocillation (689).

Science of forces: Dynamics, Statics.

(*Verbs*). To be strong, etc., to be stronger, to overmatch.

To render strong, etc., to give strength, tone, etc., to strengthen, invigorate, brace, fortify, harden, case-harden, steel, gird, screw up, wind up, set up, tone up.

(*Phrase*). Set on one's legs.

To reinforce, refit, recruit, vivify, restore (660), refect, refocillate (689).

(*Adjectives*). Strong, mighty, vigorous, robust, sturdy, powerful, puissant, adamantine, invincible, able-bodied, athletic, Herculean, muscular, brawny, sinewy, made of iron, strapping, well-set, well-knit, stalwart, gigantic, irresistible; strengthening, etc., invigorative, tonic.

Manly, manlike, masculine, male, virile, manful, full-blooded.

Unweakened, unallayed, unwithered, unshaken, unworn, unexhausted, unrelaxed, undiluted, unwatered, neat.

(*Phrases*). Made of iron; strong as a lion, as a horse; sound as a roach; proof against; in fine feather; fit as a fiddle.

ness, faintness, languidness, infirmity, emasculation, effeminacy, feminality, femineity, flaccidity, softness, defencelessness.

Childhood, etc. (127, 129); orphan, chicken.

Declension, loss, failure, etc., of strength, invalidation, decrepitude, asthenia, neurasthenia, palsy, paralysis, exhaustion, collapse, prostration, syncope, deliquium, apoplexy, seizure.

A reed, a thread, a rope of sand, a house of cards.

(*Verbs*). To be weak, etc., to droop, fade, faint, swoon, languish, decline, fail, run down, drop, crock; to go by the board.

To render weak, etc., to weaken, enfeeble, debilitate, deprive of strength, relax, enervate, unbrace, unman, emasculate, castrate, geld, hamstring, disable, unhinge, cripple, cramp, paralyse, maim, sprain, exhaust, prostrate, blunt the edge of, deaden, dilute, water, water down.

(*Adjectives*). Weak, feeble, debile, strengthless, nerveless, imbecile, unnerved, relaxed, unstrung, unbraced, enervated, nervous, sinewless, lustless, effeminate, feminine, womanly, unmanned, emasculated, castrated, crippled, maimed, lamed, shattered, broken, halting, shaken, crazy, shaky, paralysed, palsied, paralytic, decrepit, drooping, languid, faint, sickly, flagging, dull, slack, limp, spent, effete, weather-beaten, worn, seedy, exhausted, languishing, wasted, washy, vincible, untenable, laid low, asthenic, neurasthenic, neurotic, rickety, invertebrate, feckless.

Unstrengthened, unsustained, unsupported, unaided, unassisted,

(*Adverbs*). Strongly, forcibly, etc., by main force, *vi et armis*, by might and main, tooth and nail, hammer and tongs.

defenceless, indefensible, unfortified, unfriended, fatherless, etc.

(*Phrases*). On one's last legs; weak as a child, as a baby, as a chicken, as a cat, as water, as water-gruel, as milk and water; good or fit for nothing.

3°. POWER IN OPERATION

161. PRODUCTION (*Substantives*), creation, formation, construction, fabrication, manufacture, building, architecture, edification, coinage, organisation, putting together, establishment, setting up, performance (729), workmanship, output.

Development, genesis, generation, *epigenesis*, procreation, propagation, bringing forth, parturition, growth, proliferation.

Theory of development: Evolution, Heredity, Mendelism (154), Eugenics.

(*Verbs*). To produce, effect, perform, operate, do, make, gar, form, construct, fabricate, frame, manufacture, weave, forge, coin, carve, chisel, build, raise, edify, rear, erect, run up, establish.

To constitute, compose, organise, work out, realise, bring to bear, bring to pass, accomplish, bring off, bear fruit.

To create, generate, engender, beget, bring into being, breed, bear, procreate, give birth to, bring forth, yean, hatch, develop, bring up.

To induce, superinduce, suscitate, *see* Cause (153).

(*Adjectives*). Produced, etc., producing, productive of, etc., formative, parturient, genetic; eugenic.

163. REPRODUCTION (*Substantives*), renovation, recon-

162. Non-production.

DESTRUCTION (*Substantives*), waste, dissolution, breaking up, consumption, disorganisation, falling to pieces, crumbling, etc.

Fall, downfall, ruin, perdition, crash, smash, havoc, *délabrement*, desolation, *bouleversement*, *débacle*, upset, wreck, shipwreck, cataclysm, extinction, annihilation; doom, destruction of life, *see* Death (360).

Demolition, demolishment, overthrow, subversion, suppression, dismantling, cutting up, corrosion, erosion, crushing, upsetting, abolition, abolishment, sacrifice, immolation, holocaust, dilapidation, devastation, *razzia*, extermination, eradication, extirpation, rooting out, averruncation, sweeping, etc., death-blow, *coup de grâce*, the crack of doom.

(*Verbs*). To be destroyed, etc., waste, fall to pieces, break up, crumble, break down, double up.

(*Phrases*). To go to the dogs; to go to pot; to go by the board; to be all over with; one's doom being sealed.

To destroy, do away with, demolish, overturn, upset, throw down, overthrow, overwhelm, subvert, put an end to, uproot, eradicate, extirpate, root out, grub up, break up, pull down, crumble, smash, crash, crush, quell, quash, squash, cut up, shatter, shiver, batter, tear or

struction, revival, regeneration, revivification, resuscitation, re-animation, resurrection, reappearance, palingenesis, reincarnation, phœnix (660).

(*Verbs*). To reproduce, revive, renovate, rebuild, reconstruct, regenerate, revivify, resurrect, resuscitate, reincarnate, quicken; come again into life, reappear.

(*Phrase*). Spring up like a mushroom.

(*Adjectives*). Reproduced, etc., renascent, reappearing.

shake to pieces, nip, tear to tatters, pick to pieces, put down, suppress, strike out, throw or knock down, cut down, knock on the head, stifle, dispel, fell, sink, swamp, scuttle, engulf, corrode, erode, consume, sacrifice, immolate, burke, blow down, sweep away, erase, expunge, wipe out, mow down, blast.

To waste, lay waste, ravage, dilapidate, dismantle, disorganise, devour, swallow up, desolate, devastate, sap, mine, blow up, stifle, dispatch, extinguish, quench, annihilate, kill (361), unroot, root out, rout out, averruncate, deracinate.

(*Phrases*). To lay the axe to the root of; make a clean sweep of; to make mincemeat of; to scatter to the winds; cut up root and branch; knock on the head; knock into a cocked hat; sap the foundations of; nip in the bud; strike at the root of; pluck up by the root; ravage with fire and sword.

(*Adjectives*). Unproduced, unproductive, undestroyed, etc., done for, dished, etc.

---

164. PRODUCER (*Substantives*), originator, author, founder, workman, doer, performer, etc., forger, agent (690), builder, architect, factor.

165. DESTROYER (*Substantives*), extinguisher, exterminator, assassin (361), executioner (975), ravager, annihilator, subverter, etc.

166. PATERNITY (*Substantives*), parentage, parent, father, sire, paterfamilias, pater, dad; mother, dam; materfamilias, mater, procreator, progenitor, ancestor, ancestry, forefathers, forbears, grandsire; house, parent stem, trunk, stock, pedigree; motherhood, maternity; papa, mamma.

167. POSTERITY (*Substantives*), progeny, breed, issue, offspring, brood, seed, spawn, scion, offset, child, son, daughter, bantling, shoot, sprout, sprig, slip, branch, line, lineage, filiation, family, offshoot, ramification, descendant.

Straight descent, sonship, primogeniture, ultimogeniture.

(*Phrase*). A chip of the old block.

---

168. PRODUCTIVENESS (*Substantives*), fecundity, fruitfulness, fertility, prolificness.

Pregnancy, gestation, pullulation, fructification, multiplication, propagation, procreation.

169. UNPRODUCTIVENESS (*Substantives*), infertility, barrenness, sterility, unfruitfulness, unprofitableness, infecundity, *see* Inutility (645), non-agency.

(*Verb*). To be unproductive, etc.

A milch cow, a rabbit, a warren, a hydra.

(*Verbs*). To procreate (161), multiply, teem, pullulate, fructify, proliferate, generate.

(*Adjectives*). Productive, prolific, teeming, fertile, fruitful, luxuriant, fecund, pregnant, gravid, *enceinte*, with child, with young.

Procreant, procreative, generative, propagable, life-giving.

(*Adjectives*). Unproductive, inoperative, barren, addle, unfertile, unprolific, sterile, unfruitful, hungry, teemless, infecund, issueless, unprofitable (645).

170. AGENCY (*Substantives*), operation, force, working, strain, function, office, hand, intervention, exercise, work, swing, play, causation (153), impelling force, mediation (631); *see* Action (680).

Modus operandi, quickening power, maintaining power.

(*Verbs*). To be in action, to operate, work, act, perform, play, support, sustain, strain, maintain, take effect, quicken, strike, strike hard, strike home, bring to bear.

(*Phrases*). To come into play; to make an impression.

(*Adjectives*). Acting, operating, etc., operative, efficient, efficacious, effectual, in force.

Acted upon, wrought upon.

171. Physical ENERGY (*Substantives*), activity, keenness, intensity, sharpness, pungency, vigour, strength, acrimony, causticity, virulence, corrosiveness, acritude, poignancy, harshness, severity, edge, point, raciness, metal, mettle, vim.

Seasoning, mordant, pepper, mustard, cayenne, caviare (392).

Mental energy (*see* 604), mental excitation (824), voluntary energy (682).

Exertion, activity, stir, bustle, agitation, effervescence, fermentation, ferment, ebullition, splutter, perturbation, briskness, voluntary activity (682), quicksilver.

(*Verbs*). To give energy, energise, stimulate, galvanise, electrify, intensify, excite, exert (173).

(*Adjectives*). Strong, energetic, active, keen, vivid, intense, severe, sharp, acute, irritating, pungent, poignant, mordant,

172. Physical INERTNESS (*Substantives*), inertia, *vis inertiæ*, passiveness, inactivity (683), torpor, latency, torpidity, dullness, deadness, heaviness, flatness, slackness, tameness, slowness, languor, lentor, quiescence (265), sleep (683), intermission (141).

Mental inertness, *see* 605, 683, 826.

(*Verbs*). To be inert, inactive, passive, etc.; to hang fire, to let alone, to smoulder.

(*Phrase*). To sit on the fence.

(*Adjectives*). Inert, inactive, passive, torpid, flaccid, limp, lymphatic, sluggish, dull, heavy, flat, slack, tame, slow, blunt, lifeless, etc.

Latent, dormant, smouldering, unexerted, unstrained, uninfluential.

(*Adverbs*). Inactively, in suspense, in abeyance.

acrid, acrimonious, vitriolic, virulent, caustic, corrosive, racy, brisk, ebullient, harsh, double-edged, double-barrelled, double-distilled, drastic, escharotic, intensive, trenchant.

(*Phrases*). *Fortiter in re*; with telling effect; with full steam; at high pressure.

173. VIOLENCE (*Substantives*), inclemency, vehemence, might, impetuosity, boisterousness, abruptness, ebullition, turbulence, horse-play, bluster, uproar, riot, rumpus, fierceness, rage, wildness, fury, heat, exacerbation, exasperation, malignity, fit, paroxysm, orgasm, force, brute force, *coup de main*, strain, shock, spasm, convulsion, throe, shindy.

Outbreak, burst, outburst, dissilience, discharge, volley, explosion, blow-up, blast, detonation, eruption, displosion, torrent.

Turmoil, tumult, storm, tempest, squall, hurricane, tornado, earthquake, volcano, thunderstorm, typhoon, cyclone.

A rowdy (949), berserk (or baresark or berserker).

A fury, dragon, demon, tiger, beldam, Tisiphone, Megæra, Alecto, Mænad.

(*Phrase*). *Sturm und Drang.*

(*Verbs*). To be violent, etc., to run high, ferment, effervesce, run wild, run riot, run amuck, rush, tear, rush headlong, bluster, rage, rampage, riot, storm, boil, fume, let off steam, foam, wreak, bear down.

Spread like wildfire.

To break out, fly out, bounce, explode, displode, fly, fulminate, detonate, blow up, flash, flare, burst, burst out, shock, shog, strain; to see red.

To render violent, sharpen, stir up, quicken, excite, incite, stimulate, kindle, lash, suscitate, urge, accelerate, foment, aggravate, exasperate, exacerbate, con-

174. MODERATION (*Substantives*), gentleness, temperateness, calmness, mildness, softness, sobriety, slowness, tameness, quiet (740), restfulness, reason.

Relaxation, remission, measure mitigation, tranquillisation, assuagement, soothing, allaying, etc., contemperation, pacification (723), restraint, check (751), lullaby, sedative, lenitive, demulcent, opiate, anodyne, milk, opium.

Mental calmness, *see* 826.

(*Verbs*). To be moderate, etc., to keep within bounds or within compass, to settle down, to keep the peace, to sober down, remit, relent.

To moderate, soften, soothe, mitigate, appease, temper, attemper, contemper, mollify, lenify, tame, dull, take off the edge, blunt, obtund, tone down.

To tranquillise, assuage, appease, lull, smooth, compose, still, calm, quiet, hush, quell, sober, pacify, damp, lay, allay, rebate, slacken, smooth, soften, alleviate, rock to sleep, deaden (376), check, restrain, slake, curb, bridle, rein in, hold in, repress, smother, counteract (179).

(*Phrases*). To pour oil on the waves; pour balm into.

(*Adjectives*). Moderate, gentle, mild, sober, temperate, reasonable, tempered, calm, unruffled, tranquil, smooth, untroubled, unirritating, soft, bland, oily, demulcent, lenitive, cool, quiet, anodyne, hypnotic, sedative, peaceful, peaceable, pacific, lenient, tame, halcyon, restful.

vulse, infuriate, madden, lash into fury, inflame, explode, let off, discharge.

(*Phrases*). To break the peace; to out-herod Herod; add fuel to the flame.

(*Adjectives*). Violent, vehement, warm, acute, rough, rude, boisterous, impetuous, ungentle, abrupt, rampant, knock-about, rampageous, bluff, turbulent, blustering, riotous, rowdy, noisy, thundering, obstreperous, uproarious, outrageous, frantic, phrenetic, headstrong, rumbustious, disorderly (59).

Savage, fierce, ferocious, fiery, fuming, excited, unquelled, unquenched, unextinguished, unrepressed, boiling, boiling over, furious, outrageous, raging, running riot, storming, hysteric, hysterical, wild, running wild, ungovernable, unappeasable, immitigable, uncontrollable, insuppressible, irrepressible, raging, desperate, mad, rabid, infuriate, exasperated.

Tempestuous, stormy, squally, spasmodic, convulsive, galvanic, bursting, explosive, detonating, etc., volcanic, meteoric, seismic.

(*Phrases*). Fierce as a tiger; all the fat in the fire.

(*Adverbs*). Violently, etc., by force, by main force, like mad, etc.

(*Phrases*). By might and main; tooth and nail; *vi et armis*; at the point of the sword; at one fell swoop.

(*Phrases*). Gentle as a lamb; mild as mother's milk; milk and water.

(*Adverbs*). Moderately, gently, softly, etc.

(*Phrases*). *Suaviter in modo; est modus in rebus.*

———

4°. INDIRECT POWER

175. INFLUENCE (*Substantives*), weight, pressure, prevalence, sway, predominance, predominancy, dominance, prepotency, reign, ableness, capability, etc. (157).

Footing, hold, foothold, purchase, fulcrum, stance, *point d'appui, pou sto, locus standi,* leverage, vantage-ground, ascendancy.

(*Phrase*). A tower of strength.

175A. Absence of INFLUENCE, see 172, 158, 160.

(*Verb*). To have no influence.

(*Adjectives*). Uninfluential.

———

Independence, voluntary influence (737), protection, patronage, auspices.

(*Verbs*). To have influence, etc., to have a hold upon, etc., to have a pull, to gain a footing, work upon, take root, take hold, prevail, dominate, predominate, outweigh, overweigh, to bear upon.

(*Phrases*). To be in the ascendant; to spread like wild-fire.

(*Adjectives*). Influential, valid, weighty, prevailing, prevalent, dominant, regnant, predominating, predominant, prepotent, ascendant, rife.

(*Adverb*). With telling effect.

176. TENDENCY (*Substantives*), aptness, proneness, proclivity, conduciveness, bent, bias, quality, inclination, trend, propensity, conducement, subservience (641).

(*Verbs*). To tend, contribute, conduce, lead, dispose, incline, trend, verge, bend to, affect, carry, promote, redound to, subserve to (644), bid fair to, make for.

(*Adjectives*). Tending, contributing, conducing, conducive, working towards, calculated to, disposing, inclining, bending, leading, carrying to, subservient, subsidiary (644, 707).

(*Adverbs*). For, whither, in a fair way to.

177. LIABILITY (*Substantives*), subjection to, dependence on, exposure to, contingency, *see* Chance (156), susceptivity, susceptibility, obnoxiousness.

(*Verbs*). To be liable, etc., incur, to lay oneself open to, lie under, expose oneself, etc., stand a chance, to open a door to.

(*Adjectives*). Liable, subject, open to, incident to, exposed to, dependent on, obnoxious to.

Contingent, incidental, guardless (665), unexempt.

(*Phrases*). Within range of; at the mercy of.

5°. COMBINATIONS OF CAUSES

178. CONCURRENCE (*Substantives*), co-operation, union, agreement, pulling together, alliance.

Voluntary concurrence (709).

(*Verbs*). To concur, co-operate, conspire, agree, conduce, contribute, unite, to pull together, to join forces.

(*Phrases*). To have a hand in; to be in the same boat; to go hand in hand (709).

(*Adjectives*). Concurring, concurrent, co-operating, conspiring, agreeing, pulling together, etc., in alliance with, with one consent, with one accord.

————

179. COUNTERACTION (*Substantives*), opposition, antagonism, polarity, clashing, etc., collision, resistance, interference, friction.

Neutralisation, nullification, compensation (30).

Reaction, retroaction (277), *contrecoup*, repercussion, rebound, recoil, ricochet, counterblast.

Check, obstacle, hindrance (706), *vis inertiæ*.

Voluntary counteraction (708).

(*Verbs*). To counteract, oppose, contravene, antagonise, interfere with, collide with, clash, neutralise, nullify, render null, withstand, resist, hinder, etc. (706), repress, control, curb, check, rein in (174).

To react (277), countervail, counterpoise, etc. (30), over-poise.

(*Adjectives*). Counteracting, opposing, etc., antagonistic, opposite, retroactive, cohibitive, counter, contrary (14).

(*Adverbs*). Counter, notwithstanding, nevertheless, nathless, none the less, yet, still, although, though, albeit, howbeit, maugre, at all events.

But, even, however, *quoad minus*, *quand même*, in spite of, in defiance of, in the teeth of, in the face of, in spite of, in despite of, *non obstante*, against, *see* 708.

(*Phrases*). For all that; all the same; be that as it may; even so; in spite of one's teeth.

CLASS II

WORDS RELATING TO SPACE

SECTION I.—SPACE IN GENERAL

1°. ABSTRACT SPACE

180. Indefinite space.

SPACE (*Substantives*), extension, extent, expanse, room, scope, range, way, expansion, compass, sweep, play, latitude, field, swing, spread; spare room, headway, elbow-room, freedom, house-room, stowage, roomage, margin.

Open space, void space, vacuity (4), opening, waste, wilderness, moor, moorland, campagna, tundra.

Abyss, unlimited space, the four winds, *see* Infinity (105), Ubiquity (186).

(*Adjectives*). Spatial, two-dimensional, three-dimensional.

Spacious, roomy, extensive, expansive, capacious, ample.

Boundless, unlimited, unbounded, limitless, infinite, ubiquitous, shoreless, trackless, pathless, illimitable.

(*Adverbs*). Extensively, etc., wherever, everywhere.

(*Phrases*). The length and the breadth of the land; far and near, far and wide; all over; all the world over; from China to Peru; in every quarter; in all quarters; in all lands; here, there, and everywhere; from pole to pole; throughout the world; under the sun.

180A. INEXTENSION (*Substantives*), mathematical point.

(*Adjective*). One-dimensional.

181. Definite space.

REGION (*Substantives*), sphere, ground, area, realm, quarter, district, orb, circuit, circle, compartment, domain, tract, department, territory, country, canton, county, shire, parish, province, *arrondissement, commune*, principality, duchy, kingdom.

Arena, precincts, *enceinte*, walk, patch, plot, paddock, enclosure, field, compound.

Clime, climate, zone, meridian.

(*Adjectives*). Regional, territorial, zonal, climatic, departmental, etc.

Limited space, locality.

182. PLACE (*Substantives*), lieu, spot, point, nook, corner, recess, hole, niche, compartment, premises, precinct, station, pitch, venue, latitude and longitude, abode (189).

Indefinite place.

(*Adverbs*). Somewhere, in some place, wherever it may be.

2°. Relative Space

183. Situation (*Substantives*), position, locality, status, latitude and longitude, footing, standing, post, stage, bearings, aspect, attitude, posture, lie, emplacement.

Place, site, station, pitch, seat, *venue*, the whereabouts, direction, azimuth, etc. (278).

Topography, Geography, Chorography.

A map, chart, plan (554).

(*Verbs*). To be situated, to lie, to have its seats in.

(*Adjectives*). Local, topical, situate.

(*Adverbs*). *In situ*, here and there, *passim*, whereabouts.

184. Location (*Substantives*), localisation, lodgment, deposition, reposition, stowage, establishment, settlement, fixation, grafting, insertion (300), lading, encampment, billet, installation.

A colony, settlement, cantonment.

A habitation, residence, dwelling (189).

(*Phrases*). *Genius loci*; the spirit of the place.

(*Verbs*). To place, situate, locate, localise, put, lay, set, seat, station, lodge, post, instal, house, stow, establish, fix, root, plant, graft, stick in, tuck in, insert, wedge in, shelve, pitch, camp, posit, deposit, reposit, cradle, encamp, moor, pack, embed, vest, stock, populate, people, colonise, domicile.

To billet on, quarter upon.

To pocket, put up, bag, load.

To inhabit, reside (186), domesticate, put up at, colonise.

(*Phrase*). To pitch one's tent.

185. Displacement (*Substantives*), dislodgment, eviction, ejectment (297), deportation, exile.

Removal, remotion, transposition, etc., relegation, *see* Transference (270) and Exhaustion (638).

(*Verbs*). To displace, dislodge, unhouse, unkennel, break bulk, take off, eject, evict, chuck out, hoof out, expel, etc. (297), exile, relegate, oust, ostracise, remove, transfer, transpose, transplant, transport (270), empty, clear, clear out, sweep off, sweep away, do away with, get rid of, root out, disestablish, unpeople, depopulate.

To vacate, leave (293), get out, heave out, bale, lade, pour out (297).

(*Phrase*). To make a clean sweep of.

(*Adjectives*). Displaced, etc., unhoused, houseless.

(*Adjectives*). Placed, located, etc., situate, situated, posited, nestled, embosomed, housed, moored, rooted, unremoved.

3°. Existence in Space

186. Presence (*Substantives*), occupancy, occupation, attendance, whereness.

187. Nullibiety.[1]

Absence (*Substantives*), non-existence (2), non - residence,

[1] Bishop Wilkins.

Diffusion, permeation, pervasion, dissemination (73).

Ubiquity, ubiety, ubiquitousness, omnipresence.

(*Verbs*). To exist in space, to be present, attend, remain.

To occur in a place, lie, stand, occupy, colonise.

To inhabit, dwell, reside, live, abide, lodge, nestle, perch, roost, put up at, hang out at, stay at, squat, hive, burrow, camp, encamp, bivouac, anchor, settle, take up one's quarters, pitch one's tent, get a footing, frequent, haunt, tenant, take root, strike root, revisit.

To fill, pervade, permeate, be diffused through, be disseminated through, overspread, run through.

(*Adjectives*). Present, occupying, inhabiting, etc., moored, at anchor, resiant, resident, residentiary, domiciled.

Ubiquitous, omnipresent.

(*Adverbs*). Here, there, where? everywhere, aboard, on board, at home, afield, etc., on the spot.

(*Phrases*). Here, there, and everywhere; at every turn.

non-attendance, alibi, absenteeism.

Emptiness, void, vacuum, voidness, vacuity, vacancy, vacuousness.

An absentee, nobody, nobody on earth.

(*Verbs*). To be absent, not present, etc., vacate, to keep away, to keep out of the way.

(*Phrases*). Make oneself scarce; absent oneself; take oneself off; stay away; be conspicuous by one's absence.

(*Adjectives*). Absent, not present, away, gone, from home, missing, non-resident.

(*Phrases*). Nowhere to be found; *non est inventus*; not a soul; nobody present; the bird being flown.

Empty, void, vacant, blank, untenanted, tenantless, empty, uninhabited, deserted, devoid, unoccupied.

(*Adverbs*). Without, minus, nowhere, elsewhere, *sans*.

(*Phrases*). One's back being turned; behind one's back.

---

188. INHABITANT (*Substantives*), resident, residentiary, dweller, indweller, occupier, occupant, lodger, boarder, paying guest, inmate, tenant, sojourner, settler, squatter, backwoodsman, colonist, denizen, citizen, cit, cockney, townsman, burgess, countryman, villager, cottar, compatriot, garrison, crew, population.

Native, indigene, aborigines, autochthones, son of the soil.

A colony, settlement, household.

Newcomer (57).

(*Adjectives*). Indigenous, native, autochthonous, domestic,

189. Place of habitation.

ABODE (*Substantives*), dwelling, lodging, domicile, residence, address, habitation, berth, seat, lap, sojourn, housing, quarters, accommodation, headquarters, resiance, throne, ark, tabernacle.

Nest, *nidus*, lair, haunt, eyrie (or aerie), den, hole, rookery, hive, habitat, haunt, resort, retreat, nidification, perch, roost.

Bivouac, camp, encampment, cantonment, castrametation, tent, marquee, wigwam, teepee, awning.

Cave, cavern, cell, grove, grot, grotto, alcove, bower, arbour, cove, chamber, etc. (191).

domiciliated, **domesticated,** do- | Home, fatherland, country,
miciliary. | homestead, homestall, fireside,
                                     | snuggery, hearth, lares and pe-
           ——— | nates, household gods, roof,
                                       | household, housing; "dulce do-
                                       | mum."

Building, structure, edifice, fabric, erection, pile, tenement, messuage, farm, farm-house, grange.

Cot, cabin, hut, chalet, croft, shed, hangar, penthouse, lean-to, booth, stall, hovel, outhouse, barn, bawn, hole, kennel, sty, dog-hole, cote, stable, garage, offices.

House, mansion, villa, maisonnette, cottage, box, lodge, *pied-à-terre*, bungalow, hermitage, folly, rotunda, tower, temple, *château*, castle, pavilion, hotel, court, hall, palace, kiosk, house-boat.

Inn, hostel, hotel, tavern, caravansary, hospice, barrack, casemate, lodging-house, guest-house, doss-house, lodgings, apartments, diggings.

Hamlet, village, thorp, dorp, ham, kraal, borough, burgh, municipality, town, city, garden city, metropolis, suburb (227), province, country.

Street, place, terrace, parade, road, row, lane, alley, court, wynd, close, yard, passage, rents, slum; square, polygon, quadrant, circus, crescent, mall, place, piazza, arcade, gardens.

Anchorage, roadstead, dock, basin, wharf, quay, port.

(*Adjectives*). Urban, civic, metropolitan, municipal, provincial, rural, rustic, countrified; home-like, homy.

190. Things contained.

CONTENTS (*Substantives*), cargo, lading, freight, load, burden, ware (798).

191. RECEPTACLE (*Substantives*), recipient, receiver, reservatory, compartment, *see* 636.

Cell, cellule, loculus, follicle, hole, corner, niche, recess, nook, crypt, stall, dog-hole, pigeon-hole, lodging (*see* 189), bed, berth, bunk, doss, etc. (215), pew, store-room, strong-room, wardrobe.

Capsule, vesicle, cyst, *cancelli*, bladder, utensil.

Stomach, belly, paunch, ventricle, crop, craw, maw, gizzard, bread-basket, ovary, womb (221).

Pocket, pouch, sporran, fob, sheath, scabbard, socket, bag, sac, sack, wallet, scrip, poke, kit, knapsack, *rucksack*, haversack, sabretache, satchel, reticule, powder-box, vanity-bag, portfolio, budget.

Chest, box, hutch, coffer, case, casket, caddy, pyx (or pix), *caisson*, desk, bureau, cabinet, reliquary, trunk, portmanteau, saratoga, bandbox, valise, hold-all, attaché-case, suit-case, dressing-case, kit-bag, brief-bag, gladstone bag, boot, imperial, creel, crate, packing-case, cage, hutch, snuff-box, mull.

Vessel, vase, bushel, barrel, canister, jar, can, pottle, basket, pannier, corbeille, punnet, hamper, tray, hod.

For liquids: cistern, reservoir, tank, vat, caldron, barrel, cask, keg, runlet, firkin, kilderkin, demijohn, carboy, amphora, bottle, jar, decanter, carafe, tantalus, ewer, cruse, crock, kit, canteen, flagon, flask, flasket, thermos flask, stoup, noggin, vial (or phial), cruet, caster, urn, samovar, billy.

Tub, bucket, pail, pot, tankard, beaker, jug, pitcher, mug, noggin, pipkin, gallipot, matrass, receiver, alembic, retort, test-tube, pipette, bolthead, capsule, kettle, spittoon.

Bowl, basin, jorum, punch-bowl, cup, goblet, chalice, tumbler, glass, horn, can, pan, plate, dish, trencher, tray, salver, patera, calabash, porringer, saucepan, skillet, casserole, tureen, saucer, platter, hod, scuttle, shovel, trowel, spoon, spatula, ladle.

Closet, commode, cupboard, cellaret, chiffonier, locker, bin, buffet, press, safe, sideboard, whatnot, drawer, chest of drawers, till.

Chamber, flat, story, apartment, room, cabin, bower, office, court, hall, saloon, *salon*, parlour, state-room, presence-chamber, reception-room, drawing-room, sitting-room, living-room, gallery, cabinet, closet, boudoir, library, study, snuggery, *adytum*, sanctum, lumber-room (636), dormitory, bedroom, dressing-room, refectory, dining-room, breakfast-room, billiard-room, smoking-room, pew, harem, zenana.

Attic, loft, garret, cockloft, belfry, cellar, vault, hold, cockpit, ground-floor, *rez-de-chaussée*, basement, kitchen, pantry, scullery, offices.

Portico, porch, veranda, lobby, court, hall, vestibule, corridor, *loggia*, passage, anteroom, antechamber.

(*Adjectives*). Capsular, saccular, sacculate, recipient, ventricular, cystic, vascular, celled, cellular, cellulous, cellulose, camerated, chambered, locular, multilocular, roomed, two-roomed, etc., poly-gastric, marsupial.

SECTION II.—DIMENSIONS

1°. GENERAL DIMENSIONS

192. SIZE (*Substantives*), mag-nitude, dimension, bulk, volume, largeness, greatness (31), ex-panse, amplitude, mass, massive-ness.

Capacity, capaciousness, ton-nage (or tunnage), calibre, scant-ling.

Average size, stock size.

Turgidity, turgidness, expan-sion (194), corpulence, adiposity,

193. LITTLENESS (*Substan-tives*), smallness (32), minuteness, diminutiveness, exiguity, inex-tension, puniness, dwarfishness, epitome, duodecimo, rudiment, microcosm.

Leanness, emaciation, thinness (203), macilency, flaccidity, mea-greness, marcor.

A dwarf, runt, pygmy, Lilli-putian, chit, bantam, urchin,

obesity, chubbiness, plumpness, *embonpoint*, stoutness, out-size, hypertrophy; corporation, flesh and blood, brawn, brawniness.

Hugeness, vastness, enormousness, enormity, immensity, monstrousness, monstrosity; infinity (105).

A giant, Brobdignagian, Antæus, Gargantua, monster, whale, leviathan, elephant, mammoth, porpoise, colossus, tun, lump, chunk, bulk, block, boulder, mass, bushel, whacker, thumper, whopper, spanker, behemoth.

(*Phrases*). A Triton among the minnows; the lion's share; Benjamin's mess.

A mountain, mound, heap (72).

(*Verbs*). To be large, etc., to become large, *see* Expansion (194).

(*Adjectives*). Large, big, great, considerable, bulky, voluminous, ample, massive, massy, capacious, comprehensive, mighty.

Corpulent, stout, fat, plump, buxom, lusty, strapping, bouncing, portly, burly, brawny, fleshy, beefy, goodly, in good case, chopping, jolly, chubby, full-grown, chub-faced, lubberly, hulking, unwieldy, lumpish, gaunt, stalwart, spanking.

Overgrown, bloated, tumid, turgid, hypertrophied, swollen, pot-bellied, swag-bellied, puffy, distended, œdematous, dropsical.

Squab, dumpy, squat, squabby, tubby, roly-poly, podgy, pursy, blowsy.

Huge, immense, enormous, mighty, unbounded, vast, vasty, amplitudinous, stupendous, inordinate, preposterous, thumping, whacking, whopping, monstrous, monster; gigantic, giant-like, colossal, mountainous, elephantine, Gargantuan, Falstaf-

elf, doll, puppet, skeleton, ghost, spindle-shanks, shadow, Tom Thumb, manikin.

Animalcule, mite, insect, emmet, fly, gnat, shrimp, minnow, worm, grub, tit, tomtit, runt, mouse, small fry, mushroom, pollard, millet-seed, mustard-seed, grain of sand, mole-hill.

Atom, point, speck, dot, mote, ace, jot, iota, tittle, whit, thought, idea, look, particle, corpuscle, electron, molecule, monad, granule, grain, crumb, globule, nut-shell, minim, drop, droplet, mouthful, thimbleful, sprinkling, dash, *soupçon*, minimum, powder (330), driblet, patch, scrap, chip, inch, mathematical point; minutiæ.

The shadow of a shade.

(*Verbs*). To be small, etc., to become small, *see* Contraction (195).

(*Adjectives*). Little, small, minute, diminutive, inconsiderable, exiguous, puny, tiny, wee, petty, minikin, hop-o'-my-thumb, miniature, pigmy, undersized, dwarf, stunted, dwarfed, dwarfish, pollard, Lilliputian; pocket, portative, portable, duodecimo.

(*Phrases*). In a small compass; in a nutshell; on a small scale.

Microscopic, evanescent, impalpable, imperceptible, invisible, inappreciable, infinitesimal, homœopathic, atomic, corpuscular, molecular, rudimentary, rudimental.

Lean, thin, gaunt, meagre, emaciated, lank, macilent, ghostly, starved, starveling, fallen away, scrubby, reduced, shrunk, shrunken, attenuated, extenuated, shrivelled, tabid, flaccid, starved, skinny, stunted, wizen, wizened, scraggy, lanky, raw-boned, spindle-shanked, lantern-jawed (203).

fian, Brobdignagian; indefinite, infinite, unbounded.

(*Phrases*). Large as life; plump as a partridge; fat as a pig; fat as a quail; fat as butter; fat as brawn; [1] plump as a dumpling; fat as bacon.

(*Phrases*). Thin as a lath; worn to a shadow; skin and bone; lean as a rake; thin as a wafer; thin as a shadow.

---

194. EXPANSION (*Substantives*), enlargement, extension, augmentation, increase of size, amplification, a m p l i a t i o n, aggrandisement, spread, increment, growth, development, pullulation, swell, dilatation, rarefaction, turgescence, turgidity, thickening, tumefaction, intumescence, swelling, diastole, distension, puffing, inflation.

Overgrowth, hypertrophy, over-distension, tympany.

Bulb, knot, knob (249).

Superiority of size.

(*Verbs*). To become larger, to expand, enlarge, extend, grow, increase, swell (202), gather, fill out, deploy, dilate, stretch, largen, spread, mantle, bud, shoot, spring up, sprout, germinate, vegetate, pullulate, open, burst forth, put on flesh, outgrow.

To render larger, to expand, aggrandise, etc., distend, develop, open out, broaden, thicken, largen, amplify, magnify, rarefy, inflate, puff, blow up, stuff, cram, pad, fill out.

To be larger than, to surpass, exceed, be beyond, cap, o'ertop, *see* Height (206) and Superiority (33).

(*Adjectives*). Expanded, enlarged, increased, etc., swelled out, b u l b o u s; exaggerated, bloated, etc., full-blown, full-grown, full-formed.

195. CONTRACTION (*Substantives*), reduction, diminution, or decrease of size, defalcation, lessening, decrement, shrinking, shrivelling, systole, collapse, emaciation, attenuation, tabefaction, tabes, consumption, marasmus, atrophy, hour-glass, neck (203).

Condensation, compression, squeezing, friction (331).

Inferiority of size.

Corrugation, contractility, astringency.

(*Verbs*). To become smaller, to lessen, diminish, decrease, dwindle, shrink, contract, shrivel, collapse, wither, wilt, lose flesh, wizen, fall away, decay, purse up, waste, wane, ebb, to grow less.

(*Phrases*). To grow "small by degrees, and beautifully less" (659); to be on the wane.

To render smaller, to contract, lessen, etc., draw in, to condense, reduce, clip, compress, squeeze, attenuate, chip, dwarf, bedwarf, stunt, cut short (201), corrugate, purse up, pinch (203), deflate.

To be smaller than, to fall short of, not to come up to.

(*Phrase*). To hide its diminished head.

(*Adjectives*). Contracting, etc., astringent, tabid, contracted, lessened, etc., shrivelled, wasted, wizened, stunted, waning, ebbing, etc., neap, condensed.

(*Phrase*). *Multum in parvo.*

Unexpanded, **contractile**, compressible.

---

[1] Psalm cxix. v. 70.

196. Distance (*Substantives*), remoteness, farness, longinquity, elongation, offing, removedness, parallax, reach, span.

Antipodes, outpost, outskirt, aphelion, horizon.

(*Phrases*). *Ultima Thule*; *ne plus ultra*; the uttermost parts of the earth; the back of beyond.

Separation (44), transference (270).

Diffusion, dispersion (73).

(*Verbs*). To be distant, etc.; to extend to, stretch to, reach to, spread to, go to, get to, stretch away to; outgo, outstep (303); to go great lengths.

To remain at a distance, keep away, stand off, keep off, keep clear, stand aloof, hold off.

(*Adjectives*). Distant, far, far off, remote, distal, wide of, clear of, yon, yonder, at arm's length, apart, aloof, asunder, ulterior, transalpine, ultramundane, hyperborean, hull down.

Inaccessible, out of the way, unapproachable, unreachable; incontiguous.

(*Adverbs*). Far, away, far away, afar, off, a long way off, afar off, wide away, aloof, wide of, clear of, out of the way, a great way off, out of reach, abroad.

(*Phrases*). Far and near; far and wide; over the hills and far away; from end to end; from pole to pole; from China to Peru; from Dan to Beersheba; to the ends of the earth; out of the sphere of; wide of the mark; *à perte de vue.*

Apart, asunder, few and far between.

Yonder, farther, beyond, *longo intervallo*, wide apart, poles apart; 'from Indus to the pole."

---

197. Nearness (*Substantives*). nighness, propinquity, vicinity, vicinage, neighbourhood, adjacency, closeness; perihelion.

A short distance, a step, an earshot, close quarters, a stone's throw, a hair's breadth, a span, bowshot, gunshot.

Purlieus, neighbourhood, environs (227), vicinity, *alentours*, suburbs, the whereabouts, *banlieue*, borderland.

A bystander, neighbour.

Approach, approximation, appropinquation, appulse (286), junction (43), concentration, convergence (290).

Meeting, *rencontre* (292).

(*Verbs*). To be near, etc., to adjoin, hang about, trench on, border upon, stand by, approximate, tread on the heels of, cling to, clasp, hug, get near, etc., to approach (287), to meet (290).

To bring near, to crowd, pack, huddle together.

(*Adjectives*). Near, nigh, close, close at hand, neighbouring, proximate, approximate, adjacent, adjoining, intimate, bordering upon, close upon, hard upon, trenching on, treading on the heels of, verging on, at hand, handy, near the mark, home, at the point of, near run, in touch with, nearish.

(*Adverbs*) Near, nigh, hard by, fast by, close to, next door to, within reach, within call, within hearing, within an ace of, close upon, at hand, on the verge of, near the mark, in the environs, etc., at one's elbow, at close quarters, within range, pistolshot, a stone's throw, etc., cheek by jowl, beside, alongside, at the heels of, at the threshold.

About, hereabouts, thereabouts, in the way, in presence of, in round numbers, approximately, as good as, *à peu près, see* 32.

198. INTERVAL (*Substantives*), interspace, *see* Discontinuity (70), break, gap, opening (260), chasm, hiatus, cæsura, interstice, lacuna, cleft, foss, mesh, crevice, chink, creek, cranny, crack, slit, fissure, scissure, chap, rift, flaw, gash, cut, leak, dike (350), ha-ha, fracture, solution of continuity, breach, rent, oscitation, gaping, yawning, pandiculation, insertion (300), gorge, defile, ravine, canyon (or cañon), crevasse, chimney, *couloir, bergschrund,* gulf, gully, frith, furrow, *see* 259.

Thing interposed, a go-between, interjacence (228).

(*Verbs*). To separate (44), gape.

---

199. CONTIGUITY (*Substantives*), contact, proximity, apposition, no interval, juxtaposition, touching, tangency, tangent, osculation, meeting (292), syzygy, coincidence, register, co-existence, adhesion (46).

Confine, frontier, demarcation (233), border.

(*Verbs*). To be contiguous, etc., to touch, meet, adhere (46), osculate, coincide, register, co-exist, abut on, graze, border.

(*Adjectives*). Contiguous, touching, bordering on, meeting, in contact, conterminous, osculating, osculatory, tangential, proximate.

(*Phrases*). Hand to hand; end to end; *tête-à-tête*; next door to; in juxtaposition, apposition, etc.; in register.

2°. LINEAR DIMENSIONS

200. LENGTH (*Substantives*), longitude, span, stretch.

A line, bar, rule, stripe, spoke, radius.

Lengthening, elongation, prolongation, production, producing, protraction, tension, stretching.

(*Verbs*). To be long, etc., to extend to, reach, stretch to.

To render long, lengthen, extend, elongate, prolong, produce, stretch, draw out, protract, spin out, drawl.

(*Phrase*). To drag its slow length along.

(*Adjectives*). Long, longsome, lengthy, tedious, tiresome, wire-drawn, outstretched, lengthened, produced, etc., alexandrine, sesquipedalian, interminable, unending, there being no end of.

201. SHORTNESS (*Substantives*), brevity, briefness, a span, etc., *see* Smallness (193).

Shortening, abbreviation, abbreviature, abridgment, curtailment, reduction, contraction, compression (195), retrenchment, elision, ellipsis, compendium (596), conciseness (in style) (572).

(*Verbs*). To be short, brief, etc.

To render short, to shorten, curtail, abridge, abbreviate, epitomise, reduce, contract, compress, scrimp, skimp, boil down.

To retrench, cut short, cut down, pare down, whittle down, clip, dock, lop, poll, prune, crop, bob, shingle, snub, truncate, cut, hack, hew, etc.; (in drawing) to foreshorten.

(*Adjectives*). Short, brief, curt,

Linear, lineal, longitudinal, oblong.

(*Phrases*). As long as my arm; as long as to-day and to-morrow.

(*Adverbs*). Lengthwise, longitudinally, in a line, along, from end to end, endways, fore and aft, from head to foot, from top to toe.

compendious, compact, stubby, skimpy, stumpy, pug, snub.

Oblate, elliptical.

Concise (572), summary.

---

202. BREADTH (*Substantives*), width, latitude, amplitude, diameter, bore, calibre, superficial extent, expanse.

THICKNESS, crassitude (192), thickening, expansion, dilatation, etc. (194).

(*Verbs*). To be broad, thick, etc.

To broaden, to swell, dilate, expand, outspread, etc. (194); to thicken, incrassate.

(*Adjectives*). Broad, wide, ample, extended, fan-like, outstretched, etc.

Thick, dumpy, squab, squat, thick-set.

(*Phrases*). Wide as a church door; thick as a rope.

---

203. NARROWNESS (*Substantives*), slenderness, closeness, scantiness, exility, lankness, lankiness, fibrousness.

A line (205), a hair's breadth, a finger's breadth, streak, vein.

THINNESS, tenuity, leanness, meagreness.

A shaving, a slip (205), a mere skeleton, a shadow, an anatomy.

A middle constriction, stricture, neck, waist, isthmus, wasp, hour-glass, ridge, ravine, defile, gorge, pass.

Narrowing, coarctation, tapering, compression, squeezing, etc. (195).

(*Phrases*). A bag of bones; a living skeleton.

(*Verbs*). To be narrow, etc., to taper, contract, shrink.

To render narrow, etc., to narrow, contract, coarctate, attenuate, constrict, constringe, cramp, pinch, squeeze, compress, tweak, corrugate, warp.

To shave, pare, shear, etc.

(*Adjectives*). Narrow, slender, thin, fine, filiform, filamentary, filamentous, fibrous, funicular, capillary, stringy, wiredrawn, fine-spun, anguine, taper, dapper, slim, slight, gracile, scant, spare, delicate.

Meagre, lean, emaciated, lank, lanky, starveling, attenuated, skinny, scraggy, gaunt, skin and bone, raw-boned, spindle-shanked (193), spidery, spindly, reedy.

(*Phrases*). Thin as a lath; thin as a whipping-post; lean as a rake; thin as a thread-paper; thin as a wafer; thin as a shadow.

---

204. LAYER (*Substantives*), stratum, bed, zone, substratum, slab, escarpment, floor, flag, stage, story, tier.

205. FILAMENT (*Substantives*), line, fibre, fibril, hair, gossamer, wire, thread, cord, rope, yarn, etc. (*see* 45), cilium, gimp.

Plate, lamina, lamella, sheet, flake, scale, coat, pellicle, membrane, film, slice, shive, cut, shaving, rasher, board, plank, platter, trencher, spatula, leaf.

Stratification, scaliness, a nest of boxes, coats of an onion.

(*Verbs*). To slice, shave, etc.

(*Adjectives*). Lamellar, laminated, lamelliform, laminiferous, scaly, filmy, membranous, flaky, foliated, foliaceous, stratified, stratiform, tabular.

Strip (51), shred, slip, spill, list, string, band, fillet, fascia, ribbon (or riband); roll, lath, slat, splinter, shiver, shaving; arborescence, *see* 256; strand.

A hair-stroke.

(*Adjectives*). Filamentary, fibrous, hairy, capillary, thread-like, wiry, funicular, stringy.

---

206. HEIGHT (*Substantives*), altitude, elevation, eminence, pitch, loftiness, sublimity.

Stature, tallness, procerity, culmination, *see* Summit (210).

A giant, grenadier, guardsman, colossus, giraffe.

Alps, mountain, mount, hill, hillock, monticule, fell, moorland, hummock, knap, knoll, cape, headland, foreland, promontory, ridge, *arête*, pike, uplands, highlands, rising ground, downs, dune, mound, mole, steeps, bluff, cliff, crag, vantage-ground, tor, eagle's nest, crow's nest.

Orography, Orology.

Tower, pillar, column, obelisk, monument, steeple, spire, *flèche*, campanile, minaret, turret, cupola, pilaster, sky-scraper.

Pole, pikestaff, maypole, flagstaff, topmast, topgallant mast, crow's nest.

207. LOWNESS (*Substantives*), lowlands, depression, a molehill, recumbency, prostration, *see* Horizontality (213).

A ground-floor, basement, *rez de chaussée* (191), hold.

(*Verbs*). To be low, etc., crouch, slouch, lie flat.

To lower, depress (306), take down a peg, prostrate, subvert.

(*Adjectives*). Low, neap, nether, prostrate, flat, level with the ground, grovelling, crouched, crouching, subjacent, underlying, squat.

(*Adverbs*). Under, beneath, underneath, below, down, adown, over head and ears, downwards, underfoot, at the foot of, underground, at a low ebb.

Ceiling, roof, awning, canopy (*see* 210), attic, loft, garret, housetop.

Growth, upgrowth (194).

(*Verbs*). To be high, etc., to tower, soar, ride, beetle, hover, cap, overtop, culminate, overhang, hang over, impend, overlie, bestride, mount, surmount, to cover (222), perch.

To render high, to heighten, exalt, *see* Elevate (307).

To become high, grow, upgrow, soar, tower, rise (305).

(*Adjectives*). High, elevated, eminent, exalted, lofty, supernal, tall, towering, beetling, soaring, stalwart, colossal, gigantic, Patagonian, culminating, raised, elevated, etc., perched up, hanging (gardens), crowning.

Upland, moorland, hilly, mountainous, cloud-touching, heaven-kissing, cloud-topt, cloud-capt, Alpine, subalpine, aerial; orographical.

Upper, uppermost (210), topgallant.

Overhanging, impending, incumbent, overlying, superincumbent, supernatant, superimposed, hovering.

(*Phrases*). Tall as a maypole; tall as a steeple; tall as a poplar.

(*Adverbs*). On high, high up, aloft, above, aloof, overhead, in the clouds, on tiptoe, on stilts, on the shoulders of, over head and ears.

Over, upwards, from top to bottom, from top to toe, from head to foot, cap-à-pie, *a capite ad calcem.*

---

208. DEPTH (*Substantives*), deepness, profundity, profoundness, depression, bathos, anticlimax, depth of water, draught.

A hollow, pit, shaft, well, crater, gulf, abyss, abysm, bottomless pit, hell.

209. SHALLOWNESS (*Substantives*), shoaliness, shoals.

(*Adjectives*). Shallow, skin-deep, superficial, shoaly.

Soundings, submersion, plunge, dive (310).

Bathymetry.

(*Verbs*). To be deep, etc.

To render deep, etc., to deepen, sink, submerge, plunge, dip, dive (310).

To dig, scoop out, hollow, sink, delve (252).

(*Adjectives*). Deep, deep-seated, profound, sunk, buried, submerged, etc., subaqueous, submarine, subterranean, underground, subterrene, abysmal; bathymetrical, bathymetric.

Bottomless, soundless, fathomless, unfathomed, unsounded, unplumbed, unfathomable.

(*Phrases*). Deep as a well; ankle-deep; knee-deep; breast-deep; chin-deep.

(*Adverbs*). Beyond one's depth, out of one's depth, underground.

(*Phrase*). Over head and ears.

---

210. SUMMIT (*Substantives*), top, vertex, apex, zenith, pinnacle, acme, climax, culminating point, pitch, meridian, sky, pole, watershed.

Tip, tip-top, crest, crow's nest, eagle's nest, peak, turning-point, pole.

Crown, brow, nib, head, nob, noddle, pate.

211. BASE (*Substantives*), basement, plinth, foundation, substratum, ground, earth, pavement, floor, paving, flag, ground floor, deck, substructure, footing, groundwork.

The bottom, rock-bottom, nadir, foot, sole, toe, root, keel.

(*Adjectives*). Bottom, under-

Capital, cornice, sconce, architrave, pediment, entablature, frieze.

Roof, ceiling, thatch, tiling, slating, awning, canopy, *see* Cover (222).

(*Adjectives*). Top, topmost, uppermost, tip-top, culminating, meridian, capital, head, polar, supreme, crowning.

most, nethermost, fundamental, basic.

---

212. VERTICALITY (*Substantives*), erectness, uprightness, perpendicularity, aplomb, right angle, normal, azimuth, circle.

Wall, precipice, cliff.

Erection, raising, rearing.

(*Verbs*). To be vertical, etc., to stand up, to stand on end, to stand erect, to stand upright, to stick up.

To render vertical, to set up, stick up, erect, rear, raise up, cock up, prick up, raise on its legs.

(*Adjectives*). Vertical, upright, erect, perpendicular, normal, straight, standing up, etc., up on end, bolt upright, rampant.

(*Adverbs*). Up, vertically, etc., on end, up on end.

---

213. HORIZONTALITY (*Substantives*), a level, plane, dead level, flatness (251).

Recumbency, lying, lying down, reclination, decumbence, decumbency, supination, resupination, prostration, azimuth.

A plain, floor, flat, platform, bowling-green, plateau, terrace, estrade, esplanade, parterre, table-land, *see* 204, 215.

(*Verbs*). To be horizontal, recumbent, etc., to lie, recline, lie down, couch, sit down, squat, lie flat, lie prostrate, sprawl, loll.

To render horizontal, etc., to lay, lay down, level, flatten, prostrate, knock down, floor.

(*Adjectives*). Horizontal, level, plane, flat, even, discoid.

Recumbent, decumbent, lying, prone, supine, couchant, couching, jacent, prostrate, squat, squatting, on one's back, on all fours, on one's hunkers, sitting, reclining.

(*Adverbs*). Horizontally, etc., on one's back, etc.

---

214. PENDENCY (*Substantives*), dependency, suspension, hanging.

A pendant (*see* 849), pedicel, peduncle, tail, train, flap, skirt, pig-tail, queue, pendulum.

A peg, knob, button, hook, nail, ring, staple, knot (45), tenter-hook.

(*Verbs*). To be pendent, etc., to hang, swing, dangle, swag, daggle, flap, trail.

To suspend, hang, sling, hook up, hitch, fasten to.

(*Adjectives*). Pendent, pendulous, pensile, hanging, dependent,

215. SUPPORT (*Substantives*), ground, foundation, base, basis, *terra firma*, fulcrum, foothold, *point d'appui*, *pou sto*, *locus standi*, landing, landing-place, resting-place, groundwork, substratum, floor, bed, stall, berth, lap, mount.

A supporter, prop, stand, anvil, stay, shore, truss, sleeper, staff, stick, walking-stick, crutch, stirrups, stilts, alpenstock, baton.

Post, pillar, shaft, column, pediment, pedicle, pedestal, plinth (211), baluster, banister.

swinging, etc., suspended, etc., loose, flowing, caudal.

Having a peduncle, etc., ped-unculate, tailed, caudate.

(*Adverbs*). Dingle-dangle.

————

A frame, framework, scaffold, scaffolding, skeleton, cadre, beam, rafter, lintel, joist, corner-stone, stanchion, summer, girder, cantilever, outrigger, tie-beam (45), columella, backbone, keystone, axle, axle-tree, axis, fuselage chassis.

A board, form, ledge, platform, floor, stage, shelf, hob, bracket, arbor, rack, mantel, mantelpiece, mantel-shelf, counter, slab, console, dresser, flange, corbel, table, trestle, shoulder, perch, truss, horse, easel, desk.

A seat, throne, dais, divan, musnud, chair, arm-chair, easy chair, hammock-chair, deck-chair, bench, sofa, lounge, settee, chesterfield, couch, *fauteuil*, stool, tripod, footstool, *tabouret*, trivet, woolsack, ottoman, settle, squab, bench, saddle, pillion, dicky, hassock, cushion, howdah.

Bed, bedstead, chair-bedstead, bedding, pillow, bolster, mattress, shake-down, tester, pallet, hammock, crib, cradle, cot, palliasse.

Atlas, Persides, Atlantes, Caryatides, Hercules, Ygdrasil.

(*Verbs*). To be supported, etc., to lie, sit, recline, lean, loll, lounge, abut, bear, rest, stand, step, repose, etc., on, be based on, bestride, straddle, bestraddle.

To support, bear, carry, hold, sustain, shoulder, uphold, hold up, upbear, prop, underprop, shore up, underpin, pillow.

To give, furnish, afford, supply, lend, etc., support or foundations, to bottom, to found, embed.

(*Adjectives*). Supported, etc., astride on, astraddle; fundamental, basic.

216. PARALLELISM (*Substantives*), coextension.

(*Verbs*). To be parallel, etc.

(*Adjectives*). Parallel, coextensive.

(*Adverbs*). Alongside, abreast, beside.

(*Phrases*). Side by side; cheek by jowl.

————

217. OBLIQUITY (*Substantives*), inclination, slope, leaning, slant, crookedness, bias, bend, bevel, tilt, swag, cant, lurch, skew, skewness, bevelling, squint.

(*Phrase*). The tower of Pisa.

Acclivity, uphill, rise, ascent, gradient, rising ground, bank.

Declivity, downhill, fall, devexity.

A gentle or rapid slope, easy ascent or descent, chute, switchback, *montagnes russes*.

Steepness, precipitousness, cliff, precipice, talus, scarp, escarp, escarpment, measure of inclination, clinometer.

Diagonal, zigzag, distortion, hypotenuse, *see* Angle (244).

(*Verbs*). To be oblique, etc., to slope, slant, lean, incline, shelve, stoop, descend, bend, heel, careen, sag, swag, slouch, cant, sidle, skew.

To render oblique, etc., to slope, tilt, scarp, escarp, bevel, bend, incline, etc., distort.

(*Adjectives*). Oblique, inclined, leaning, recumbent, sloping, shelving, skew, askew, slant, aslant, slanting, slantendicular, plagioclastic, indirect, distorted, wry, awry, ajee, drawn, crooked, canted, tilted, biased, saggy, bevel, slouched, slouching, etc., out of the perpendicular, backhanded.

Uphill, rising, ascending.

Downhill, falling, descending, declining, anticlinal.

Steep, abrupt, precipitous, break-neck.

Diagonal, transverse, athwart, transversal, antiparallel.

(*Adverbs*). Obliquely, etc., on one side, askew, edgewise, askant, askance, sideways, aslope, slopewise, all on one side, crinkum-crankum, asquint.

(*Phrase*). *Facilis descensus Averni.*

---

218. INVERSION (*Substantives*), contraposition, overturn, somerset (somersault or summerset), *culbute*, subversion, retroversion, reversion, introversion, eversion, transposition, anastrophy, pronation and supination, overturn, antipodes (237).

(*Verbs*). To be inverted, etc., to turn turtle.

To render inverted, etc., to invert, reverse, upset, overset, overturn, turn over, upturn, subvert, retrovert, transpose, turn topsy-turvy, tilt over, *culbuter*, keel over, topple over, capsize.

(*Adjectives*). Inverted, inverse, upside down, topsy-turvy, top-heavy.

(*Adverbs*). Inversely, topsy-turvy, etc., inside out.

(*Phrases*). The cart before the horse; head over heels; the wrong side up; *hysteron proteron.*

219. CROSSING (*Substantives*), intersection, decussation, transversion.

Reticulation, network, inosculation, anastomosis, interweaving, twining, intertwining, matting, plaiting, interdigitation, mortise (or mortice).

Net, knot, *plexus*, web, mesh, twill, skein, hank, felt, lace, tulle, wicker, mat, trellis, lattice, grille, *cancelli*, grid, griddle, grating, gridiron, tracery, fretwork, filigree, reticle, diaper.

Cross, chain, wreath, braid, cat's-cradle, dovetail, Greek cross, Latin cross, Maltese cross, cross of St. Anthony, St. Andrew's cross, swastika, fylfot.

(*Verbs*). To cross, lace, intersect, decussate, interlace, intertwine, intertwist, entwine, enlace, enmesh, weave, interweave, inweave, twine, twist, wreathe, interdigitate, interlock, anastomose, inosculate, dovetail (43).

To mat, plait, plat, braid, felt, twill, tangle, entangle, ravel, net, knot (43), dishevel, raddle.

(*Adjectives*). Crossing, intersecting, etc., crossed, intersected, matted, etc., crucial, cruciform.

Retiform, reticulate, areolar, areolate, cancellated, grated, barred, streaked, traceried.

(*Adverbs*). Across, thwart, athwart, transversely, crosswise.

3°. CENTRICAL DIMENSIONS [1]

1. *General*

220. EXTERIORITY (*Substantives*), externality, outness, the outside, the exterior, surface, superficies, superstratum, eccentricity, extremity, frontage.

Disk, face, facet, front (234), skin, etc. (222).

(*Verbs*). To be exterior, etc.

To place exteriorly, or outwardly, to turn out.

(*Adjectives*). Exterior, external, outer, outward, outlying, outdoor, outside, superficial, skin-deep, frontal, discoid, eccentric, extrinsic.

(*Adverbs*). Externally, etc., out, without, outwards, outdoors.

(*Phrases*). Out of doors; *extra muros*; *ab extra*; in the open air; *sub Jove*; *à la belle étoile*; al fresco.

———

222. COVERING (*Substantives*), cover, roof, canopy, baldachin, awning, tarpaulin, tilt, tent (189), lid, hatch, operculum (263), shed.

Integument, skin, tegument, pellicle, fleece, cuticle, scarf-skin, epidermis, hide, pelt, peel, crust, bark, rind, cortex, husk, scale, shell, carapace, capsule, coat, tunic, tunicle, sheath, case, calyx, theca, sheathing, scabbard, wrapping, wrapper, envelope, veneer, blanket, rug, quilt, counterpane.

Superposition, coating, paint, varnish, anointing, inunction, incrustation, plaster, stucco, wash, parget, patina.

221. INTERIORITY (*Substantives*), the inside, interior, hinterland, interspace, substratum, subsoil.

Vitals, viscera, pith, marrow, heart, bosom, breast, entrails, bowels, belly, intestines, guts, inwards, womb, lap, backbone, *penetralia*, inmost recesses, cave, cavern, etc. (191).

(*Verbs*). To be interior, internal, within, etc.

To place or keep within, to enclose, circumscribe, *see* 231, 232.

(*Adjectives*). Interior, internal, inner, inside, inward, inlying, inmost, innermost, deep-seated, intestine, intestinal, intercostal, inland, interstitial, subcutaneous; up country.

Home, domestic, indoor.

(*Adverbs*). Internally, inwards, inwardly, within, inly, therein, *ab intra*, withinside, indoors, within doors, at home, *chez soi.*

223. CENTRALITY (*Substantives*), centre (68), middle, focus, hub, core, kernel, nucleus, nucleolus, heart, pole, axis, bull's-eye, nave, umbilicus, omphalos; concentration, centralisation.

(*Verbs*). To be central, etc.

To render central, centralise, concentrate.

To bring to a focus.

(*Adjectives*). Central, centrical, middle, median, azygous, axial, focal, umbilical, concentric.

(*Adverbs*). Midway, centrally, etc.

224. LINING (*Substantives*), coating, facing, internal incrusta-

---

[1] That is, Dimensions having reference to a centre.

(*Verbs*). To cover, superpose, superimpose, overspread, over-canopy, wrap, lap, overlap, face, case, encase, veneer, pave, upholster.

To coat, paint, varnish, pave, plaster, beplaster, daub, bedaub, encrust, stucco, dab, smear, anoint, do over, gild, japan, lacquer (or lacker), plate, electroplate, parget.

(*Phrase*). To lay it on thick.

(*Adjectives*). Covering, etc., cutaneous, dermal, cortical, cuticular, tegumentary, skinny, scaly, squamous, imbricated, epidermal, loricated.

tion, puddle, stalactite, stalagmite, wainscot, dado, wall.

Filling, stuffing, wadding.

(*Verbs*). To line, encrust, stuff, face, puddle, bush.

(*Adjectives*). Lined, encrusted, stuffed, wadded.

---

225. INVESTMENT (*Substantives*), dress, clothing, raiment, drapery, costume, attire, toilet, trim, rig, rig-out, fig, habiliment, vesture, apparel, underwear, full dress, evening dress, fancy dress, accoutrement, outfit, wardrobe, trousseau, uniform, regimentals, kit, equipment, livery, gear, harness, turn-out, caparison, suit, dress suit, lounge suit, etc., rigging, trappings, slops, traps, duds, togs, kit, frippery, bloomers, haberdashery, housing.

Dishabille, morning dress, dressing-gown, undress, mufti, rags, *negligé*, tea-gown.

Clothes, garment, garb, garniture, vestment, pontificals, robe, tunic, paletot, habit, gown, coat, dress-coat, claw-hammer, frock, stole, blouse, toga, haik, smock-frock, kimono.

Cloak, opera-cloak, cape, mantle, mantlet, dolman, shawl, scarf, wrap, wrapper, veil, fichu, yashmak, tippet, kirtle, plaid, mantilla, tabard, burnous, roquelaure, overcoat, great-coat, surtout, spencer, rain-coat, ulster, mackintosh, waterproof, poncho, surplice, alb, cassock, pallium, etc., mask, domino, cardinal, pelerine.

226. DIVESTMENT (*Substantives*), nudity, bareness, nakedness, baldness, undress, dishabille, threadbareness.

Denuding, denudation, stripping, uncovering, decortication, peeling, flaying, excoriation, desquamation, moulting, exfoliation.

(*Verbs*). To divest, uncover, denude, bare, strip, unclothe, undress, unrobe, disrobe, disapparel, disarray, take off, doff, cast off, peel, pare, decorticate, husk, uncoif, unbonnet, excoriate, skin, flay, expose, exfoliate, lay open, unroof, uncase, unsheathe, moult.

(*Adjectives*). Bare, naked, nude, stripped, denuded, undressed, unclothed, unclad, undraped, uncovered, unshod, unbonneted, exposed, in dishabille, in buff, bald, threadbare, ragged, callow, roofless.

(*Phrases*). In a state of nature; stark-naked; *in puris naturalibus*; stripped to the buff; bald as a coot; as bare as the back of one's hand; out at elbows.

Jacket, vest, under-vest, singlet, jerkin, waistcoat, cardigan, sweater, doublet, gaberdine, camisole, combinations, stays, corset, corsage, cestus, petticoat, kilt, filibeg, stomacher, skirt, kirtle, crinoline, farthingale, underskirt, slip, apron, pinafore.

Trousers, trews, breeches, galligaskins, knickerbockers, knickers, drawers, pantaloons, pants, overalls, dungarees, unmentionables, inexpressibles, smalls, tights, bags, breeks, slacks.

Cap, hat, top-hat, bowler, panama, slouch-hat, deerstalker, billycock, wide-awake, beaver, castor, bonnet, toque, sunbonnet, hood, head-gear, head-dress, kerchief, scarf, *coiffure*, coif, tartan, skull-cap, calotte, biretta, cowl, chaplet, capote, calash, pelt, wig, peruke, periwig, toupee, transformation, chignon, caftan, turban, puggaree, fez, helmet, shako, busby, *képi*, casque.

Shirt, smock, shift, chemise, chemisette, nightshirt, nightdress, pyjamas, bed-jacket, bed-gown, collar, cravat, neck-cloth, neck-tie, stock, handkerchief.

Shoe, pump, high-low, Oxford shoe, sabot, brogue, boot, jack-boot, slipper, galosh, overshoe, legging, puttee, buskin, greaves, galligaskins, mocassin, gambado, gaiter, spatterdash, spat, stocking, sock, hose, sandal, clog, babouche.

Glove, gauntlet, mitten, muff.

(*Verbs*). To invest, cover, envelop, lap, involve, drape, enwrap, wrap up, lap up, sheathe, vest, clothe, array, enrobe, dress, dight, attire, apparel, accoutre, trick out, rig, fit out, fig out, caparison, adonise, don, put on, wear, have on, huddle on, slip on, roll up in, muffle, perk up, mantle, swathe, swaddle, equip, harness.

(*Adjectives*). Invested, clothed, arrayed, dight, etc., clad, shod, etc.; sartorial.

---

227. Circumjacence (*Substantives*), circumambiency, encompassment, atmosphere, medium, outpost, skirt, outskirts, boulevards, suburbs, purlieus, precincts, faubourgs, environs, entourage, *banlieue*.

(*Verbs*). To lie around, surround, beset, set about, compass, encompass, environ, enclose, encircle, embrace, lap, gird, begird, engirdle, orb, enlace, skirt, twine round, *see* 231.

(*Adjectives*). Circumjacent, ambient, circumambient, surrounding, etc., circumfluent, cir-

228. Interjacence (*Substantives*), interlocation, intervention, insertion, interposition, interdigitation, interpolation, interlineation, intercurrence, intrusion, obtrusion, insinuation, intercalation, insertion, interference, permeation, infiltration.

An intermedium, intermediary, a go-between, bodkin, intruder, interloper, parenthesis, gag, flyleaf, entresol, *see* Mean (68).

A partition, septum, panel, diaphragm, party-wall.

A half-way house.

(*Verbs*). To lie, come, or get

cumferential, suburban, extra-mural, landlocked, begirt, buried in (363), immersed in (300), embosomed, in the bosom of.

(*Adverbs*). Around, about, without, on every side, on all sides, right and left, all around, round about.

229. OUTLINE (*Substantives*), circumference, perimeter, periphery, ambit, circuit, lines, tournure, contour, profile, silhouette.

Zone, belt, girth, band, baldric, zodiac, cordon, girdle, cingulum, clasp, *see* 247.

230. EDGE (*Substantives*), verge, brink, brow, brim, margin, border, skirt, rim, side, mouth, jaws, lip, muzzle, door, porch, portal (260), coast.

Frame, flounce, frill, ruffle, *jabot*, list, fringe, valance, edging, hem, selvedge, welt, furbelow.

(*Verbs*). To border, edge, skirt, coast, verge on.

(*Adjectives*). Border, marginal, coastal, skirting.

between, intervene, intrude, butt in, slide in, permeate, put between, put in, interpose, interject, throw in, wedge in, thrust in, foist in, insert, intercalate, interpolate, parenthesise, interline, interleave, interlard, interdigitate, do ve tail, sand wich, worm in, insinuate, obtrude (300), intersperse, infiltrate; to gag.

(*Adjectives*). Interjacent, intervening, etc., intermediary, intermediate, intercalary, interstitial, parenthetical, mediterranean.

(*Adverbs*). Between, betwixt, 'twixt, among, amongst, amid, amidst, midst, betwixt and between, sandwich - wise, parenthetically, between the lines.

231. CIRCUMSCRIPTION (*Substantives*), limitation, enclosure, confinement, shutting up, circumvallation, entombment.

Imprisonment, incarceration (751).

(*Verbs*). To circumscribe, limit, delimit, localise, bound, confine, enclose, surround (227), compass about, impound, restrict, restrain (751), shut in, shut up, lock up, bottle up, hem in, hedge in, wall in, rail in, fence, picket, pen, enfold, coop, corral, encage, cage, entomb, bury, immure, encase, pack up, seal up, wrap up (225), etc.

(*Adjectives*). Circumscribed, etc., imprisoned, pent up (754).

(*Phrase*). Not room to swing a cat in.

232. ENCLOSURE (*Substantives*), envelope, case, box, etc. (191), pen, penfold, pound, paddock, enclave, *enceinte*, corral, wall, hedge, hedgerow, espalier.

Barrier, bar, gate, gateway, door, barricade, cordon.

Dike (or dyke), ditch, fosse, moat.

Fence, pale, paling, balustrade, rail, railing, hurdle, palisade, battlement, rampart, embankment, groyne, etc. (717), circumvallation, contravallation.

233. LIMIT (*Substantives*), boundary, bounds, confine, term, bourne, kerb-stone, line of demarcation, termination, stint, frontier, precinct, marches, line of circumvallation, the pillars of Hercules, the Rubicon, the turning-point, the last word, the *ne plus ultra*.

(*Adjectives*). Definite, conterminal, terminal, frontier.

2. *Special*

234. FRONT (*Substantives*), face, anteriority, fore-part, front rank, foreground, van, vanguard, advanced guard, outpost, proscenium, façade, preface, frontispiece, disk.

Forehead, visage, physiognomy, phiz, countenance, mug, beak, rostrum, bow, stem, prow.

Pioneer, avant-courier (64).

(In a medal), the obverse.

(*Verbs*). To be in front, etc., to front, face, envisage, confront, bend forward, etc.

(*Adjectives*). Fore, anterior, front, frontal, facial.

(*Adverbs*). Before, in front, ahead, right ahead, in the van, foremost, vis-à-vis, in the foreground, face to face, before one's eyes, in the lee of.

---

235. REAR (*Substantives*), back, posteriority, the rear rank, rear-guard, the background, heels, tail, scut, rump, croup, crupper, breech, backside, buttocks, haunches, hunkers, hind quarters, *dorsum*, dorsal region, stern, poop, after-part, heel-piece, wake.

(In a medal), the reverse.

(*Verbs*). To be in the rear, behind, etc., to fall astern, to bend backwards, to back on.

(*Phrases*). Turn the back upon; bring up the rear.

(*Adjectives*). Back, rear, postern, hind, hinder, hindmost, posterior, dorsal, after.

(*Adverbs*). Behind, in the rear.

(*Phrases*). In the background; behind one's back; at the heels of; at the tail of; at the back of.

After, aft, abaft, astern, sternmost, aback, rearward.

---

236. LATERALITY (*Substantives*), side, flank, quarter, hand, cheek, jowl, wing, profile, temple, loin, haunch, hip, broadside, lee-side, lee.

East, orient.

West, occident.

(*Verbs*). To be on one side, etc., to flank, outflank, to sidle, skirt.

(*Adjectives*). Lateral, sidelong, collateral, sideling, many-sided, oriental, occidental, eastward, westward.

(*Adverbs*). Sideways, side by side (216), sidelong, abreast, alongside, aside, by the side of, to windward, or to leeward.

(*Phrase*). Cheek by jowl.

---

237. ANTIPOSITION (*Substantives*), opposite side, contraposition, reverse, inverse, antipodes, opposition, inversion (218).

Polarity, opposite poles, North and South Poles.

(*Verbs*). To be opposite, etc., subtend.

(*Adjectives*). Opposite, reverse, inverse, antipodal, subcontrary.

Fronting, facing, diametrically opposite, *vis-à-vis*.

Boreal, arctic, austral, antarctic.

(*Adverbs*). Over, over the way, over against, facing, against, fronting (234), face to face, subtending.

238. DEXTRALITY (*Substantives*), right, right hand, dexter, off-side, starboard, recto.

(*Adjectives*). Dextral, right-handed, ambidextral.

239. SINISTRALITY (*Substantives*), left, left hand, sinister, near side, larboard, port, verso.

(*Adjectives*). Sinistral, left-handed.

SECTION III.—FORM

1°. GENERAL FORM

240. FORM (*Substantives*), figure, shape, configuration, make, formation, frame, construction, conformation, cut, set, trim, build, make, stamp, cast, mould, fashion, structure.

Feature, lineament, phase, turn, attitude, posture, pose.

Science of form: Morphology.

Similarity of form, isomorphism.

Formation, figuration, efformation, sculpture.

(*Verbs*). To form, shape, figure, fashion, carve, cut, chisel, hew, rough - hew, cast, rough - cast, hammer out, block out, trim, lick into shape, knock together, mould, sculpture, stamp.

(*Adjectives*). Formed, etc., receiving form, plastic, fictile.

Giving form, formative, plastic, plasmatic, plasmic.

241. Absence of form.

AMORPHISM (*Substantives*), amorphousness, formlessness, shapelessness, disfigurement, defacement, mutilation, *see* Deformity (846).

Vandalism, vandal.

(*Verbs*). To destroy form, deform, deface, disfigure, disfeature (*see* 846), mutilate.

(*Adjectives*). Shapeless, amorphous, formless, unhewn, rough, unfashioned, unshapen, misshapen, inchoate.

242. Regularity of form.

SYMMETRY (*Substantives*), shapeliness, uniformity, finish, *see* Beauty (845), arborescence (256).

(*Adjectives*). Symmetrical, regular, shapely, well-set, uniform, finished, etc., arborescent (256).

Teres atque rotundus.

243. Irregularity of form.

DISTORTION (*Substantives*), twist, kink, wryness, asymmetry, gibbosity, contortion, malformation, *see* Ugliness (846), teratology.

(*Verbs*). To distort, twist, wrest, writhe, wring, contort, kink, buckle.

(*Adjectives*). Irregular, unsymmetrical, asymmetrical, distorted, twisted, wry, awry, askew, crooked, on one side, humpbacked, hunch-backed, gibbous, gibbose.

(*Phrase*). All manner of ways.

2°. SPECIAL FORM

244. ANGULARITY (*Substantives*), angulation, angle, cusp, bend, elbow, knee, knuckle, groin, crinkle, crankle, hook, crook, kink, crotch, crutch, crane, fluke, scythe, sickle, zigzag, anfractuosity, refraction; Fold (*see* 258), Corner (*see* 182).

Fork, bifurcation, dichotomy.

A right angle, *see* Perpendicularity (212), salient and re-entrant angles, acute and obtuse angles.

A polygon, square, triangle, etc., lozenge, diamond, rhomb, etc., gore, gusset, wedge.

T-square, protractor, etc.

(*Verbs*). To bend, refract, diffract, crook, hook, fork, bifurcate, angulate, crinkle, crankle, splay.

(*Adjectives*). Angular, bent, crooked, hooked, aduncous, aquiline, jagged, serrated, falciform, falcated, furcated, forked, bifurcate, zigzag; dovetailed, knock-kneed, crinkled, akimbo, geniculated, polygonal, etc., fusiform, sagittate, arrow-headed, wedge-shaped, cuneate, cuneiform, splayed, angulate.

245. CURVATURE (*Substantives*), curvation, incurvity, incurvation, bend, flexure, flexion, camber, bending, deflexion, inflexion, arcuation, diffraction, turn, deviation, detour, sweep, sinuosity, curl, curling, winding, recurvature, recurvation, refraction, flexibility (324).

A curve, arc, parabola, hyperbola, arch, arcade, vault, bow, crescent, half - moon, lunette, horse-shoe, loop, bight, crane-neck, conchoid, ogee, etc.

(*Verbs*). To be curved, etc., to bend, curve, etc., decline, turn, trend, deviate, re-enter, sweep.

To render curved; to bend, curve, incurvate, camber, deflect, inflect, crook, turn, round, arch, arcuate, bow, curl, recurve, loop, frizzle.

246. STRAIGHTNESS (*Substantives*), rectilinearity, directness.

A straight line, a right line, a direct line; inflexibility (323).

(*Verbs*). To be straight, etc.

To render straight, to straighten, rectify, set or put straight, take the curl out of, unbend, unfold, uncurl, uncoil, unroll, unwind, unravel, untwist, unwreathe, unwrap.

(*Adjectives*). Straight, rectilinear (or rectilineal), direct, even, right, in a line; unbent; not inclining, bending, turning, or deviating to either side; undeviating, unturned, undistorted, unswerving.

(*Phrases*). Straight as an arrow; as the crow flies.

(*Adjectives*). Curved, bent, etc., curvilinear, curviform, recurved, recurvous, parabolic, hyperbolic, bowed, crooked, bandy, arched, vaulted, arcuated, hooked, falcated, falciform, crescent-shaped, semilunar, semicircular, conchoidal, lunular, lunulate, cordiform, heart-shaped, reniform; bow-kneed, bow-legged, bandy-legged, knock-kneed, devious.

247. Simple circularity.

CIRCULARITY (*Substantives*), roundness.

A circle, circlet, ring, areola, hoop, roundlet, *annulus*, annulet, bracelet, bangle, ringlet, eye, loop, wheel, cycle, orb, orbit, rundle, zone, belt, cordon, band, sash, girdle, cestus, cincture, baldric, fillet, cummerbund, fascia, wreath, garland, crown, corona, coronal, coronet, chaplet, necklace, rivière; noose, lasso.

An ellipse, oval, ovule, ellipsoid, cycloid, epicycloid, epicycle, etc.

(*Verbs*). To round, to circle, encircle, environ, etc. (227).

(*Adjectives*). Round, rounded, circular, annular, orbicular.

Oval, elliptical, elliptic, ovate, egg - shaped; cycloidal, etc., moniliform.

248. Complex circularity.

CONVOLUTION (*Substantives*), winding, wave, undulation, circuit, tortuosity, anfractuosity, sinuosity, involution, sinuation, circumvolution, meandering, circumbendibus, twist, twirl, curl, curlicue, crimp, frizz, frizzle, windings and turnings, *ambages*, inosculation, peristalsis.

A coil, reel, spiral, helix, corkscrew, worm, volute, scroll, cartouche, rundle, scollop (or scallop).

Serpent, eel, maze, labyrinth.

(*Verbs*). To be convoluted, etc.

To wind, twine, turn and twist, twirl, wave, undulate, meander, scallop, curl, crimp, frizz, frizzle, inosculate, entwine (219), enlace, twist together, goffer.

(*Adjectives*). Convoluted, winding, twisting, contorted, waving, waved, wavy, curly, undulating, undated, serpentine, anguilline, mazy, tortuous, sinuous, flexuous, snaky, involved, sigmate, sigmoid, vermiform, vermicular, peristaltic, meandering; scolloped (or scalloped), wreathed, wreathy, crisped, crimped, frizzed, frizzy, frizzled, frizzly, ravelled, twisted, dishevelled.

Spiral, coiled, helical, turbinate.

(*Adverb*). In and out.

---

249. ROTUNDITY (*Substantives*), cylindricity; cylinder, barrel, drum, cylindroid, roll, roller, rouleau, column, rolling-pin, rundle.

Cone, conoid; pear-shape, bell-shape.

Sphericity, spheroidity, globosity; a sphere, globe, ball, spheroid, ellipsoid, drop, spherule, globule, vesicle, bulb, bullet, pellet, pill, clue, marble, pea, knob, pommel.

(*Verbs*). To form into a sphere, render spherical, to sphere, ensphere, to roll into a ball, round off, give rotundity, etc.

(*Adjectives*). Rotund, cylindric, cylindrical, cylindroid, columnar, lumbriciform; conic, conical, conoidal.

Spherical, spheral, spheroidal, globular, globated, globous, globose, ovoid, egg-shaped, gibbous, bell-shaped, campaniliform, campaniform, campanulate, fungiform, bead - like, moniliform, pyriform, cigar-shaped.

(*Phrases*). Round as an apple; round as a ball; *teres atque rotundus.*

3°. Superficial Form

250. Convexity (*Substantives*), prominence, projection, swelling, gibbosity, bulge, protuberance, intumescence, tumour, tuberosity, tubercle, tooth, knob, excrescence, elbow, process, condyle, bulb, nub, nubble, node, nodule, nodosity, tongue, *dorsum*, hump, hunch, hunk, bunch, boss, embossment, bump, lump, clump, sugar-loaf, point (253), bow, bagginess.

Pimple, wen, wheal, papula, pustule, carbuncle, corn, wart, furuncle, fungus, fungosity, bleb, blister, blain.

Papilla, nipple, teat, pap, udder, mamilla, proboscis, nose, neb, beak, snout, nozzle, belly, back, shoulder, elbow, lip, flange.

Peg, button, stud, ridge, crimp, weal, rib, jetty, snag, eaves; mole, cupola, dome, balcony.

Cameo, high and low relief, bas-relief, *basso rilievo*, *alto rilievo*; repoussé work.

Mount, hill, etc. (206); cape, promontory, foreland, headland, point of land, hummock, spur, hog's back, ridge, offset.

(*Verbs*). To be prominent, etc., to project, bulge, belly, jut out, bristle up, to hang over, overhang, beetle, bend over, protrude, stand out, stick out, poke out, stick up, start up, cock up, shoot up, swell.

To render prominent; to raise (*see* 307), to emboss, stud, bestud, ridge, crimp.

(*Adjectives*). Prominent, projecting, bulging, etc., bowed, bold, tuberous, tuberculous, bossed, bossy, knobby, nubbly, lumpy, etc., embossed, gibbous, salient, mamilliform, in relief, bowed, arched, bellied, baggy, cornute, odontoid, ridged, ridgy.

251. Flatness (*Substantives*), plane; *see* Horizontality (213), Layer (204), and Smoothness (255); plate, platter.

(*Verbs*). To render flat, flatten, smooth, level.

(*Adjectives*). Flat, plane, level, etc., flush, scutiform, scutellate.

(*Phrases*). Flat as a pancake; flat as a flounder; flat as a board; flat as my hand; a dead flat; a dead level.

252. Concavity (*Substantives*), depression, hollow, hollowness, indentation, intaglio, cavity, dent, dint, dimple, follicle, pit, *sinus*, *alveolus*, lacuna, honeycomb, excavation, trough (259).

Cup, basin, crater, chalice, etc. (191), bowl, socket, thimble.

Valley, vale, dale, dell, dingle, coombe, strath, corrie, glade, glen, cave, cell, cavern, cove, grotto, alcove, gully (198), *cul-de-sac*.

(*Verbs*). To be depressed, etc., to retire.

To depress, hollow, scoop, dig, delve, excavate, dent, dint, mine, undermine, burrow, tunnel.

(*Adjectives*). Depressed, concave, hollow, stove in, retiring, retreating, cavernous, honeycombed, alveolar, funnel-shaped, infundibular, bell-shaped, campaniliform.

253. SHARPNESS (*Substantives*), keenness, pointedness, acuteness, acuity, acumination, spinosity, prickliness.

A point, spike, spine, spicule, needle, *aiguille*, pin, prickle, prick, arrow, spear, bayonet, spur, rowel, barb, spit, cusp, horn, snag, tag, thorn, brier, bramble, thistle, nib, tooth, tusk, spoke, cog, ratchet, staple, bristle, beard, awn, crag, *arête*, *chevaux de frise*, crest, cone, peak, spire, pyramid, steeple, porcupine, hedgehog, vandyke.

Cutting edge, wedge, edge-tool, knife, jack-knife, pen-knife, razor, scalpel, axe, adze, etc., bill-hook, cleaver, etc.

Sharpener, knife-sharpener, strop, hone, grinder, grind-stone, whetstone, etc.

(*Verbs*). To be sharp, etc., to taper to a point, to bristle with.

To render sharp, etc., to sharpen, point, aculeate, whet, strop, hone, grind, barb, bristle up.

(*Adjectives*). Sharp, keen, pointed, conical, acute, acicular, aculeated, arrowy, needle-shaped, spiked, spiky, spicular, spiculate, ensiform, peaked, acuminated, salient, cusped, cornute, prickly, spiny, spinous, thorny, bristling, muricate, pectinated, studded, thistly, briery, cragged, craggy, snaggy, digitated, barbed, spurred, two-edged, tapering, fusiform, denticulated, toothed, cutting, trenchant, sharp-edged.

Starlike, stellated, stelliform.

(*Phrases*). Sharp as a needle, as a razor.

254. BLUNTNESS (*Substantives*), obtuseness, dullness.

(*Verbs*). To be blunt, etc., to render blunt, etc., to obtund, dull, take off the point or edge, turn.

(*Adjectives*). Blunt, obtuse, dull, bluff.

---

255. SMOOTHNESS (*Substantives*), evenness, level, etc. (213), polish, gloss, glossiness, sleekness, slipperiness, lubricity, lubrication (332), down, velvet, enamel, macadam.

(*Verbs*). To smooth, smoothen, plane, polish, burnish, calender, enamel, glaze, iron, file, lubricate, macadamise.

(*Adjectives*). Smooth, even, level, plane, sleek, slick, polished, glazed, glossy, sleeky, silken, silky, satiny, velvety, glabrous, slippery, oily, soft, unwrinkled.

(*Phrases*). Smooth as glass, as velvet, as satin, as oil; slippery as an eel.

256. ROUGHNESS (*Substantives*), unevenness, asperity, rugosity, ruggedness, scabrousness, salebrosity, scragginess, cragginess, craggedness, corrugation, nodosity, crispness, plumosity, villosity.

Arborescence, branching, ramification.

Brush, bur, beard, nap, shag, whisker, dundreary, mutton-chop, down, goatee, imperial, moustache, feather, plume, crest, tuft, *panache*, byssus, hair, chevelure, wool, fur, mane, cilia, fringe, *fimbriæ*, tress, moss, plush, velvet, stubble.

(*Verbs*). To be rough, etc.

To render rough, to roughen, crisp, crumple, corrugate, rumple.

(*Adjectives*). Rough, uneven, scabrous, gnarled, rugged, rugose, rugous, salebrous, unpolished, rough-hewn, craggy, cragged, scraggy, prickly, scrubby.

Arborescent, dendriform, arboriform, branching, ramose, ramulose, dendroid.

Feathery, plumose, tufted, fimbriated, hairy, ciliated, hirsute, flocculent, bushy, hispid, tomentous, downy, woolly, velvety, villous (or villose), bearded, pilous, shaggy, shagged, stubbly, fringed, befringed, setaceous, filamentous.

(*Phrases*). Rough as a bear; like quills upon the fretful porcupine.

257. Notch (*Substantives*), dent, dint, nick, indent, indentation, dimple.

Embrasure, battlement, machicolation, machicoulis, saw, tooth, sprocket, crenelle.

(*Verbs*). To notch, nick, cut, dent, indent, dint, jag.

(*Adjectives*). Notched, etc., jagged, crenated, crenulated, dented, dentated, denticulated, toothed, palmated, indented, fimbriated, serrated.

258. Fold (*Substantives*), plication, plait, ply, crease, flexion, flexure, joint, elbow, doubling, duplicature, gather, wrinkle, crow's-foot, rimple, crinkle, crankle, crumple, rumple, rivel, ruck, ruffle, ruche, dog's-ear, corrugation, flounce, pucker, crimp.

(*Verbs*). To fold, double, plicate, plait, crease, wrinkle, crinkle, crankle, curl, cockle up, cocker, rimple, frizz, frizzle, rumple, flounce, rivel, twill, corrugate, ruffle, crimp, crumple, pucker, to turn down, turn under, tuck, ruck.

(*Adjective*). Folded, etc.

259. Furrow (*Substantives*), groove, rut, scratch, streak, stria, crack, score, rib.

Channel, gutter, trench, ditch, dike, moat, fosse, trough, kennel, chamfer, ravine (*see* 198), fluting.

(*Verbs*). To furrow, etc., flute, plough.

(*Adjectives*). Furrowed, etc., ribbed, striated, striate, sulcated, fluted, canaliculate, bisulcate, trisulcate, etc., corduroy, corrugated.

260. Opening (*Substantives*), hole, *foramen*, perforation, window, eye, eyelet, keyhole, loophole, porthole, mouse-hole, pigeon-hole, eye of a needle, pinhole, puncture.

Aperture, hiatus, yawning, oscitancy, dehiscence, patefaction, *see* Interval (198).

Orifice, inlet, intake, outlet, mouth, throat, muzzle, gullet, weasand, nozzle, portal, porch,

261. Closure (*Substantives*), occlusion, blockade, shutting up, filling up, plugging, sealing, obstruction, impassableness, blocking up, obstipation, constipation, blind alley, blind corner, *cul-de-sac*, impasse, cæcum.

Imperforation, imperviousness, impermeability, imporosity.

(*Verbs*). To close, occlude, plug, block up, fill up, blockade, obstruct, stop, bung up, seal,

gate, gateway, door, embouchure, doorway, exit, vomitory, arcade.

Channel (350), passage, pass, tube, pipe, vessel, tubule, canal, thoroughfare, gut, fistula, a jutage, tap, chimney, flue, funnel, gully, tunnel, main, adit, pit, shaft, gallery, alley, aisle, glade, vista, bore, mine, calibre, pore, follicle, porosity, porousness, lacuna.

Sieve, cullender, colander, strainer, tamis, riddle, screen, honeycomb.

plumb, cork up, shut up, choke, throttle, ram down, dam up, cram, stuff up.

(*Adjectives*). Closed, shut, unopened, occluded, etc., impervious, imperforate, cæcal, impassable, invious, pathless, untrodden, unpierced, unventilated, impermeable, imporous, operculated, air-tight, hermetic.

(*Phrase*). Hermetically sealed.

———

Apertion, perforation, piercing, boring, mining, terebration, drilling, etc., impalement, pertusion, puncture, acupuncture, penetration (302).

(*Verbs*). To open, gape, yawn.

To perforate, lay open, pierce, empierce, bore, mine, drill, scoop out, canalise, tunnel, transpierce, transfix, enfilade, rake, impale, spike, spear, gore, stab, pink, stick, prick, puncture, riddle, punch, jab; to stave in.

(*Phrase*). To cut a passage through.

To uncover, unrip, stave in.

(*Adjectives*). Open, pierced, perforated, etc., perforate, wide open, ajar, unclosed, unstopped, patulous, gaping, yawning, patent.

Tubular, tubulate, tubuliform, cannular, fistulous, fistular, fistulate, pervious, permeable, foraminous, porous, follicular, cribriform, honeycombed, infundibular, windowed, fenestrated.

———

262. PERFORATOR (*Substantives*), borer, auger, gimlet, stylet, drill, wimble, awl, bradawl, scoop, terrier, corkscrew, dibble, trepan, probe, bodkin, needle, stiletto, lancet, punch, spike, bit, gouge, fleam.

(*Verbs*). To s p i k e, g o u g e, scoop, punch, lance.

263. STOPPER (*Substantives*), stopple, plug, cork, bung, spigot, spike, spile, stopcock, tap, stopgap, rammer, ramrod, piston, wad, wadding, tompion, stuffing, tourniquet.

Cover, lid, operculum, covering, covercle, door, etc. (*see* 222), valve.

A janitor, door-keeper, concierge, porter, warder, beadle, Cerberus.

SECTION IV.—MOTION

1°. MOTION IN GENERAL

264. Successive change of place.[1]

MOTION (*Substantives*), movement, transit, transition, move, going, etc., passage, course, stir.

Science of motion: Kinematics.

Step, gait, port, footfall, carriage, transference (270), locomotion (266).

Mobility, restlessness, unrest, movability, movableness, inquietude, flux.

(*Verbs*). To be moving, etc., to move, go, stir, hie, gang, budge, pass, flit, shift, glide, roll, roll on, flow (347, 348), sweep along, wander (279), change or shift one's place or quarters, dodge, keep going.

(*Adjectives*). Moving, in motion, on the move, going, transitional; kinematic.

Shifting, movable (270), mobile, restless, nomadic, wandering, vagrant, discursive, erratic (279), mercurial, unquiet.

(*Adverbs*). *In transitu*, under way, on the road.

————

265. QUIESCENCE (*Substantives*), rest, stillness, stagnation, stagnancy, fixedness, immobility, catalepsy.

Quiet, tranquillity, calm, calmness, sedentariness, *quietum*, peace; steadiness, balance, equilibrium.

Pause, suspension, suspense, lull, stop, stoppage, interruption, stopping, stand, standstill, standing still, lying to, repose (687), respite; goose-step.

Lock, deadlock, dead stop, embargo.

Resting-place, anchorage, moorings, bivouac, port, post (189, 666), bed, pillow, etc. (215).

(*Verbs*). To be quiescent, etc., to remain, stand, stand still, lie to, pull up, hold, halt, stop, anchor, stop short, stop dead, heave to, rest, pause, repose, keep quiet, take breath, stagnate, settle; to mark time.

To stay, tarry, sojourn, dwell (186), pitch one's tent, cast anchor, settle, encamp, bivouac, moor, tether, picket, plant oneself, alight, land, etc. (292), ride at anchor.

(*Phrases*). Not to stir a peg or step; to go to bed; to come to a standstill; to come to a deadlock.

To stop, suspend, arrest, lay to, hold one's hand, interrupt, intermit, discontinue (142), put a stop to, quell, becalm.

(*Phrases*). To bring to a standstill; to lay an embargo on.

(*Adjectives*). Quiescent, still, motionless, moveless, at rest, stationary, untravelled, at a stand, stock-still, standing still,

---

[1] A thing cannot be said to *move* from one place to another unless it passes in succession through every intermediate place: hence motion is only such a change of place as is *successive*. "Rapid or swift as thought" are therefore incorrect expressions.

sedentary, undisturbed, unruffled, fast, stuck fast, fixed, transfixed, rooted, moored, aground, at anchor, tethered, becalmed, stagnant, quiet, calm, breathless, peaceful, unmoved, unstirred, immovable, immobile, restful, cataleptic, irremovable, stable, steady, steadfast.

(*Phrases*). Still as a statue; still as a post; quiet or still as a mouse.

(*Adverbs*). At a stand, at a standstill, etc., *tout court*; at anchor.

(*Interjections*). Soho! stop! stay! avast! halt! hold hard! hold on! whoa!

266. Locomotion by land.

JOURNEY (*Substantives*), travel, travelling, excursion, expedition, tour, trip, trek, circuit, peregrination, discursion, ramble, pilgrimage, Odyssey, course, ambulation, march, marching, walk, walking, promenade, stroll, saunter, trot, tramp, stalk, noctambulation, perambulation, ride, equitation, drive, jog-trot, airing, constitutional, spin, jaunt, joy-ride, change of scene.

Roving, vagrancy, flit, flitting, migration, emigration, immigration, intermigration; *Wanderlust*.

Plan, itinerary, road-book, guide, Baedeker, Bradshaw.

Procession, caravan, cavalcade.

Organs and instruments of locomotion; legs, feet, pins, skate, ski, snow-shoe, locomotive, vehicle (272, 273), velocipede, bicycle, cycle, tricycle, scooter.

(*Phrase*). Shanks's mare.

(*Verbs*). To travel, journey, trek, walk, ramble, roam, rove, course, wander, itinerate, perambulate, stroll, straggle, expatiate, range, gad about, gallivant, knock about, to go or take a walk, journey, tour, turn, trip, etc.; to prowl, stray, saunter, tour, make a tour, knock about, emigrate, flit, migrate.

267. Locomotion by water, or air.

NAVIGATION (*Substantives*), voyage, sail, cruise, circumnavigation, periplus, sea-faring.

Natation, swimming, drifting.

Flight, flying, volitation, aerostation, aeronautics, aerostatics, ballooning, aviation.

Wing, pinion, fin, flipper; oar, sail, paddle, punt-pole, screw, turbine.

(*Verbs*). To sail, make sail, warp, put to sea, navigate, take ship, get under way, spread sail, spread canvas, carry sail, plough the waves, plough the deep, walk the waters, scud, boom, drift, course, cruise, coast, circumnavigate, aviate.

To row, paddle, scull, punt, steam.

To swim, float, buffet the waves, skim, *effleurer*, dive, wade.

To fly, be wafted, hover, soar, glide, wing; to flush.

(*Phrases*). To take wing; to take flight.

(*Adjectives*). Sailing, etc., sea-faring, under way, under sail, on the wing, volant, nautical, aerostatic.

To walk, march, step, tread, pace, wend, wend one's way, promenade, perambulate, circumambulate, take a walk, go for a walk, take the air, trudge, stalk, stride, straddle, strut, foot it, hoof it, stump, clump, peg along, bundle, toddle, patter, shuffle on, tramp, traverse, bend one's steps, thread one's way, make one's way, find one's way, tread a path, take a course, take wing, take flight, defile, file off.

(*Phrase*). To pad the hoof.

Ride, jog on, trot, amble, canter, gallop, take horse, prance, frisk, tittup, caracole, to have a run.

To drive, slide, glide, skim, skate, toboggan, ski.

To go to, repair to, resort to, hie to.

(*Adjectives*). Travelling, etc., ambulatory, itinerant, peripatetic, discursive, vagrant, migratory, nomadic, on the wing, etc., circumforanean, overland.

(*Adverbs*). By the way, *chemin faisant*, on the road, *en passant*, *en route*, on foot, afoot.

---

268. TRAVELLER (*Substantives*), wayfarer, voyager, itinerant, passenger, tourist, tripper, wanderer, rover, straggler, rambler, bird of passage, gad-about, globe-trotter, vagrant, tramp, vagabond, rolling-stone, nomad, pilgrim, hadji, palmer, runner, courier, pedestrian, peripatetic, emigrant, fugitive.

Rider, horseman, equestrian, cavalier, jockey, postilion, rough-rider, scout, motorist.

Mercury, Iris, Ariel, comet.

269. MARINER (*Substantives*), navigator, seaman, sailor, seafarer, shipman, tar, bluejacket, marine, jolly, boatman, *voyageur*, ferryman, waterman, longshoreman, crew, oarsman.

An aerial navigator, aeronaut, balloonist, aviator, airman, flying man.

---

270. TRANSFERENCE (*Substantives*), displacement, metathesis, transposition (148), remotion, removal (185), relegation, deportation, extradition, conveyance, draft, carriage, carrying, convection, conduction, export, import.

Transmission, passage, transit, ferry, transport, gestation, portage, porterage, cartage, carting, shovelling, shipment, transhipment, freight, wafture, transportation, transumption, transplantation, translation, shifting, dodging, dispersion (73), traction (285), transfusion.

(*Verbs*). To transfer, convey, transmit, transport, carry, bear, carry over, pass forward, remove, etc. (185), transpose, shift, export, import, convey, conduct, convoy, send, relegate, extradite, turn over to, deliver, waft, ship, tranship, ferry over.

To bring, fetch, reach, draft.

To load, lade, charge, unload, shovel, ladle, decant, empty, break bulk.

(*Adjectives*). Transferred, etc., movable, portable, portative.

(*Adverbs*). From hand to hand, *in transitu*, from pillar to post.

271. CARRIER (*Substantives*), porter, bearer, coolie, *hammal*, conveyer, transport-worker, stevedore (690), conductor, locomotive (285).

Beast of burden, cattle, horse, blood-horse, arab, steed, nag, palfrey, galloway, charger, courser, racer, race-horse, hunter, pony, filly, colt, barb, jade, hack, *bidet*, pad, cob, tit, punch, roadster, goer, pack-horse, draught-horse, cart-horse, post-horse, shelty, bayard, mare, stallion, gelding, gee-gee, stud.

Ass, donkey, jackass, mule, hinny, sumpter-mule.

Camel, dromedary, llama, zebra, elephant, carrier-pigeon.

272. VEHICLE (*Substantives*), conveyance.

Carriage, caravan, van, motor-van, furniture van, pantechnicon, waggon, stage-waggon, railway train, goods train, train, wain, dray, cart, trolley, sledge, sleigh, bob-sleigh, *luge*, toboggan, truck, tumbril, pontoon, barrow, wheelbarrow, hand-barrow, lorry.

Equipage, turn-out, carriage, coach, chariot, chaise, phaeton, curricle, tilbury, coupé, whisky, victoria, landau, brougham, clarence, gig, calash, dog-cart, governess-cart, buggy, carriole, jingle, tandem, shandrydan, kibitka, berlin, stage, stage-coach, car, motor-car, touring car, torpedo, landaulette, limousine, side-car, motor-cycle, Pullman car, omnibus, bus, char-à-banc, break, cabriolet, cab, hackney cab, four-wheeler, hansom, taxi-cab, taxi, sedan chair, palanquin (or palankeen), litter, jinricksha (or rickshaw), brancard, stretcher, perambulator, baby-carriage.

Shovel, spoon, spatula, ladle, hod.

---

273. SHIP (*Substantives*), vessel, bottom, craft, shipping, marine, fleet, flotilla, squadron, armada, navy, H.M.S., man-of-war, ironclad, dreadnought, cruiser, gunboat, torpedo-boat, destroyer, submarine, ship of the line, first-rate, flag-ship, frigate, brig, schooner, sloop, cutter, corvette, yacht, skiff, yawl, ketch, smack, hoy, lugger, barge, bark (or barque), wherry, lighter, hulk, buss, packet, transport.

Liner, merchantman, fire-ship, slaver, steamer, steamboat, steam-packet, tug, collier, whaler, galley, bilander, coaster, brigantine, barquentine, dogger, clipper.

Argosy, bireme, trireme, etc., galleon, galliot, polacca, tartane, junk, praam, saic, dhow, proa, sampan, xebec.

Boat, motor-boat, long-boat, pinnace, launch, yacht, shallop, jolly-boat, gig, funny, dinghy, bumboat, fly-boat, wherry, coble, cock-boat, punt, cog, kedge, outrigger, catamaran, fishing-boat, coracle, hooker, life-boat, gondola, felucca, dahabeeyah, caïque, canoe, dug-out, raft, float.

Balloon, air-balloon, aerostat, Montgolfier, pilot balloon, kite, airship, aircraft, dirigible, Zeppelin, aeroplane, monoplane, biplane, hydroplane, waterplane, helicopter, glider.

(*Adverbs*). Afloat, aboard.

2°. Degrees of Motion

274. VELOCITY (*Substantives*), speed, celerity, swiftness, rapidity, fleetness, expedition, speediness, quickness, nimbleness, briskness, agility, promptness, promptitude, dispatch, acceleration.

Gallop, canter, trot, run, rush, scamper, scoot, scorch, handgallop, amble, lope; flight, dart, bolt, spurt, sprint, flying, etc.

Haste, hurry, scurry, bounce, bolt, precipitation, precipitancy, etc. (684), forced march, race, steeplechase, Marathon race, full gallop.

Rate, pace, step, gait, course, progress.

Lightning, light, cannon-ball, wind, rocket, arrow, dart, quicksilver, telegraph, express train, clipper.

An eagle, antelope, courser, race-horse, racer, gazelle, greyhound, hare, squirrel.

Mercury, Ariel, Camilla.

(*Verbs*). To move quickly; to trip, speed, haste, hie, hasten, hurry, press, press on, press forward, post, push, push on, whip, scamper, run, sprint, race, scud, scour, scurry, scuttle, spin, scoot, scorch, rip, clip, shoot, tear, whisk, sweep, skim, brush, glance, cut along, dash on, dash forward, trot, gallop, amble, lope, rush, bound, bounce, flounce, frisk, tittup, bolt, flit, spring, boom, dart, scramble.

(*Phrases*). Fly off at a tangent; carry sail; crowd sail; take to one's heels; clap spurs to one's horse; to run like mad; ride hard; outstrip the wind; to make rapid strides; wing one's way; be off like a shot; run a

275. SLOWNESS (*Substantives*), tardiness, dilatoriness, slackness, lentor, languor, drawl, *see* Inactivity (683).

Hobbling, creeping, lounging, etc., shambling, claudication, halting, jog-trot, dog-trot, mincing steps, foot-pace, crawl, etc.

A slow-goer, dawdle, dawdler, lingerer, slowcoach, drone, tortoise, snail, slug, sluggard, slacker.

Retardation, slackening, slowing down.

(*Verbs*). To move slowly, to creep, crawl, lag, slug, drawl, dawdle, linger, loiter, plod, trudge, flag, saunter, lounge, lumber, trail, drag, grovel, glide, laze, steal along, jog on, rub on, bundle on, toddle, waddle, shuffle, halt, hobble, limp, claudicate, shamble, mince, falter, totter, stagger.

(*Phrases*). To "drag its slow length along"; to hang fire; to march in slow time, in funeral procession; to lose ground.

To retard, slacken, relax, check, rein in, curb, strike sail, reef, slow up, slow down.

(*Phrases*). Put on the drag; apply the break; clip the wings; take in sail; take one's time; ca' canny.

(*Adjectives*). Slow, slack, tardy, dilatory, easy, lazy, languid, drowsy, sleepy, heavy, drawling, leaden, sluggish, snail-like, creeping, crawling, etc., dawdling, lumbering, hobbling, tardigrade.

(*Adverbs*). Slowly, etc., gingerly, softly, leisurely, deliberately, gradually, etc. (144), *piano, adagio, largo,* lamely, etc.

(*Phrases*). Under easy sail; at

race; stir one's stumps; do a scoot; get a move on.

To hasten, accelerate, expedite, urge, whip, forward, buck up, express, speed-up, hurry, precipitate, quicken pace, gather way, ride hard.

To keep up with, keep pace with, race, race with, outpace, leave behind, outrun, outstrip, gain ground.

(*Adjectives*). Fast, speedy, swift, rapid, full-drive, quick, fleet, nimble, agile, expeditious, prompt, brisk, frisky, hasty, hurried, flying, etc., precipitate, furious, light-footed, nimble-footed, winged, eagle-winged, mercurial, electric, telegraphic, light-legged; accelerative.

(*Phrases*). Swift as an arrow, as a doe, as a lamplighter; off like a shot; quick as lightning; quick as thought.[1]

(*Adverbs*). Swiftly, with speed, speedily, trippingly, etc., full-tilt, full speed, apace, post-haste, *presto*, tantivy, by express, by telegraph, slap, slap-dash, headlong, hurry-scurry, hand over hand, at a round trot.

(*Phrases*). Under press of sail, or canvas; *velis et remis*; on eagle's wings; in double-quick time; with giant, or gigantic steps; *à pas de géant*; in seven-league boots; whip and spur; *ventre à terre*; as fast as one's legs or heels will carry one; *sauve qui peut*; the devil take the hindmost; *vires acquirit eundo*; with rapid strides; at top speed; on top gear; like greased lightning.

a snail's pace; "as slow as a lame snail"; with mincing steps; with clipped wings; *haud passibus œquis*; lamely, etc.

3°. MOTION CONJOINED WITH FORCE

276. IMPULSE (*Substantives*), momentum, impetus, push, impulsion, thrust, shove, fling, jog, jolt, brunt, booming, throw, volley, explosion (173).

Percussion, collision, concussion, clash, encounter, cannon, carambole, appulse, shock, crash, bump, foul.

Blow, stroke, knock, tap, fillip, pat, rap, dab, dig, jab, smack, slap, hit, putt, cuff, bang, whack, thwack, slog, wipe, clout, swipe, squash, dowse, punch, thump, pelt, kick, lunge, buffet, beating (972); impact.

Hammer, mallet, flail, cudgel,

277. RECOIL (*Substantives*), retroaction, revulsion, reaction, rebound, repercussion, *ricochet*, rebuff, reverberation, reflux, springing back, etc., ducks and drakes.

A boomerang, spring, etc., *see* Elasticity (325).

(*Verbs*). To recoil, react, spring back, fly back, bound back, rebound, reverberate, repercuss.

(*Adjectives*). Recoiling, etc., on the recoil, etc., refluent, repercussive.

------

[1] See Note on 264.

bludgeon, cane, stick, club, racket, bat, driver, putter, cleek, niblick, etc., ram, battering-ram, monkey-engine, catapult, ballista, pile-driver, rammer, sledge-hammer, steam hammer.

Propulsion (284): Science of mechanic forces, Dynamics.

(*Verbs*). To impel, push, give impetus, etc., drive, urge, hurtle, boom, thrust, elbow, shoulder, jostle, justle, hustle, shove, jog, jolt, encounter, collide, clash, cannon, foul.

To strike, knock, tap, slap, dab, pat, slam, hit, bat, putt, rap, prod, jerk, dig, cuff, smite, butt against, impinge, thump, bethump, beat, bang, punch, thwack, whack, lay into, shin, slog, clout, wipe, swipe, batter, dowse, baste, pummel, pelt, patter, drub, buffet, belabour, cane, whip, etc. (*see* 972), poke at, hoof, jab, pink, lunge, kick, recalcitrate.

To throw, etc., *see* Propel (284), to set going, mobilise.

(*Adjectives*). Impelling, etc., impulsive, impellent, impelled, etc., booming, dynamic, dynamical.

4°. MOTION WITH REFERENCE TO DIRECTION

278. DIRECTION (*Substantives*), bearing, course, route, bent, inclination, drift, tenor, tendency, incidence, set, leaning, bending, trend, dip, steerage, tack, steering, aim, collimation.

A line, bee-line, path, road, aim, range, quarter, point of the compass, rhumb, azimuth, line of collimation.

(*Verbs*). To tend towards, go to, point to, or at; trend, verge, incline, conduct to, determine.

To make for, or towards, aim at, take aim, level at, steer for, keep or hold a course, be bound for, bend one's steps towards, direct or shape one's course.

To ascertain one's direction, orientate oneself, to see which way the wind blows.

(*Adjectives*). Directed, etc., determinate, point-to-point.

(*Adverbs*). Towards, to, *versus*, thither, directly, straight, point-blank, before the wind, near the wind, close to the wind, whither, in a line with, as the crow flies.

279. DEVIATION (*Substantives*), swerving, aberration, obliquation, *ambages*, warp, bending, refraction, sidling, side-slip, straying, straggling, warping, etc., digression, circuit, detour, departure from, divergence (291), desultory motion; googly.

Motion sideways, side-step.

(*Verbs*). To alter one's course, divert, deviate, depart from, turn, bend, swerve, break, switch, skid, side-slip, zoom, jib, shift, warp, stray, straggle, sidle, diverge (291), digress, wander, meander, veer, tack, turn aside, turn a corner, turn away from, face about, wheel, wheel about, steer clear of, ramble, rove, go astray, step aside, shunt, side-track.

(*Phrases*). To fly off at a tangent; to face to the right-about.

To go out of one's way; to lose one's way.

(*Adjectives*). Deviating, etc., aberrant, discursive, devious, desultory, erratic, vagrant, stray,

In all directions, *quaquaversum*, in all manner of ways.

—————

undirected, circuitous, roundabout, crab-like.

(*Adverbs*). Astray from, round about.

(*Phrases*). To the right-about; all manner of ways; knight-like (chess).

280. Going before.

PRECESSION (*Substantives*), leading, heading.

Precedence in order (62).

(*Verbs*). To precede, lead, head, go ahead.

(*Phrases*). Go in the van; take the lead; lead the way; have the start; to get before; steal a march.

(*Adjectives*). Preceding, leading, etc.

(*Adverbs*). In advance, before (62), in the van, ahead.

—————

281. Going after.

SEQUENCE (*Substantives*), following, pursuit, chase, hunt.

A follower, pursuer, attendant, shadow, satellite, duenna.

Sequence in order (63).

(*Verbs*). To follow, pursue, chase, hunt, hound, shadow.

(*Phrases*). Go in the rear, or in the wake of; tread in the steps of; tread on the heels of; go after; fly after; to follow as a shadow; to lag behind; to bring up the rear; to fall behind; to tail off.

(*Adjectives*). Following, etc., in the wake of, in the rear of, on the heels of.

(*Adverbs*). Behind, in the rear, etc., *see* 63.

282. Motion forwards.

PROGRESSION (*Substantives*), advance, progress (658, 682), ongoing, progressiveness, progressive motion, flood-tide, headway, advancing, etc., pursuit, steeplechase, *see* 622.

(*Verbs*). To advance, proceed, progress, go, move, bend or pass forward, go on, move on, pass on, get on, get along, jog on, push on, go one's way, go ahead, make head, make way, make headway, work one's way, press forward, edge forward, get over the ground, gain ground, make progress, keep or hold on one's course, keep up with, get forward, distance.

(*Phrases*). To make up leeway; to go with the stream; to make rapid strides; to push

283. Motion backwards.

REGRESSION (*Substantives*), regress, recess, retrogression, retrogradation, crab - like motion, refluence, reflux, retroaction, return, reflexion, reflex, ebb, countermovement, countermarch, veering, regurgitation, backwash.

(*Verbs*). To recede, retrograde, return, rebound, back, fall back, fall or drop astern, lose ground, put about, go back, turn back, double, countermarch, turn tail, draw back, get back, retrace one's steps, wheel about, back water, regurgitate, yield, give.

(*Phrases*). Dance the back step; beat a retreat.

(*Adjectives*). Receding, etc., retrograde, retrogressive, regressive, refluent, reflex, recidivous, crab-like.

or elbow one's way; to go full tilt at.

(*Adjectives*). Advancing, etc., progressive, go-ahead, profluent, undeviating.

(*Adverbs*). Forward, onward, forth, on, in advance, ahead, under way, straightforward.

(*Phrase*). *Vestigia nulla retrorsum.*

(*Adverbs*). Backwards, reflexively, to the right-about, *à reculons, à rebours.*

284. Motion given to an object in front.

PROPULSION (*Substantives*), push, pushing, projection, jaculation, ejaculation, throw, fling, toss, shot, discharge, shy.

Science of propulsion: projectiles, ballistics, gunnery; *vis a tergo.*

Things thrown: a missile, projectile, shot, shell, ball, bolt, dart, arrow, bullet, stone, shaft, brickbat.

Bow, sling, pea-shooter, catapult, etc. (727).

(*Verbs*). To propel, project, throw, fling, cast, pitch, chuck, toss, lob, loft, jerk, lance, jaculate, ejaculate, hurl, bolt, drive, sling, flirt, flip, flick, shy at, dart, send, roll, send off, let off, discharge, fire off, shoot, launch, let fly, dash, punt, volley, heave.

To bowl, trundle, roll along (312).

To put in motion, start, give an impulse, impel (276), expel (297).

(*Phrases*). To carry off one's legs; to put to flight.

(*Adjectives*). Propelling, etc., propulsive, projectile, etc.

285. Motion given to an object behind.

TRACTION (*Substantives*), drawing, draught, pull, pulling, towage, haulage.

Traction engine, locomotive; hauler, haulyer; trailer.

(*Phrase*). A long pull, a strong pull, and a pull all together.

(*Verbs*). To draw, pull, haul, lug, drag, tug, tow, trail, train, wrench, jerk, twitch, yank.

(*Phrase*). To take in tow.

(*Adjectives*). Drawing, etc., tractile.

286. Motion towards.

APPROACH (*Substantives*), approximation, appropinquation, appulse, afflux, affluxion, pursuit (622), collision (276).

(*Verbs*). To approach, draw near, approximate, to near, drift; to come, get, go, etc., near, set in towards, make up to, snuggle up to, gain upon, gain ground upon.

(*Phrases*). To tread on the heels of; to hug the shore.

287. Motion from.

RECESSION (*Substantives*), retirement, withdrawal, retreat, retrocession (283), departure (293), recoil (277), decampment, flight, stampede.

A runaway, a fugitive.

(*Verbs*). To recede, go, move or fly from, retire, retreat, withdraw, come away, go or get away, draw back, shrink, move away.

To move off, stand off, draw

(*Adjectives*). Approaching, etc., approximative.

———

leave; to cut and run; take to one's heels; to hop the twig; to give leg-bail; take one's hook; *sauve qui peut*; the devil take the hindmost; beat a retreat; make oneself scarce; do a bolt; make tracks; cut one's lucky.

(*Adjectives*). Receding, etc., fugitive, runaway (671).

off, fall back, turn tail, march off, decamp, sheer off, bolt, slip away, run away, pack off, fly, remove, abscond, sneak off, slink away.

(*Phrases*). To take French

288. Motion towards, actively.
ATTRACTION (*Substantives*), drawing to, pulling towards, adduction, attractiveness.

A loadstone, magnet.

(*Verbs*). To attract, draw, pull, drag, etc., towards, adduce.

(*Adjectives*). Attracting, etc., adducent, attrahent, adductive, attractive.

(*Interjections*). Come! come hither! approach! come near!

289. Motion from, actively.
REPULSION (*Substantives*), push, driving from, repulse, *see* Impulse (276).

(*Verbs*). To repel, push, drive, etc., from, drive away, send packing, send to the right-about (678), abduce.

(*Adjectives*). Repelling, etc., repellent, repulsive.

(*Interjections*). Begone! be off! avaunt! etc. (293).

290. Motion nearer to.
CONVERGENCE (*Substantives*), appulse, meeting, confluence, concourse, conflux, congress, concurrence, concentration.

Resort, assemblage, synod (72), focus (74), asymptote.

(*Verbs*). To converge, come together, unite, meet, fall in with, close in upon, centre in, enter in, to meet, come across.

To gather together, unite, concentrate, etc.

(*Adjectives*). Converging, etc., convergent, confluent, concurring, concurrent, centripetal, asymptotical.

291. Motion farther off.
DIVERGENCE (*Substantives*), aberration, peregrination, wandering, divarication, radiation, separation (44), dispersion, diffusion, dissemination (73).

Oblique motion: deviation (279).

(*Verbs*). To diverge, divaricate, wander, stray (279), radiate, branch off, file off, draw aside.

To spread, disperse, scatter, distribute, decentralise, diffuse, disseminate, shed, sow broadcast, broadcast, sprinkle.

To sidle, swerve, deviate, heel.

To part, part company, turn away from, wander from, separate.

(*Phrase*). To go or fly off at a tangent.

(*Adjectives*). Diverging, etc., divergent, radiant, wandering, aberring, aberrant, centrifugal.

(*Adverb*). Broadcast.

292. Terminal motion at.

ARRIVAL (*Substantives*), advent, reception, welcome, return, disembarkation, debarkation, remigration.

Home, goal, resting - place, destination, harbour, haven, port, landing-place, terminus, station.

Meeting, rencontre, rencounter, encounter.

(*Verbs*). To arrive, get to, come, come to, reach, attain, come up with, come up to, catch up, make, fetch, overtake, overhaul.

To light, alight, land, dismount, disembark, debark, detrain, put in, put into, visit, cast anchor.

To come upon, light upon, pitch upon, hit, drop in, pop upon, bounce upon, plump upon, bump against, run against, run across, close with.

(*Phrase*). To be in at the death.

To come back, return, get back, get home, sit down.

To meet, encounter, rencounter, come in contact (199).

(*Adjectives*). Arriving, etc.

(*Adverbs*). Here, hither.

(*Interjections*). Welcome! hail! all hail! good day! good morrow! etc.

---

294. Motion into.

INGRESS (*Substantives*), ingoing, entrance, entry, introgression, admission, admittance, intromission, introduction, insinuation, insertion (300), intrusion, inroad, incursion, influx, irruption, invasion, penetration, interpenetration, infiltration, import, importation, immigration.

293. Initial motion from.

DEPARTURE (*Substantives*), outset, removal, exit, exodus, decampment, embarkation, flight, hegira.

Valediction, adieu, farewell, good-bye, leave-taking, send-off.

A starting point or post, place of departure or embarkation.

(*Phrase*). The foot being in the stirrup.

(*Verbs*). To depart, go, set out, set off, start, start off, issue, go forth, sally, debouch, sally forth, set forward, be off, move off, pack off, begone, get off, sheer off, clear out, vamose, absquatulate.

To leave a place, quit, retire, withdraw, go one's way, take wing, flit, entrain, embark, go on board, set sail, put to sea, weigh anchor, slip cable, decamp (671).

(*Phrases*). To take leave; bid or take adieu; bid farewell; to say good-bye; make one's exit.

(*Adjectives*). Departing, etc., valedictory.

(*Adverbs*). Whence, hence, thence.

(*Interjections*). Go! begone! get you gone! go along! off with you! avaunt! go thy way! aroynt! away with you! go about your business! be off!

Farewell! adieu! good-bye! bye! bye-bye! *au revoir!* fare you well! God bless you! *ave atque vale!* so-long!

---

295. Motion out of.

EGRESS (*Substantives*), exit, issue, emersion, emergence.

Exudation, extravasation, transudation (348), leakage, percolation, distillation, oozing, effluence, efflux, effusion, drain, dropping, dripping, dribbling, drip, dribble, drainage, filtering, defluxion, gush, trickling, erup-

A mouth, door, etc., *see* Opening (260); an entrant.

(*Verbs*). To enter, go into, come into, set foot in, intrude, invade, flow into, pop into, insinuate itself, penetrate, interpenetrate, infiltrate, soak into; to put into, etc., bring in, insert, drive in, run in, wedge in, ram in (300), intromit, introduce, import, smuggle.

(*Phrases*). To find one's way into; creep into; worm oneself into; to darken one's door; to open the door to.

(*Adjectives*). Ingoing, penetrative, penetrant.

(*Adverb*). Inwards.

296. Motion into, actively.

RECEPTION (*Substantives*), admission, importation, immission, ingestion, imbibition, absorption, resorption, ingurgitation, inhalation, *see* Insertion (300).

Eating, swallowing, deglutition, devouring, gulp, gulping, gorge, gorging, carousal.

Drinking, potation, sipping, suction, sucking, draught, libation; smoking, snuffing.

Mastication, manduction, chewing.

(*Verbs*). To admit, receive, intromit, import, ingest, absorb, resorb, imbibe, inhale, let in, take in, readmit, resorb, reabsorb, snuff up, sop up, suck, suck in, swallow, take down, gulp, bolt, snap, get down, ingurgitate, engulf.

(*Phrase*). To give entrance to.

To eat, fare, feed, devour, tuck in, pick, peck, gorge, engorge, fall to, stuff, cram, gobble, guttle, wolf, raven, eat heartily, do justice to, overeat, gormandise (957), discuss.

To feed upon, live on, feast

tion, outpouring, emanation, aura.

Export, expatriation, emigration, remigration, repatriation.

An outlet, vent, spout, flue, chimney, pore, drain, sewer (350).

(*Verbs*). To emerge, emanate, issue, go, come, move, pass, pour, flow, etc., out of, pass off, evacuate.

To transude, exude, leak, percolate, transcolate, strain, distil, drain, ooze, filter, filtrate, dribble, trickle, drizzle, drip, gush, spout, run, flow out, effuse, extravasate, disembogue (348), seep.

(*Adjectives*). Dripping, etc., oozy, leaky, trickly, dribbly.

297. Motion out of, actively.

EJECTION (*Substantives*), emission, effusion, rejection, expulsion, detrusion, extrusion, eviction.

Discharge, egestion, evacuation, vomition.

Deportation, exile, rustication, banishment, relegation, extradition.

(*Verbs*). To be let out, etc., to ooze, percolate, fall out, to emit, eject, expel, export, reject, discharge, give out, let out, cast out, clear out, sweep out, clean out, gut, wipe off, turn out, chuck out, elbow out, kick out, hoof out, drive out, root out, pour out, shed, void, evacuate, disgorge, extrude, empty, detrude, throw off, spit, spit out, expectorate, spirt, spill, slop, empty, drain.

To vomit, spue, cat, puke, cast up, keck, retch, spatter, splutter, slobber, slaver, slabber, squirt, eructate, belch, give vent to, tap, open the sluices, heave out, bale out, shake off.

To unpack, unlade, unload (270).

upon, carouse, batten upon, fatten upon, dine, etc., browse, graze, crop, chew, champ, munch, gnaw, nibble, crunch, masticate, manducate, mumble.

(*Phrase*). To refresh one's inner man.

To drink, quaff, guzzle, swill, swig, booze, drench, sip, sup, lap, drink up, drain up, toss off, drain the cup, tipple (959), smoke.

(*Phrases*). To wet one's whistle; empty one's glass; crook or lift one's elbow.

(*Adjectives*). Admitting, etc., admitted, etc., admissible; absorbent, absorptive.

To banish, exile, deport.

(*Adjectives*). Emitting, etc., emitted, etc.

(*Phrase*). The rogue's march.

---

298. Food (*Substantives*), pabulum, aliment, nutriment, sustenance, sustentation, nurture, subsistence, provender, fodder, provision, prey, forage, pasture, pasturage, keep, fare, rations, diet, regimen.

Comestibles, eatables, victuals, prog, grub, meat, bread, breadstuffs, *cerealia*, viands, cates, delicacy, *delicatessen*, dainty, creature comforts, belly-timber, contents of the larder, dish, flesh-pots, pottage, pudding, ragout, omelet, etc.

299. Excretion (*Substantives*), discharge, emanation, exhalation, exudation, secretion, extrusion, effusion, extravasation, evacuation, fæces, excrement (653), perspiration, diaphoresis, etc.

(*Verbs*). To emanate, exhale, excern, excrete, exude, effuse, secrete, secern, extravasate, evacuate, discharge, etc. (297).

Table, board, commons, good cheer, bill of fare, commissariat, table d'hôte, ordinary, cuisine.

Canteen, restaurant, chop-house, café, tea-shop, coffee-house, coffee-stall, public-house, pot-house, ale-house, wine-shop, bodega, tavern (189).

Meal, repast, feed, mess, spread, course, regale, regalement, entertainment, feast, banquet, junket, refreshment, refection; breakfast, *déjeuner*, lunch, bever, luncheon, tiffin, tea, afternoon tea, five-o'clock tea, dinner, supper, whet, appetiser, bait, dessert, *entremet*, *hors d'œuvre*, picnic, wayzgoose, bean-feast blow-out, tuck-in, tuck-out, snack, pot-luck, table d'hôte, *déjeuner à la fourchette*.

Mouthful, bolus, gobbet, sip, sop, tot, dram, peg, cocktail (615), nip, *chasse*, liqueur.

Drink, tipple, beverage, liquor, broth, soup, etc., symposium.

(*Phrases*). A good tuck-in; a modest quencher.

(*Adjectives*). Eatable, edible, esculent, comestible, alimentary, cereal, culinary, nutritious, nutritive, nutrient, nutrimental, succulent, potable, drinkable.

298A. TOBACCO, the weed, bacca, baccy, honeydew, cavendish, bird's-eye, shag, virginia, latakia, perique, plug, twist, etc.

Cigar, cheroot, havana, manila, weed, whiff, cigarette, fag, gasper.

Snuff, rappee.

A smoke, pinch, *prise*, quid, chaw.

(*Adjective*). Nicotian.

300. Forcible ingress,

INSERTION (*Substantives*), putting in, implantation, introduction, interjection, insinuation, planting, intercalation, embolism, injection, inoculation, vaccination, importation, intervention (228), dovetailing, wedge.

Immersion, dip, plunge, bath, submersion, souse, duck, soak.

Interment, burying, etc. (363).

(*Verbs*). To insert, introduce, put into, import, throw in, interlard, inject, interject, intercalate, infuse, instil, inoculate, vaccinate, pasteurise, impregnate, imbue, imbrue, graft, engraft, bud, plant, implant, obtrude, foist in, worm in, thrust in, stick in, ram in, plough in, let in, dovetail, mortise, insinuate, wedge in, press in, impact, drive in, run in, empierce (260).

To immerse, dip, steep, immerge, merge, submerge, bathe, plunge, drop in, souse, douse, soak, duck, drown.

To inter, bury, etc. (363).

(*Adjectives*). Inserting, inserted, implanted, embedded, etc., ingrowing.

301. Forcible egress.

EXTRACTION (*Substantives*), taking out, removal, elimination, extrication, evulsion, avulsion, wrench.

Expression, squeezing.

(*Verbs*). To extract, take out, draw, draw out, pull out, tear out, pluck out, wring from, prise, wrench, rake out, rake up, grub up, root up, dredge, remove, get out (185), elicit, extricate, eliminate.

To express, squeeze out, wring out, pick out, disembowel, eviscerate, exenterate.

(*Adjectives*). Extracted, etc.

302. Motion through.

PASSAGE (*Substantives*), transmission, permeation, penetration, interpenetration (294), percolation, osmosis, osmose, capillary attraction, endosmose, exosmose, intercurrence, way, thoroughfare.

Terebration, impalement, etc. (260).

(*Verbs*). To pass, pass through, traverse, terebrate, stick, pierce, impale, spear, spike, spit (260), penetrate, permeate, thread, thrid, enfilade, go through, go across, go over, pass over, get over, clear, negotiate, cut across, pass and repass, work, thread or worm one's way, force a passage; to transmit.

(*Adjectives*). Passing, intercurrent, penetrative, etc.

303. Motion beyond.

TRANSCURSION (*Substantives*), transilience, transgression, tres-

304. Motion short of.

SHORTCOMING (*Substantives*), failure, falling short (732), defal-

pass, encroachment, infringement, extravagation, transcendence, enjambement, overrunning.

(*Verbs*). To transgress, overstep, surpass, overpass, overrun, overgo, outgo, outstep, outrun, overreach, overleap, outleap, pass, go by, strain, overshoot the mark, overjump, overskip, overlap, go beyond, outpace, outmarch, transcend, distance, encroach, exceed, trespass, infringe, trench upon.

(*Phrases*). To stretch a point; to pass the Rubicon; to shoot ahead of.

(*Adverbs*). Beyond the mark, out of bounds.

305. Motion upwards.

ASCENT (*Substantives*), rise, climb, ascension, upgrowth, leap (309).

A rocket, sky-rocket, lark, sky-lark; a climber, mountaineer.

(*Verbs*). To ascend, rise, mount, arise, uprise, go up, get up, climb, clamber, swarm, shin, scale, scramble, escalade, surmount, aspire, over-ride, start up, overreach.

(*Phrase*). Get up on one's hind legs.

To tower, soar, hover, spire, plane, swim, float, surge.

To leap, jump, take off, buck, buck-jump, hop, skip, vault, bound, dance, bob, curvet, romp, caracole, caper, cut capers.

(*Adjectives*). Rising, etc., scandent, buoyant, floating, supernatant, superfluitant, leaping, etc., saltatory, frisky, rampant.

(*Adverbs*). Uphill, on the up grade.

(*Interjection*). Excelsior!

cation, lee-way, incompleteness (53).

(*Verbs*). To fall short of, not to reach, keep within bounds, keep within compass, to stop short.

(*Adjectives*). Unreached, deficient (53), short, *minus*.

(*Adverbs*). Within the mark, within compass, within bounds, etc., behindhand.

306. Motion downwards.

DESCENT (*Substantives*), fall, descension, declension, declination, drop, cadence, subsidence, lapse, downfall, tumble, tilt, toppling, trip, lurch, *culbute*, spill.

Titubation, shamble, shambling, stumble.

An avalanche, débâcle, slump. The fate of Icarus.

(*Verbs*). To descend, go down, fall, sink, drop, drop down, droop, come down, dismount, alight, settle, subside, slide, slip, slither, glissade, toboggan, coast, volplane.

To stoop, bend, bow, curtsy, bob, bend the head or knee, dip, crouch, cower, lout.

To recline, lie, lie down, sit, sit down, couch, squat.

To tumble, slip, trip, stumble, pitch, lurch, swag, topple, topple over, swoop, tilt, sprawl, plump down, measure one's length, heel over, careen (217), slump.

To alight, dismount, get down.

(*Adjectives*). Descending, etc., descendent, decurrent, decursive.

(*Phrase*). Nodding to its fall.

(*Adverbs*). Downhill, on the down grade.

307. ELEVATION (*Substantives*), raising, lifting, erection, lift, uplift, upheaval, upcast.

(*Verbs*). To elevate, raise, lift, uplift, upraise, set up, erect, stick up, rear, uprear, upbear, upcast, hoist, uphoist, heave, upheave, weigh, exalt, give a lift, help up, prick up, perk up.

To drag up, fish up, dredge.

(*Adjective*). Elevated, etc.

(*Adverbs*). On stilts, on the shoulders of.

———

309. LEAP (*Substantives*), jump, hop, spring, bound, vault, saltation.

Dance, caper, curvet, caracole, *entrechat*, gambade, gambado, capriole; hop.

(*Phrases*). Skip and jump; hop, skip and a jump.

Kangaroo, jerboa, chamois, goat, frog, grasshopper, flea, buck-jumper.

308. DEPRESSION (*Substantives*), lowering, abasement, abasing, detrusion, reduction.

Overthrow, upset, prostration, subversion, overset, overturn, precipitation.

(*Verbs*). To depress, lower, let down, take down, sink, debase, abase, reduce, detrude, let fall, cast down, to grass, send to grass.

(*Phrase*). To take down a peg.

To overthrow, overturn, upset, overset, subvert, prostrate, level, raze, fell; cast, take, throw, fling, dash, pull, cut, knock, hew, etc., down.

(*Phrase*). To pull about one's ears (218).

(*Adjectives*). Depressed, sunk, prostrate, etc.

———

310. PLUNGE (*Substantives*), dip, dive, ducking, header.

(*Verbs*). To plunge, dip, souse, duck, dive, plump, plop, submerge, submerse, squash, douse, sink, engulf.

———

311. Curvilinear motion.

CIRCUITION (*Substantives*), turn, wind, circuit, curvet, detour, excursion, circumbendibus, circumvention, circumnavigation, north-west passage, circulation.

Turning, winding, twist, twisting, wrench, evolution, twining, coil, circumambulation, meandering.

(*Verbs*). To turn, bend, wheel, put about, heel, switch, go round, or round about, circumambulate, turn a corner, double a point, wind, whisk, twirl, twist, twill, raddle.

(*Phrases*). To lead a pretty dance; to go the round.

(*Adjectives*). Turning, etc., circuitous, circumforaneous, circumfluent.

(*Adverb*). Round about.

312. Motion in a continued circle.

ROTATION (*Substantives*), revolution, gyration, roll,

313. Motion in a reverse circle.

EVOLUTION (*Substantives*), unfolding, etc., development, introversion, reversion, eversion.

circumrotation, circumgyration, gurgitation, pirouette, circumvolution, convolution, whir, whirl, eddy, vortex, whirlpool, cyclone, anticyclone, tornado, surge, a dizzy round, maelstrom, Charybdis.

A wheel, screw, reel, whirligig, rolling stone, windmill, top, teetotum, merry - go - round, roundabout, gyroscope, gyrostat.

(*Verbs*). To evolve, unfold, unroll, unwind, uncoil, untwist, unfurl, develop, introvert, reverse.

(*Adjectives*). Evolving, evolved, etc.

(*Adverbs*). Against.

_____

Axis, spindle, pivot, pin, hinge, pole, swivel, gimbals.

(*Verbs*). To rotate, roll, revolve, spin, turn, turn round, circumvolve, circulate, gyre, gyrate, wheel, reel, whirl, twirl, thrum, trundle, troll, twiddle, bowl, roll up, furl, wallow, welter.

(*Phrases*). To box the compass; to spin like a top.

(*Adjectives*). Rotating, etc., rotatory, rotary, circumrotatory, trochoid, vortiginous, vortical, gyratory.

(*Adverbs*). Head over heels; clockwise, with the sun, deiseal (or deisil); counter-clockwise, against the sun, withershins (or widdershins).

314. Reciprocating motion, motion to and fro.

OSCILLATION (*Substantives*), vibration, undulation, pulsation, pulse, systole, diastole, libration, nutation, swing, beat, shake, seesaw, going and coming, wag, evolution, vibratiuncle; vibratility.

Fluctuation, vacillation, dance, lurch, dodge, rolling, pitching, tossing, etc.

A pendulum, see-saw, rocker, rocking-chair, rocking-horse, etc.

(*Verbs*). To oscillate, vibrate, undulate, librate, wave, rock, swing, sway, pulsate, beat, wag, waggle, nod, bob, tick, play, wamble, wabble, waddle, dangle, swag, curtsy.

To fluctuate, vacillate, dance, curvet, reel, quake, quaver, roll, top, pitch, flounder, stagger, totter, brandish, shake, flourish, move up and down, to and fro, backwards and forwards, to pass and repass, to beat up and down.

(*Adjectives*). Oscillating, etc., oscillatory, vibratory, vibratile, vibrant, vibrational, undulatory, pulsatory, pendulous, libratory, systaltic.

(*Adverbs*). To and fro, up and down, backwards and forwards, see-saw, zigzag, wibble-wabble.

315. Irregular motion.

AGITATION (*Substantives*), stir, tremor, shake, ripple, jog, jolt, jar, succussion, trepidation, quiver, quaver, dance, jactitation, jactitancy, restlessness, shuffling, twitter, flicker, flutter, bobbing.

Disturbance, perturbation, commotion, turmoil, welter, bobbery; turbulence, tumult, tumultuation, jerk, throe, convulsion, spasm

(173), twitch, tic, *subsultus*, staggers, St. Vitus's dance, epilepsy, writhing, ferment, fermentation, effervescence, hurly-burly, splatter-dash; ground swell.

(*Verbs*). To be agitated, to shake, tremble, quiver, quaver, shiver, dither, twitter, twire, writhe, toss about, tumble, stagger, bob, reel, wag, waggle, dance, wriggle, squirm, stumble, flounder, shuffle, totter, dodder, shamble, flounce, flop, curvet, prance, throb, pulsate, beat, palpitate, go pit-a-pat, flutter, flitter, flicker, bicker, twitch.

(*Phrases*). To jump like a parched pea; to be all of a tremble; to shake like an aspen leaf; to drive from pillar to post.

To agitate, shake, convulse, toss, tumble, bandy, wield, brandish, flap, flourish, whisk, switch, jerk, hitch, jolt, jog, joggle, jostle, hustle, disturb, shake up, churn, jounce, ferment, effervesce, boil.

(*Adjectives*). Shaking, etc., agitated, tremulous, shivery, tottery, jerky, shaky, quivery, quavery, trembly, choppy, rocky, wriggly, desultory, subsultory, shambling, giddy-paced, saltatory.

(*Adverbs*). By fits and starts; subsultorily, *per saltum* (139).

CLASS III

WORDS RELATING TO MATTER

SECTION I.—MATTER IN GENERAL

316. MATERIALITY (*Substantives*), corporeity, corporality, materialness, substantiality, physical condition.

Matter, body, substance, brute matter, stuff, element, principle, parenchyma, material, substratum, frame, *corpus pabulum*, stocks and stones.

Science of matter: Physics, Somatology, Somatics, Natural Philosophy, Physiography, Physical Science, Experimental Philosophy, Positivism, Materialism.

(*Verbs*). To materialise, embody.

(*Adjectives*). Material, bodily, corporeal or corporal, physical, somatic, somatological, materialistic, sensible, tangible, ponderable, objective, bodied.

317. IMMATERIALITY (*Substantives*), incorporeity, spirituality, spirit, etc. (450), inextension.

Personality, I, myself, ego.

Spiritualism, Spiritism, Docetism, Immaterialism.

(*Verbs*). To disembody, spiritualise, immaterialise.

(*Adjectives*). Immaterial, incorporeal, unextended, bodiless, unbodied, disembodied, spiritual, astral, psychical, psychic, extramundane, unearthly, pneumatoscopic, spiritualistic, Docetic.

Personal, subjective.

———

318. WORLD (*Substantives*), nature, universe; earth, globe; the wide world, cosmos, sphere, macrocosm.

The heavens, sky, welkin, empyrean, starry heaven, firmament, ether; the vault or canopy of heaven; the celestial spaces, the starry host, the heavenly bodies, stars, asteroids, constellations, galaxy, Milky Way, *via lactea*, nebulæ, etc., sun, moon, planets, planetoids, satellites.

Science of the heavenly bodies: Astronomy, Astrophysics, Uranography, Uranology, Cosmology, Cosmography, Cosmogony; orrery.

An astronomer, star-gazer, cosmographer.

(*Adjectives*), Cosmic, cosmical, mundane, terrestrial, terraqueous, terréne, sublunary, under the sun, subastral.

Celestial, heavenly, spheral, starry, stellar, nebular, etc., sidereal, sideral, astral, solar, lunar.

319. GRAVITY (*Substantives*), weight, heaviness, gravitation, ponderosity, ponderousness, pressure, load, burden, ballast; a lump, mass, weight; ponderability.

Lead, a millstone, mountain.

(*Phrase*). Pelion on Ossa.

Science of gravity: Statics.

(*Verbs*). To be heavy, to gravitate, weigh, press, cumber, load.

(*Adjectives*). Weighty, heavy, ponderous, gravitating, weighing, etc., ponderable, lumpish, cumbersome, massive, unwieldy, cumbrous, incumbent, superincumbent; gravitational.

(*Phrase*). Heavy as lead.

320. LEVITY (*Substantives*), lightness, imponderability, subtlety, buoyancy, airiness, portability, volatility.

A feather, dust, mote, down, thistle-down, flue, cobweb, gossamer, straw, cork, bubble; a float, buoy; ether; a feather-weight.

(*Verbs*). To be light, to float, swim, be buoyed up.

(*Adjectives*). Light, subtle, airy, vaporous, imponderous, astatic, weightless, imponderable, ethereal, sublimated, floating, swimming, buoyant, portable, uncompressed, volatile.

(*Phrases*). Light as a feather; light as thistle-down; "trifles light as air."

SECTION II.—INORGANIC MATTER

1°. SOLID MATTER

321. DENSITY (*Substantives*), solidity, impenetrability, incompressibility, cohesion, coherence, cohesiveness (46), imporosity, impermeability, closeness, compactness, constipation, consistence, spissitude, thickness.

Specific gravity: hydrometer, aræometer.

Condensation, consolidation, solidification, concretion, coagulation, petrifaction, lapidification, vitrification, crystallisation, precipitation, inspissation, thickening, grittiness, knottiness.

Indivisibility, indiscerptibility, indissolubility.

322. RARITY (*Substantives*), tenuity, absence of solidity, subtility, sponginess, compressibility; hollowness (252).

Rarefaction, expansion, dilatation, inflation, subtilisation.

Ether, vapour, air, gas (334).

(*Verbs*). To rarefy, expand, dilate, subtilise.

(*Adjectives*). Rare, subtle, thin, fine, tenuous, compressible.

Porous, cavernous, spongy, bibulous, spongious, spongeous.

Rarefied, expanded, dilated, subtilised, unsubstantial, hollow (252).

———

A solid body, mass, block, knot, lump, concretion, concrete, cake, clot, stone, curd, coagulum, clinker, nugget.

(*Verbs*). To be dense, etc.

To become or render solid; solidify, solidate, concrete, set, consolidate, congeal, coagulate, curdle, curd, fix, clot, cake, cohere, crystallise, petrify, vitrify, condense, thicken, inspissate, compress, squeeze, ram down, constipate.

(*Adjectives*). Dense, solid, solidified, consolidated, etc., coherent, cohesive, compact, close, thick-set, substantial, massive, lumpish, impenetrable, incompressible, impermeable, imporous, constipated, concrete, knotted, gnarled, crystalline, crystallisable, vitreous, coagulated, thick, incrassated, inspissated, curdled, clotted, grumous.

Undissolved, unmelted, unliquefied, unthawed.

Indivisible, indiscerptible, infrangible, indissolvable, indissoluble, insoluble.

---

323. HARDNESS (*Substantives*), rigidity, rigescence, firmness, renitence, inflexibility, stiffness, starchiness, starchedness, temper, callosity, induration, grittiness, petrifaction, etc. (321), ossification, sclerosis.

A stone, pebble, flint, marble, rock, granite, iron, steel, adamant, callus.

Tenseness, stretching (200).

(*Verbs*). To render hard, harden, stiffen, indurate, petrify, temper, ossify.

(*Adjectives*). Hard, horny, rigid, rigescent, stiff, firm, starch, stark, unbending, unyielding, inflexible, tense, indurate, indurated, gritty, etc., proof, adamantean, adamantine.

(*Phrases*). Hard as iron, etc.; hard as a brick; hard as a nail; hard as a deal board; stiff as buckram; stiff as a poker.

---

324. SOFTNESS (*Substantives*), tenderness, flexibility, pliancy, pliableness, pliantness, litheness, pliability, suppleness, sequacity, ductility, malleability, tractility, extensibility, plasticity, inelasticity, laxity, limpness.

Clay, wax, butter, dough; a cushion, pillow, featherbed, down.

Mollification, softening, etc.

(*Verbs*). To render soft, soften, mollify, relax, temper, mash, knead, squash.

To bend, yield, relent, relax.

(*Adjectives*). Soft, tender, supple, pliable, limp, limber, flexible, flexile, lithe, lissom, *svelte*, willowy, pliant, plastic, waxen, ductile, tractile, tractable, malleable, extensile, sequacious.

Yielding, bending, flabby, lymphatic, flocculent, downy, flimsy, spongy, œdematous, doughy, argillaceous, mellow; emollient, softening, etc.

(*Phrases*). Soft as butter; soft as down; soft as silk; yielding as wax; tender as a chicken.

---

325. ELASTICITY (*Substantives*), springiness, spring, resilience, renitency, contractility (195), compressibility.

India-rubber, caoutchouc, whalebone, elastic.

(*Verbs*). To be elastic, etc., to spring back, fly back, rebound, recoil (277).

---

326. INELASTICITY (*Substantives*), want or absence of elasticity, *see* 324.

(*Adjectives*). Inelastic, ductile, limber, etc.

(*Adjectives*). Elastic, tensile, springy, resilient, buoyant.

327. TENACITY (*Substantives*), toughness, strength, cohesion (46), stubbornness.

(*Verbs*). To be tenacious, etc., to resist fracture.

(*Adjectives*). Tenacious, tough, stubborn, cohesive, strong, resisting, coriaceous.

(*Phrase*). Tough as leather.

328. BRITTLENESS (*Substantives*), fragility, crispness, friability, frangibility, fissility.

(*Verbs*). To be brittle, break, crack, snap, split, shiver, splinter, fracture, crumble, break short, burst, fly.

(*Adjectives*). Brittle, frangible, fragile, frail, gimcrack, shivery, fissile, splitting, splintery, crisp, short, crumbling.

(*Phrase*). Brittle as glass.

329. TEXTURE (*Substantives*), structure, organisation, organism, anatomy, frame, mould, fabric, framework, carcass, architecture, *compages*, substance, parenchyma, constitution, intertexture, contexture, tissue, grain, web, warp, woof, nap (256).

Fineness or coarseness of grain.

Science of textures: Histology.

(*Adjectives*). Textural, structural, organic, anatomic, anatomical. Fine, delicate, subtle, fine-grained.

Coarse, rough-grained, coarse-grained.

Flimsy, unsubstantial, gossamery, filmy, gauzy.

330. PULVERULENCE (*Substantives*), state of powder, powderiness, efflorescence, sandiness, friability.

Dust, powder, sand, shingle, sawdust, grit, meal, bran, flour, limature, filings, débris, detritus, moraine, scobs, crumb, seed, grain, particle, flocculence.

Reduction to powder, pulverisation, comminution, granulation, disintegration, weathering, subaction, contusion, trituration, levigation, abrasion, filing, etc. (331).

Instruments for pulverisation: a mill, grater, rasp, file, pestle and mortar.

(*Verbs*). To reduce to powder, to pulverise, comminute, granulate, triturate, levigate, scrape, file, abrade, rub down, grind, grate, rasp, mill, pound, bray, contuse, contund, beat, crush, crunch, scrunch, crumble, disintegrate, weather.

(*Adjectives*). Powdery, granular, mealy, floury, branny, farinaceous, furfuraceous, flocculent, dusty, sandy, sabulous, arenaceous, gritty, efflorescent, impalpable, pulverisable, pulverulent, friable, crumbly, shivery, pulverised, etc., attrite.

331. FRICTION (*Substantives*), attrition, rubbing, massage, abrasion, rub, etc., scouring, limature, filing, rasping, frication.

Grindstone, etc., *see* 253.

(*Verbs*). To rub, abrade, etc., scrape, scrub, grate, fray, rasp, pare, scour, polish, massage, shampoo, rub out.

332. Absence of friction.

LUBRICATION (*Substantives*), prevention of friction, oiling, synovia, etc.

Lubricant, oil, lard, grease, etc.

(*Verbs*). To lubricate (355), smooth (255).

(*Adjective*). Lubricated, etc.

2°. FLUID MATTER

1. *Fluids in general*

333. FLUIDITY (*Substantives*), fluid (including both inelastic and elastic fluids).

Inelastic fluid.

Liquidity, liquidness, aquosity, a liquid, liquor, lymph, humour, juice, sap, serum, serosity, gravy, rheum, ichor, sanies; solubility.

Science of liquids at rest: Hydrology, Hydrostatics, Hydrodynamics.

(*Verbs*). To be fluid or liquid, to flow, run.

(*Adjectives*). Liquid, fluid, fluent, running, flowing, serous, juicy, succulent, sappy, lush.

Liquefied, uncongealed, melted, etc. (335).

334. Elastic fluid.

Gaseity, vaporousness, gas, air, vapour, ether, steam, fume, reek, effluvium.

Smoke, cloud (353).

Science of elastic fluids: Pneumatics, Aerostatics, Aerodynamics.

(*Verbs*). To emit vapour, to steam, fume, reek, smoke, puff, smoulder.

To aerate (338).

(*Adjectives*). Gaseous, aeriform, ethereal, aerial, airy, vaporous, vapoury, volatile, evaporable.

335. LIQUEFACTION (*Substantives*), fusion, melting, thaw, deliquation, deliquescence.

Solution, dissolution, decoction, infusion, etc., liquescence.

Solvent, menstruum.

(*Verbs*). To render liquid, to liquefy, run, melt, thaw, fuse, solve, dissolve, resolve, to hold in solution.

(*Adjectives*). Liquefied, melted, unfrozen, molten, liquescent, liquefiable, deliquescent, diffluent, soluble, dissoluble.

336. VAPORISATION (*Substantives*), volatilisation, evaporation, distillation, sublimation, exhalation, volatility.

Vaporiser (353).

(*Verbs*). To render gaseous, vaporise, volatilise, evaporate, exhale, distil, sublime, sublimate.

(*Adjectives*). Volatilised, etc., volatile, evaporable, vaporisable.

2. *Specific Fluids*

337. WATER (*Substantives*), serum, lymph, rheum, whey.

Dilution, immersion, maceration, humectation, infiltration, sprinkling, spraying, aspersion, affusion, irrigation, douche, balneation, bath, shower-bath, inundation, deluge (*see* 348), a diluent.

338. AIR (*Substantives*), common air, atmospheric air.

The atmosphere, the sky, the ether, the open air, weather, climate.

Exposure to the air or weather, airing, weathering (330).

(*Verbs*). To aerate, oxygenate, arterialise.

Sprinkler, sprayer, spray, atomiser, aspergillum, aspersorium,
water-cart, watering-pot.

(*Verbs*). To be watery, etc., to
reek.

To add water, to water, wet,
moisten (339), dilute, dip, immerse, plunge, merge, immerge,
steep, souse, duck, submerge,
drown, soak, sop, macerate, pickle, wash, sprinkle, asperge,
asperse, dabble, bedabble, affuse, splash, splatter, spray,
swash, douse, drench, slop, slobber, irrigate, inundate, deluge,
flood.

To take a bath, to tub, bathe (300), paddle.

To syringe, inject.

(*Adjectives*). Watery, aqueous, aquatic, lymphatic, diluted,
etc., reeking, dripping, sodden, drenched, soaking, sopping.

Wet, washy, sloppy, squashy, splashy, soppy, soggy, slob-
bery, diluent, balneal.

(*Phrases*). Wet as a drowned rat; wet as a rag; wet through.

(*Adjectives*). Containing air,
windy, flatulent, effervescent.

Atmospheric, airy, alfresco,
aerial, aeriform.

(*Adverbs*). In the open air, *à la
belle étoile*, alfresco, *sub Jove*.

————

339. Moisture (*Substantives*),
moistness, humidity, dampness,
damp, wetness, wet, humectation, madefaction, dew, muddiness.

(*Verbs*). To be moist, etc.

To moisten, wet, humectate,
damp, dampen, bedew, imbue,
infiltrate, imbrue.

(*Adjectives*). Moist, damp,
watery, humid, wet, dank,
muggy, dewy, roral, rorid, roscid,
juicy, swampy, muddy; humec-
tant.

(*Phrase*). Wringing wet.

340. Dryness (*Substantives*),
siccity, aridity, drought.

Exsiccation, desiccation, are-
faction, drainage.

(*Verbs*). To be dry, etc.

To render dry, to dry, dry
up, sop up, exsiccate, desiccate,
drain, parch.

(*Adjectives*). Dry, anhydrous,
arid, dried, etc., unwatered, un-
damped, waterproof, husky, juice-
less, sapless; siccative, desicca-
tive.

(*Phrases*). Dry as a bone; dry
as dust; dry as a stick; dry as
a mummy; dry as a biscuit; dry
as a limekiln.

341. Ocean (*Substantives*), sea,
main, the deep, brine, salt water,
tide, wave, surge, ooze, etc. (348);
archipelago.

Hydrography, Oceanography.

Neptune, Thetis, Triton, Ocea-
nid, Nereid, etc., mermaid; tri-
dent.

(*Phrases*). The vasty deep; the
briny.

(*Adjectives*). Oceanic, marine,

342. Land (*Substantives*),
earth, ground, terra firma, con-
tinent, mainland, p e n i n s u l a,
delta, tongue of land, oasis.

Coast, shore, seaboard, seaside,
sea-bank, strand, beach, bank,
lea.

(*Phrase*). An iron-bound coast.

Cape, promontory, etc. (250),
headland, point of land, highland.

Soil, glebe, clay, humus, loam.

maritime, thalassic, pelagic, pelagian, archipelagian.

(*Adverbs*). At sea, on sea.

marl, clod, clot, rock, crag, etc. (206), mould, subsoil.

(*Adjectives*). Terrene, continental, earthy, terraqueous, terrestrial.

Littoral, riparian, midland.

(*Adverbs*). Ashore, on shore, on land.

---

343. GULF (*Substantives*), bay, inlet, bight, estuary, arm of the sea, armlet, sound, frith, firth, fiord, lough, lagoon, cove, creek, strait, Euripus.

(*Adjective*). Estuarine.

LAKE (*Substantives*), loch, mere, tarn, llyn, plash, broad, pond, dew-pond, pool, puddle, well, standing water, dead water, a sheet of water, fish-pond, ditch, dike, backwater.

(*Adjective*). Lacustrine.

344. PLAIN (*Substantives*), table-land, open country, the face of the country, champaign country, basin, downs, waste, wild, weald, steppe, pampas, savanna, llano, prairie, heath, common, wold, moor, moorland, the bush; plateau, flat.

(*Phrase*). A weary waste.

Meadow, mead, haugh, pasturage, park, field, lawn, terrace, esplanade, sward, turf, sod, heather, lea, grounds, pleasure-grounds, playing-fields.

(*Adjectives*). Alluvial, champaign, lawny.

---

345. MARSH (*Substantives*), swamp, morass, moss, fen, bog, quagmire, slough, wash.

(*Adjectives*). Marshy, marish, swampy, boggy, plashy, poachy, paludal.

346. ISLAND (*Substantives*), isle, islet, ait, holm, reef, atoll.

(*Adjectives*). Insular, sea-girt.

---

3. *Fluids in motion*

347. Fluid in motion.

STREAM (*Substantives*), flow, current, jet, undercurrent, course.

(*Verbs*). To flow, stream, issue, run.

348. Water in motion.

RIVER (*Substantives*), running water, jet, spirt, squirt, spout, splash, rush, gush, water-spout, sluice, linn, waterfall, cascade, catadupe, cataract, débâcle, avalanche, spate.

Rain, shower, scud, driving rain, downpour, drencher, soaker, cloud-burst, mizzle, drizzle, drip-

349. Air in motion.

WIND (*Substantives*), draught, flatus, afflatus, breath, air, breath of air, puff, whiff, zephyr, blow, drift, aura.

Gust, blast, breeze, squall, gale, storm, tempest, hurricane, whirlwind, tornado, blizzard, simoom, samiel, harmattan, monsoon, trade-wind, sirocco, mis-

ping, stillicidium, flux, flow, profluence, effluence, efflux, effluxion, defluxion.

Irrigation (337).

Spring, fountain, rill, rivulet, gill, gullet, rillet, streamlet, runnel, sike, burn, beck, brook, stream, river, torrent, rapids, flush, flood, swash, tide, spring tide, high tide, bore, eagre, freshet, current, indraught, reflux, eddy, whirlpool, regurgitation.

Confluence.

Wave, billow, surge, swell, ripple, ground swell, surf, breaker.

Inundation, cataclysm.

Science of fluids in motion: Hydraulics, Hydrodynamics, Hydrography.

(*Verbs*). To flow, run, meander, gush, spout, roll, billow, surge, jet, well, drop, drip, trickle, dribble, ooze (295), percolate, distil, transude, stream, sweat, perspire (299), overflow, flow over, splash, swash, guggle, gurgle, sputter, spurt, regurgitate, surge.

tral, *bise, tramontana, föhn,* pampero; windiness, ventosity.

Anemometer, anemograph, wind-guage.

(*Phrase*). A capful of wind.

Insufflation, sufflation, perflation, blowing, fanning, ventilation, blowing up, inflation, afflation, respiration, inspiration, expiration, sneezing, sternutation.

Æolus, Boreas, Auster, the cave of Æolus.

Bellows, blowpipe, fan, ventilator, punka.

(*Verbs*). To blow, waft, blow hard, blow a hurricane, breathe, respire, inspire, expire, insufflate, puff, whiff, sough, whiffle, wheeze, snuffle, sniffle, sneeze, cough.

To fan, ventilate, inflate, perflate, blow up.

(*Phrase*). To blow great guns.

(*Adjectives*). Blowing, etc., windy, breezy, gusty, squally, puffy, stormy, tempestuous, blustering.

———

To rain, rain hard, pour with rain, drizzle, spit, mizzle, set in.

To flow into, fall into, open into, discharge itself, disembogue, disgorge, meander.

(*Phrases*). To rain cats and dogs; to rain in torrents.

To cause a flow, to pour, drop, distil, splash, squirt, spill, drain, empty, discharge, pour out, open the sluices or floodgates; shower down, irrigate (337).

To stop a flow, to stanch, dam, dam up (261), intercept.

(*Adjectives*). Fluent, profluent, affluent, tidal, flowing, etc., babbling, bubbling, gurgling, meandering.

Fluviatile, fluvial, riverine, streamy, showery, drizzly, rainy, pluvial, pouring.

350. Channel for the passage of water.

CONDUIT (*Substantives*), channel, duct, watercourse, watershed, race, adit, aqueduct, canal,

351. Channel for the passage of air.

AIR-PIPE (*Substantives*), air-tube, shaft, flue, chimney, vent, blow-hole, nostril, nozzle, throat,

sluice, dike, main, gully, moat, ditch, lode, leat, rhine, trough, gutter, drain, sewer, culvert, cloaca, sough, kennel, siphon, pipe, emunctory, gully-hole, artery, aorta, pore, spout, scupper, ajutage, waste-pipe, hose, gargoyle, artesian well.

Flood-gate, dam, water-gate, lock, valve.

weasand, trachea, windpipe, spiracle, ventiduct.

Ventilator, louvre, register.

Tobacco - pipe, pipe, briar, meerschaum, calabash, corncob, clay pipe, clay, churchwarden, dudeen, nose-warmer, cutty, hookah, hubble - bubble, chibouque, narghile, calumet.

3°. IMPERFECT FLUIDS

352. SEMILIQUIDITY (*Substantives*), pulpiness, viscidity, viscosity, ropiness, sliminess, gumminess, gummosity, siziness, clamminess, mucosity, spissitude, lentor, thickness, crassitude.

Inspissation, thickening, incrassation.

Jelly, mucilage, gelatine, mucus, gum, colloid, albumen, size, milk, cream, emulsion, soup, squash, mud, slush, dope, glycerine.

(*Verbs*). To inspissate, thicken, incrassate, jelly, jellify, mash, squash, churn, beat up, pulp.

(*Adjectives*). Semi-fluid, semiliquid, milky, emulsive, creamy, curdy, thick, succulent, squashy.

Gelatinous, albuminous, gummy, colloid, amylaceous, mucilaginous, glairy, slimy, ropy, stringy, clammy, glutinous (46), slab, slabby, sizy, lentous, tacky.

353. Mixture of air and water.

BUBBLE (*Substantives*), foam, froth, head, spume, lather, bleb, spray, spindrift, surf, yeast, barm, suds.

Cloud, vapour, fog, mist, haze, scud, rack, cumulus, cirrus, stratus, etc.

Science of clouds, Nephelology.

Effervescence, foaming, mantling, fermentation, frothing, etc.

A spray, atomiser, vaporiser.

(*Verbs*). To bubble, boil, foam, froth, mantle, sparkle, guggle, gurgle, effervesce, ferment.

(*Adjectives*). Bubbling, etc., frothy, yeasty, barmy, nappy, effervescent, boiling, fermenting, sparkling, mantling, *mousseux*.

———

viscid, viscous, sticky,

354. PULPINESS (*Substantives*), pulp, paste, dough, curd, pap, pudding, poultice, soup, squash, mud, slush, rob, jam, preserve.

———

355. UNCTUOUSNESS (*Substantives*), unctuosity, oiliness, greasiness, slipperiness, lubricity.

Lubrication (332), anointment, unction.

(*Verbs*). To oil, grease, anoint, wax, lubricate.

(*Adjectives*). Unctuous, oily, oleaginous, adipose, sebaceous, fat, fatty, greasy, waxy, butyraceous, soapy, saponaceous, pinguid, lardaceous.

356. OIL (*Substantives*), fat, butter, margarine, cream, grease, tallow, suet, lard, dripping, blubber, pomatum, pomade, stearin, lanoline, vaseline, soap, wax, spermaceti, adipocere, ointment, unguent, liniment; paraffin, kerosene, petroleum, petrol, etc.

SECTION III.—ORGANIC MATTER

1°. VITALITY

1. *Vitality in general*

357. ORGANISATION (*Substantives*), the organised world, organised nature, living nature, animated nature, living beings.

The science of living beings: Biology, Œcology, Natural History,[1] Organic Chemistry. *See* 368, 369.

359. LIFE[2] (*Substantives*), vitality, animation, viability, the vital spark or flame, the breath of life, life-blood.

(*Phrase*). The breath of one's nostrils.

Vivification, revivification.

The science of life: Physiology, metabolism.

(*Verbs*). To be living, alive, etc., to live, breathe, fetch breath, respire, draw breath, to be born.

(*Phrases*). To see the light; to come into the world; to draw breath.

To come to life, to revive, come to.

To give birth to, *see* 161.

To bring, restore, or recall to life, to vivify, revive, revivify, reanimate, vitalise.

(*Phrase*). To keep body and soul together.

358. INORGANISATION (*Substantives*), the mineral world or kingdom, unorganised, inorganic, brute or inanimate matter.

The science of the mineral kingdom: Mineralogy, Geognosy, Petrology, Lithology, Geology, Metallurgy, etc.

360. DEATH (*Substantives*), decease, dissolution, demise, departure, obit, expiration, termination, close or extinction of life, existence, etc., mortality, fall, doom, fate, release, rest, quietus, loss, bereavement, euthanasia, katabolism.

Last breath, last gasp, last agonies, the death-rattle, dying breath, agonies of death, dying agonies.

(*Phrases*). The ebb of life; the jaws of death; the swan-song; the Stygian shore; the sleep that knows no waking.

(*Verbs*). To die, perish, expire.

(*Phrases*). Breathe one's last; cease to live; depart this life; be no more; go off; drop off; pop off; lose one's life; drop down dead; resign, relinquish, or surrender one's life; drop or

---

[1] The term *Natural History* is also used as relating to all the objects in Nature, whether organic or inorganic, and including therefore *Mineralogy, Geology,* and *Meteorology.*
[2] Including the life both of *plants* and *animals.*

(*Adjectives*). Living, alive, in life, above ground, breathing, quick, viable.

Vital, vivifying, vivified, Promethean, metabolic.

(*Phrases*). Alive and kicking, in the land of the living.

_____

sink into the grave; close one's eyes; break one's neck; to give up the ghost; to be all over with one; to pay the debt to nature; to take one's last sleep; to shuffle off this mortal coil; to go to one's last home; to go the way of all flesh; to kick the bucket; to hop the twig; to cross the Stygian ferry; to go to the wall; to snuff out; to go off the hooks; to go to one's account; to go aloft; to join the majority; to go west; to be numbered with the dead; to die a natural death; to make one's will; to hand in one's checks; to pass away or over.

(*Adjectives*). Dead, lifeless, deceased, demised, gone, departed, defunct, exanimate, inanimate, out of the world, mortuary, katabolic, azoic.

Dying, expiring, moribund, *in articulo*, *in extremis*, in the agony of death, etc., going, life ebbing, going off, life failing, *aux abois*, having received one's death warrant.

(*Phrases*). Dead and gone; dead as a door-nail, as mutton, as a door-post, as a herring; stone-dead; launched into eternity; gone to one's last home; gathered to one's fathers; gone to Davy Jones's locker; gone west.

At death's door; on one's death-bed; in the jaws of death; death staring one in the face; one's hour being come; one's days being numbered; one foot in the grave; on one's last legs; life hanging by a thread; going to one's last account; at one's last gasp.

(*Adverbs*). Post-mortem, post-obit.

361. Destruction of life, violent death.

KILLING (*Substantives*), homicide, manslaughter, murder, assassination, blood, gore, bloodshed, slaughter, carnage, butchery, massacre, fusillade, noyade, Thuggism; Aceldama.

Death-blow, *coup de grâce*, grace-stroke.

Suicide, *felo de se*, *hara-kiri*, happy despatch; execution, *see* 972.

Destruction of animals, slaughtering, etc., Phthisozoics.[1]

Slaughter-house, shambles, abattoir.

A butcher, slayer, murderer, assassin, cut-throat, bravo, Thug, Moloch, executioner, *see* 975.

(*Verbs*). To kill, put to death, do to death, slay, murder, assassinate, slaughter, butcher, immolate, massacre, take away or deprive of life, make away with, dispatch, burke, lynch, settle, do for, do in, brain, spifficate.

To strangle, throttle, bowstring, choke, garrotte, stifle, suffocate, smother, asphyxiate, drown, hang, turn off.

To commit suicide, to make away with oneself.

[1] Bentham, *Chrestomathia*.

To cut down, sabre, cut to pieces, cut off, cut the throat, stab, shoot, behead, decapitate, execute (972).

(*Phrases*). To put to the sword; put to the edge of the sword; run through the body; blow the brains out; commit suicide; give the death blow, the *coup de grâce*; launch into eternity; give a quietus to.

(*Adjectives*). Killing, etc., murderous, slaughterous, sanguinary, blood-stained, blood-guilty.

Mortal, fatal, deadly, lethal, internecine, suicidal.

362. CORPSE (*Substantives*), corse, carcass, bones, skeleton, carrion, defunct, relic, remains, ashes, earth, clay, mummy, food for worms.

Shade, ghost, *manes*; the dead, the majority, the great majority.

363. INTERMENT (*Substantives*), burial, sepulture, inhumation, obsequies, exequies, funeral, wake, lyke-wake, pyre, funeral pile, cremation.

Funeral rite or solemnity, knell, passing-bell, tolling, dirge, requiem, epicedium, obit, death-march, dead march, lying in state.

Grave-clothes, a shroud, winding-sheet, cerecloth, cerement.

Coffin, shell, sarcophagus, urn, pall, bier, hearse, catafalque.

Grave, pit, sepulchre, tomb, vault, catacomb, mausoleum, house of death, burial-place, cemetery, necropolis, churchyard, graveyard, burial-ground, cromlech, dolmen, barrow, tumulus, cairn, ossuary, charnel-house, morgue, mortuary, crematorium, cinerator; Valhalla.

Exhumation, disinterment.

(*Verbs*). To inter, bury, lay in the grave, consign to the grave or tomb, entomb, inhume, cremate, lay out.

To exhume, disinter.

(*Adjectives*). Buried, etc., funereal, funebrial, funerary, mortuary, sepulchral.

2. *Special Vitality*

364. ANIMALITY (*Substantives*), animal life, animality, animation, breath, animalisation.

Flesh, flesh and blood.

(*Verb*). To animalise.

366. ANIMAL (*Substantives*), the animal kingdom, fauna, avifauna.

A beast, brute, creature, created being; creeping or living thing, dumb creature, flocks and herds, flight.

Cattle, kine, etc.

Game. *Fera natura*, wild life.

(*Phrases*). The beasts of the field; fowls of the air; denizens of the deep.

365. VEGETABILITY (*Substantives*), vegetable life, vegetation.

———

367. PLANT (*Substantives*), vegetable, the vegetable kingdom, flora.

Tree, fruit-tree, shrub, bush, creeper, herb, herbage, grass, fungus, lichen, moss, seaweed, alga; annual, biennial, perennial; exotic.

Forest, wood, hurst, holt, greenwood, woodland, bush, brake, grove, copse, coppice, hedgerow, boscage, plantation,

Mammal, quadruped, bird, reptile, fish, mollusc, worm, insect, zoophyte, animalcule, etc.

Menagerie, fossil remains.

(*Adjectives*). Animal, organic, zoological, piscatory, fishy, molluscous, vermicular, etc., feral.

thicket, underwood, brushwood, jungle, clump of trees, garden, espalier, herbaceous border, shrubbery, parterre, rock-garden, park, chase, weald.

Foliage, florescence, etc.

Hortus siccus, herbarium, herbal.

(*Adjectives*). Vegetable, vegetal, arboreal, herbaceous, herbal, botanic, sylvan, woodland, woody, wooded, well-wooded, shrubby, verdant.

368. The science of animals.

ZOOLOGY (*Substantives*), Zoography, Anatomy, Zootomy, Comparative Anatomy, Physiology, Morphology.

Palæontology.

Ornithology, Ichthyology, Herpetology, Ophiology, Malacology, Helminthology, Entomology.

369. The science of plants.

BOTANY (*Substantives*), Phytography, Phytology, Vegetable Physiology, Herborisation, Dendrology, Mycology, Pomona.

(*Verbs*). To botanise, herborise.

370. The economy or management of animals.

CICURATION (*Substantives*), Zohygiastics.[1]

Domestication, domesticity.

Training, breaking in.

Manège, fishery.

Menagerie, aviary, apiary, vivarium, aquarium, etc.

Destruction of animals, Phthisozoics.[1]

(*Verbs*). To tame, domesticate, train, tend, etc., break in.

371. The economy or management of plants.

AGRICULTURE (*Substantives*), cultivation, culture, intensive cultivation, husbandry, geoponics, georgics, tillage, gardening, horticulture, forestry, vintage, etc., arboriculture, floriculture, the topiary art.

Vineyard, vinery, garden, nursery, bed, hothouse, greenhouse, conservatory, orchard, winter garden, pinery, arboretum.

A husbandman, horticulturist, gardener, florist, agriculturist, agriculturalist, forester, farmer, cultivator.

(*Verbs*). To cultivate, till, garden, farm.

(*Adjectives*). Agricultural, agrarian, arable, pastoral, bucolic, agrestic.

372. MANKIND (*Substantives*), the human race or species; man, human nature, humanity, mortality, flesh, generation; Everyman.

The science of man: Anthropology, Anthropography, Ethnology, Ethnography, Demography, Sociology, Social Economics; Civics.

[1] Bentham.

Anthropomorphism.

Human being, person, individual, creature, fellow - creature, mortal, body, somebody, one, someone, a soul, living soul, earthling, party, personage, inhabitant.

Dramatis personœ.

People, persons, folk, population, public, world, society, community, the million, nation, state, realm, community, commonwealth, republic, commonweal, polity, nationality; civilised society, civilisation.

Anthropologist, ethnologist, sociologist, etc.

(*Phrases*). The lords of creation; the body politic.

(*Adjectives*). National, civic, public, human, mortal, personal, individual, social, cosmopolitan, ethnic, racial; sociological, anthropological, ethnological; anthropomorphic, anthropomorphous, anthropoid, manlike.

---

373. Man (*Substantives*), manhood, virility, he, menfolk.

A human being, man, male, mortal, person, body, soul, individual, fellow creature, one, someone, somebody, so-and-so.

Personage, a gentleman, sir, master, yeoman, citizen, denizen, burgess, cosmopolite, wight, swain, fellow, blade, bloke, beau, chap, cove, gossoon, buffer, gaffer, goodman.

(*Adjectives*). Human, manly, male, masculine, manlike, mannish, virile, mortal, personal, individual, cosmopolitan.

(*Phrase*). The spear side.

---

374. Woman (*Substantives*), female, feminality, femininity, womanhood, muliebrity, she, womenfolk.

Womankind, the sex, the fair, the fair sex, the softer sex, the weaker vessel, a petticoat.

Dame, madam, madame, ma'am, mistress, lady, donna, belle, matron, dowager, goody, gammer, good woman, goodwife.

Damsel, girl, lass, lassie, maid, maiden, *demoiselle*, flapper, miss, missie, nymph, wench, jade, dona, grisette, colleen.

(*Adjectives*). Female, feminine womanly, womanish, ladylike, matronly, maidenly, girlish.

(*Phrase*). The distaff side.

2°. Sensation

(1) *Sensation in general*

375. Physical Sensibility (*Substantives*), sensitiveness, feeling, perceptivity, acuteness, etc.

Sensation, impression, consciousness (490).

The external senses, sensation. Science: Æstho-physiology.

(*Verbs*). To be sensible of, to

376. Physical Insensibility (*Substantives*), obtuseness, dullness, apathy, callousness (823), paralysis, anæsthesia.

Anæsthetic agent: Opium, ether, chloroform, cocaine, etc. Science: Anæsthetics.

(*Verbs*). To be insensible, etc.

To render insensible, to blunt,

feel, perceive, be conscious of, respond to, react to.

To render sensible, to sharpen.

To cause sensation, to impress, excite, or produce an impression.

(*Adjectives*). Sensible, conscious, sensitive, sensuous, æsthetic, perceptive.

Hypersensitive, thin-skinned, neurotic.

Acute, keen, vivid, lively, impressive.

dull, obtund, benumb, paralyse, anæsthetise, dope, hocus, gas.

(*Adjectives*). Insensible, unfeeling, senseless, impercipient, impassible, thick-skinned, apathetic, obtuse, dull, anæsthetic, paralytic, etc., unaffected, untouched, etc.

(*Phrase*). Having a rhinoceros hide.

---

377. PHYSICAL PLEASURE (*Substantives*), bodily enjoyment, gratification, luxury, voluptuousness, sensuousness, sensuality.

(*Phrases*). The flesh-pots of Egypt; creature comforts; a bed of roses; a bed of down, velvet, clover, *see* 827.

(*Verbs*). To feel, experience, receive, etc., pleasure, to enjoy, relish, luxuriate, revel, riot, bask, wallow in.

To cause or give physical pleasure, to gratify, tickle, regale, etc., *see* 829.

(*Adjective*). Enjoying, etc.

378. PHYSICAL PAIN (*Substantives*), bodily pain, suffering, sufferance, dolour, ache, aching, smart, smarting, shoot, shooting, twinge, twitch, gripe, headache, etc., sore, *see* 828.

Spasm, cramp, nightmare, crick, convulsion, throe.

Pang, anguish, agony, torment, torture, rack, cruciation, crucifixion, martyrdom.

(*Verbs*). To feel, experience, suffer, etc. pain; to suffer, ache, smart, bleed, tingle, shoot, twinge, lancinate, wince, writhe, twitch.

(*Phrases*). To sit on thorns; to sit on pins and needles.

To give or inflict pain; to pain, hurt, chafe, sting, bite, gnaw, pinch, tweak, grate, gall, fret, prick, pierce, gripe, etc., wring, torment, torture, rack, agonise, break on the wheel, etc., convulse.

(*Adjectives*). In pain, in a state of pain, etc., pained, etc.

Painful, aching, etc., sore, raw, agonising, excruciating, etc.

---

(2) *Special Sensation*

1. *Touch*

379. Sensation of pressure.

TOUCH (*Substantives*), taction, tactility, feeling, palpation, manipulation, palpability.

Organ of touch: hand, finger, forefinger, thumb, paw, feeler, antenna.

(*Verbs*). To touch, feel, handle, finger, thumb, paw, fumble, grope, grabble, scrabble; pass, or run the fingers over, manipulate.

(*Phrase*). To throw out a feeler.

(*Adjectives*). Tactual, tangible, palpable, tactile.

(*Adjectives*). Fragrant, aromatic, redolent, balmy, scented, sweet-smelling, sweet-scented, perfumed, musky.

(*Adjectives*). Fetid, strong-smelling, smelly, malodorous, noisome, offensive, rank, rancid, reasty, mouldy, fusty, musty, stuffy, frowsty, foul, frowzy, olid, nidorous, stinking, rotten, putrescent, putrid, putrefying, mephitic, empyreumatic.

5. Sound

(1) SOUND IN GENERAL

402. SOUND (*Substantives*), noise, strain, voice (580), accent, twang, intonation, resonance; sonority, sonorousness, audibleness, audibility.

Science of Sound: Acoustics, Phonics, Phonetics, Phonology, Diacoustics.

(*Verbs*). To produce sound; to sound, make a noise, give out or emit sound, to resound.

(*Adjectives*). Sonorous, sounding, sonorific, soniferous, resonant, canorous, audible.

403. SILENCE (*Substantives*), stillness, quiet, peace, calm, hush, lull; muteness (581).

A silencer, mute, damper, sordine.

(*Verbs*). To be silent, etc.

(*Phrases*). To keep silence; to hold one's tongue; to hold one's peace.

To render silent, to silence, still, hush, stifle, muffle, muzzle, mute, damp, gag.

(*Adjectives*). Silent, still, noiseless, soundless, inaudible, hushed, etc., mute, mum, solemn, awful, deathlike.

(*Phrases*). Still as a mouse; deathlike silence; silent as the grave.

(*Adverbs*). Silently, softly, etc., *sub silentio*.

(*Interjections*). Hush! silence! soft! mum! whist! chut! tut!

404. LOUDNESS (*Substantives*), din, clangour, clang, roar, uproar, racket, hubbub, flourish of trumpets, tucket, tantara, taratantara, *tintamarre*, peal, swell, blast, echo, fracas, clamour, hullaballoo, chorus, hue and cry, shout, yell, whoop, charivari, shivaree, vociferation; lungs, Stentor, Boanerges.

Speaking-trumpet, megaphone, loud-speaker; microphone, resonator.

405. FAINTNESS (*Substantives*), lowness, faint sounds, whisper, undertone, breath, underbreath, murmur, mutter, hum, susurration.

Hoarseness, huskiness, raucity.

(*Verbs*). To whisper, breathe, murmur, mutter, purl, hum, croon, gurgle, ripple, babble, flow.

(*Phrases*). Steal on the ear; melt, float on the air.

(*Adjectives*). Inaudible, scarcely audible, low, dull, stifled, muffled, hoarse, husky, gentle, breathed,

Artillery, cannon, thunder.

(*Verbs*). To be loud, etc., to resound, echo, re-echo, peal, swell, clang, boom, blare, thunder, fulminate, roar, whoop, shout, *s'égosiller*, deafen, stun (411).

(*Phrases*). To din in the ear; to pierce, split, or rend the ears, or head; to shout, or thunder at the pitch of one's breath, or at the top of one's voice; *faire le diable à quatre*.

(*Adjectives*). Loud, resounding, etc., high-sounding, big-sounding, deep, full, swelling, clamorous, blatant, plangent, vocal, vociferous, stunning, piercing, splitting, rending, deafening, ear-deafening, ear-piercing, obstreperous, blaring, deep-mouthed, open-mouthed, trumpet-tongued, uproarious, stentorian; in full cry.

(*Phrase*). Enough to split the head or ears.

(*Adverbs*). Loudly, aloud, etc., *forte, fortissimo*.

(*Phrases*). At the top of one's voice; in full cry.

etc., soft, floating, purling, etc., liquid, mellifluous, dulcet, flowing, soothing.

(*Adverbs*). In a whisper, with bated breath, under one's breath, *sotto voce*, between the teeth, aside, *piano, pianissimo, à la sourdine*.

---

(2) SPECIFIC SOUNDS

406. Sudden and violent sounds.

SNAP (*Substantives*), knock, click, clash, slam, clack, crack, crackling, crepitation, decrepitation, report, pop, plop, bang, ping, zip, clap, burst, explosion, discharge, crash, detonation, firing, salvo, atmospherics.

Squib, cracker, gun, pop-gun.

(*Verbs*). To snap, knock, etc., brustle.

(*Adjective*). Snapping, etc.

---

407. Repeated and protracted sounds.

ROLL (*Substantives*), rumble, rumbling, hum, humming, shake, trill, chime, tick, beat, toll, ticking, tick-tack, patter, tattoo, ding-dong, drumming, quaver, tremolo, ratatat, rataplan, rat-tat, clatter, clutter, rattle, racket, rub-a-dub.

(*Phrases*). The devil's tattoo; tuck of drum.

(*Verbs*). To roll, beat, tick, toll, drum, etc., drum, or din in the ear.

(*Adjectives*). Rolling, rumbling, etc.

408. RESONANCE (*Substantives*), ring, ringing, jingle, chink, tinkle, tink, tintinnabulation, gurgle, chime, toot, tootle, *see* 404.

Reflection, **reverberation**, echo.

409. Hissing sounds.

SIBILATION (*Substantives*), hiss, buzz, whiz, rustle, fizz, fizzle, wheeze, whistle, snuffle, sneeze, sternutation.

(*Verbs*). To hiss, buzz, etc.

(*Verbs*). To resound, ring, jingle, clink, etc.

(*Adjectives*). Resounding, resonant, tintinnabular, ringing, etc.

(*Phrase*). Clear as a bell.

BASS, low, flat or grave note, chest-note, baritone, deep - toned, deep - sounding, deep-mouthed, hollow, sepulchral, *basso profundo*.

(*Adjectives*). Sibilant, hissing, buzzing, etc.

HIGH notes, *see* 410.

———

410. Harsh sounds.

STRIDOR (*Substantives*), jar, grating, creak, clank, twang, jangle, jarring, creaking, rustling, roughness, gruffness, sharpness, cacophony.

High note, shrillness, acuteness, soprano, falsetto, treble, penny trumpet, head-note.

(*Verbs*). To creak, grate, jar, burr, pipe, twang, jangle, rustle, clank; to shrill, stridulate.

(*Phrases*). To set the teeth on edge; to grate upon the ear.

(*Adjectives*). Strident, stridulous, jarring, etc., harsh, hoarse, discordant, scrannel (414), cacophonous, rough, gruff, sepulchral, grating.

Sharp, high, acute, shrill, piping, screaming.

411. Human sounds, *see* Voice (580).

CRY (*Substantives*), vociferation, outcry, roar, shout, bawl, brawl, halloo, hullaballoo, hoop, whoop, yell, cheer, hoot, howl, chorus, scream, screech, screak, shriek, squeak, squawk, squeal, skirl, squall, whine, pule, pipe, grumble, plaint, groan, moan, snore, snort.

(*Verbs*). To vociferate, roar, shout, bawl, etc., raise or lift up the voice.

(*Adjective*). Vociferating, etc., stertorous.

———

412. Animal sounds.

ULULATION (*Substantives*, latration, cry, roar, bellow, reboation, bark, yelp, howl, bay, baying, yap, growl, grunt, gruntle, snort, neigh, nicker, whinny, bray, croak, snarl, howl, caterwauling, mew, mewl, miaow, miaul, purr, pule, bleat, baa, low, moo, boo, caw, coo, croodle, cackle, gobble, quack, gaggle, squeak, squawk, squeal, chuckle, chuck, cluck, clack, chirp, chirrup, crow, wood-note, twitter, peep.

Insect cry, drone, buzz, hum. Cuckoo, screech-owl.

(*Verbs*). To cry, bellow, re-bellow, etc., give tongue.

(*Phrases*). To bay the moon; to roar like a bull or lion.

(*Adjectives*). Crying, etc., blatant, latrant, remugient.

(3) MUSICAL SOUND

413. MELODY (*Substantives*), melodiousness, *melos*.

Pitch, note, interval, tone, intonation, timbre; high or low, acute or grave notes, treble, alto,

———

414. DISCORD (*Substantives*), discordance, dissonance, jar, jarring, cacophony.

Hoarseness, croaking, etc. (410).

tenor, bass, soprano, mezzo-soprano, contralto, counter-tenor, baritone, *basso profondo*.

Scale, gamut, diapason; diatonic, chromatic, enharmonic, whole-tone, etc., scales; key, clef; major, minor, Dorian, Phrygian, Lydian, etc., modes; tetrachord, hexachord, pentatonic scale; tuning, modulation, temperament; solmisation, solfeggio, sol-fa.

Staff (or stave), lines, spaces, brace; bar, double bar, rest.

Confused sounds Babel: Dutch, concert, cat's concert, marrowbones and cleavers, charivari (404).

(*Verbs*). To be discordant, etc., to croak, jar (410).

(*Adjectives*). Discordant, dissonant, out of tune, sharp, flat, tuneless, absonant, unmusical, inharmonious, unmelodious, untuneful, untunable, singsong.

Cacophonous, harsh, hoarse, croaking, jarring, stridulous, etc. (410).

Notes of the scale: sharps, flats, naturals, accidentals; breve, semibreve, minim, crotchet, quaver, semiquaver, demi-semiquaver, etc.

Tonic, key-note, supertonic, mediant, subdominant, dominant, submediant, leading note, octave; primes, seconds, triads, etc.

Harmonic, overtone, partial, fundamental note, hum-note.

Harmony, harmoniousness, concord, concordance, unison, homophony, chord, chime, consonance, euphony; counterpoint, polyphony; tonality, atonality.

Science of music: Harmony, thorough-bass, figured bass; Counterpoint.

Rhythm, time, *tempo* ; common, duple, triple, six-eight, etc., time; *tempo rubato*, syncopation, rag-time, jazz.

(*Verbs*). To harmonise, chime, be in unison, etc.

(*Adjectives*). Harmonious, harmonic, harmonical, in harmony, in tune, etc., unisonant, unisonal, univocal, symphonic, homophonous; contrapuntal, chordal; diatonic, chromatic, enharmonic, tonal, atonal.

Measured, rhythmical, in time, on the beat, etc.

Melodious, musical, tuneful, tunable, sweet, dulcet, canorous, mellow, mellifluous, silver-toned, silvery, euphonious, euphonic, euphonical; enchanting, ravishing, etc., Orphean.

---

415. MUSIC (*Substantives*), tune, air, lilt, melody, refrain, cadence, theme, motive, *motif*, *leit-motiv*, subject, counter-subject, episode, modulation, introduction, finale, etc.

Composition, work, opus, score, full score, vocal score, etc.

Solo, duet, trio, quartet, etc., concerted music, chorus, chamber music.

Instrumental music: Symphony, *sinfonietta*, symphonic poem, tone-poem, concerto, sonata, sonatina; allegro, andante, largo, scherzo, rondo, etc.; overture, prelude, intermezzo, postlude, voluntary; ballade, nocturne, serenade, aubade, barcarolle, *berceuse*, etc.; fugue, fugato, canon; variations, humoresque, rhapsody, caprice, *capriccio*, fantasia, impromptu; arrangement, pot-pourri; march, pibroch, minuet, gavotte, waltz, mazurka, etc. (840); accompaniment, *obbligato*; programme-music.

Vocal music: chant, plain-song, Gregorian music, neume, psalmody, psalm, hymn, anthem, motet, antiphon, canticle, introit, etc., service; song, ballad, *lied, chanson*, cavatina, canzonet, serenade, lullaby, ditty, chanty, folk-song; dithyramb; part-song, glee, catch, canon, madrigal, chorus, cantata, oratorio, etc.; opera, *see* Drama (599).

Dirge, requiem, *nenia*, knell, lament, coronach, dead march.

Musical ornament; grace-note, appoggiatura, trill, shake, turn, beat, mordent, etc.; cadenza, roulade, bravura, colorature, *coloratura*.

Scale, run, arpeggio, chord; five-finger exercise, study, *étude*, toccata.

Performance, execution, technique, touch, expression, tone-colour, rendering, interpretation; voice-production, *bel canto*; *embouchure*, lipping, bowing.

Concert, recital, performance, ballad-concert, etc., singsong.

Minstrelsy, musicianship, musicality, musicalness, an ear for music; composition, composing, orchestration, scoring, filling in the parts.

Apollo, the Muses, Erato, Euterpe, Terpsichore.

(*Verbs*). To play, fiddle, bow, strike, strike up, thrum, strum, grind, touch, tweedle, scrape, blow, pipe, tootle, blare, etc.; to execute, perform, render, interpret, conduct, accompany, vamp, arrange, prelude, improvise (612).

To sing, chant, vocalise, warble, carol, troll, hum, croon, chirp, chirrup, twitter, quaver, trill, shake, whistle, yodel.

To compose, set to music, score, harmonise, orchestrate.

To put in tune, tune, attune, accord, string, pitch.

(*Adjectives*). Musical, harmonious, etc. (413), instrumental, orchestral, pianistic, vocal, choral, operatic, etc.; musicianly, having a good ear.

(*Phrase*). *Fanatico per la musica.*

(*Adverbs*). Adagio, largo, larghetto, *andante, andantino, maestoso, moderato, allegretto, con moto, vivace, veloce, allegro, presto, prestissimo, strepitoso*, etc.; *scherzando, legato, staccato, crescendo, diminuendo, morendo, sostenuto, sforzando, accelerando, stringendo, più mosso, meno mosso, allargando, rallentando, ritenuto, a piacere*, etc. ; *arpeggiando, pizzicato, glissando, martellato, da capo.*

416. MUSICIAN (*Substantives*), minstrel, performer, player, soloist, virtuoso, maestro.

Organist, pianist, violinist, fiddler, 'cellist, harper, harpist, flautist, fifer, clarinettist, trombonist, etc., trumpeter, bugler, piper, drummer, timpanist; campanologist; band, orchestra, brass band, military band, string band, etc., waits; conductor, bandmaster, leader, *chef d'orchestre*, etc., accompanist.

Vocalist, singer, songster, songstress, chanter, chantress, *cantatrice*, *lieder*-singer, ballad-singer, etc.; troubadour, minnesinger, gleeman; nightingale, Philomel, thrush, throstle, Orpheus.

Chorus, choir.

(*Phrase*). The tuneful Nine.

417. MUSICAL INSTRUMENTS.

1. Stringed instruments: Monochord, polychord, harp, lyre, lute, theorbo, mandolin, guitar, gittern, cithern, banjo, balalaika, etc.

Violin, fiddle, Cremona, Stradivarius (or Strad), kit, viola (or tenor), violoncello (or 'cello), double-bass (or bass-viol), viol, viola d'amore, viola da gamba, violone, rebeck, psaltery, etc.

Pianoforte (or piano), harpsichord, clavier, clavichord, clavicembalo, spinet, cembalo, virginal, zither, dulcimer, etc.

2. Wind instruments: Organ, siren, pipe, pitch-pipe, Pan-pipes; piccolo, flute, bass-flute, oboe (or hautboy), oboe d'amore, cor anglais, clarinet, basset-horn, bass-clarinet, bassoon, double-bassoon, saxophone, horn, French horn, tuba, trumpet, cornet, cornet-à-piston, trombone, euphonium; fife, flageolet, whistle, pennywhistle, ocarina, bugle, serpent, ophicleide, clarion, bagpipe, musette; harmonium, American organ, seraphina, concertina, accordion, mouth-organ, etc.; great, swell, choir, solo and echo organs.

3. Vibrating surfaces: Cymbal, bell, carillon, gong, tabor, tambourine, timbrel, drum, side-drum, bass-drum, kettle-drum, timpano, military drum, tom-tom, castanet; musical glasses, harmonica, glockenspiel; sounding-board, etc.

4. Vibrating bars: Tuning-fork, triangle, xylophone, Jew's harp, etc.

5. Mechanical instruments: Musical box, hurdy-gurdy, barrel-organ, piano-organ, orchestrion, piano-player, pianola, etc.; gramophone, phonograph.

Key, string, bow, drumstick, bellows, sound-box, pedal, stop; loud or sustaining pedal, soft pedal, mute, sordine, *sourdine*, damper, swell-box; keyboard, finger-board, console; organ-loft, concert-platform, orchestra, choir, singing-gallery, belfry, campanile.

(4) PERCEPTION OF SOUND

418. Sense of sound.

HEARING (*Substantives*), audition, auscultation, listening, eavesdropping; audibility.

Acuteness, nicety, delicacy, of ear.

Ear, acoustic organs, auditory apparatus, ear-drum, tympanum; lug.

419. DEAFNESS (*Substantives*), hardness of hearing, surdity.

(*Verbs*). To be deaf, to shut, stop, or close one's ears.

To render deaf, to stun, to deafen.

(*Phrase*). To turn a deaf ear to.

(*Adjectives*). Deaf, hard of hearing, earless, surd, dull of

Telephone, speaking-tube, ear-trumpet, audiphone, ear-phone, phone, receiver.

A hearer, auditor, listener, eavesdropper, auditory, audience.

(*Verbs*). To hear, overhear, hark, listen, list, hearken, give or lend an ear, prick up one's ears, give a hearing or audience to, listen in.

hearing, deaf-mute, stunned, deafened, having no ear.

(*Phrases*). Deaf as a post; deaf as a beetle; deaf as a trunk-maker.

Inaudible, out of hearing.

(*Phrases*). To hang upon the lips of; to be all ears.
To become audible, to catch the ear, to be heard.
(*Adjectives*). Hearing, etc., auditory, auricular, acoustic.
(*Interjections*). Hark! list! hear! listen!
(*Adverb*). *Arrectis auribus.*

6. *Light*

(1) LIGHT IN GENERAL

420. LIGHT (*Substantives*), ray, beam, stream, gleam, streak, pencil, sunbeam.

Day, daylight, sunshine, sunlight, the light of day, the light of heaven, noontide, noonday, noontide light, broad daylight.

Glimmer, glimmering, phosphorescence, lambent flame, play of light.

Flush, halo, glory, corona.

Meteor, northern lights, aurora borealis, fire-drake, *ignis fatuus*, jack-o'-lantern, will-o'-the-wisp, friar's lantern, afterglow.

Spark, sparkle, scintilla, sparkling, scintillation, flame, flash, blaze, coruscation, fulguration, lightning, flood of light, glint.

Lustre, shine, sheen, gloss, tinsel, spangle, brightness, brilliancy, refulgence, dazzlement, resplendence, luminousness, luminosity, luminescence, lucidity, lucidness, incandescence, radiance, illumination, irradiation, glare, flare, glow, flush, effulgence, fluorescence, lucency, lambency.

Science of light: Optics,

421. DARKNESS (*Substantives*), night, midnight, obscurity, dusk, duskiness, gloom, gloominess, murkiness, shadow, shade, umbrage, shadiness, penumbra, Erebus.

Obscuration, adumbration, obumbration, obtenebration, obfuscation, extinction, eclipse, gathering of the clouds, dimness (422).

(*Verbs*). To be dark, etc.

To darken, obscure, shade, shadow, dim, bedarken, overcast, overshadow, obfuscate, obumbrate, adumbrate, cast in the shade, becloud, overcloud, bedim, put out, snuff out, extinguish, dout, douse.

To cast, throw, spread a shade or gloom.

(*Phrase*). To douse the glim.

(*Adjectives*). Dark, unenlightened, obscure, darksome, tenebrous, tenebrific, rayless, beamless, sunless, pitch-dark, pitchy, Stygian, Cimmerian, darkling.

Sombre, dusky, unilluminated, unillumined, unlit, **unsunned,**

Photology, Photometry, Dioptrics, Catoptrics.

Radioactivity, radiography, radiograph, radiometer, etc.

(Verbs). To shine, glow, glitter, glisten, glister, glint, twinkle, gleam, flare, glare, beam, irradiate, shoot beams, shimmer, sparkle, scintillate, coruscate, flash, blaze, fizzle, daze, dazzle, bedazzle; to clear up, to brighten.

(Phrase). To hang out a light.

To illuminate, illume, illumine, lighten, enlighten, light, light up, irradiate, flush, shine upon, cast lustre upon, cast, throw, or shed a light upon, brighten, clear, relume.

(Phrase). To strike a light.

(Adjectives). Luminous, shining, glowing, etc., lambent, glossy, lucid, lucent, luculent, lustrous, lucific, glassy, clear, bright, scintillant, lightsome, unclouded, sunny, orient, noonday, noontide, beaming, beamy, vivid, alight, splendent, radiant, radiating, cloudless, clear, unobscured; radioactive, fluorescent.

Garish, resplendent, refulgent, fulgent, effulgent, in a blaze, ablaze, relucent, splendid, blazing, rutilant, meteoric, burnished.

(Phrases). Bright as silver, as day, as noonday.

nocturnal, dingy, lurid, overcast, cloudy, murky, murksome, shady, shadowy, umbrageous.

(Phrases). Dark as pitch; dark as a pit; dark as Erebus; darkness visible; the palpable obscure.

422. DIMNESS (Substantives), paleness, glimmer, glimmering, owl-light, nebulousness, nebulosity, nebula, cloud, film, mist, haze, fog, smoke, haziness, eclipse, dusk, cloudiness, dawn, aurora, twilight, crepuscule, gloaming, half-light, moonlight.

(Verbs). To be dim, etc., to glimmer, loom, lour, twinkle.

To grow dim, to pale, to render dim, to dim, obscure, pale.

(Adjectives). Dim, dull, lacklustre, dingy, darkish, glassy, faint, confused.

(Phrase). Shorn of its beams.

Cloudy, misty, hazy, foggy, brumous, muggy, fuliginous, nebulous, lowering, overcast, crepuscular, muddy, lurid, looming.

---

423. Source of light, self-luminous body.

LUMINARY (Substantives), sun, Phœbus, star, orb, meteor, galaxy, constellation, blazing star, glow-worm, fire-fly.

Artificial light, flame, gas-light, incandescent gas-light, electric light, limelight, acetylene, torch, candle, flash-light, flambeau, link, light, taper, lamp, arc lamp, lantern (or lanthorn), rushlight, farthing rushlight, night-light, firework, rocket, blue lights, fizgig, bude light, flare.

Chandelier, candelabra, girandole, lustre, sconce, gasbracket, gas-jet, gas-burner, batswing.

424. SHADE (Substantives), screen, curtain, veil, mantle, mask, gauze, blind, cloud, mist.

A shadow, chiaroscuro, umbrage, penumbra.

(Adjectives). Shady, umbrageous, etc.

Lighthouse, pharos, beacon, watch-fire, cresset, brand.
(*Adjectives*). Self-luminous, phosphoric, phosphorescent.

425. TRANSPARENCY (*Substantives*), pellucidity, diaphaneity, translucency, lucidity, limpidity, clarity.

Glass, crystal, lymph, water.

(*Verbs*). To be transparent, etc., to transmit light.

(*Adjectives*). Transparent, pellucid, diaphanous, translucent, relucent, limpid, clear, crystalline, vitreous, transpicuous, glassy, hyaline.

(*Phrase*). Clear as crystal.

426. OPACITY (*Substantives*), thickness, opaqueness, turbidity, turbidness, muddiness.

Cloud, film, haze.

(*Verbs*). To be opaque, etc., not to transmit, to obstruct the passage of light.

(*Adjectives*). Opaque, turbid, thick, muddy, opacous, obfuscated, fuliginous, cloudy, hazy, misty, foggy, impervious to light.

427. SEMITRANSPARENCY, opalescence, gauze, milkiness.

(*Adjectives*). Semitransparent, opalescent, gauzy, pearly, milky.

(2) SPECIFIC LIGHT

428. COLOUR (*Substantives*), hue, tint, tinge, dye, complexion, shade, spectrum, tincture, blazonry, cast, livery, coloration, glow, flush, tone, key.

Pure or positive colour: primary colour.

Broken colour: secondary, tertiary colour.

Science of colour: Chromatics.

A pigment, colouring matter, paint, dye, wash, stain, distemper, mordant.

(*Verbs*). To colour, dye, tinge, stain, tinct, tincture, paint, wash, illuminate, blazon, emblazon, bedizen, imbue, distemper.

(*Adjectives*). Coloured, colorific, chromatic, prismatic, full-coloured, lush, dyed; tinctorial.

Bright, vivid, florid, fresh, high-coloured, unfaded, gay, showy, gaudy, garish, flaunting, vivid, gorgeous, glaring, flaring, flashy, raw, intense, double-dyed, loud, noisy.

Mellow, harmonious, pearly.

429. Absence of colour.

ACHROMATISM (*Substantives*), decoloration, discoloration, paleness, pallidity, pallidness, etiolation, anæmia, chlorosis, albinism, neutral tint, colourlessness.

A spot, blot, etc. (848).

(*Verbs*). To lose colour, to fade, fly, become colourless.

To deprive of colour, discolour, bleach, tarnish, decolour, decolorate, decolorise, achromatise.

(*Adjectives*). Colourless, uncoloured, untinged, untinctured, achromatic, aplanatic, hueless, undyed, pale, pallid, pale-faced, pasty, etiolated, anæmic, chlorotic, faint, faded, dull, cold, muddy, wan, sallow, dead, dingy, ashy, ashen, cadaverous, glassy, lack-lustre, tarnished, bleached, discoloured, mat.

(*Phrases*). Pale as death, as ashes, as a witch, as a ghost, as a corpse.

430. WHITENESS (*Substantives*), milkiness, hoariness.

Etiolation.

Snow, paper, chalk, milk, lily, sheet, ivory, silver, alabaster.

(*Verbs*). To be white, etc.

To render white, whiten, bleach, whitewash, blanch, etiolate.

(*Adjectives*). White, milk-white, snow-white, cream-coloured, chalky, hoary, hoar, silvery, argent, pearly, fair, blonde, etiolated, albescent.

(*Phrases*). White as the driven snow; white as a sheet.

431. BLACKNESS (*Substantives*), swarthiness, dinginess, lividity, inkiness, pitchiness, nigritude.

Nigrification.

Jet, ink, ebony, coal, pitch, charcoal, soot, sloe, smut, raven, negro, nigger, blackamoor.

(*Verbs*). To be black, etc.

To render black, to blacken, nigrify, denigrate, blot, blotch.

(*Adjectives*). Black, sable, swarthy, swart, sombre, inky, ebon, livid, coal-black, fuliginous, dingy, dusky, Ethiopic, nocturnal, nigrescent.

(*Phrases*). Black as my hat; black as a crow; black as thunder.

432. GREY (*Substantives*), dun, drab, dingy, sombre, tawny, mouse-coloured, ash, cinereous, cineritious, slate, stone, grizzly, grizzled.

———

433. BROWN (*Substantives*), bay, dapple, auburn, chestnut, nut-brown, umber, cinnamon, fawn, russet, olive, hazel, tawny, fuscous, chocolate, liver-colour, tan, brunette, maroon, khaki, bronze, bistre.

(*Phrases*). Brown as a berry, as mahogany, as a gipsy.

(*Verbs*). To render brown, to tan, bronze, etc.

(*Adjectives*). Brown, etc., brindled, brindle, sallow, foxy, bronzed, sunburnt, tanned.

Primitive Colours

434. REDNESS (*Substantives*), scarlet, vermilion, crimson, carmine, pink, lake, maroon, carnation, damask, ruby, rose, rubescence, rosiness, rufescence, ruddiness, rubicundity, blush colour, peach colour, flesh colour, gules, solferino.

Lobster.

Erubescence, rubefaction.

(*Verbs*). To become red, to blush, flush, mantle, redden, colour, incarnadine.

435. GREENNESS (*Substantives*), verdure, viridescence.

Emerald, jasper, verd-antique, verdigris, beryl, aquamarine.

(*Adjectives*). Green, verdant, pea-green, grass-green, apple-green, sea-green, turquoise-green, olive-green, bottle-green, glaucous, virescent, æruginous.

(*Phrase*). Green as grass.

———

To render red, redden, rouge, rubefy, rubricate.

(*Adjectives*). Red, ruby, crimson, pink, etc., ruddy, rufous, florid, rosy, roseate, auroral, rose-coloured, blushing, mantling, etc., erubescent, blowzy, rubicund, stammel, blood-red, ensanguined, rubiform, cardinal, cerise, *sang-de-bœuf*, murrey, carroty, sorrel, brick-coloured, lateritic.

(*Phrases*). Red as fire, as blood, as scarlet, as a turkey-cock, as a cherry.

436. YELLOWNESS (*Substantives*), buff colour, flesh colour, gamboge, crocus, saffron, topaz.

(*Adjectives*). Yellow, citron, gold, golden, aureate, citrine, fallow, fulvous, saffron, croceate, lemon, sulphur, amber, straw-coloured, sandy, lurid, Claude-tint, luteous, primrose-coloured, cream-coloured, buff, chrome.

(*Phrases*). Yellow as a quince, as a guinea, as a crow's foot.

437. PURPLE (*Substantives*), violet, plum, prune, lavender, lilac, peach colour, puce, gride-lin, lividness, lividity, bishop's purple, magenta, mauve.

Amethyst, murex.

(*Adjectives*). Purple, violet, livid, etc.

438. BLUENESS (*Substantives*), bluishness, azure, indigo, ultra-marine, Prussian blue, mazarine, bloom, bice.

(*Adjectives*). Blue, cerulean, sky-blue, sky-coloured, sky-dyed, watchet, azure, bluish, sapphire, Garter-blue, lapis lazuli.

439. ORANGE (*Substantives*), gold, flame, copper, brass, apricot colour, aureolin, nacarat.

(*Adjectives*). Orange, golden, etc., buff, flesh-coloured.

440. VARIEGATION (*Substantives*), dichroism, trichroism, irides-cence, play of colours, *reflet*, variegatedness, patchwork, maculation, spottiness, marquetry, inlay, buhl, striæ, spectrum.

A rainbow, iris, tulip, peacock, chameleon, butterfly, tortoiseshell, leopard, zebra, harlequin, mother-of-pearl, opal, marble.

(*Verbs*). To be variegated, etc.

To variegate, speckle, stripe, streak, chequer, bespeckle, fleck, freckle, inlay.

(*Adjectives*). Variegated, varicoloured, many-coloured, versicolor, many-hued, divers-coloured, particoloured, polychromatic, bi-colour, tricolour, dichromatic.

Iridescent, prismatic, opaline, nacreous, pearly, opalescent, shot, *chatoyant, gorge de pigeon*, all manner of colours, pied, piebald, skewbald, motley, mottled, veined, marbled, paned, dappled, clouded, cymophanous.

Mosaic, inlaid, tessellated, chequered, tortoiseshell.

Dotted, spotted, bespotted, spotty, speckled, bespeckled, punc-tate, maculated, freckled, fleckered, flecked, studded, tattooed.

Striped, striated, streaked, barred, veined, brinded, brindled, tabby, roan, grizzled, listed, stippled.

(3) PERCEPTIONS OF LIGHT

441. VISION (*Substantives*), sight, optics, eyesight, view, espial, glance, glimpse, peep, gaze, stare, leer, perlustration, contemplation, regard, survey, reconnaissance, introspection, inspection, speculation, watch, *coup d'œil*, bo-peep, ocular demonstration, autopsy, visualisation, envisagement, *see* 457.

A point of view, gazebo, vista, loop - hole, belvedere, field of view, watch - tower, theatre, amphitheatre, horizon, arena, commanding view, coign of vantage, observatory, periscope.

The organ of vision, eye, the naked or unassisted eye, retina, optics, peepers.

Perspicacity, penetration, discernment, lynx, eagle, Argus.

(*Verbs*). To see, behold, discern, have in sight, descry, catch a sight, glance, or glimpse of, spy, espy, to get a sight of.

To look, view, eye, open one's eyes, glance on, cast or set one's eyes on, look on or upon, turn or bend one's looks upon, turn the eyes to, envisage, visualise, peep,

442. BLINDNESS (*Substantives*), cecity, *amaurosis*, ablepsy, nictitation, wink, blink.

A blinkard.

(*Verbs*). To be blind, etc., not to see, to lose sight of.

Not to look, to close or shut the eyes, to look another way, to turn away or avert the eyes, to wink, blink, nictitate.

To render blind, etc., to put out the eyes, to blind, blindfold, hoodwink, daze, dazzle.

(*Phrases*). To throw dust into the eyes; *jeter de la poudre aux yeux.*

(*Adjectives*). Blind, purblind, eyeless, sightless, visionless, dark, stone-blind, sand-blind, stark-blind, mope-eyed, dazzled, hoodwinked, blindfolded, undiscerning.

(*Phrases*). Blind as a bat, as a buzzard, as a beetle, as a mole, as an owl.

(*Adverbs*). Blindly, etc., blindfold.

———

peer, pry, scan, survey, reconnoitre, contemplate, regard, inspect, recognise, mark, discover, distinguish, see through, speculate; to see sights, lionise.

(*Phrases*). To have an eye upon; keep in sight; look about one; glance round; run the eye over; lift up one's eyes; see at a glance, or with half an eye; keep a look-out for; to see with one's own eyes; to see through.

To look intently, strain one's eyes, be all eyes, look full in the face, gaze, pore over, gloat on, leer, to see with half an eye, to blink, goggle, ogle; to play at bo-peep.

(*Adjectives*). Visual, ocular, optic, optical.

Seeing, etc., the eyes being directed to, fixed, riveted upon.

Clear-sighted, sharp-sighted, quick-sighted, eagle-eyed, hawk-eyed, lynx-eyed, keen-eyed, Argus-eyed, piercing, penetrating.

(*Phrase*). The scales falling from one's eyes.

(*Adverbs*). Visibly, etc., at sight, in sight of, to one's face, before one's face, with one's eyes open, at a glance, at first sight, at sight.

(*Interjections*). Look! behold! see! lo! mark! observe! lo and behold!

443. Imperfect vision.

DIM-SIGHTEDNESS (*Substantives*), lippitude, confusion of vision, scotomy, failing sight, short-sightedness, myopia, nictitation, long-sightedness, presbyopia, hypermetropia, astigmatism, squint, strabismus, wall-eye, cast of the eye, double sight; an albino.

Fallacies of vision: *deceptio visus*, refraction, false light, phantasm, anamorphosis, distortion, looming, mirage, *fata Morgana*, the spectre of the Brocken, *ignis fatuus*, phantasmagoria, dissolving views, etc.

Colour-blindness, Daltonism.

Limitation of vision: blinker, screen.

(*Verbs*). To be dim-sighted, etc., to see double, to squint, goggle, look askant, or askance, to see through a prism, wink, nictitate.

To glare, dazzle, loom.

(*Adjectives*). Dim-sighted, half-sighted, short-sighted, near-sighted, myopic, long-sighted, hypermetropic, presbyopic, moon-eyed, mope-eyed, blear-eyed, goggle-eyed, wall-eyed, one-eyed, nictitating, winking, monoculous, amblyopic.

(*Phrases*). *Nimium ne crede colori* ; *fronti nulla fides*; things are seldom what they seem.

444. SPECTATOR (*Substantives*), looker-on, bystander, inspector, spy, beholder, observer, star-gazer, etc., scout.

(*Verbs*). To witness, behold, etc.

445. OPTICAL INSTRUMENTS (*Substantives*), lens, meniscus, magnifier, microscope, megascope, spectacles, glasses, barnacles, goggles, *pince-nez*, lorgnette, folders, eye-glass, monocle, periscope, telescope, spy-glass, field-glass, opera-glass, glass, view-finder.

Mirror, reflector, speculum, looking-glass, pier-glass, cheval-glass, kaleidoscope.

Prism, camera lucida, camera obscura, magic lantern, phantasmagoria, thaumatrope, chromatrope, stereoscope, pseudoscope, bioscope.

Photometer, polariscope, spectroscope, collimator, polemoscope, eriometer, actinometer, lucimeter.

446. VISIBILITY (*Substantives*), perceptibility, conspicuousness, distinctness, conspicuity, appearance, exposure.

(*Verbs*). To be visible, etc., to appear, come in sight, come into view, heave in sight, open to the

447. INVISIBILITY (*Substantives*), indistinctness, inconspicuousness, imperceptibility, non-appearance, delitescence, concealment (526).

(*Verbs*). To be invisible, etc., to lie hidden, concealed, etc., to

view, catch the eye, show its face, present itself, show itself, manifest itself, produce itself, discover itself, expose itself, come out, come to light, come forth, come forward, arise, peep out, peer out, start up, loom, burst forth, break through the clouds, glare, reveal itself, betray itself.

(*Phrases*). To show its colours; to tell its own tale; *cela saute aux yeux*; to stare one in the face.

(*Adjectives*). Visible, perceptible, discernible, in sight, apparent, plain, manifest, patent, obvious, clear, distinct, definite, well-defined, well-marked, recognisable, evident, unmistakable, palpable, naked, bare, bare-faced, ostensible, conspicuous, prominent, staring, glaring, notable, notorious, overt, periscopic, panoramic.

(*Phrases*). Open as day; clear as day; plain as a pikestaff; there is no mistaking; plain as the nose on one's face; *oculis subjecta fidelibus*; above-board; exposed to view; under one's nose; in bold relief; in the limelight.

Intelligible, etc., see 518.

be in or under a cloud, in a mist, in a haze, etc.; to lurk, lie in ambush, skulk.

Not to see, etc., to be blind to.

To render invisible, to hide, conceal, etc. (528).

(*Adjectives*). Invisible, imperceptible, unseen, unbeheld, undiscerned, viewless, undiscernible, indiscernible, sightless, undescried, unespied, unapparent, non-apparent, inconspicuous, hidden, concealed, etc. (528), covert.

Confused, dim, obscure, dark, misty, hazy, foggy, indistinct, ill-defined, indefinite, ill-marked, blurred, shadowy, nebulous, shaded, screened, veiled, masked.

Unintelligible, etc., see 519.

---

448. APPEARANCE (*Substantives*), phenomenon, sight, spectacle, show, premonstration, scene, species, view, *coup d'œil*, look-out, prospect, outlook, vista, perspective, bird's-eye view, scenery, landscape, picture, tableau, display, exposure, exhibition, manifestation.

Pageant, raree-show, panorama, diorama, cosmorama, georama, spectacle, *coup de théâtre*, *jeu de théâtre*.

Bioscope, biograph, cinematograph (or kinematograph).

Phantasm, phasma, phantom, spectrum, apparition, spectre, mirage, etc. (4, 443).

Aspect, phase, *phasis*, seeming, guise, look, complexion, shape,

449. DISAPPEARANCE (*Substantives*), evanescence, eclipse, occultation.

Dissolving views, fade-out.

(*Verbs*). To disappear, vanish, dissolve, fade, melt away, pass, be gone, be lost, etc.

(*Phrase*). To go off the stage.

To efface, blot, blot out, erase, rub out, expunge (552).

(*Adjectives*). Disappearing, etc., lost, vanishing, evanescent, missing.

Inconspicuous, unconspicuous.

(*Phrases*). Lost in the clouds; leaving no trace; out of sight.

(*Interjections*). Begone! away! avaunt! vanish! disappear! see 293.

---

mien, air, cast, carriage, port, demeanour, presence, expression, first blush.

Lineament, feature, trait, lines, outline, contour, face, countenance, physiognomy, visage, phiz, mug, profile, *tournure*.

(*Verbs*). To seem, look, appear; to present, wear, carry, have, bear, exhibit, take, take on, or assume the appearance of; to look like, to be visible, to reappear; to materialise.

To show, to manifest.

(*Adjectives*). Apparent, seeming, etc.

(*Adverbs*). Apparently, to all appearance, etc., on the face of it, *prima facie*, at the first blush, at first sight.

CLASS IV

WORDS RELATING TO THE INTELLECTUAL FACULTIES

DIVISION I.—FORMATION OF IDEAS

SECTION I.—OPERATIONS OF INTELLECT IN GENERAL

450. INTELLECT (*Substantives*), mind, understanding, reason, thinking principle, nous, noesis, sense, common sense, consciousness, capacity, intelligence, percipience, intellection, intuition, instinct, conception, judgment, genius, parts, wit, wits, shrewdness, archness, intellectuality; the five senses; rationalism; *see* Skill (698) and Wisdom (498).

Subconsciousness, the subconscious mind.

Soul, spirit, psyche, ghost, inner man, heart, breast, bosom, *penetralia mentis, divina particula auræ.*

Organ or seat of thought: *sensorium*, sensory, brain, head, head-piece, pate, noddle, nut, skull, brain-pan, pericranium, cerebrum, cerebellum, cranium.

Science of mind: Metaphysics, Psychology, Psychics, Psycho-analysis, Ideology, Idealism, Ideality, Pneumatology, Immaterialism, Intuitionism, Realism, etc.

Metaphysician, psychologist, psycho-analyst, etc.

(*Adjectives*). Relating to intellect: intellectual, noetic, gnostic, mental, spiritual, subjective, metaphysical, psychical, psychological, noumenal, ghostly, immaterial (317), cerebral; subconscious, subliminal, Freudian.

ABSENCE or want of intellect, *see* 499, materialism.

(*Adjectives*). Material, objective, etc.

———

451. THOUGHT (*Substantives*), reflection, cogitation, cerebration, consideration, meditation, study, lucubration, speculation, deliberation, pondering, head-work, application, attention (457).

Abstraction, contemplation, musing, reverie (458), Platonism; depth of thought, workings of

452. Absence or want of thought.

INCOGITANCY (*Substantives*), vacancy, fatuity (*see* 499), thoughtlessness, *see* Inattention (458).

(*Verbs*). Not to think, to take no thought of, not to trouble oneself about, to put away

the mind, inmost thoughts, self-counsel, self-communing, self-examination, introspection; succession, flow, train, current, etc., of thought or of ideas, brain-wave.

Afterthought, second thoughts, reconsideration, retrospection, retrospect (505), examination, *see* Inquiry (461).

Thoughtfulness, pensiveness, intentness.

Telepathy, thought-transference, mind-reading.

(*Verbs*). To think, reflect, cogitate, excogitate, consider, deliberate, speculate, contemplate, meditate, introspect, ponder, muse, ruminate, think over, brood over, animadvert, con, con over, study, bend or apply the mind, digest, discuss, hammer at, puzzle out, weigh, perpend.

thought; to dismiss, discard, or discharge from one's thoughts, or from the mind; to drop the subject, set aside, turn aside, turn away from, turn one's attention from, abstract oneself, dream; to indulge in reverie or daydreams.

To unbend, relax, divert the mind.

(*Adjectives*). Vacant, unintellectual (*see* 499), unoccupied, unthinking, inconsiderate, thoughtless, idealess, absent, *distrait*, abstracted, inattentive (458), diverted, distracted, unbent, etc.

(*Phrase*). *In nubibus.*

Unthought of, unconsidered, incogitable, undreamed, off one's mind.

————

(*Phrases*). Take into account; take into consideration; to take counsel; to commune with oneself; to collect one's thoughts; to advise with one's pillow; to sleep on or over it; to chew the cud upon; revolve in the mind; turn over in the mind; to rack one's brains; to put on one's thinking-cap.

To harbour, entertain, cherish, nurture, etc., an idea, or a thought, a notion, a view, etc.

To occur, present itself, pass in the mind, suggest itself; to fancy, trow, dream of.

(*Phrases*). To flash on the mind; to flit across the view; to enter the mind; come into the head; come uppermost; run in one's head.

To make an impression; to sink or penetrate into the mind; fasten itself on the mind; to engross one's thoughts.

(*Adjectives*). Thinking, etc., thoughtful, pensive, meditative, reflective, ruminant, introspective, wistful, contemplative, speculative, deliberative, studious, abstracted, introspective, reflex, Platonic, conceptual.

Close, active, diligent, mature, deliberate, laboured, steadfast, deep, profound, intense, etc., thought, study, reflection, etc.

Intent, engrossed, absorbed, deep-musing, wrapped, rapt, abstracted; sedate.

(*Phrases*). Having the mind on the stretch; the mind or head running upon.

453. Object of thought.

IDEA (*Substantives*), notion, conception, concept, thought, fancy, conceit, impression, perception, percept, ideation, image, eidolon, sentiment, *see* Opinion (484), fantasy, flight of fancy.

Point of view, light, aspect, field of view, standpoint.

Fixed idea, *see* 481, 606.

———

454. Subject of thought, νοήματα.

TOPIC (*Substantives*), subject, matter, theme, thesis, text, subject-matter, point, proposition, theorem, business, affair, matter in hand, question, argument, motion, resolution, moot point (461), head, chapter; nice or subtle point, quodlibet.

(*Adverbs*). In question, on the carpet, *sur le tapis*, relative to (*see* 9), concerning, touching.

SECTION II.—PRECURSORY CONDITIONS AND OPERATIONS

455. The desire of knowledge.

CURIOSITY (*Substantives*), curiousness, inquisitiveness.

A quidnunc, Paul Pry, newsmonger, gossip.

(*Verbs*). To be curious, etc., to take an interest in, to stare, gape, to lionise.

(*Adjectives*). Curious, inquisitive, inquiring, all agog, staring, gaping, agape, over-curious, nosy.

(*Adverbs*). With open mouth, on tiptoe, *arrectis auribus*.

456. Absence of curiosity.

INCURIOSITY (*Substantives*), incuriousness, insouciance, want of interest, indifference.

(*Verbs*). To be incurious, etc., to have no curiosity, take no interest in, etc., not to care, not to mind, etc.

(*Phrases*). Not to trouble oneself about; the devil may care.

(*Adjectives*). Incurious, *sans souci*, insouciant, uninterested.

457. ATTENTION (*Substantives*), advertence, advertency, observance, observation, interest, notice, heed, look, regard, view, remark, inspection, introspection, mindfulness, look-out, watch, vigilance, circumspection, surveillance, consideration, scrutiny, revision, recension, review, revise, particularity, *see* Care (459).

Close, intense, deep, profound, etc., attention, application, or study.

(*Verbs*). To be attentive, etc.; to attend, advert to, mind, observe, look, look at, see, view, look to, see to, remark, heed, notice, spot, twig, take heed, take notice, mark; give or pay

458. INATTENTION (*Substantives*), inconsideration, inconsiderateness, inadvertence, inadvertency, non-observance, inobservance, disregard, unmindfulness, giddiness, respectlessness, thoughtlessness, *see* Neglect (460), insouciance, wandering, distracted, etc., attention.

Absence of mind, abstraction, preoccupation, distraction, reverie, brown study, day-dream, day-dreaming, wool-gathering.

(*Phrases*). The wits going wool-gathering; the attention wandering.

(*Verbs*). To be inattentive, etc., to overlook, disregard, pass by, slur over, pass over, gloss

attention to; give heed to, have an eye to; turn, apply, or direct the mind, the eye, or the attention to; look after, give a thought to, animadvert on, occupy oneself with, be interested in, devote oneself to, give oneself up to, see about.

(*Phrases*). To trouble one's head about; lend or incline an ear to; to take cognisance of; to prick up one's ears; to have one's eyes open.

To examine cursorily; to glance at, upon, or over; cast or pass the eyes over, run over, turn over the leaves, dip into, skim, perstringe.

(*Phrase*). To take a cursory view of.

To examine closely or intently, scrutinise, consider, give one's mind to, overhaul, pore over, note, mark, inspect, review, have one's eyes open, fix the eye, mind, thoughts, or attention on, keep in view, contemplate, revert to, etc. (451).

(*Phrases*). To have one's eyes about one; to bear in mind; to come to the point; to take into account.

over, blink, miss, skim, skim the surface, *effleurer* (460).

(*Phrases*). To take no account of; to come in at one ear and go out of the other; to reckon without one's host.

To call off, draw off, call away, divert, etc., the attention; to distract; to disconcert, put out, discompose, confuse, perplex, bewilder, bemuse, moither, bemuddle, muddle, dazzle, obfuscate, flummox, befog.

(*Adjectives*). Inattentive, mindless, unobservant, unmindful, uninterested, inadvertent, heedless, regardless, respectless, careless (*see* 460), insouciant, unwatchful, listless, cursory, blind, deaf, etc.

Absent, abstracted, *distrait*, absent-minded, lost, preoccupied, dreamy, moony, napping.

(*Phrase*). Caught napping.

Disconcerted, put out, etc., dizzy, muzzy, *see* 460.

(*Adverbs*). Inattentively, etc., cavalierly.

———

To fall under one's notice, observation, etc., to catch the eye; to catch, awaken, wake, invite, solicit, attract, claim, excite, engage, occupy, strike, arrest, fix, engross, monopolise, preoccupy, obsess, absorb, rivet, etc., the attention, mind, or thoughts; to interest.

(*Adjectives*). Attentive, mindful, heedful, regardful, alive to, bearing in mind, occupied with, engaged, taken up with, interested, engrossed, wrapped or rapt in, absorbed.

Awake, watchful, on the watch (459), broad awake, wide awake, agape, intent on, with eyes fixed on, open-eyed, unwinking, undistracted, with bated breath, breathless, upon the stretch.

(*Interjections*). *Nota bene!* see! look! mark! lo! behold!

459. CARE (*Substantives*), caution, heed, heedfulness, wariness, prudence, discretion, watch,

460. NEGLECT (*Substantives*), negligence, omission, laches, heedlessness, carelessness, per-

watchfulness, vigil, vigilance, circumspection, watch and ward, deliberation, forethought, predeliberation, solicitude, precaution (673), scruple, scrupulousness, scrupulosity, particularity, surveillance.

(*Phrases*). The eyes of Argus; *l'œil du maître*.

(*Verbs*). To be careful, etc., to take care, have a care, look to it, heed, take heed, provide for, see to, see after, keep watch, keep watch and ward, look sharp, look about one, set watch, take precautions, see about.

(*Phrases*). To have all one's eyes about one; to mind one's P's and Q's; to speak by the card; to pick one's steps; keep a sharp look out; keep one's weather eye open.

(*Adjectives*). Careful, cautious, heedful, wary, guarded, on one's guard, on the alert, on the watch, watchful, on the look out, *aux aguets*, awake, vigilant, circumspect, broad awake, having the eyes open, Argus-eyed.

(*Phrase*). On the *qui vive*.

Discreet, prudent, sure-footed, provident, scrupulous, particular, meticulous.

(*Adverbs*). Carefully, etc., with care, etc., gingerly, considerately.

(*Phrases*). Let sleeping dogs lie; catching a weasel asleep.

(*Interjections*). Look out! mind your eye!

————

functoriness, remissness, imprudence, secureness, indiscretion, *étourderie*, incautiousness, indiscrimination, rashness (863), recklessness, nonchalance.

In dress: A slattern, slut, sloven.

In rhetoric, Paralipsis.

(*Verbs*). To be negligent, etc., to neglect, scamp, pass over, omit, pretermit, set aside, cast or put aside.

To overlook, disregard, slight, pay no regard to, make light of, trifle with, blink, wink at, connive at; take or make no account of; gloss over, slur over, slip over, skip, jump over, shirk (623), discount.

(*Phrases*). To give to the winds; take no account of; not to mind; think no more of; set at naught; give the go-by to.

To render neglectful, etc., to put or throw off one's guard.

(*Adjectives*). Neglecting, etc., unmindful, heedless, careless, *sans souci*, negligent, neglectful, slovenly, remiss, perfunctory, thoughtless, unthoughtful, unheedful, off one's guard, unwary, incautious, unguarded, indiscreet, inconsiderate, imprudent, improvident, rash, headlong, reckless, heels over head, witless, hare-brained, giddy-brained, offhand, slapdash, happy-go-lucky, cursory, brain-sick, scatter-brained.

Neglected, unheeded, unperceived, unseen, unobserved, unnoticed, unnoted, unmarked, unattended to, untended, unwatched, unthought of, overlooked, unmissed, unexamined, unsearched, unscanned, unweighed, unsifted, untested, unweeded, undetermined.

(*Phrases*). In an unguarded moment; buried in a napkin.
(*Adverbs*). Negligently, etc., hand over head.

461. INQUIRY (*Substantives*), search, research, quest, pursuit, examination, scrutiny, investigation, indagation, perquisition, perscrutation, discussion, symposium, inquest, inquisition, exploration, exploitation, sifting, calculation, analysis, dissection, resolution, induction; the Baconian method; a searching inquiry; *scire facias, ad referendum.*

Questioning, asking, interrogation, interpellation, interrogatory, the Socratic method, examination, cross-examination, cross-questioning, catechism.

Reconnoitring, reconnaissance, prying, spying, espionage, the lantern of Diogenes, searchlight.

Subject of inquiry: QUESTION, moot point, query, difficulty, problem, desideratum, point to be solved; point or matter in dispute; moot point, question at issue, plain question, fair question, open question, knotty point, vexed question, crux.

462. ANSWER (*Substantives*), response, reply, replication, riposte, rejoinder, rebutter, retort, repartee, rescript, antiphony, rescription, acknowledgment.

Explanation, solution, deduction, resolution, exposition, rationale, interpretation (522).

A key, master-key, open sesame, *passepartout,* clue.

Œdipus, *see* Oracle (513).

(*Verbs*). To answer, respond, reply, rebut, retort, rejoin, return for answer, acknowledge, echo.

(*Phrases*). To turn the tables upon; *mutato nomine de te fabula narratur.*

To explain, solve, resolve, expound, decipher, spell, interpret (522), to unriddle, unlock, cut the knot, unravel, pick or open the lock, discover, fish up, to find a clue to.

(*Adjectives*). Answering, responding, etc., responsive, respondent.

Enigma, riddle, conundrum, a bone to pick, quodlibet, Gordian knot, *dignus vindice nodus.*

An inquirer, querist, questioner, heckler, inquisitor, examiner, analyst, quidnunc, newsmonger, gossip (527, 532); investigator, detective, bloodhound, sleuth-hound, sleuth, inquiry agent, Sherlock Holmes, busy.

(*Verbs*). To inquire, seek, search, look for, look about for, look out for, cast about for, beat up for, grope for, feel for, reconnoitre, explore, sound, rummage, ransack, pry, look round, look over, look through, peruse.

(*Phrases*). To look, peer, or pry into every hole and corner; to beat the bushes; to leave no stone unturned; to seek a needle in a bundle of hay; to scratch the head.

To pursue, hunt, track, trail, mouse, dodge, trace, shadow, dog (622), nose out, hunt up.

To investigate, take up, follow up, institute, pursue, conduct, carry on, prosecute, etc., an inquiry, etc., to overhaul, to examine, study, consider, fathom, take into consideration, dip into, look into, calculate, pre-examine, dive into, to delve into, rake, rake over, discuss, canvass, thrash out, probe, fathom, sound, scrutinise, analyse, anatomise, dissect, sift, winnow, torture, resolve, traverse, see into.

(Phrases). To subject to examination; to grapple with a question; to put to the proof; pass in review; take into consideration; to ventilate a question; seek a clue; throw out a feeler.

To undergo examination; to be in course of inquiry; to be under consideration.

To ask, question, query, demand, put, propose, propound, moot, raise, stir, suggest, put forth, start, pop, etc., a question, interrogate, catechise, pump, cross-question, cross-examine, heckle, dodge, require an answer, *see* 765.

(Adjectives). Inquiring, etc., inquisitive, requisitive, requisitory, catechetical, inquisitorial, heuristic, analytic, in search of, in quest of, on the look out for, interrogative.

Undetermined, untried, undecided, to be resolved, etc., in question, in dispute, *sub judice*, moot, proposed, doubtful.

(Adverbs). Why? wherefore? whence? *quære?* how comes it? how happens it? how is it? what is the reason?

463. EXPERIMENT *(Substantives)*, essay, trial, tentative method, *tâtonnement*, verification, probation, *experimentum crucis*, proof, criterion, test, touchstone, pyx, assay, ordeal; empiricism, rule of thumb, method of trial and error.

A feeler, a pilot-balloon, a messenger-balloon; a pilot-engine; a straw to show the wind.

(Verbs). To essay, try, explore, grope, beat the bushes; feel or grope one's way; to thread one's way; to make an experiment, make trial of.

To subject to trial, etc., to experiment upon, try over, give a trial to, put, bring, or submit to the test or proof; to prove, verify, test, assay, touch, practise upon.

To feel the pulse, *aller à tâtons*, to throw out a feeler.

(Adjectives). Experimental, crucial, tentative, probationary, empirical, *sub judice*.

(Adverb). A *tâtons*.

464. COMPARISON *(Substantives)*, collation, contrast, identification.

A comparison, simile, similitude, analogy, metaphor, allegory (521).

(Verbs). To compare to or with; to collate, confront, place side by side, or in juxtaposition, to draw a parallel, institute a comparison, contrast, balance, identify.

(Phrase). *Parvis componere magna.*

(Adjectives). Comparative, metaphorical, figurative, allegorical, compared with, pitted against, placed by the side of.

465. DISCRIMINATION *(Substantives)*, distinction, differentiation, perception or appreciation of difference, taste (850), judgment, nice perception, tact, critique.

465A. INDISCRIMINATION *(Substantives)*, indistinctness, indistinction (460).

(Verbs). Not to distinguish or discriminate, neglect, overlook, lose sight of a distinction.

(*Phrases*). To split hairs; to cut blocks with a razor.

(*Verbs*). To discriminate, distinguish, differentiate, to separate or winnow the chaff from the wheat.

(*Adjectives*). Discriminating, etc., discriminative, distinctive, diagnostic, judicial.

(*Adjectives*). Indiscriminate, undistinguished, undistinguishable, unmeasured.

————

466. MEASUREMENT (*Substantives*), admeasurement, mensuration, survey, valuation, appraisement, assessment, assize, estimation, reckoning, evaluation; mileage, voltage, etc.

Geometry, geodetics, geodesy, orthometry, gauging, altimetry, sounding, surveying, weighing, ponderation, trutination, dead reckoning, metrology.

A measure, standard, rule, compass, callipers, gauge, meter, line, rod, plumb-line, plummet, log, log-line, sound, sounding-rod, sounding-line, index, flood-mark, check.

Scale, graduation, graduated scale, vernier, quadrant, theodolite, etc., balance, scales, steelyard, beam, weather-glass, barometer, aneroid, barograph, aræometer, altimeter, clinometer, graphometer, thermometer, tachometer, pedometer, ammeter, voltmeter, micrometer, etc.

(*Verbs*). To measure, mete, value, assess, rate, appraise, estimate, form an estimate, set a value on, appreciate, span, pace, step, apply the compass, rule, scale, etc., gauge, plumb, probe, sound, fathom, heave the log, survey, weigh, poise, balance, hold the scales, take an average, graduate, evaluate, size up, to place in the beam, to take into account, price.

(*Adjectives*). Measuring, etc., metrical, ponderable, measurable.

SECTION III.—MATERIALS FOR REASONING

467. EVIDENCE (*Substantives*) on one side, premises, data, *prœcognita*, indication (550).

Testimony, testimonial, deposition, declaration, attestation, testification, authority, warrant, warranty, guarantee, surety, handwriting, autograph, signature, endorsement, seal, sigil, signet, superscription, entry, finger-print.

Voucher, *pièce justificative*, credential, certificate, deed, indenture, docket, dossier, probate,

468. Evidence on the other side, on the other hand.

COUNTER-EVIDENCE (*Substantives*), disproof, contradiction, rejoinder, rebutter, answer (462), weak point, conflicting evidence, see Refutation (479).

(*Phrases*). A *tu quoque* argument; the other side of the shield.

(*Verbs*). To countervail, oppose, rebut, check, weaken, invalidate, contradict, contravene.

(*Phrase*). To tell another story.

(*Adjectives*). Countervailing,

affidavit, attestation, diploma; admission, concession, allegation, deposition, citation, quotation, reference; admissibility.

Criterion, test, reagent, touchstone, check, prerogative, fact, argument, shibboleth.

(*Phrases*). A case in point; *ecce signum*; *ex pede Herculem*; *ex ungue leonem*.

A witness, eye-witness, indicator, ear-witness, deponent, telltale, sponsor, special pleader.

Assumption, presumption, show of reason, postulation, postulate, lemma.

Reason, proof, *see* Demonstration (478), circumstantial evidence.

Ex-parte evidence, one-sided view.

Secondary evidence, confirmation, corroboration, ratification, support, approval.

(*Verbs*). To be evidence, etc., to evince, show, indicate (550), imply, involve, entail, necessitate, argue, admit, allow, concede, homologate, certify, testify, attest, bear testimony, depose, witness, vouch for, sign, seal, set one's hand and seal to, endorse, confirm, ratify, corroborate, support, bear upon, bear out, warrant, guarantee.

(*Phrases*). To hold good; hold water; to speak volumes; to speak for itself; tell its own tale.

To adduce, cite, quote, refer to, appeal to, call, bring forward, produce, bring into court, confront witnesses, collect, bring together, rake up evidence, to make a case, authenticate, substantiate, go bail for.

To allege, plead, assume, postulate, posit, presume; to beg the question.

(*Adjectives*). Showing, etc., indicating, indicative, indicatory, evidential, evidentiary, following, deducible, consequential, collateral, corroborative, confirmatory, good for.

Postulatory, presumptive.

Sound, logical, strong, valid, cogent, decisive, persuasive, persuasory, demonstrative, irrefragable, irresistible, etc. (578).

etc., contradictory, unattested, unvouched for.

(*Adverbs*). Although, though, but, *per contra*.

(*Phrase*). *Audi alteram partem.*

469. QUALIFICATION (*Substantives*), limitation, modification, allowance, grains of allowance, consideration, extenuating circumstance, condition, proviso, exception (83), assumption (514).

(*Verbs*). To qualify, limit, modify, tone down, discount, allow for, make allowance for, take into account, introduce new conditions, admit exceptions, take exception.

(*Adjectives*). Qualifying, etc., conditional, exceptional (83), postulatory, hypothetical.

(*Adverbs*). Provided, if, unless, but, yet, according as, conditionally, admitting, supposing; on the supposition, assumption, presumption, allegation, hypothesis, etc., of; with the understanding, even, although, for all that, at all events, after all.

(*Phrases*). With a grain of salt; *cum grano salis*; *exceptis excipiendis*.

(*Adverbs*). According to, witness, admittedly, confessedly, *à fortiori*, still more, still less, etc., *raison de plus*, all the more reason for.

Degrees of Evidence

470. POSSIBILITY (*Substantives*), potentiality, contingency, *see* Chance (156), what may be, what is possible, etc.

Practicability, feasibility (705), compatibility (23).

(*Verbs*). To be possible, etc., to admit of, to bear; may, may be, mayhap.

To render possible, etc., to put into the way of.

(*Adjectives*). Possible, contingent.

Practicable, feasible, achievable, attainable, obtainable, compatible.

(*Adverbs*). Possibly, by possibility, maybe, perhaps, *in posse* (156).

(*Phrases*). Wind and weather permitting; within the bounds of possibility; on the cards; D.V.

471. IMPOSSIBILITY (*Substantives*), what cannot be, what can never be, hopelessness (859), a dead lift.

Impracticability, incompatibility (704), incredibility.

(*Verbs*). To be impossible, etc., to have no chance whatever.

(*Phrases*). To make a silk purse out of a sow's ear; *prendre la lune avec les dents*; to square the circle; to eat one's cake and have it too.

(*Adjectives*). Impossible, contrary to reason, inconceivable, unreasonable, incredible, marvellous, desperate, hopeless, unheard of, unthinkable.

Impracticable, unattainable, unachievable, unfeasible, infeasible, beyond control, unobtainable, unprocurable, ideal.

(*Phrases*). Out of the question; sour grapes.

472. PROBABILITY (*Substantives*), likelihood, *vraisemblance*, verisimilitude, plausibility, a show of, credibility, reasonable chance, favourable chance, fair chance, presumptive evidence, circumstantial evidence, the main chance, a prima facie case.

Probabilism, probabiliorism.

(*Verb*). To be probable, etc.

(*Phrases*). To bid fair; to stand fair for; to stand a good chance; to stand to reason.

(*Adjectives*). Probable, likely, hopeful, well-founded.

(*Phrases*). Likely to happen; in a fair way; appearances favour-

473. IMPROBABILITY (*Substantives*), unlikelihood, unfavourable chances, small chance, off-chance, etc., incredibility.

(*Verbs*). To be improbable, etc., to have or stand a small, little, poor, etc., chance; to whistle for.

(*Adjectives*). Improbable, incredible, unlikely.

(*Phrases*). Contrary to all reasonable expectation; having scarcely a chance, etc.

ing; according to every reasonable expectation; the odds being in favour of.

Plausible, specious, ostensible, colourable, standing to reason, reasonable, credible, tenable, easy of belief, presumable, presumptive, *ben trovato*.

(*Adverbs*). Probably, etc., belike, in all probability, or likelihood, apparently, to all appearance, on the face of it, in the long run, *prima facie*, very likely, like enough, ten to one.

---

474. CERTAINTY (*Substantives*), certitude, positiveness, a dead certainty, infallibleness, infallibility, gospel, scripture, surety, assurance, indisputableness, moral certainty, *see* Truth (494).

Fact, matter of fact, *fait accompli*.

(*Verbs*). To be certain, etc., to believe (484).

(*Phrase*). To stand to reason.

To render certain, etc., to ensure, to assure.

(*Phrase*). To make assurance doubly sure.

(*Adjectives*). Certain, sure, assured, solid, absolute, positive, flat, determinate, categorical, unequivocal, inevitable, unavoidable, avoidless, unerring, infallible, indubitable, indubious, indisputable, undisputed, uncontested, undeniable, incontestable, incontrovertible, undoubted, doubtless, without doubt, beyond a doubt, past dispute, unanswerable, decided, unquestionable, beyond all question, unquestioned, questionless, demonstrable (478), authoritative, official, trustworthy (939).

(*Phrases*). Sure as fate; *à coup sûr*; sure as a gun; clear as the sun at noonday; sure as death and taxes; *cela va sans dire*; that's flat; a dead certainty.

(*Adverbs*). Certainly, assuredly,

475. UNCERTAINTY (*Substantives*), incertitude, *see* Doubt (485), doubtfulness, dubiety, dubiousness, suspense, precariousness, indefiniteness, indetermination, slipperiness, fallibility, perplexity, ambiguity, hesitation, equivoque, vagueness, peradventure, touch-and-go.

(*Phrases*). A blind bargain; a moot point; an open question.

(*Verbs*). To be uncertain, etc.

(*Phrases*). To be in a state of uncertainty; to be at fault; to lose the scent.

To render uncertain, etc., to perplex, embarrass, confuse, confound, bewilder, disorientate.

(*Phrases*). To tremble in the balance; to hang by a thread.

(*Adjectives*). Uncertain, doubtful, dubious, precarious (665), chancy, casual, random, contingent, indecisive, dependent on circumstances, undecided, pending, pendent, vague, indeterminate, indefinite, ambiguous, undefined, equivocal, undefinable, puzzling, enigmatic, questionable, apocryphal, problematical, hypothetical, controvertible, fallible, fallacious, suspicious, fishy, slippery, ticklish, debatable.

Unauthentic, unconfirmed, undemonstrated, undemonstrable.

---

etc., for certain, *in esse*, sure, surely, sure enough, of course, as a matter of course, yes (*see* 488), depend upon it, that's so, by all manner of means, beyond a peradventure.

Section IV.—Reasoning Processes

476. Reasoning (*Substantives*), ratiocination, dialectics, induction, generalisation.

Argumentation, discussion *pourparler*, controversy, polemics, debate, wrangling, logomachy, disputation, disceptation.

(*Phrases*). A paper war; a war of words; a full-dress debate.

The art of reasoning, logic, process, train or chain of reasoning, argument, lemma, proposition, terms, premises, postulate, data, starting - point, principle, inference, result, conclusion.

Syllogism, prosyllogism, enthymeme, sorites, dilemma, *perilepsis*, a comprehensive argument.

Correctness, soundness, force, validity, cogency, conclusiveness.

(*Phrases*). The horns of a dilemma; *onus probandi*.

A disputant, controversialist, wrangler, arguer, debater.

(*Verbs*). To reason, argue, discuss, debate, dispute, wrangle; bandy words or arguments; hold or carry on an argument, controvert, contravene, comment upon, moralise upon, spiritualise.

(*Phrases*). To open a discussion or case; to moot; to join issue; to stir, agitate, torture, or ventilate a question; to talk it over; to have it out; to take up a side or case.

To chop logic; to try conclusions; to impale on the horns of a dilemma; to cut the matter short; to have the last word.

(*Adjectives*). Reasoning, etc., argumentative, controversial, dialectic, polemical, discursory, discursive, debatable, contro-

477. The absence of reasoning. Intuition (*Substantives*), instinct, presentiment.

False or vicious reasoning, show of reason.

Sophistry (*Substantives*), paralogy, fallacy, perversion, casuistry, jesuitry, quibble, equivocation, evasion, chicanery, special pleading, quiddity, mystification.

Sophist, Jesuit, quibbler, casuist, *advocatus diaboli*.

(*Phrases*). Begging the question; *petitio principii*; *ignoratio elenchi*; reasoning in a circle; *post hoc, ergo propter hoc*; *non constat*; *non sequitur*.

Misjudgment, miscalculation (481).

Sophism, solecism, paralogism, quibble, elenchus, fallacy, quodlibet, subterfuge, subtlety, quillet, inconsistency, antilogy.

Speciousness, plausibility, illusiveness, irrelevancy, invalidity.

(*Phrases*). The meshes or cobwebs of sophistry; a flaw in an argument; an argument falling to the ground.

(*Verbs*). To envisage, to judge intuitively, etc.

To reason ill, falsely, etc.; to pervert, quibble, equivocate, mystify, evade, elude, gloss over, varnish, misjudge, miscalculate (481).

To refine, subtilise, sophisticate, mislead.

(*Phrases*). To split hairs; to cut blocks with a razor; throw off the scent; to beg the question; reason in a circle; beat about the bush; lose one's reckoning.

vertible, disputatious; correct, just, fair, sound, valid, cogent, logical, demonstrative (478), relevant, pertinent, subtle (9).

(*Phrases*). To the point; in point; to the purpose; *ad rem*; fine-spun.

Rem acu tetigisti.

(*Adverbs*). For, because, for that reason, forasmuch as, inasmuch as, whereas, considering, therefore, consequently, *ergo*, then, thus, accordingly, wherefore, *a fortiori, ex concesso*.

(*Phrases*). In consideration of; in conclusion; in fine; after all; *au bout du compte*; on the whole; taking one thing with another.

————

478. Demonstration (*Substantives*), proof, conclusiveness, probation, comprobation, *experimentum crucis*, test, etc. (463).

(*Verbs*). To demonstrate, prove, establish, show, evince, verify, substantiate.

(*Phrases*). Make good; set at rest; settle the question; reduce to demonstration; to make out a case; bring home to; bear out.

(*Adjectives*). Demonstrating, etc., demonstrative, probative, demonstrable, unanswerable, conclusive, final, apodictic (or apodeictic), irrefutable, irrefragable, unimpeachable, categorical, decisive, crucial.

Demonstrated, etc., unconfuted, unrefuted; evident, self-evident, axiomatic.

(*Phrases*). *Probatum est*; it

(*Adjectives*). Intuitive, instinctive, impulsive, independent of, or anterior to reason.

Sophistical, illogical, false, unsound, not following, inconsequent, unwarranted, untenable, inconclusive, incorrect, fallacious, groundless, fallible, unproved, indecisive, deceptive, illusive, illusory, specious, plausible, irrelevant.

(*Epithets*). Weak, feeble, poor, flimsy, trivial, trumpery, trashy, puerile, childish, irrational, silly, foolish, imbecile, absurd (499), extravagant, far-fetched, hair-splitting.

(*Phrases*). *Non constat*; *non sequitur*; not holding water; away from the point; foreign to the purpose or subject; having nothing to do with the matter; *nihil ad rem*; not bearing upon the point in question; not the point; beside the mark.

479. Confutation (*Substantives*), refutation, disproof, conviction, redargution, invalidation, exposure, exposition; demolition of an argument; a clincher, retort.

(*Phrases*). *Reductio ad absurdum*; a knock-down argument; a *tu quoque* argument.

(*Verbs*). To confute, refute, disprove, redargue, expose, show the fallacy of, knock the bottom out of, rebut, defeat, overthrow, demolish, explode, overturn, invalidate, silence, reduce to silence.

(*Phrases*). To clinch an argument or question; to give one a set-down.

(*Adjectives*). Confuting, etc., confuted, etc., capable of refutation, refutable, confutable, etc., exhaustive; unproved, etc.

stands to reason; there being nothing more to be said; *Q.E.D.*

(*Adverbs*). Of course, in consequence, consequently, as a matter of course, no wonder.

(*Phrases*). Having exhausted the subject; at the end of one's tether; *au bout de son Latin; cadit quæstio.*

SECTION V.—RESULTS OF REASONING

480. JUDGMENT (*Substantives*), conclusion, determination, deduction, inference, result, illation, corollary, consectary.

Estimation, valuation, appreciation, judication, arbitrament, arbitration, assessment, review, ponderation.

Decision, sentence, verdict, moral, finding; detection, discovery, estimate; *chose jugée.*

A judge, umpire, arbiter, arbitrator, assessor, censor, referee, reviewer.

(*Verbs*). To judge, deduce, conclude, draw a conclusion, infer, make a deduction, draw an inference, put two and two together; come to, arrive or jump at a conclusion; to derive, gather, collect.

To estimate, appreciate, value, count, assess, rate, account, rank, regard, review, settle, decide, pronounce, arbitrate, perpend, size up.

(*Phrases*). To sit in judgment; to hold the scales; to pass an opinion; to pass judgment.

To ascertain, determine, find, find out, make out, detect, discover, elicit, recognise, trace, get at; get or arrive at the truth; meet with, fall upon, light upon, hit upon, fall in with, stumble upon, pop upon, lay the finger on, smoke, spot, solve, resolve, unravel, fish out, worm out, ferret out, root out, nose out, disinter,

481. MISJUDGMENT (*Substantives*), obliquity of judgment, *see* Error (495), presumption.

Prejudgment, prejudication, prejudice, prenotion, *parti pris*, prevention, preconception, prepossession, preapprehension, presentiment, *esprit de corps*, party spirit, partisanship.

Bias, warp, twist, narrow-mindedness, bigotry, dogmatism, intolerance, tenacity, obstinacy (606), blind side; one-sided, partial, narrow or confined views, ideas, conceptions, or notions; *idée fixe*, fixed idea, obsession, monomania.

(*Verbs*). To misjudge, misestimate, misconceive, misreckon, etc., *see* 495.

To jump at a conclusion.

To prejudge, forejudge, prejudicate, dogmatise, have a bias, etc., presuppose, presume.

(*Phrases*). *Jurare in verba magistri*; to look only at one side of the shield; to view with jaundiced eye; to run away with the notion.

To produce a bias, twist, etc.; to bias, warp, twist, prejudice, etc.

(*Adjectives*). Prejudging, etc., prejudiced, jaundiced, narrow-minded, dogmatic, intolerant, besotted, infatuated, fanatical, *entêté*, positive, obstinate, tenacious, pig-headed, having a bias, twist, etc., warped, partial, one-sided, biased, tendentious, opin-

grub up, fish up, *see* Investigate (461).

To be near the truth, to burn.

(*Adjectives*). Judging, etc., deducible (467); impartial, unbiased, unprejudiced, unwarped, unbigoted, equitable, fair, sound, rational, judicious, shrewd.

(*Interjection*). *Eureka !*

482. OVERESTIMATION (*Substantive*), exaggeration.

(*Verbs*). To overestimate, estimate too highly, overrate, overvalue, overprize, overpraise, overweigh, outreckon; exaggerate, extol, make too much of, overstrain.

(*Phrase*). To set too high a value upon.

(*Adjectives*). Overestimated, etc.

ionated, opinionative, opinioned, self-opinioned, self-opinionated.

(*Phrase*). Wedded to an opinion.

483. UNDERESTIMATION (*Substantives*), depreciation, disparagement, detraction, underrating, undervaluing, etc.

(*Verbs*). To depreciate, disparage, detract, underrate, underestimate, undervalue, underreckon, underprize, misprize, not to do justice to, make light of, slight; make little, or make nothing of, hold cheap, cheapen, disregard, to care nothing for, despise, set at naught, minimise, discount, deride, derogate, decry, cry down, crab, denigrate, vilipend, run down (934).

To scout, deride, pooh-pooh, mock, scoff at, laugh at, whistle at, play with, trifle with, fribble, niggle, ridicule (856).

(*Phrases*). To snap one's fingers at; throw into the shade; not to care a pin, rush, etc., for; to damn with faint praise; *see* 643.

(*Adjectives*). Depreciating, etc., derogatory, cynical.
Depreciated, etc., unvalued, unprized.

484. BELIEF (*Substantives*), credence, faith, trust, troth, confidence, credit, dependence on, reliance, assurance.

Opinion, notion, idea (453), conception, apprehension, impression, conceit, mind, view, persuasion, conviction, convincement, sentiment, voice, judgment, estimation, self-conviction.

System of opinions, creed, doctrine, tenet, dogma, principle, articles of belief, way of thinking, popular belief, *vox populi*, public opinion, *esprit de corps*, partisanship; ism.

485. UNBELIEF (*Substantives*), disbelief, misbelief, discredit, agnosticism.

DOUBT, dubitation, scepticism, *diaporesis*, misgiving, demur, suspense; shade or shadow of doubt, distrust, mistrust, misdoubt, suspicion, shyness, embarrassment, hesitation, uncertainty (475), scruple, qualm, dilemma; casuistry, paradox; schism (489), incredulity (487).

(*Phrase*). Doubting Thomas.

(*Verbs*). To disbelieve, discredit, not to believe; refuse to admit, or believe; misbelieve,

Change of opinion (607), proselytism, propagandism (537).

A convert, pervert, vert.

(*Verbs*). To believe, credit, give faith to, give credit to, rely upon, make no doubt, reckon, doubt not, confide in, count upon, depend upon, calculate upon, take upon trust, swallow, gulp down, take one's word for, take upon credit, swear by.

To think, hold, take, look upon, take it, consider, esteem.

(*Phrases*). To pin one's faith to; to take at one's word.

To be of opinion, to opine, to have, hold, possess, entertain, adopt, imbibe, embrace, foster, nurture, cherish, etc., a notion, idea, opinion, etc.; to think, look upon, view, consider, take, take it, hold, trow, ween, conceive, fancy, apprehend, regard, esteem, deem, account; meseems, methinks.

(*Phrases*). To take it into one's head; to run away with the notion; to come round to an opinion.

To cause to be believed, thought, or esteemed; to satisfy, persuade, assure, convince, convert, bring over, win over, indoctrinate, proselytise, evangelise, *see* Teach (537); to vert.

(*Phrases*). To cram down the throat; to carry conviction; pass current; pass muster; to go down.

controvert; put or set aside; join issue, dispute, etc.

To doubt, be doubtful, etc., diffide, distrust, mistrust, suspect, smoke; have, harbour, entertain, etc., doubts; demur, stick at, pause, hesitate, scruple, question, query, call in question, look askant or askance.

(*Phrases*). Not to know what to make of; to smell a rat; to hang in doubt; to have one's doubts; to float in a sea of doubts.

To cause, raise, suggest, or start a doubt; to pose, stagger, floor, startle, embarrass, puzzle (704); shake, or stagger one's faith or belief.

(*Adjectives*). Unbelieving, etc., sceptical, shy of belief, at sea, at a loss (487, 491).

Doubting, etc., doubtful, dubious, scrupulous, suspicious; *see* Uncertain (475).

Unworthy or undeserving of belief, hard to believe, doubtful, dubious, unreliable, fishy, staggering, puzzling, etc., paradoxical, incredible, inconceivable.

(*Phrases*). With grains of allowance; *cum grano salis*; *fronti nulla fides*; *nimium ne crede colori*; *timeo Danaos et dona ferentes*; the cowl does not make the monk.

———

(*Adjectives*). Believing, etc., impressed with, imbued with, wedded to, unsuspecting, unsuspicious, void of suspicion, etc., credulous (486), convinced, etc.

Believed, etc., credited, accredited, unsuspected, received, current, popular.

Worthy or deserving of belief, commanding belief, believable, reliable, dependable, trustworthy (939), credible, *see* Probable (472), fiducial, fiduciary; relating to belief, doctrinal.

(*Epithets*). Firm, implicit, steadfast, fixed, rooted, deep-rooted, staunch, unshaken, inveterate; calm, sober, dispassionate, impartial.

(*Adverbs*). In the opinion of, in the eyes of, on the strength of, *me judice*.

486. CREDULITY (*Substantives*), credulousness, gullibility, infatuation, self-delusion, superstition, gross credulity, self-deception, dogmatism.

A credulous person, gull, *gobemouche* ; dupe (547).

(*Verbs*). To be credulous, etc., to follow implicitly, swallow, etc.

To impose upon, practise upon, palm upon, cajole, etc., see Deceive (545).

(*Phrases*). *Jurare in verba magistri* ; *credo quia absurdum* ; the wish being father to the thought.

(*Adjectives*). Credulous, gullible, easily deceived, cajoled, etc., green, verdant, superstitious, simple, unsuspicious, etc. (484), over-credulous, over-confident.

487. INCREDULITY (*Substantives*), scepticism, pyrrhonism, nihilism, suspicion (485), suspiciousness, scrupulousness, scrupulosity.

An unbeliever, sceptic, misbeliever,[1] pyrrhonist; nihilist.

(*Verbs*). To be incredulous, etc., to distrust, *see* 485.

(*Phrases*). Let those believe who may; tell that to the marines ; it won't wash ; *credat Judæus Apella.*

(*Adjectives*). Incredulous, hard of belief, sceptical, unbelieving, inconvincible, shy of belief, doubting, *see* 485.

soft, childish, silly, stupid,

---

488. ASSENT (*Substantives*), acquiescence, admission, assentation. nod, consent, concession, accord, accordance, agreement, concordance, concurrence, ratification, confirmation, recognition, acknowledgment, acceptance, granting, avowal, confession.

Unanimity, chorus; affirmation (535), common consent, consensus.

(*Verbs*). To assent, acquiesce, agree, yield assent, accord, concur, consent, nod assent, accept, coincide, go with, go along with, chime in with, strike in with, close with, conform with, defer to; say yes, amen, etc.

(*Phrase*). To go or be solid for.

To acknowledge, own, avow, confess, concede, subscribe to, admit, allow, recognise, grant, endorse, approve.

489. DISSENT (*Substantives*), dissidence, discordance, denial (536), dissonance, disagreement; difference or diversity of opinion, recusancy, contradiction, nonconformity, schism, secession; protest.

(*Phrases*). Shake of the head; shrug of the shoulders.

A dissentient, dissenter, nonconformist, recusant, heretic.

(*Verbs*). To dissent, demur, deny, disagree, refuse assent, say no, etc., ignore, protest, contradict, secede, refuse to admit.

(*Phrases*). To shake the head; to shrug the shoulders; to join issue; to give the lie; to differ *toto cælo*; to join issue.

(*Adjectives*). Dissenting, etc., dissentient, dissident, discordant, protestant, nonconforming,

---

[1] The word *miscreant*, which originally meant simply *misbeliever*, has now quite another meaning (949). *See* Trench, *On the Study of Words.*

(*Adjectives*). Assenting, etc., acquiescent, content, consentient, willing; approved, agreed; uncontradicted, unquestioned, uncontroverted.

(*Phrase*). Of one mind.

(*Adverbs*). Affirmatively, in the affirmative (535).

Yes, yea, ay, aye, well, very well, even so, just so, to be sure, all right, right oh! right you are, exactly, precisely, truly, certainly, certes, verily, very true (494), quite so, *ex concesso*.

Be it so, so be it, by all means, by all manner of means, *à la bonne heure*, amen, willingly, etc. (602).

Agreed, with one accord, *una voce*, unanimously, in chorus, with one voice, as one man, to a man, *nem. con.* or *nemine contradicente, nemine dissentiente, nemine discrepante, en bloc*, without a dissentient voice, one and all, on all hands.

recusant; unconvinced, unconverted, unavowed, unacknowledged, non-content.

Unwilling, reluctant, extorted, etc.

(*Adverbs*). Negatively, in the negative (536), at variance with.

No, nay, not, not so, not at all, nohow, nowise, not in the least, not a bit, not a whit, not a jot, by no means, by no manner of means, not for the world, on no account, in no respect.

(*Phrases*). Many men, many minds; *quot homines, tot sententiæ; tant s'en faut; nullius addictus jurare in verba magistri; il s'en faut bien.*

(*Interjections*). God forbid! forbid it, heaven! not if I know it! your humble servant! pardon me! I beg your pardon!

———

490. KNOWLEDGE (*Substantives*), cognisance, cognition, cognoscence, gnosis, acquaintance, ken, privity, insight, familiarity, comprehension, understanding, recognition; discovery (480), appreciation; knowability.

Intuition, clairvoyance, consciousness, conscience, perception, precognition, light, enlightenment, glimpse, inkling, glimmer, dawn, scent, suspicion; conception, notion, idea (453).

Self-consciousness, self-knowledge, apperception.

System or body of knowledge: science, philosophy, pansophy, pandect, doctrine, theory, ætiology, literature, *belles - lettres, literæ humaniores*, the humanities, humanism; ology.

Erudition, learning, lore,

491. IGNORANCE (*Substantives*), nescience, unacquaintance, unconsciousness, darkness, blindness, incomprehension, incognisance, inexperience, emptiness.

(*Phrases*). Crass ignorance; monumental ignorance; *tabula rasa; terra incognita.*

Imperfect knowledge, smattering, sciolism, glimmering; bewilderment, perplexity; incapacity.

Affectation of knowledge, pedantry, dilettantism.

(*Verbs*). To be ignorant, etc., not to know, to know not, to know not what, not to be aware of, to be at a loss, to be out of it, to be at fault, to ignore, to be blind to, etc., not to understand, etc.

(*Phrases*). To be caught trip-

scholarship, book-learning, book-ishness, bibliomania, education, instruction, information, acquisitions, acquirements, accomplishments, proficiency, cultivation, culture; a liberal education, encyclopædic knowledge, omniscience.

Elements, rudiments, abecedary (542), cyclopædia, encyclopædia, school, etc., academy.

Depth, extent, profoundness, profundity, stores, etc., solidity, accuracy, etc., of knowledge.

(*Phrases*). The march of intellect; the progress, advance, etc., of science; the schoolmaster being abroad.

(*Verbs*). To know, be aware of, ken, wot, ween, weet, trow, have, possess, perceive, conceive, apprehend, ideate, understand, comprehend, make out, recognise, be master of, know full well, possess the knowledge of, experience, discern, perceive, see, see through, have in one's head.

(*Phrases*). Connaître le dessous des cartes ; to know what's what; to know how the wind blows; to know the ropes; to have at one's finger-tips or -ends.

(*Adjectives*). Knowing, aware of, etc., cognisant of, acquainted with, privy to, conscious of, no stranger to, au fait, au courant, versed in, up in, up to, alive to, conversant with, proficient in, read in, familiar with.

(*Phrases*). Behind the scenes; in the know; at home in; the scales fallen from one's eyes.

Apprised of, made acquainted with, led into, informed of.

ping; not to know what to make of; to know nothing of; not to be able to make head or tail of; not to know a hawk from a handsaw; to lose one's bearings.

(*Adjectives*). Ignorant, unknowing, unconscious, unaware, unwitting, witless, a stranger to, unacquainted, unconversant, unenlightened, unilluminated, incognisant, unversed, uncultivated, in the dark.

Uninformed, uninstructed, untaught, unapprised, untutored, unschooled, unguided.

Shallow, superficial, green, verdant, rude, half-learned, illiterate, unread, uneducated, unlearned, uncultured, Philistine, unlettered, empty-headed, rude, having a smattering, etc., pedantic.

Confused, puzzled, bewildered, bemused, muddled, bemuddled, lost, benighted, belated, at sea, at fault, posed, blinded, abroad, distracted, in a maze, hoodwinked, in the dark, at a loss, désorienté, caught tripping.

(*Phrases*). Having a film over the eyes; au bout de son Latin ; having no idea of.

Unknown, novel, unapprehended, unexplained, unascertained, uninvestigated, unexplored, untravelled, uncharted, chartless, unheard of, unperceived, unknowable.

(*Adverbs*). Ignorantly, unwittingly, unawares; for anything one knows; for aught one knows.

(*Phrase*). A little knowledge is a dangerous thing.

————

Undeceived, unbenighted, unbigoted.

Erudite, instructed, learned, well-read, lettered, literate, educated, cultivated, cultured, knowledgeable, enlightened, well-informed, shrewd, bookish, scholastic, deep-read, clair-voyant; self-taught, well-grounded, well-conned.

Known, etc., recognised, received, notorious, proverbial, familiar; hackneyed, trite, commonplace; cognoscible, knowable; experiential.

Extensive, vast, encyclopædical, monumental, deep, profound, accurate, solid.

(*Adverbs*). To one's knowledge, to the best of one's knowledge.

(*Phrase*). *Experto crede.*

492. SCHOLAR (*Substantives*), savant, scientist, humanist, intellectual, pundit, schoolman, professor, lecturer, graduate, doctor, gownsman, philosopher, philomath, clerk, encyclopædist.

Linguist; *littérateur, literati, dilettanti, illuminati,* intelligentsia.

Pedant, pedagogue, bookworm, *helluo librorum,* bibliomaniac, blue - stocking, *bas - bleu,* highbrow, big-wig, bookman.

(*Phrases*). Man of letters; man of learning; at the feet of Gamaliel; a walking dictionary.

493. IGNORAMUS (*Substantives*), sciolist, smatterer, novice, greenhorn, half - scholar, schoolboy, booby, dunce (501); bigot (481); doctrinaire, ideologist, visionary; Philistine, obscurant, obscurantist.

(*Adjectives*). Bookless, shallow (499), ignorant, etc. (491), prejudiced (481), obscurantist.

---

494. Object of knowledge.

TRUTH (*Substantives*), verity, actual existence (1), reality, fact, matter of fact, actuality, nature, principle, orthodoxy, gospel, substantiality, genuineness, authenticity.

Accuracy, exactness, exactitude, precision, preciseness, nicety, delicacy, fineness, strictness, rigour, punctuality.

(*Phrases*). The plain truth; the honest truth; the naked truth; the sober truth; the very thing; a stubborn fact; not a dream, fancy, illusion, etc.; the exact truth, etc.; the real Simon Pure.

(*Verbs*). To be true, real, etc., to hold good.

To render true, legitimatise, legitimise, substantiate, realise, actualise; to make good, establish.

To get at the truth, *see* 480.

(*Phrases*). *Vitam impendere*

495. Untruth, *see* 546.

ERROR (*Substantives*), mistake, miss, fallacy, misconception, misapprehension, misunderstanding, inaccuracy, incorrectness, inexactness, misconstruction (523), miscomputation, miscalculation (481).

Fault, blunder, bull, bloomer, slip of the tongue, *lapsus linguæ,* Spoonerism, slip of the pen, equivoque, cross purposes, oversight, flaw, misprint, erratum; heresy, misstatement, misreport, bad shot.

Illusion, delusion, self-deceit, self-deception, hallucination, monomania, aberration; fable, dream, shadow, fancy, bubble, false light, the mists of error, will-o'-the-wisp, jack-o'-lantern, *ignis fatuus,* chimera, *maya.*

(*Verbs*). To be erroneous, false, etc., to cause error, to mislead, lead astray, lead into error,

vero ; magna est veritas et præ-valebit.

(*Adjectives*). True, real, verit-able, actual, certain, positive, absolute, existing (1), substantial, categorical, factual; unrefuted, unconfuted, unideal, unimagined.

Exact, accurate, definite, pre-cise, well-defined, just, correct, strict, hard-and-fast, literal, rigid, rigorous, scrupulous, conscienti-ous, religious, punctilious, nice, mathematical, axiomatic, de-monstrable, scientific, unerring, faithful, *bona fide*, curious, deli-cate, meticulous.

Genuine, authentic, legitimate, orthodox, official, *ex officio*, pure, sound, sterling, hall-marked, unsophisticated, unadulterated, unvarnished; solid, substantial, undistorted, undisguised, un-affected, unexaggerated, unro-mantic.

(*Phrases*). Just the thing; neither more nor less; to a hair.

(*Adverbs*). Truly, verily, verit-ably, troth, certainly, certes, assuredly, in truth, in good truth, of a truth, really, indubitably, in sooth, forsooth, in reality, in fact, in point of fact, as a matter of fact, strictly speaking, *de facto*, indeed, in effect, actually, *ipso facto*, positively, virtually, at bottom, *au fond.*

Precisely, accurately, *ad amussim*, etc., mathematically, to a nicety, to a hair, to a T, to an inch; to the letter, *au pied de la lettre.*

In every respect, in all respects, *sous tous les rapports*, at any rate, at all events, by all means.

(*Phrases*). Joking apart; in good earnest; in sober earnest; sooth to say; at the bottom of the well.

delude, give a false impression, idea, etc., to falsify, misstate, misrelate, misrepresent **(544)**, deceive (545), beguile.

To be in error, to mistake, to receive a false impression; to lie or labour under an error, mistake, etc., to blunder, be at fault, to misapprehend, mis-conceive, misunderstand, mis-remember, misreckon, miscalcu-late, miscount, misestimate, mis-judge, misthink, flounder, trip.

(*Phrases*). To take the shadow for the substance; to go on a fool's errand.

(*Adjectives*). Erroneous, un-true, false, unreal, unsubstantial, baseless, groundless, ungrounded, heretical.

Inexact, incorrect, illogical, partial, one-sided, unreasonable, absonous, absonant, indefinite, unscientific, inaccurate, aberrant.

In error, mistaken, etc., trip-ping, floundering, etc.

(*Phrases*). Wide of the mark; on the wrong scent; out of it; without a leg to stand upon.

Illusive, illusory, ideal, imagin-ary, fanciful, chimerical, vision-ary, shadowy, mock, futile.

Spurious, illegitimate, pseudo, bastard, meretricious, deceitful, sophisticated, adulterated.

---

496. MAXIM (*Substantives*), aphorism, apophthegm, dictum, saying, adage, gnome, saw, pro-verb, sentence, precept, rule,

497. ABSURDITY (*Substantives*), absurdness, nonsense, folly, para-dox, inconsistency, quibble, so-phism **(477)**, stultiloquy, stul-

formula, tag, code, motto, word, byword, moral, sentiment, phylactery, conclusion, reflection, thought, golden rule, axiom, theorem, scholium, lemma, truism.

Catechism, creed, profession of faith.

(*Adjectives*). Aphoristic, gnomic, proverbial, phylacteric, axiomatic, conclusive.

(*Epithets*). Wise, sage, true, received, admitted, recognised; common, hackneyed, trite, commonplace.

(*Phrase*). "Wise saws and modern instances."

———

tiloquence, bull, Irishism, Hibernicism, sciamachy, imbecility.

Jargon, gibberish, rigmarole, double-Dutch, galimatias, fustian, rant, bombast, bathos, amphigouri, rhapsody, extravagance, rodomontade, romance; nonsense verse, Limerick.

Twaddle, twattle, fudge, rubbish, piffle, verbiage, trash, truism, stuff, balderdash, slipslop, *bavardage*, palaver, *baragouin*, moonshine, fiddlestick, wish-wash, platitude, *niaiserie*, flummery, inanity, fiddle-faddle, rot, tommy-rot, bosh, tosh, blether, tripe, bilge.

Vagary, foolery, tomfoolery, mummery, monkey-trick, *boutade*, lark, escapade, rag.

(*Phrases*). A cock-and-bull story; a mare's nest; a wild-goose chase; "a tale told by an idiot, full of sound and fury, signifying nothing"; clotted nonsense; arrant rot.

(*Adjectives*). Absurd, nonsensical, foolish, etc. (*see* 499), sophistical, inconsistent, extravagant, cock-and-bull, quibbling, trashy, washy, wishy-washy, twaddling, etc.; topsyturvy, Gilbertian.

498. INTELLIGENCE (*Substantives*), capacity, nous, parts, talent, sagacity, sagaciousness, wit, mother-wit, *esprit*, gumption, quick parts, grasp of intellect.

Acuteness, acumen, shrewdness, astuteness, arguteness, sharpness, aptness, aptitude, quickness, receptiveness, subtlety, archness, penetration, perspicacity, perspicaciousness, clear-sightedness, discrimination, discernment, flair, refinement.

Head, brains, head-piece, a long head.

WISDOM, sapience, sense, good sense, common sense, plain sense, horse-sense, reason, reasonableness, judgment, judiciousness, solidity, depth, profoundness, catholicity, breadth of view, en-

499. IMBECILITY (*Substantives*), incapacity, vacancy of mind, poverty of intellect, shallowness, dullness, stupidity, asininity, obtuseness, stolidity, hebetude, doltishness, muddle-headedness, vacuity, short-sightedness, incompetence.

Silliness, simplicity, childishness, puerility, babyhood; dotage, second childhood, fatuity, idiocy, idiotism (503).

FOLLY, absurdity, infatuation, irrationality, senselessness, foolishness, inconsistency, lipwisdom, conceit, giddiness, extravagance, oddity, eccentricity, ridiculousness, desipience.

Act of folly (497), imprudence (699), rashness, fanaticism.

(*Phrases*). The fool's para-

larged views, reach or compass of thoughts.

Genius, inspiration, the fire of genius.

Wisdom in action: prudence, discretion, aplomb (698), sobriety, tact, ballast.

(*Phrase*). Discretion being the better part of valour.

(*Verbs*). To be intelligent, wise, etc., to reason (476), to discern (441), discriminate (465), to penetrate, to see far into.

(*Adjectives*). Applied to persons: Intelligent, sagacious, receptive, quick, sharp, acute, shrewd, gumptious, canny, astute, sharp-sighted, quick-sighted, quick-eyed, keen, keen-eyed, keen-sighted, keen-witted, sharp-witted, needle-witted, penetrating, piercing, clear-sighted, discerning, discriminating, discriminative, clever, knowledgeable.

Wise, sage, sapient, sagacious, reasonable, rational, sound, common-sense, sane, sensible, judicious, judgmatic, enlightened, impartial, catholic, broad-minded, open-minded, unprejudiced, unbiased, unprepossessed, undazzled, unperplexed, judicial, progressive.

Cool, cool-headed, long-headed, long-sighted, calculating, thoughtful, reflective, oracular, heaven-directed, heaven-born.

Prudent, discreet, sober, staid, solid, considerate, provident, politic, diplomatic, tactful.

(*Phrases*). Wise as a serpent; wise as Solomon; wise as Solon.

Applied to actions: Wise, sensible, reasonable, judicious, well-judged, well-advised, prudent, prudential, politic (646), expedient.

———

dise; one's wits going wool-gathering; *mentis gratissimus error*.

(*Verbs*). To be imbecile, foolish, etc., to trifle, drivel, ramble, dote, *radoter*, blether; to fool, to monkey, to footle.

(*Phrases*). To play the fool; to play the giddy goat; to make an ass of oneself; to go on a fool's errand; to pursue a wild-goose chase; *battre la campagne*; to strain at a gnat; to reckon without one's host; to quarrel with one's bread and butter; *semel insanivimus omnes*; *aliquando bonus dormitat Homerus*.

(*Adjectives*). Applied to persons: Unintelligent, unintellectual, witless, reasonless, imbecile, shallow, *borné*, weak, soft, sappy, spoony, weak-headed, weak-minded, feeble-minded, half-witted, short-witted, half-baked, not all there, shallow-pated, shallow-brained, dull, stupid, heavy, obtuse, stolid, doltish, asinine, addle-headed, dull-witted, blunt, dull-brained, dim-sighted, vacuous.

Childish, infantine, infantile, babyish, childlike, puerile, callow; anile.

Fatuous, idiotic, lack-brained, drivelling, blatant, brainless, blunt-witted, beef-witted, fat-witted, fat-headed, insulse, having no head or brains, thick-skulled, blockish, Bœotian.

Foolish, silly, senseless, irrational, insensate, nonsensical, blunder-headed, chuckle-headed, puzzle-headed, muddle-headed, muddy-headed, undiscerning, unenlightened, unphilosophical; prejudiced, bigoted, purblind, narrow-minded, wrong-headed, tactless, crotchety, conceited, self-opinionated, pig-headed, mulish, unprogressive, one-ideaed, stick-in-the-mud, besotted, infatuated, unreasoning.

Wild, giddy, thoughtless, eccentric, odd, extravagant, quixotic, light-headed, rantipole, high-flying, crack-brained, cracked, cranky, hare-brained, scatter-brained, scatter-pated, unballasted, ridiculous, frivolous, balmy.

Applied to actions: Foolish, unwise, injudicious, improper, imprudent, unreasonable, nonsensical, absurd, ridiculous, silly, stupid, asinine, ill-imagined, ill-advised, ill-judged, ill-devised, tactless, inconsistent, irrational, unphilosophical, extravagant, preposterous, egregious, imprudent, indiscreet, improvident, impolitic, improper (645, 647), footling.

(*Phrases*). Without rhyme or reason; penny-wise and pound-foolish.

---

500. Sage (*Substantives*), wise man, *savant*, expert, luminary, adept, authority.

Oracle, a shining light, *esprit fort*, intellectual, high-brow, pundit, academist, academician, philomath, schoolman, magi, a *Magnus Apollo*, a Solomon, Nestor, Solon, a second Daniel.

(*Epithets*). Venerable, reverend, authoritative.

(*Phrase*). "A Daniel come to judgment."

(*Ironically*). Wiseacre, big-wig.

---

501. Fool (*Substantives*), blockhead, idiot, tom-fool, wise-acre (ironically), simpleton, witling, ass, goose, ninny, dolt, booby, noodle, muff, mug, muggins, juggins, owl, cuckoo, numskull, noddy, goose-cap, half-wit, imbecile, ninnyhammer, *badeau*, driveller, idiot, cretin, natural, lack-brain, *niais*, child, infant, baby, innocent, greenhorn, zany, dunce, lout, loon, oaf, lown, dullard, duffer, doodle, calf, colt, buzzard, block, stick, stock, numps, clod-poll, clot-poll, clod-hopper, clod, lubber, bull-calf, bull-head, fat-head, thick-skull,

dunderhead, addle-head, dizzard, hoddydoddy, looby, nincompoop, a poor head, *un sot à triple étage*, loggerhead, sot, jolthead, shallow-brain, jobbernowl, changeling, dotard, driveller, moon-calf, giddy-head, *gobe-mouche*, rantipole, muddler, stick-in-the-mud, old woman, April fool, Cyclops.

(*Phrases*). One who is not likely to set the Thames on fire; one who did not invent gunpowder; one who is no conjuror; *qui n'a pas inventé la poudre*; who could not say "Boh" to a goose; one with his upper story to let.

Men of Gotham; men of Bœotia.

---

502. Sanity (*Substantives*), rationality, being in one's senses, in one's right mind, in one's sober senses; sobriety, lucidity, lucid interval.

(*Verbs*). To be sane, etc.,

503. Insanity (*Substantives*), lunacy, madness, unsoundness, derangement, psychosis, alienation, aberration, dementia, paranoia, mania, calenture, frenzy, raving, monomania, megalo-

to retain one's senses, reason, etc.

To become sane, come to one's senses, sober down.

To render sane, bring to one's senses, to sober.

(*Adjectives*). Sane, rational, reasonable, *compos*, in one's sober senses, in one's right mind, sober-minded.

(*Adverbs*). Sanely, soberly, etc.

———

mania, disordered intellect, incoherence, wandering, delirium, hallucination, lycanthropy, vertigo, dizziness, swimming, dementation; Bedlam.

(*Verbs*). To be or become insane, etc., to lose one's senses, wits, reason, faculties, etc., to run mad, run amuck, go off one's head, rave, dote, ramble, wander, drivel.

(*Phrases*). *Battre la campagne ; avoir le diable au corps.*

To render, or drive mad; to madden, dementate, turn the brain, addle the wits, turn one's head, befool, infatuate, craze.

(*Adjectives*). Insane, mad, lunatic, crazy, crazed, *non compos*, cracked, cranky, of unsound or abnormal mind, touched, deficient, out of one's mind, off one's head or nut, bereft of reason, unsettled in one's mind, unhinged, insensate, reasonless, beside oneself, demented, daft, dotty, possessed, maddened, moonstruck, mad-brained, maniacal, delirious, incoherent, rambling, doting, doited, wandering, frantic, phrenetic, paranoiac, raving, corybantic, dithyrambic, rabid, light-headed, giddy, vertiginous, wild, haggard, flighty, distracted, distraught, hag-ridden, *écervelé*, *tête montée.*

(*Phrases*). The head being turned; having a bee in one's bonnet; far gone; stark staring mad; mad as a March hare; the devil being in one; dizzy as a goose; candidate for Bedlam; like one possessed.

The wits going wool-gathering, or bird's-nesting.

504. MADMAN (*Substantives*), lunatic, maniac, bedlamite, energumen, raver, monomaniac, dreamer, visionary, a high-flier, madcap, megalomaniac, psychopath, *malade imaginaire*, crank, mænad.

SECTION VI.—EXTENSION OF THOUGHT

1°. *To the Past*

505. MEMORY (*Substantives*), remembrance, reminiscence, recognition, anamnesis, retention, retentiveness, readiness, tenacity.

Recurrence, recollection, retrospection, retrospect.

(*Phrase*). The tablets of the memory.

506. OBLIVION (*Substantives*), forgetfulness, amnesia, obliteration (552), a short memory, the memory failing, being in fault, or deserting one, the waters of Lethe, Nepenthe, *tabula rasa.*

(*Verbs*). To forget, lose, unlearn, discharge from the memory.

Suggestion (514), hint.

Token of remembrance: memorial, memento, souvenir, keepsake, relic, reliquary, memorandum, remembrancer, flapper.

Things to be remembered, *memorabilia.*

Art of memory, artificial memory, mnemonics; Mnemosyne.

(*Verbs*). To remember, retain, mind, bear or keep in mind, have or carry in the memory, know by heart or by rote; recognise.

To be deeply impressed, to live, remain, or dwell in the memory, to be stored up, bottled up, to sink in the mind, to rankle, etc.

To slip, escape, fade, die away from the memory, to sink into oblivion.

(*Phrases*). To cast behind one's back; to have a short memory; to have no head: to apply the sponge; *non mi ricordo*; let bygones be bygones.

(*Adjectives*). Forgotten, etc., lost, effaced, blotted out, obliterated, discharged, sponged out, buried or sunk in oblivion, clean out of one's head or recollection, past recollection, unremembered.

Forgetful, oblivious, mindless, out of mind.

———

(*Phrases*). To have at one's fingers' ends; *manet alta mente repostum*; *olim meminisse juvabit.*

To occur to the mind (514), recollect, call to mind, bethink oneself, recall, call up, retrace, carry one's thoughts back, look back, rake up, brush up, think upon, call to remembrance, tax the memory.

To suggest, prompt, hint, recall to mind, put in mind, remind, whisper, call up, summon up, renew, commend to.

(*Phrases*). Jog or refresh the memory; pull by the sleeve; bring back to the memory; to lash the memory; to keep the memory alive; to keep the wound green; to reopen old sores; put in remembrance; *infandum renovare dolorem*; *tangere ulcus.*

To say by heart, repeat by rote, say one's lesson, repeat as a parrot.

To commit to memory, get or learn by heart or rote, memorise, con, con over, repeat, to fix, imprint, impress, stamp, grave, engrave, store, treasure up, bottle up, embalm, enshrine, etc., in the memory; to load, store, stuff, or burden the memory with.

(*Adjectives*). Remembering, etc., mindful, remembered, etc., fresh, green, unforgotten, present to the mind, living in, being in, or within one's memory, indelible, ineffaceable, green in remembrance, reminiscential.

(*Epithets*). The memory being retentive, ready, correct, exact, faithful, trustworthy, capacious, encyclopædic.

(*Adverbs*). By heart, by rote, *memoriter*, without book.

2°. To the Future

507. EXPECTATION (*Substantives*), expectance, anticipation, forestalling, foreseeing (510); reckoning, calculation.

Contemplation, prospect, perspective, hope, trust (858), abeyance, waiting, etc. (121).

(*Verbs*). To expect, look for, look out for, look forward to, anticipate, contemplate, flatter oneself, to dare to say, foresee (510), forestall, reckon upon, count upon, lay one's account to, to calculate upon, rely upon, build upon, make sure of, prepare oneself for, not to wonder at.

(*Phrase*). To count one's chickens before they are hatched.

To wait, tarry, lie in wait, watch for, abide, to bide one's time.

To hold out, raise, or excite expectation, to bid fair, to promise, to augur, etc. (511); we shall see, *nous verrons*.

(*Phrase*). To have in store for.

(*Adjectives*). Expectant, expecting, etc., prepared for, gaping for, ready for, agog.

Expected, anticipated, foreseen, etc., long expected; in prospect; anxious, ardent, eager, breathless, sanguine.

(*Adverbs*). With breathless expectation, on tenter-hooks.

(*Phrases*). On the tiptoe of expectation; looming in the distance; the wish father to the thought.

508. INEXPECTATION (*Substantives*), non-expectation; *see* Surprise (870).

False or vain expectation, miscalculation.

(*Phrase*). A bolt from the blue.

(*Verbs*). Not to expect, not to look for, etc., to be taken by surprise, to come upon, to fall upon, not to bargain for, to miscalculate.

(*Phrases*). To reckon without one's host; to trust to a broken reed.

To be unexpected, etc., to crop up, pop up, to come unawares, suddenly, abruptly, like a thunderbolt, burst upon, bounce upon, startle.

(*Phrase*). To drop from the clouds.

(*Adjectives*). Non - expectant, unexpected, unanticipated, unlooked for, unhoped for, unforeseen, beyond expectation, abrupt, sudden, contrary to or against expectation, unannounced, unheralded; backhanded.

Surprised, taken by surprise, unwarned, startled, etc., taken aback.

(*Adverbs*). Suddenly, abruptly, unexpectedly, plump, pop, *à l'improviste*, unawares, without notice or warning (113).

509. Failure of expectation.

DISAPPOINTMENT (*Substantives*), vain expectation, surprise, astonishment (870).

(*Phrase*). "There's many a slip 'twixt cup and lip."

A balk, an afterclap, a miscalculation.

(*Verbs*). To be disappointed, etc., to miscalculate; to look blank, to look blue, to look aghast.

To disappoint, balk, let down, dumbfound, dash one's hope (859), sell.

(*Adjectives*). Disappointed, aghast, blue.

Happening contrary to or against expectation.

(*Phrases*). *Rusticus exspectat*, etc.; *dis aliter visum*; *parturiunt montes, nascetur ridiculus mus*.

510. FORESIGHT (*Substantives*), prospiscience, prescience, foreknowledge, forethought, forecast, prevision, prognosis, precognition, second-sight, clairvoyance.

Anticipation, foretaste, prenotion, presentiment, foregone conclusion, providence, sagacity.

Announcement, prospectus, programme.

(*Verbs*). To foresee, foreknow, forejudge, forecast, anticipate, look forwards or beyond, look, peep, or pry into the future.

(*Phrase*). To keep a sharp look out for.

(*Adjectives*). Foreseeing, etc., prescient, weather-wise, far-sighted, far-seeing; rational, sagacious, perspicacious.

511. PREDICTION [1] (*Substantives*), announcement, prognosis, prophecy, vaticination, mantology, prognostication, haruspicy, auguration, bodement, omination, augury, foreboding, abodement, aboding, horoscope, nativity, genethliacs, fortune - telling, palmistry, soothsaying, ominousness, *see* Necromancy (992).

Place of prediction: adytum, tripod.

(*Verbs*). To predict, prognosticate, prophesy, vaticinate, presage, augur, bode, forebode, foretell, croak, soothsay, auspicate.

To foretoken, betoken, prefigure, portend, foreshadow, foreshow, usher in, herald, signify, premise, announce, point to, lour, admonish, warn, forewarn, advise.

(*Adjectives*). Predicting, etc., predictive, prophetic, fatidical, vaticinal, oracular, Sibylline.

[1] Divination:—By oracles; Theomancy. By the Bible; Bibliomancy. By the stars; Astrology, Sideromancy, Horoscopy, Judicial Astrology. By ghosts; Psychomancy. By spirits seen in a magic lens; Crystallomancy. By shadows or manes; Sciomancy. By appearances in the air; Aeromancy, Chaomancy. By meteors; Meteoromancy. By winds; Austromancy. By sacrificial appearances; Aruspicy (or Haruspicy), Hieromancy, Hieroscopy. By the entrails of animals sacrificed; Hieromancy. By the entrails of a human sacrifice; Anthropomancy. By the entrails of fishes; Ichthyomancy. By sacrificial fire; Pyromancy. By smoke from the altar; Capnomancy. By mice; Myomancy. By birds; Ornithomancy. By herbs; Botanomancy. By water; Hydromancy. By fountains; Pegomancy. By a wand; Rhabdomancy. By dough of cakes; Crithomancy. By meal; Aleuromancy. By salt; Halomancy. By dice; Cleromancy. By arrows; Belomancy. By a balanced hatchet; Axinomancy. By a balanced sieve; Coscinomancy. By a suspended ring; Dactyliomancy. By dots made at random on paper; Geomancy. By precious stones; Lithomancy. By nails reflecting the sun's rays; Onychomancy. By names; Onomancy. By pebbles; Pessomancy. By pebbles drawn from a heap; Psephomancy. By mirrors; Catoptromancy. By writings in ashes; Tephramancy. By dreams; Oneiromancy. By the hand; Palmistry, Chiromancy. By numbers; Arithmancy. By the letters forming the name of the person; Onomancy, or Nomancy. By the mode of laughing; Geloscopy. By ventriloquism; Gastromancy. By walking in a circle; Gyromancy. By a cock picking up grains; Alectryomancy (or Alectoromancy).

Ominous, portentous, augural, auspicious, monitory, premonitory, significant of, pregnant with, weatherwise, bodeful.

(*Phrase*). "Coming events cast their shadows before."

512. OMEN (*Substantives*), portent, presage, prognostic, augury, auspice, sign, forerunner, precursor (64), harbinger, herald, monition, warning, avant-courier, pilot-balloon, handwriting on the wall, rise and fall of the barometer, a bird of ill omen, a sign of the times.

513. ORACLE (*Substantives*), prophet, seer, soothsayer, fortune-teller, palmist, gipsy, witch, geomancer, Sibyl, Python, Pythoness, *Pythia*, Pythian oracle, Old Moore, Zadkiel, Mother Shipton, haruspex, Sphinx, Tiresias, Cassandra, Œdipus.

SECTION VII.—CREATIVE THOUGHT

514. SUPPOSITION (*Substantives*), conjecture, surmise, presurmise, guess, guess-work, shot, divination, conceit; assumption, postulation, hypothesis, presupposition, postulate, *postulatum*, presumption, theory; suggestion, allusion, proposition, motion, proposal, allusion, insinuation, innuendo.

(*Phrases*). A rough guess; a lucky shot.

(*Verbs*). To suppose, conjecture, surmise, guess, divine, theorise, give a guess, make a shot, hazard a conjecture, throw out a conjecture, etc., presuppose, fancy, wis, take it, dare to say, take it into one's head, assume, postulate, posit, presume, presurmise.

To suggest, hint, insinuate, put forth, propound, propose, start, allude to, prompt, put a case, move, make a motion.

(*Phrase*). To put it into one's head.

To suggest itself, occur to one, come into one's head; to run in the head; to haunt (505).

(*Phrase*). "Thereby hangs a tale."

(*Adjectives*). Supposing, etc., supposed, supposititious, suppositive, putative, suggestive, allusive, conjectural, presumptive, hypothetical, theoretical, warranted, authorised, given, fair, reasonable, just, natural, conjecturable, supposable.

Unwarranted, gratuitous, baseless, wild, hazardous, rash, untenable, extravagant, unreasonable, unauthorised, unsatisfactory, loose, vague, unconnected.

(*Adverbs*). If, if so be, an, maybe, perhaps, on the supposition, *ex hypothesi, quasi*.

515. IMAGINATION (*Substantives*), fancy, conception, ideality, idealism, inspiration, afflatus, verve, dreaming, somnambulism, frenzy, ecstasy, excogitation, liveliness of fancy, reverie, *Schwärmerei*, trance, vision; Pegasus.

(*Phrases*). Flight of fancy; fumes of fancy; fine frenzy; thick-coming fancies; coinage of the brain; the mind's eye; castle-building; a stretch of imagination; "such stuff as dreams are made on."

Invention, inventiveness, originality, fertility, conceit, maggot, figment, coinage, fiction, romance, novel (594), myth, Arabian Nights, fairyland, the man in the moon, dream, day-dream, vapour, phantom, phantasy, fantasia, whim, whimsy, vagary, rhapsody, extravaganza, air-drawn dagger, bugbear, men in buckram, castle in the air, air-built castle, castle in Spain, will-o'-the-wisp, ignis fatuus, jack-o'-lantern, Utopia, Atlantis, millennium, *fata Morgana* (443).

A visionary, romancer, rhapsodist, high-flyer, enthusiast, idealist, energumen, dreamer, seer, fanatic, knight-errant, Don Quixote.

(*Verbs*). To imagine, fancy, conceive, ideate, idealise, realise, objectify; fancy or picture to oneself; create, originate, devise, invent, coin, fabricate, make up, mint.

(*Phrases*). To take into one's head; to figure to oneself; to strain or crack one's invention; to strike out something new; to give a loose to the fancy; to give the reins to the imagination; to set one's wits to work; to rack or cudgel one's brains.

(*Adjectives*). Imagining, imagined, etc.; ideal, unreal, unsubstantial, imaginary, *in nubibus*, fabulous, fictitious, *ben trovato*, fanciful, air-drawn, air-built, original, fantastic, fantastical, whimsical, high-flown.

Imaginative, inventive, creative, fertile, romantic, flighty, extravagant, high-flown, fanatic, enthusiastic, Utopian, Quixotic.

Warm, heated, excited, sanguine, ardent, fiery, boiling, wild, bold, daring; playful, fertile, etc., imagination or fancy.

DIVISION II.—COMMUNICATION OF IDEAS

SECTION I.—NATURE OF IDEAS COMMUNICATED

516. Idea to be conveyed.

MEANING (*Substantives*), signification, sense, import, purport, significance, drift, gist, acceptation, acceptance, bearing, interpretation (522), reading, tenor, allusion, spirit, colouring, expression.

Literal meaning, literality, obvious meaning, grammatical sense, first blush, *prima facie* meaning; after-acceptation.

Equivalent meaning, synonym, synonymity.

Thing signified: matter, substance, pith, marrow, argument, text.

517. Absence of meaning.

UNMEANINGNESS (*Substantives*), empty sound, a dead letter, inexpressiveness, vagueness (519).

Nonsense, gibberish, rubbish, rot, *see* Absurdity (497), empty babble, empty sound, verbiage, *nugæ*, truism.

(*Verbs*). To mean nothing, to be unmeaning, etc.

(*Adjectives*). Unmeaning, void of meaning, of sense, etc., senseless, not significant, undefined, tacit, not expressed.

Inexpressible, indefinable, undefinable, unmeant, unconceived.

(*Phrases*). *Vox et præterea*

(*Verbs*). To mean, signify, express, import, purport, convey, breathe, imply, bespeak, bear a sense, involve, declare (527), insinuate, allude to, point to, drive at; to come to the point, give vent to; to stand for.

To take, understand, receive, or accept in a particular sense.

(*Adjectives*). Meaning, etc., significant, significative, significatory, pithy, pointed, epigrammatic, telling, striking, full of meaning, pregnant with meaning.

Synonymous, equivalent, tantamount; the same thing as.

(*Epithets*). Plain, simple, natural, *prima facie*, obvious, explicit, precise, downright, definite, distinct, defined, literal, ostensible, overt, broad, naked, unstrained, undisguised, positive, formal, honest, emphatic, *bona fide*, true.

Implied, tacit, understood, implicit, inferred, latent.

(*Adverbs*). Literally, etc., *videlicet* (522).

(*Phrases*). *Au pied de la lettre*; so to speak; so to express oneself; as it were; that is to say; *façon de parler*.

nihil; "a tale told by an idiot, full of sound and fury, signifying nothing"; "sounding brass and tinkling cymbal."

(*Adverb*). Tacitly.

---

518. INTELLIGIBILITY (*Substantives*), clearness, lucidity, perspicacity, explicitness, distinctness, plain speaking, expressiveness, legibility, visibility (446).

(*Phrases*). A word to the wise; *verbum sapienti*.

Intelligence, comprehension, understanding, learning (539).

(*Verbs*). To be intelligible, etc.

To render intelligible, etc., to simplify, to throw light upon.

(*Phrases*). *Cela saute aux yeux*; he who runs may read; to stand to reason; to speak for itself.

To understand, comprehend, take, take in, catch, catch on to, twig, get the hang of, grasp, collect; master, tumble to.

(*Phrases*). To come to an understanding; to see with half an eye.

(*Adjectives*). Intelligible, clear, lucid, understandable, explicit, expressive, significant, express, distinct, precise, definite, well-defined, perspicuous, transpicuous, striking, plain, obvious,

519. UNINTELLIGIBILITY (*Substantives*), incomprehensibility, inconceivability, darkness (421), obscurity, confusion, perplexity, *imbroglio*, indistinctness, mistiness, indefiniteness, vagueness, ambiguity, looseness, uncertainty, mysteriousness (526), paradox, inexplicability, incommunicability, spinosity.

Jargon, gibberish, rigmarole, rodomontade, etc. (497).

(*Phrases*). *Obscurum per obscurius; lucus a non lucendo.*

High Dutch, Greek, Hebrew, etc.

(*Verbs*). To be unintelligible, etc., to pass comprehension.

To render unintelligible, etc., to perplex, confuse, confound, bewilder, darken, moither.

Not to understand, etc., to lose, miss, etc., to lose the clue.

(*Phrases*). Not to know what to make of; not to be able to make either head or tail of; to play at cross purposes; to beat about the bush.

manifest, palpable, glaring, transparent, above-board, unambiguous, unmistakable, legible, open, positive, unconfused, unequivocal, pronounced, graphic, readable.

(*Phrases*). Clear as day; clear as noonday; not to be mistaken; plain as a pikestaff; in plain English.

(*Adjectives*). Unintelligible, incognisable, inapprehensible, incomprehensible, inconceivable, unimaginable, unknowable, above or past or beyond comprehension, inexplicable, illegible, undecipherable, inscrutable, beyond one's depth, paradoxical, insoluble, impenetrable.

Obscure, dark, confused, indistinct, indefinite, misty, nebulous, indefinite, undefined, ill-defined, perplexed, loose, vague, ambiguous, disconnected, incoherent, unaccountable, enigmatical, hieroglyphic, mysterious, mystic, mystical, intricate, at cross purposes.

Hidden, recondite, abstruse, crabbed, transcendental, far-fetched, *in nubibus*, searchless, unconceived, unimagined.

(*Phrases*). Greek to one; without rhyme or reason; *obscurum per obscurius*.

520. Having a double sense.

EQUIVOCALNESS (*Substantives*), double meaning, quibble, equivoque, equivocation, *double-entendre*, amphibology, prevarication, tergiversation, slip of the tongue, *lapsus linguæ*, a pun, play on words.

Having a doubtful meaning, ambiguity (*see* 475), homonymy.

Having a false meaning (*see* 544), *suggestio falsi*.

(*Verbs*). To be equivocal, etc., to have two senses, etc., to equivocate, prevaricate, tergiversate, palter to the understanding, to pun.

(*Adjectives*). Equivocal, ambiguous, amphibolous, amphibological, double-tongued, double-edged, left-handed, equivocatory, paltering.

(*Adverb*). Over the left.

521. METAPHOR (*Substantives*), figure, metonymy, trope, catachresis, synecdoche, figure of speech, figurativeness, image, imagery, metalepsis, type (22), symbol, symbolism (550), tropology.

Personification, prosopopœia, allegory, apologue, parable.

Implication, inference, allusion, adumbration, hidden meaning.

Allegorist, tropist, symbolist.

(*Verbs*). To employ metaphor, etc., to personify, allegorise, adumbrate, shadow forth, imply, understand, apply, allude to.

(*Adjectives*). Metaphorical, figurative, catachrestical, typical, tropical, parabolic, allegorical, allusive, symbolic (550), symbolistic, implied, inferential, implicit, understood.

(*Phrases*). Where more is meant than meets the ear; *façon de parler*; in a Pickwickian sense.

522. INTERPRETATION (*Substantives*), exegesis, explanation, explication, expounding, exposition, rendition, reddition.

523. MISINTERPRETATION (*Substantives*), misapprehension, misunderstanding, misacceptation, misconstruction, misspelling,

Translation, version, rendering, construction, reading, spelling, restoration, metaphrase, paraphrase.

Comment, commentary, inference, illustration, exemplification, definition, *éclaircissement*, elucidation, crib, gloss, glossary, annotation, *scholium*, marginalia, note, clue, key, side-light, master-key (631), rationale, *dénouement*, answer (462), object-lesson.

Palæography, dictionary, glossology, etc. (562), semasiology, oneirocritics, oneirocriticism, hermeneutics.

(*Verbs*). To interpret, expound, explain, clear up, construe, translate, render, do into, turn into, transfuse the sense of.

To read, spell, make out, decipher, decode, unfold, disentangle, elicit the meaning of, make sense of, find the key of, unriddle, unravel, resolve (480), restore.

To elucidate, illustrate, exemplify, comment upon, define, unfold.

(*Adjectives*). Explanatory, expository, explicatory, exegetical, hermeneutic, constructive, inferential.

misapplication, catachresis, mistake, cross-reading, cross-purpose.

Misrepresentation, perversion, falsification, misquotation, garbling, exaggeration (549), false colouring, abuse of terms, parody, travesty, misstatement, etc. (544).

(*Verbs*). To misinterpret, misapprehend, misunderstand, misconceive, misdeem, misspell, mistranslate, misconstrue, misapply, mistake (495).

To misstate, etc. (544); to pervert, falsify, distort, torture, travesty, stretch, strain, wring, or wrest the sense or meaning; to put a bad or false construction on; to misquote, garble, belie, explain away.

(*Phrases*). To make neither head nor tail of; to play at cross-purposes; to put a false construction on.

(*Adjectives*). Misinterpreted, etc., untranslated, untranslatable.

(*Phrase*). *Traduttori traditori.*

Paraphrastic, metaphrastic; literal, plain, simple, strict.

(*Adverbs*). That is to say, *id est, videlicet*, in other words, in plain words, simply, in plain English.

Literally, verbatim, *au pied de la lettre*, strictly speaking (494).

524. INTERPRETER (*Substantives*), expositor, exponent, demonstrator, scholiast, commentator, palæographer, spokesman, speaker, mouthpiece, guide, dragoman, cicerone, *trucheman*, oneirocritic; Œdipus (513).

SECTION II.—MODES OF COMMUNICATION

525. MANIFESTATION (*Substantives*), expression, showing, etc., indication, exposition, demonstration, exhibition, production, display, showing off.

526. LATENCY (*Substantives*), secrecy, secretness, privacy, invisibility (*see* 447), occultness, darkness, reticence, silence, closeness, reserve, inexpression; a

An exhibit, an exhibitor.

Openness, frankness (543), publicity (531).

(*Verbs*). To manifest, show, express, indicate, point out, bring forth, bring forward, trot out, set forth, exhibit, expose, produce, bring into view, set before one, hold up to view, lay open, lay bare, expose to view, set before one's eyes, show up, shadow forth, bring to light, display, demonstrate, unroll, unveil, unmask, disclose, *see* 529.

(*Phrases*). Hold up the mirror; draw, lift up, raise, or remove the curtain; throw off the mask.

To elicit, educe, draw out, bring out, unearth, disinter.

To be manifested, etc., to appear, transpire, come to light, *see* Visibility (446), to come out, to crop out.

(*Phrases*). To speak for itself; to tell its own tale; to give vent to.

(*Adjectives*). Manifest, clear, apparent, evident, visible (446), prominent, in the foreground, conspicuous, palpable, open.

Manifested, shown, expressed, etc., disclosed (529), frank, capable of being shown, producible.

(*Adverbs*). Openly, before one's eyes, face to face, above-board, in open court, in open daylight, in the open streets, on the stage, on show.

527. INFORMATION (*Substantives*, communication, intimation, notice, notification, enunciation, announcement, annunciation, statement, specification, report, advice, monition, mention, acquaintance, acquainting, etc., outpouring, communicativeness.

sealed book; a dark horse; an undercurrent.

Retirement, delitescence, seclusion (893).

To render latent (528).

(*Verbs*). To be latent, etc., to lurk, smoulder; to keep back, reserve, suppress, keep close, keep secret, keep to oneself, keep snug, hush, hush up.

(*Phrases*). Hold one's tongue; hold one's peace; leave in the dark; to keep one's own counsel; to seal the lips; not to breathe a syllable about.

(*Adjectives*). Latent, secret, close, unapparent, unknown (491) delitescent, in the background, occult, cryptic, snug, private, privy, *in petto*, anagogic, sequestered, dormant, smouldering.

Inconspicuous, unperceived, invisible (447), unseen, unwitnessed, impenetrable, unespied, unsuspected.

Untold, unpublished, unmentioned, unbreathed, untalked of, unsung, unpronounced, unpromulgated, unreported, unexposed, unproclaimed, unexpressed, not expressed, tacit, implied, undeveloped, unsolved, unexplained, undiscovered, untraced, untracked, unexplored.

(*Phrase*). No news being good news.

(*Adverbs*). Secretly, etc., *sub silentio.*

In the background, under the table, behind the scenes.

528. CONCEALMENT (*Substantives*), hiding, etc., secrecy, stealth, stealthiness, slyness, disguise, incognito, masquerade, camouflage, mystery, mystification, freemasonry, reservation, suppression, backstairs, reserve, uncommunicativeness; secret path.

An informant, teller, tipster, spy, intelligencer, messenger, newsmonger, gossip (532).

Hint, suggestion (514), wrinkle, tip, insinuation, innuendo, wink, glance, leer, nod, shrug, gesture, whisper, implication, cue, by-play, eye-opener.

(*Phrases*). *Verbum sapienti*; a broad hint; a stage whisper.

A round robin.

(*Verbs*). To inform, acquaint, tell, mention, express, intimate, communicate, apprise, post, make known, notify, signify to, let one know, advise, state, specify, give notice, announce, annunciate, report, set forth, bring word, send word, leave word, write word, declare, certify, depose, pronounce, explain, undeceive, enlighten, set right, open the eyes of, convey the knowledge of, give an account of.

To hint, give an inkling of, give, throw out, or drop a hint, insinuate, allude to, glance at, make allusion to, to wink, to tip the wink, glance, leer, nod, shrug, give the cue, give the tip, wave, whisper, suggest, prompt, whisper in the ear, give one to understand.

To tell once for all.

To be informed, etc., of, made acquainted with, to hear of, to understand.

To come to one's ears, to come to one's knowledge, to reach one's ears.

(*Adjectives*). Informed, etc., of, made acquainted with, in the know; undeceived.

Reported, made known (531), bruited.

Expressive, significant, pregnant with meaning, etc. (*see* 516), declaratory, enunciative, nuncupatory, expository, communi-

A mask, vizor (or visor), ambush, etc. (530), enigma, etc. (533).

(*Phrases*). A needle in a bundle of hay; a skeleton in the cupboard; a family skeleton.

(*Verbs*). To conceal, hide, secrete, cover, envelop, screen, cloak, veil, shroud, enshroud, shade, muffle, mask, disguise, camouflage, ensconce, eclipse.

To keep from, lock up, bury, sink, suppress, burke, hush up, keep snug or close, etc.

(*Phrase*). To draw or close the curtain.

To keep in ignorance, blind, hoodwink, mystify, pose, puzzle, perplex, embarrass, flummox, bewilder, bamboozle, etc. (545).

To be concealed, etc., to lurk, skulk, smoulder, lie hid, lie in ambush, lie *perdu*, lie low, sneak, retire, steal into, steal along.

To conceal oneself, put on a veil, etc. (530), masquerade.

(*Phrases*). To play at bo-peep; to play at hide-and-seek; to hide under a bushel; to throw dust in the eyes.

(*Adjectives*). Concealed, hid, hidden, etc., secret, clandestine, close, private, furtive, surreptitious, stealthy, feline, underhand, sly, sneaking, skulking, hole-and-corner, undivulged, unrevealed, undisclosed, mum.

Mysterious, mystic, mystical, enigmatical, problematical, anagogical, paradoxical, occult, cryptic, gnostic, cabbalistic, esoteric, recondite, abstruse, unexplained, impenetrable, undiscoverable, inexplicable, unknowable, bewildering, baffling.

Covered, closed, shrouded, veiled, masked, screened, shaded, disguised, under cover, under a cloud, veil, etc., in a fog, haze,

catory, communicative, insinuative.

(*Adverbs*). Expressively, significantly, etc., *verbum satis*.

By post, etc. (532), messenger, etc. (534).

———

mist, etc., under an eclipse; inviolable, confidential.

(*Phrase*). Close as wax.

Reserved, uncommunicative, secretive, buttoned up, taciturn (585).

(*Adverbs*). Secretly, clandestinely, *incognito*, privily, in secret, mum, with closed doors, *à huis clos*, *à la dérobée*, under the rose, *sub rosa*, underhand, *en tapinois*, privately, in private, aside, on the sly, *sub silentio*, behind one's back, behind the curtain, behind the scenes.

Confidentially, between ourselves, between you and me, *entre nous*, *inter nos*, in strict confidence, on the strict q.t., it must go no farther.

(*Phrases*). Like a thief in the night; under the seal of secrecy, of confession; *Davus sum, non Œdipus*; "tell it not in Gath"; nobody any the wiser.

529. DISCLOSURE (*Substantives*), revealment, revelation, disinterment, exposition, effusion, outpouring.

Acknowledgment, avowal, confession; an *exposé*, *dénouement*.

A tell-tale, tale-bearer, informer.

(*Verbs*). To disclose, open, lay open, divulge, reveal, bewray, unfold, let drop, let fall, let out, let on, lay open, acknowledge, own, own up, confess, avow, unseal, unveil, unmask, uncover, unkennel, unearth (525).

530. AMBUSH (*Substantives*), hiding-place, retreat, cover, lurking-hole, secret place, recess, cache, ambuscade, *guet-apens*, *adytum*, trap, gin, see 545.

A mask, veil, vizor (or visor), cloak, screen, hoarding, curtain, shade, cover, disguise, masquerade dress, domino.

(*Verbs*). To lie in ambush, lurk, couch, lie in wait for, lay or set a trap for.

———

To blab, peach, let out, let fall, let on, betray, give away, tell tales, speak out, blurt out, vent, give vent to, come out with, round on, split.

To make public, publish, see 531.

To make no secret of, to disabuse, unbeguile, undeceive.

(*Phrases*). To let into the secret; to let the cat out of the bag; to unburden or disburden one's mind or conscience; to open one's mind; to unbosom oneself; to make a clean breast of it; to give the show away; to own the soft impeachment; to tell tales out of school; not to mince the matter; to be on the tip of the tongue; to show one's hand.

To be disclosed, revealed, etc., to come out, to transpire, to ooze out, to leak out, to creep out, to get wind, to come to light.

(*Phrase*). Murder will out.

(*Adjectives*). Disclosed, revealed, divulged, laid open, etc., unriddled, etc.; outspoken, etc. (543).

Open, public, exoteric, in the face of the day.

(*Interjection*). Out with it!

531. PUBLICATION (*Substantives*), announcement, notification, enunciation, annunciation, advertisement, promulgation, circulation, propagation, edition, redaction, proclamation, hue and cry, the Press, journalism.

Publicity, notoriety, currency, cry, bruit, rumour, fame, report, *on dit*, flagrancy, limelight, town-talk, small talk, table-talk, puffery, *réclame*, the light of day, daylight.

Notice, notification, manifesto, propaganda, advertisement, circular, placard, bill, *affiche*, poster, newspapers, gazette; agony column.

Publisher (*see* 593), publicity agent, advertising agent.

(*Phrases*). An open secret; *un secret de Polichinelle*.

(*Verbs*). To publish, make known, announce, notify, annunciate, gazette, set forth, give forth, give out, utter, advertise, circularise, placard, *afficher*, circulate, propagate, spread, spread abroad, broadcast, edit, redact, rumour, diffuse, disseminate, celebrate, blaze about; blaze or noise abroad; buzz, bandy, hawk about, trumpet, herald, puff, boom, give tongue, raise a cry, raise a hue and cry, bring, lay or drag before the public, give currency to, bring out.

(*Phrases*). To proclaim from the house-tops; to publish in the gazette; to send round the crier; *spargere auras per vulgum ambiguas*; with beat of drum.

To be published, etc., to become public, to go forth, get abroad, get about, get wind, take air, get afloat, acquire currency, get in the papers, spread, go the rounds, buzz about, blow about.

(*Phrases*). *Virum volitare per ora*; to pass from mouth to mouth; to spread like wildfire.

(*Adjectives*). Published, etc., made public, exoteric, rumoured, rife, current, afloat, notorious, flagrant, whispered, buzzed about, in every one's mouth, reported, trumpet-tongued; encyclical.

(*Phrase*). As the story runs.

(*Interjections*). Oyez! O yes!

532. NEWS (*Substantives*), piece of information, intelligence, tidings, budget of news, word, advice, message, communication, errand, embassy, dispatch, bulletin.

Report, rumour, hearsay, *on dit*, fame, talk, gossip, *oui-dire*, scandal, buzz, bruit, *chronique scandaleuse*, town-talk.

Letters, mail, post (592), tele-

533. SECRET (*Substantives*), *arcanum*, *penetralia*, profound secret, mystery, *arrière-pensée*, problem, enigma, teaser, poser, riddle, puzzle, conundrum, charade, rebus, logogriph, anagram, acrostic, cross-word, cipher, code, cryptogram, monogram, paradox, maze, labyrinth, perplexity, chaos (528), the Hercynian wood: *terra incognita*.

gram, wire, cable, wireless message, Marconigram.

Glad tidings; fresh news, old news, stale news, stale story.

Newsmonger, scandalmonger, scaremonger, tale-bearer, gossip (527), special correspondent, reporter (590).

(*Phrases*). The secrets of the prison-house; a sealed book.

534. MESSENGER (*Substantives*), envoy, nuncio, internuncio, herald, ambassador, legate, emissary, *corps diplomatique*.

Marshal, crier, trumpeter, pursuivant, *parlementaire*, courier, runner, dawk, errand-boy, Mercury, Iris, Ariel.

Narrator, etc., tale-bearer, spy, scout.

535. AFFIRMATION (*Substantives*), predication, assertion, declaration, word, averment, asseveration, protestation, swearing, protest, profession, deposition, avouchment, affirmance, assurance, allegation, acknowledgment, avowal, confession, confession of faith, oath.

Remark, observation, position, thesis, proposition, saying, dictum, theorem, sentence.

Positiveness, dogmatism, *ipse dixit*.

A dogmatist, doctrinaire.

(*Phrase*). The big bow-wow style.

(*Verbs*). To assert, make an assertion, etc., say, affirm, predicate, declare, profess, aver, avouch, put forth, advance, express, allege, pose, propose, propound, broach, set forth, maintain, contend, pronounce, pretend, pass an opinion, etc.; to reassert, reaffirm, reiterate; quoth, *dixit, dixi*.

To vouch, assure, vow, swear, take oath, depose, recognise,

536. NEGATION (*Substantives*), abnegation, denial, denegation, disavowal, disclaimer, abjuration, contradiction, *démenti*, contravention, recusation, retraction, retractation, recantation, renunciation, palinode, recusancy, protest.

(*Phrase*). A flat contradiction.

Qualification, modification, (469).

(*Verbs*). To deny, disown, contradict, negative, gainsay, contravene, disclaim, withdraw, recant, disavow, retract, revoke, abjure, negate.

(*Phrases*). To deny flatly; eat one's words; go back from, or upon one's word.

To dispute, impugn, question, call in question, give the lie to, rebut, belie.

(*Adjectives*). Denying, etc., denied, etc., contradictory, recusant.

(*Adverbs*). No, nay, not, *see* 489.

avow, acknowledge, own, confess, announce, hazard or venture an opinion.

To dogmatise, lay down, lay down the law; to call heaven to witness, protest, depose, warrant, posit, go bail for.

(*Phrases*). I doubt not; I warrant you; I'll engage; take my word for it; depend upon it; I'll be bound; I am sure; I have no doubt; sure enough; what I have said, I have said; faith! that's flat.

630

To swear till one is black in the face.

(*Adjectives*). Asserting, etc., dogmatic, positive, emphatic, predicable, pronounced, unretracted.

Positive, broad, round, express, explicit, pointed, marked, distinct, decided, formal, solemn, categorical, peremptory, emphatic, flat, pronounced.

(*Adverbs*). *Ex cathedra*, positively, avowedly, confessedly, broadly, roundly, etc., so to speak; ay, yes, indeed, etc., *see* 488.

537. TEACHING (*Substantives*), instruction, direction, guidance, tuition, culture, inculcation, inoculation, indoctrination, *éclaircissement*, explanation.

Education, co-education, initiation, preparation, training, upbringing, schooling, discipline, exercise, drill, exercitation, breaking in, taming, drilling, etc., preachment, persuasion, edification, proselytism, propagandism.

A lesson, lecture, prolusion, prelection, exercise, task; curriculum, course.

Rudiments, A B C, elements, grammar, text-book, vade-mecum, school-book (593).

(*Verbs*). To teach, instruct, enlighten, edify, inculcate, indoctrinate, instil, imbue, inoculate, infuse, impregnate, graft, infix, engraft, implant, sow the seeds of, infiltrate, give an idea of, cram, coach, put up to.

(*Phrases*). Sharpen the wits; beat into the head.

To explain, expound, lecture, hold forth, read a lecture or sermon, give a lesson, preach; sermonise, moralise, point a moral.

To educate, train, discipline, school, form, ground, tutor, prepare, qualify, prime, drill, exercise, bring up, rear, nurture, dry-nurse, breed, break in, tame, domesticate.

To direct, guide, put in the

538. MISTEACHING (*Substantives*), misdirection, misinformation, misguidance, perversion, false teaching.

Indocility, incapacity, misintelligence, dullness.

(*Verbs*). To misinform, mislead, misdirect, misguide, miscorrect, pervert, lead into error, bewilder, mystify (528), throw off the scent; to unteach.

(*Phrases*). *Piscem natare doces*; *obscurum per obscurius*; the blind leading the blind.

(*Adjectives*). Misteaching, etc., unedifying.

539. LEARNING (*Substantives*), acquisition of knowledge, acquirement, attainment, scholarship, erudition, instruction, study, etc., *see* Knowledge (490), apprenticeship.

Docility, aptitude, aptness to be taught, teachableness, persuasibility, capacity.

(*Verbs*). To learn; to acquire, gain, catch, receive, imbibe, pick up, gather, collect, glean, etc., knowledge or information.

(*Phrases*). To come to the ears of; to flash on the mind; get scent of; get on the track of.

To hear, overhear, catch hold of, take in, fish up, drink in, run away with an idea, to make oneself acquainted with, master, read, spell, turn over the leaves, run through, peruse, grind, cram,

way of, proselytise, bring round to an opinion, bring over, win over, persuade, convince, convict, set right, enlighten, give one new ideas, put one up to, bring home to.

(*Phrase*). To teach the young idea how to shoot.

(*Adjectives*). Teaching, etc., taught, etc.

Didactic, academic, doctrinal, disciplinal, disciplinary, instructive, scholastic, persuasive.

mug, swot, go to school; to get up a subject; to serve one's time or apprenticeship.

To be taught, etc.

(*Adjectives*). Docile, apt, teachable, persuasible, studious.

---

540. TEACHER (*Substantives*), instructor, apostle, master, director, tutor, preceptor, institutor, mentor, adviser, monitor, counsellor, expositor, dry - nurse, coach, crammer, grinder, governor, bear-leader, disciplinarian, martinet, guide, cicerone, pioneer; governess, duenna.

Orator, speaker, mouthpiece (582).

Professor, lecturer, reader, prælector, prolocutor, schoolmaster, usher, pedagogue, dominie, moonshee; missionary, propagandist.

541. LEARNER (*Substantives*), scholar, student, disciple, pupil, *élève*, schoolboy, beginner, tyro (or tiro), abecedarian, novice, neophyte, chela, inceptor, probationer, apprentice, freshman, undergraduate.

(*Phrase*). Freshwater sailor.

Proselyte, convert, catechumen, sectator; class, form.

Pupilage, pupilarity, pupilship, apprenticeship, novitiate, leading-strings, matriculation.

(*Phrase*). *In statu pupillari*.

---

542. SCHOOL (*Substantives*), academy, university, Alma Mater, college, seminary, lyceum, polytechnic, nursery, institute, institution, palæstra, gymnasium, hot-bed, class, propaganda, kindergarten, crèche.

Horn-book, rudiments, vade-mecum, abecedary, manual, primer, text-book.

Professorship, lectureship, chair; pulpit, ambo, theatre, amphitheatre, forum, stage, rostrum, platform, hustings.

(*Adjectives*). Scholastic, academic, collegiate.

(*Adverb*). *Ex cathedra*.

543. VERACITY (*Substantives*), truthfulness, truth, sincerity, frankness, straightforwardness, ingenuousness, candour, honesty, fidelity, openness, unreservedness, bluntness, plainness, plain speaking, plain dealing; simplicity, *bonhomie*, naïveté, artlessness (703), love of truth.

544. FALSEHOOD (*Substantives*), falseness, falsity, mendacity, falsification, perversion of truth, romance, forgery, prevarication, equivocation, shuffling, evasion, fencing, duplicity, double-dealing, unfairness, dishonesty, misrepresentation, *suggestio falsi*, *suppressio veri*, Punic faith, giv-

A plain-dealer, truth-teller, man of his word.

(*Phrase*). The Palace of Truth.

(*Verbs*). To speak the truth, speak one's mind, open out, think aloud.

(*Phrases*). Not to mince the matter; to deal faithfully with; to wear one's heart on one's sleeve.

(*Adjectives*). Truthful, true, veracious, sincere, candid, frank, open, outspoken, unreserved, free-spoken, open-hearted, honest, simple, simple-hearted, ingenuous, blunt, plain-spoken, straightforward, straight, fair, fair-minded, single-minded, artless, guileless, pure, natural, unaffected, simple-minded, undisguised, unfeigned, unflattering.

(*Adverbs*). Truly, etc. (494), above-board, broadly.

(*Phrases*). In plain English; without mincing the matter; *bona fide*; *sans phrase*.

ing the go-by, disguise, disguisement, irony, understatement.

Insincerity, dissimulation, dissembling, shiftiness, hypocrisy, cant, humbug, jesuitry, mental reservation, lip-service, simulation, acting, sham, malingering, pretending, etc., crocodile tears, false colouring, art, artfulness (702), perjury.

Deceiver, *see* 548.

(*Verbs*). To be false, etc., to play false, speak falsely, lie, fib, tell a lie or untruth, etc. (546), to mistake, misreport, misrepresent, falsify, prevaricate, equivocate, palter, shuffle, fence, hedge, understate, mince the truth.

To forswear, swear false, perjure oneself, bear false witness.

To garble, gloss over, disguise, colour, varnish, cook, wangle, gerrymander, put a false colouring or construction upon (523).

To invent, make up, fabricate, trump up, forge, fake, romance.

To dissemble, dissimulate, feign, assume, act or play a part, simulate, pass off for, counterfeit, sham, malinger, make believe, cant, put on.

(*Phrases*). To play the hypocrite; to give the go-by; to play fast and loose; to blow hot and cold; to lie like a conjuror; sham Abraham; *faire patte de velours*; to look as if butter would not melt in one's mouth; to sail close to the wind; to ring false.

(*Adjectives*). False, dishonest, faithless, truthless, trothless, unfair, uncandid, disingenuous, shady, shifty, underhand, underhanded, hollow, insincere, canting, hypocritical, jesuitical, pharisaical, tartuffian, double, double-tongued, double-faced, smooth-spoken, smooth-tongued, plausible, mealy-mouthed.

Artful, insidious, sly, designing, diplomatic, Machiavellian.

Untrue, unfounded, fictitious, invented, made up, *ben trovato*, forged, falsified, etc., counterfeit, spurious, factitious, self-styled, bastard, sham, mock, pseudo, disguised, simulated, etc., artificial, colourable, catchpenny, Brummagem, *postiche*, pinchbeck, illusory, elusory, supposititious, surreptitious, ironical, apocryphal.

(*Phrases*). All is not gold that glitters; *Parthis mendacior.*

(*Adverbs*). Falsely, etc., slyly, stealthily, underhand.

545. DECEPTION (*Substantives*), fraud, deceit, imposition, artifice, juggle, juggling, sleight of hand, legerdemain, conjuration, hocus-pocus, jockeyship, trickery, coggery, fraudulence, imposture, *supercherie*, cozenage, circumvention, ingannation, prestidigitation, subreption, collusion, complicity, guile, gullery, hanky-panky.

Quackery, charlatanism, charlatanry, empiricism, humbug, hypocrisy, gammon, flapdoodle, bunkum, *blague*, bluff, mummery, borrowed plumes.

Stratagem, trick, cheat, wile, artifice, fraud, cross, deception, take-in, camouflage, make-believe, ruse, manœuvre, finesse, hoax, canard, hum, kid, bubble, fetch, catch, spoof, swindle, plant, abuse, hocus, dodge, bite, forgery, fake, fakement, rig, delusion, stalking-horse.

Snare, trap, pitfall, decoy, gin, springe, noose, springle, hook, bait, net, meshes, mouse-trap, trap-door, ambush, ambuscade, masked battery, hush-boat; dupe, *see* 547.

(*Phrases*). A Cornish hug; a painted sepulchre; a pious fraud.

(*Verbs*). To deceive, mislead, cheat, impose upon, practise upon, circumvent, play upon, put upon, bluff, cross, dupe, mystify, blind, hoodwink, best, outreach, trick, hoax, kid, gammon, spoof, hocus, juggle, trepan, nick, entrap, beguile, lure, inveigle, decoy, lime, ensnare, entangle, lay a snare for, trip up, stuff, give the go-by.

To defraud, cheat, take in, jockey, do, do brown, cozen, diddle, chouse, welsh, bilk, bite, pluck, swindle, victimise, outwit, overreach, nobble, palm upon, work off upon, foist upon, fob off, balk, trump up.

(*Phrases*). To throw dust into the eyes; to play a trick upon; to pull one's leg; to try it on; to cog the dice; to mark the cards; to play a part; to throw a tub to the whale; to make one believe the moon is made of cream-cheese.

(*Adjectives*). Deceiving, cheating, etc.; hypocritical, Pecksniffian; deceived, duped, done, had, etc., led astray.

Deceptive, deceitful, deceptious, illusive, illusory, delusory, elusive, insidious, *ad captandum*, *ben trovato*.

(*Phrase*). *Fronti nulla fides ; timeo Danaos.*

546. UNTRUTH (*Substantives*), falsehood, lie, falsity, fiction, fabrication, fib, whopper, bouncer, cracker, crammer, taradiddle, story, fable, novel, romance, flam, bam, gammon, flim-flam, *guet-apens*, white lie, canard, nursery tale.

Falsification, perjury, forgery, false swearing, misstatement, misrepresentation.

Pretence, pretext, subterfuge, irony, evasion, blind, disguise, plea, claptrap, shuffle, make-believe, shift, mask, cloak, visor, veil, masquerade, gloss, cobweb.

(*Phrases*). A tub to the whale; a cock-and-bull story; all my eye.

547. DUPE (*Substantives*), gull, gudgeon, *gobemouche*, cully, victim, puppet, April fool, Cyclops, *see* Credulity (486).

548. DECEIVER (*Substantives*), liar, hypocrite, tale-teller, shuffler, shammer, dissembler, serpent, cockatrice, Ananias, Pharisee,

(Phrase). *Qui vult decipi, de-cipiatur.*

——

Jesuit, Janus, Tartuffe, Pecksniff, Joseph Surface, Cagliostro.

Pretender, impostor, knave, cheat, rogue, trickster, swindler, adventurer, humbug, sharper, jockey, welsher, leg, black-leg, rook, shark, guinea-dropper, confidence trickster, decoy, decoy-duck, stool-pigeon, gipsy.

Quack, charlatan, mountebank, empiric, quacksalver, *saltimbanco*, medicaster, Rosicrucian, *soi-disant*.

Actor, player, mummer, tumbler, posture-master, jack-pudding; illusionist, conjuror (994).

(Phrases). A wolf in sheep's clothing; one who lives by his wits.

549. EXAGGERATION (*Substantives*), hyperbole, overstatement, stretch, strain, colouring, bounce, flourish, vagary, bombast, yarn, figure of speech, flight of fancy, *façon de parler*, extravagance, rhodomontade, heroics, sensationalism, highfalutin; Baron Munchausen, *see* Boasting (884).

(*Verbs*). To exaggerate, amplify, overcharge, overstate, overcolour, overlay, overdo, strain, stretch, bounce, flourish, embroider; to hyperbolise, aggravate, to make the most of.

(Phrases). To stretch a point; spin a long yarn; draw the long bow; deal in the marvellous; out-herod Herod; lay it on thick; put it on; make a mountain of a mole-hill.

(*Adjectives*). Exaggerated, etc., hyperbolical, turgid, tumid, extravagant, bombastic, *outré*, highly coloured, high-flying, high-flown, highfalutin, sensational, blood-and-thunder, lurid.

(Phrases). All his geese are swans; much cry and little wool.

SECTION III.—MEANS OF COMMUNICATING IDEAS

1°. *Natural Means*

550. INDICATION (*Substantives*), symbolisation, typification, notation, connotation, prefigurement, representation (554), exposition, notice (527), trace (551), name (564).

A sign, symbol, index, placard, exponent, indicator, pointer, mark, token, symptom, type, emblem, cipher, code, device, epigraph, motto, posy.

Science of signs: Sematology.

Lineament, feature, line, stroke, dash, trait, score, stripe, streak, scratch, tick, dot, point, notch, nick, asterisk, red letter, rubric, italics, print, stamp, impress, imprint, sublineation, underlining, display, jotting.

For identification: Badge, criterion, check, countercheck, countersign, duplicate, label, book-plate, *ex-libris*, ticket, billet, card, visiting-card, *carte de visite*, bill, bill-head, facia, sign-board, witness, voucher, coupon, trade-mark, hall-mark, signature, handwriting, sign-manual, cipher, seal, sigil, signet, autograph, autography, superscription, endorsement, *visé*, title, heading, caption, docket, watchword, password, shibboleth, *mot du guet*, catchword.

Insignia: Banner, banneret, flag, colours, bunting, streamer, standard, ensign, pennon, pennant, pendant, jack, ancient, oriflamme, gonfalon, banderole; crest, arms, coat of arms, armorial bearings, shield, scutcheon, escutcheon, livery, cockade, epaulet, chevron, cordon, totem.

Indication of locality: Beacon, cairn, post, staff, flagstaff, hand, pointer, vane, guide-post, finger-post, sign-post, landmark, seamark, lighthouse, lightship, pole-star, lodestar, cynosure, guide, address, direction, rocket, blue-light, watch-fire, blaze.

Indication of an event: Signal, nod, wink, beck, cue, gesture, gesticulation, dumb-show, pantomime, touch, nudge, freemasonry, telegraph, heliograph, semaphore.

Indication of time: Time-ball, clock (114), alarm-clock, hooter, buzzer, siren.

Indication of danger: Alarm, alarum, alarm-bell, tocsin, firehooter, beat of drum, fiery cross, sound of trumpet, war-cry, warwhoop, slogan.

(*Verbs*). To indicate, point out, be the sign, etc., of, denote, betoken, connote, connotate, represent, stand for, typify, symbolise, shadow forth, argue, bear the impress of, witness, attest, testify.

To put an indication, mark, etc.; to note, mark, stamp, impress, label, ticket, docket, endorse, sign, countersign; put, append, or affix a seal or signature; dot, jot down, book, score, dash, trace, chalk, underline, italicise, print, imprint, engrave, stereotype, rubricate, star, obelise, initial.

To make a sign, signal, etc., signalise; give or hang out a signal; give notice, gesticulate, beckon, beck, nod, wink, nudge, tip the wink, give the cue, tip, or office; wave, unfurl, hoist, or hang out a banner, flag, etc., show one's colours, give or sound an alarm, beat the drum, sound the trumpets, raise a cry, etc.

(*Adjectives*). Indicating, etc., indicatory, indicative, sematic, denotative, representative, typical, typic, symbolic, symbolical, connotative, pathognomic, symptomatic, exponential, emblematic, attesting; armorial, totemistic.

Indicated, etc., typified, impressed, etc.

Capable of being denoted, denotable, indelible.

(*Phrases*). *Ecce signum*; *ex pede Herculem*; *verbum satis*; in token of.

---

551. RECORD (*Substantives*), trace, tradition, vestige, footstep, footmark, footprint, footfall, wake, trail, slot, spoor, pug, scent, *piste*, monument, relic,

552. Suppression of sign.
OBLITERATION (*Substantives*), erasure, rasure, cancel, cancellation, circumduction, deletion, application of the sponge.

remains, trophy, hatchment, achievement, obelisk, monolith, pillar, stele, column, testimonial, memorial.

Note, minute, register, registry, memorandum, jotting, document, voucher, protocol, inscription.

Paper, parchment, scroll, instrument, deed, indenture, debenture, roll, archive, schedule, file, dossier, tablet, cartulary, table, *procès verbal*, affidavit, certificate, attestation, entry, diploma, protest, round-robin, muster-roll, muster-book, note-book, commonplace-book, *adversaria*, portfolio, *see* List (86).

Chronicle, annals, gazette, newspaper, gazetteer, Blue book, almanac, calendar, ephemeris, diary, log, journal, *see* History (594).

Registration, tabulation, enrolment, entry, booking.

(*Verbs*). To record, note, register, chronicle, make an entry of, enter, book, take a note of, post, enrol, jot down, take down, mark, sign, etc. (550), tabulate, catalogue, file, index, calendar.

(*Adjective*). Registered, etc.

(*Adverbs*). Under one's hand and seal, on record.

(*Verbs*). To efface, obliterate, erase, raze, expunge, cancel, delete, blot out, take out, rub out, scratch out, strike out, elide, wipe out, wash out, black out, write off, sponge, render illegible.

(*Phrase*). To draw the pen through.

To be effaced, etc., to leave no trace.

(*Adjectives*). Obliterated, effaced, etc., printless, leaving no trace.

Unrecorded, unattested, unregistered, intestate.

(*Adverbs*). *Dele*, out with it!

---

553. RECORDER (*Substantives*), notary, clerk, registrar, registrary, prothonotary, secretary, scribe, remembrancer, journalist, historian, historiographer, annalist, etc., book-keeper.

Recordership, secretaryship, secretariat, clerkship.

---

554. REPRESENTATION (*Substantives*), delineation, representment, personification.

Art, the fine arts, the graphic arts, design, designing, illustration, imitation (19), copy (21), iconography.

An image, likeness, icon, effigy, facsimile, autotype, imagery, figure, puppet, dummy, lay figure, figure-head, doll, manikin, *mannequin*, mammet, marionette, *fantoccini* (599), waxwork.

555. MISREPRESENTATION (*Substantives*), distortion (243), caricature, burlesque, a bad likeness, daub, *croûte*, scratch, sign-painting, anamorphosis ; misprint, *erratum*.

Hieroglyphic, hieroglyph, inscription, diagram, monogram, draught (or draft), outline, scheme, *schema*, schedule.

Map, plan, chart, ground-plan, projection, elevation, ichnography, atlas ; cartography, chorography.

(*Verbs*). To represent, delineate, design, figure, shadow forth, copy, draft, mould, diagrammatise, schematise, map.

To imitate, impersonate, personate, personify, act, take off, hit off, figure as.

(*Adjectives*). Representing, etc.; artistic, imitative, figurative, hieroglyphic, hieroglyphical, diagrammatic, schematic.

556. PAINTING (*Substantives*), depicting, etc., sciagraphy, photography, etc.

Drawing in pencil, crayon, pastel, chalk, water-colour, etc.

Painting in oils, in distemper, in gouache, in fresco; encaustic painting, enamel painting, scene-painting; wash (428), body-colour, impasto.

A picture, drawing, painting, sketch, illustration, scratch, *graffito*, outline, *tableau*, cartoon, fresco, illumination; pencil, etc., drawing; oil, etc., painting; daguerreotype, calotype, talbotype, heliotype, autotype, photograph; mosaic, tapestry, etc., picture-gallery.

Portrait, portraiture, likeness, full-length, etc., miniature, kitcat, shade, profile, silhouette, photograph, snapshot.

Landscape, seascape, nocturne, view, still-life, genre, panorama, diorama.

Pre-Raphaelitism, impressionism, etc., *see* 559.

(*Verbs*). To paint, depict, portray, limn, draw, sketch, pencil, scratch, scrawl, block in, rough in, dash off, chalk out, shadow forth, adumbrate, outline, illustrate, illuminate; to take a portrait, take a likeness, to photograph, snap, kodak.

(*Adjectives*). Painted, etc.; pictorial, graphic, picturesque, Giottesque, Raphaelesque, Turneresque, etc.; like, etc. (17).

557. SCULPTURE (*Substantives*), insculpture, carving, modelling.

A statue, statuary, statuette, figure, figurine, model, bust, image, alto-rilievo, mezzo-rilievo, basso-rilievo, bas-relief, cast, marble, bronze, intaglio, anaglyph; medallion, cameo.

(*Verbs*). To sculpture, sculp, carve, cut, chisel, model, mould, cast.

(*Adjectives*). Sculptured, etc., sculptural, sculpturesque, anaglyphic, ceroplastic.

558. ENGRAVING (*Substantives*), etching, wood-engraving, process-engraving, xylography, etc., cerography; poker-work.

A print, engraving, impression, plate, cut, wood-cut, vignette.

An etching, dry-point, silver-point, copper-plate, mezzotint, aquatint, stippling, lithograph, chromolithograph, chromo, colour-plate, anastatic-printing, glyphograph, stereograph.

(*Verbs*). To engrave, etch, lithograph, print, etc.

559. ARTIST (*Substantives*), painter, limner, draughtsman, black-and-white artist, cartoonist, caricaturist, drawer, sketcher, designer, engraver, copyist, photographer.

Academician; historical, landscape, portrait, miniature, scene, sign, etc., painter; engraver; an Apelles.

Primitive, Pre-Raphaelite, old master, quattrocentist, cinque-centist, impressionist, post-impressionist, futurist, vorticist, cubist, pointillist, etc.

A sculptor, carver, modeller, *figuriste*; a Phidias, a Praxiteles.

Implements of art: pen, pencil, brush, crayon; stump, graver, style, burin; canvas, easel, palette, maul-stick, palette-knife; studio, *atelier*.

2°. *Conventional Means*

1. *Language generally*

560. LANGUAGE (*Substantives*), tongue, lingo, vernacular, mother-tongue, native tongue, the genius of a language.

Dialect, provincialism, Cockney speech, brogue, patois, patter, slang, argot, broken English, pidgin-English, lingua franca.

Universal languages: Esperanto, Volapük, Ido.

Pasigraphy, chirology, dactylology, pantomime, dumb-show, deaf-and-dumb language; linguistics, glossology, dialectology, phonetics.

Literature, letters, polite literature, belles-lettres, the muses, humanities, the republic of letters, *literæ humaniores*.

Scholarship (490), scholar (492), writer (593), glossographer.

(*Verbs*). To express by words, to couch in terms, to clothe in language.

(*Adjectives*). Literary, belletristic, linguistic, dialectal, current, polyglot, pantomimic.

(*Adverbs*). In plain terms, in king's English, in common parlance, in household words.

561. LETTER (*Substantives*), alphabet, A B C, abecedary, spelling-book, horn-book, criss-cross-row; character (591), hieroglyph, hieroglyphic; consonant, vowel, diphthong; spelling, orthography, phonetic spelling, misspelling; spelling-bee.

Syllable, monosyllable, dissyllable, polysyllable; anagram.

(*Verbs*). To spell, spell out.

(*Adjectives*). Literal, abecedarian, orthographic.

562. WORD (*Substantives*), term, vocable, monogram, cipher, terminology, etymon.

Word similarly pronounced, homonym, homophone, paronym.

A dictionary, vocabulary, lexicon, index, polyglot, glossary, thesaurus, gradus; lexicography; a lexicographer.

Derivation, etymology, glossology.

(*Adjectives*). Verbal, literal,

563. NEOLOGY (*Substantives*), neologism, slang, cant, byword, hard word, jaw - breaker, dog-Latin, monkish Latin, loan-word, Gallicism.

A pun, play upon words, paronomasia, *jeu de mots, calembour*, palindrome, conundrum, acrostic, anagram (533).

Dialect, *see* 560.

(*Verbs*). To neologise, archaise, pun.

titular, etymological, termino-
logical.

Similarly derived, conjugate,
paronymous.

(*Adverbs*). Nominally, etc., *verbatim*, word for word, literally,
sic, *totidem*, *verbis*, *ipsissimis verbis*, *literatim*, chapter and
verse.

(Phrase). To coin or mint words.

(*Adjectives*). Neological, archa-
istic, unprounceable, parono-
mastic.

---

564. NOMENCLATURE (*Substantives*), nuncupation.

A name, appellation, designation, appellative, denomination,
term, expression, noun, byword,
byname, epithet, style, title,
prenomen, forename, Christian
name, baptismal name, cogno-
men, agnomen, patronymic, sur-
name.

Synonym, namesake; euphemism, onomatopœia.

Quotation, citation, chapter
and verse.

(*Verbs*). To name, call, term,
denominate, designate, style,
clepe, entitle, dub, christen,
baptise, characterise, specify,
define.

To be called, etc., to take the
name of, pass under the name of;
to quote, cite.

(*Phrases*). To call a spade a spade; to rejoice in the
name of.

(*Adjectives*). Named, called, etc., hight, yclept, known as;
nuncupatory, nuncupative, cognominal, titular, nominal.

Literal, verbal, discriminative.

565. MISNOMER (*Substantives*),
missaying, malaprop, malaprop-
ism, antiphrasis, nickname, sob-
riquet, byname, assumed name
or title, alias, *nom de guerre*, *nom
de plume*, pen-name, pseudonym,
euphemism.

(Phrase). *Lucus a non lucendo*.

A neologist, a Mrs. Malaprop.

(*Verbs*). To misname, missay,
miscall, misterm, nickname.

To assume a name; to coin
words.

(*Adjectives*). Misnamed, etc.,
malapropian, pseudonymous, *soi-
disant*, self-called, self-styled,
new-fangled expressions.

Nameless, anonymous, without a name, having no name,
innominate, unnamed.

---

566. PHRASE (*Substantives*), expression, phraseology, paraphrase,
periphrasis, circumlocution, set phrase, round terms; mode, or
turn of expression; idiom, wording, *façon de parler*, mannerism,
plain terms, plain English.

Sentence, paragraph, motto.

Figure, trope, metaphor (521), antiphrasis, proverb.

(*Verbs*). To express, phrase, couch, clothe in words; to word.

(*Adjectives*). Expressed, etc., couched in, phraseological, paraphrastic, periphrastic, circumlocutory (573), proverbial.

(*Phrases*). As the saying is; in good set terms; *sans phrase*.

567. GRAMMAR (*Substantives*),
accidence, syntax, praxis, punc-
tuation, conjugation, declension,

568. SOLECISM (*Substantives*),
bad or false grammar, slip of
the pen or tongue, bull, *lapsus*

inflexion, philology, parts of speech.

(*Phrase*). *Jus et norma loquendi.*

(*Verbs*). To parse, conjugate, decline, inflect, punctuate.

(*Adjectives*). Grammatical, syntactic, inflexional.

――――

linguæ, barbarism, colloquialism, vulgarism.

(*Verbs*). To use bad or faulty grammar, to solecise, or commit a solecism.

(*Phrases*). To murder the king's English; to break Priscian's head.

(*Adjectives*). Ungrammatical, colloquial, slipshod, incorrect, faulty, inaccurate.

569. STYLE (*Substantives*), diction, phraseology, turn of expression, idiom, manner, strain, composition, authorship; stylist.

(*Adjective*). Stylistic.

(*Phrase*). *Le style, c'est l'homme même.*

Various Qualities of Style

570. PERSPICUITY (*Substantives*), lucidity, lucidness, clearness, clarity, perspicacity, plain speaking, intelligibility (518).

(*Adjectives*). Perspicuous, clear, lucid, intelligible, plain, transparent, explicit.

571. OBSCURITY (*Substantives*), ambiguity, etc., *see* Unintelligibility (519), involution, involvedness, vagueness.

(*Adjectives*). Obscure, confused, ambiguous, vague, unintelligible, etc., involved, wiredrawn, tortuous.

572. CONCISENESS (*Substantives*), brevity, terseness, compression, condensation, concision, closeness, laconism, pithiness, succinctness, quaintness, stiffness, ellipsis.

(*Verbs*). To be concise, etc., to condense, compress, abridge, abbreviate, cut short, curtail, abstract.

(*Adjectives*). Concise, brief, short, terse, laconic, sententious, gnomic, snappy, pithy, nervous, succinct, *guindé,* stiff, compact, close, cramped, elliptical, telegraphic, lapidary.

(*Adverbs*). In short, briefly, in a word, to the point, for short.

(*Phrases*). The long and short of it; *multum in parvo*; it comes to this; for shortness' sake; to put it in a nutshell.

――――

573. DIFFUSENESS (*Substantives*), prolixity, verbosity, pleonasm, tautology, copiousness, exuberance, laxity, looseness, verbiage, flow, flow of words, fluency, *copia verborum,* redundancy, redundance, digression, circumlocution, ambages, periphrasis, episode, expletive, *see* Length (200), journalese.

(*Verbs*). To be diffuse, etc., to expatiate, enlarge, launch out, dilate, expand, spin out, swell out, inflate, dwell, harp on, descant, digress, ramble, rant.

(*Phrases*). To beat about the bush; to spin a long yarn.

(*Adjectives*). Diffuse, wordy, verbose, prolix, copious, exuberant, flowing, fluent, bombastic, lengthy, long - winded, prosy, spun out, long - spun, loose, lax, slovenly, washy, slipslop, sloppy, frothy, flatulent, windy, digressive, discursive, excursive, tripping, rambling, ambagious, pleonastic, redundant, periphrastic, episodic, circumlocutory, roundabout.

Minute, detailed, particular, circumstantial.

(*Adverbs*). In detail, *in extenso*, about it and about, *currente calamo*, *usque ad nauseam*.

---

574. VIGOUR (*Substantives*), energy, power, force, spirit, point, vim, snap, raciness, liveliness, glow, verve, piquancy, pungency, spice, boldness, gravity, warmth, sententiousness, elevation, loftiness, sublimity, eloquence, individuality, distinction, emphasis, virility.

(*Phrase*). "Thoughts that glow and words that burn."

(*Adjectives*). Vigorous, energetic, powerful, forcible, nervous, spirited, vivid, virile, expressive, lively, glowing, racy, bold, slashing, incisive, trenchant, snappy, piquant, pungent, spicy, meaty, pithy, juicy, pointed, antithetical, sententious, emphatic, athletic, distinguished, individual, lofty, elevated, sublime, Miltonic, eloquent, full of point, poetical, etc.

575. FEEBLENESS (*Substantives*), baldness, tameness, meagreness, coldness, frigidity, poverty, puerility, childishness, dullness, jejuneness, monotony.

(*Adjectives*). Feeble, bald, tame, meagre, invertebrate, mealy-mouthed, wishy-washy, banal, uninteresting, jejune, vapid, cold, frigid, poor, dull (843), languid, anæmic, prosy, prosaic, pedestrian, platitudinous, mechanical, decadent, trashy, namby-pamby (866), emasculate.

---

576. PLAINNESS (*Substantives*), simplicity, homeliness, chasteness, chastity, neatness, dryness, monotony, severity.

(*Adjectives*). Simple, unornamented, unvarnished, straightforward, plain, unadorned, dry, costive, unvaried, monotonous, severe, etc., homespun.

577. ORNAMENT (*Substantives*), floridness, floridity, flamboyance, richness, opulence, turgidity, tumidity, pomposity, inflation, pretension, fustian, affectation, euphuism, gongorism, mannerism, metaphor, preciosity, inversion, figurativeness, *sesquipedalia verba*, rant, bombast, frothiness; flowers of speech, high-sounding words, well-rounded periods, purple patches, *see* 851.

(*Verbs*). To ornament, overcharge, overlay with ornament, lard or garnish with metaphors, lay the colours on thick, round a period, mouth.

(*Adjectives*). Ornamented, etc., ornate, florid, flamboyant, rich, opulent, golden-mouthed, figurative, metaphorical, pedantic, affected, pretentious, falsetto, euphuistic, Della Cruscan, pompous, fustian, high-sounding, mouthy, inflated, bombastic, stilted, mannered, high-flowing, frothy, flowery, luscious, turgid, tumid, swelling, rhapsodic, rhetorical,

orotund, grandiose, grandiloquent, magniloquent, sesquipedalian, Johnsonian, ponderous.

(*Adverb*). *Ore rotundo*.

578. ELEGANCE (*Substantives*),
grace, ease, nature, purity, con-
cinnity, readiness, euphony; a
purist.

(*Phrases*). A ready pen; flowing periods; *curiosa felicitas*.

(*Adjectives*). Elegant, graceful,
Ciceronian, classical, natural,
easy, unlaboured, chaste, pure,
flowing, mellifluous, euphonious,
rhythmical, puristic.

(*Phrases*). To round a period;
"to point a moral and adorn a
tale."

579. INELEGANCE (*Substantives*), stiffness, uncouthness,
barbarism, archaism, rudeness,
ruggedness, abruptness, artificiality, cacophony.

(*Phrases*). Words that dislocate the jaw, that break the
teeth.

(*Verb*). To be inelegant, etc.

(*Phrase*). To smell of the lamp.

(*Adjectives*). Inelegant, stiff,
forced, laboured, clumsy, contorted, tortuous, harsh, cramped,
rude, rugged, dislocated, crude,
uncouth, barbarous, archaic, ar-
chaistic, affected (577), artificial,
abrupt, incondite.

---

2. *Spoken Language*

580. VOICE (*Substantives*),
vocality, vocalisation, utterance,
accent, cry, strain, articulate
sound, prolation, articulation,
enunciation, delivery, vocalism,
pronunciation, orthoepy, euphony.

Cadence, accent, accentuation,
emphasis, stress, intonation, ex-
clamation, ejaculation, vociferation, ventriloquism, polyphonism.

A ventriloquist, polyphonist.

Science of voice: Phonetics,
Phonology; voice-production.

(*Verbs*). To utter, breathe,
cry, exclaim, shout, ejaculate,
vociferate; raise, lift, or strain
the voice or lungs; to vocalise,
prolate, articulate, enunciate, pronounce, aspirate, deliver, mouth,
rap out, speak out, speak up.

(*Phrase*). To whisper in the ear.

(*Adjectives*). Vocal, oral,
articulate.

Silvery, mellow, soft, *see*
Melodious (413).

581. APHONY (*Substantives*),
obmutescence, absence or want
of voice, dumbness, muteness,
mutism, speechlessness, aphasia,
hoarseness, raucity.

A dummy, a mute, deaf-mute.

(*Verbs*). To render mute, to
muzzle, to gag.

(*Phrases*). To stick in the
throat; *vox faucibus hæsit*; to
close one's lips; to shut up.

(*Adjectives*). Aphonous, dumb,
speechless, mute, tongueless,
muzzled, tongue-tied, inarticulate, inaudible, unspoken, un-
said, mum, lips closed or sealed,
wordless, raucous, hoarse, husky,
sepulchral.

(*Phrases*). Mute as a fish;
hoarse as a raven; with bated
breath; *sotto voce*; *vox et præterea nihil*; with the finger on
the lips; mum's the word.

582. SPEECH (*Substantives*), locution, talk, parlance, verbal intercourse, oral communication, word of mouth, palaver, prattle, effusion, narrative (594), tale, story, yarn, oration, recitation, delivery, say, harangue, formal speech, lecture, address, tirade, screed; soliloquy, *see* 589.

Oratory, elocution, rhetoric, declamation, eloquence, gift of the gab, *copia verborum*, grandiloquence, magniloquence, *usus loquendi*.

A speaker, spokesman, prolocutor, mouthpiece, lecturer, orator, a Cicero, a Demosthenes, a stump-orator, speechifier.

(*Verbs*). To speak, break silence, say, tell, open one's lips, give tongue, hold forth, make or deliver a speech, speechify, harangue, talk, discourse, declaim, flourish, spout, rant, recite, rattle off, intone, whisper in the ear, expatiate, run on; to lecture, address, sermonise, préachify; to soliloquise (589); quoth he.

(*Phrases*). To have a tongue in one's head; to have on the tip of one's tongue; to have on one's lips; to pass one's lips; to find one's tongue.

(*Adjectives*). Speaking, etc., oral, spoken, unwritten, outspoken.

(*Adverbs*). *Viva voce*; *ore rotundo*; by word of mouth.

583. Imperfect speech, inarticulateness.

STAMMERING (*Substantives*), stuttering, impediment in one's speech, titubancy, faltering, hesitation, lisp, drawl, jabber, gibber, sputter, splutter, mumbling, mincing, muttering, mouthing, twang, a broken or cracked voice, broken accents or sentences, tardiloquence, falsetto, a whisper, mispronunciation.

(*Verbs*). To stammer, stutter, hesitate, falter, hem, haw, hum and ha, mumble, lisp, jabber, mutter, sputter, splutter, drawl, lisp, croak, speak through the nose, snuffle, clip one's words, mispronounce, missay.

(*Phrases*). To clip the king's English; *parler à tort et à travers*; not to be able to put two words together.

To speak aside, *sotto voce*, whisper.

(*Adjectives*). Stammering, etc., inarticulate, guttural, nasal, unspeakable.

---

584. LOQUACITY (*Substantives*), loquaciousness, talkativeness, garrulity, flow of words, prate, gas, jaw, gab, gabble, jabber, chatter, prattle, cackle, clack, blether (or blather), patter, rattle, twaddle, bibble-babble, gibblegabble, talkee-talkee, gossip.

Fluency, flippancy, volubility, verbosity, *cacoethes loquendi*, anecdotage.

(*Phrases*). A thrice-told tale; a long yarn.

585. TACITURNITY (*Substantives*), closeness, reserve, muteness, silence, costiveness; aposiopesis.

(*Phrase*). A Quaker meeting.

(*Verbs*). To be silent, etc. (403), to hold one's tongue, keep silence, hold one's peace, say nothing, hold one's jaw, close one's mouth or lips, fall silent, shut up.

To render silent, silence, put to silence, seal one's lips, smother,

The gift of the gab.

A chatterer, chatter - box, babbler, wind-bag, gas-bag, rattle, ranter, tub-thumper, sermoniser, proser, driveller, gossip.

Magpie, jay, parrot, poll, Babel.

(*Verbs*). To be loquacious, etc., to prate chatter, prattle, jabber, jaw, rattle, twaddle, blether, babble, gabble, gas, out-talk, descant, dilate, dwell on, reel off, expatiate, prose, launch out, palaver, yarn, gossip, wag one's tongue, run on.

(*Phrases*). To din in the ears; to drum into the ear; *battre la campagne*; to spin a long yarn; to talk at random; to talk oneself out of breath; to talk nineteen to the dozen.

(*Adjectives*). Loquacious, talkative, garrulous, gassy, open-mouthed, chatty, chattering, etc.

Fluent, voluble, glib, flippant, hoarse with talking, long-winded, verbose, the tongue running fast.

(*Adverb*). Trippingly on the tongue.

suppress, stop one's mouth, gag, muffle, muzzle.

(*Adjectives*). Taciturn, close, reserved, mute, sparing of words, costive, buttoned up, short-spoken, close-tongued, secretive, uncommunicative, inconversable.

(*Phrases*). Not a word escaping one; not having a word to say.

(*Interjections*). Tush! silence! mum! hush! *chut !* hist! tut!

---

586. ALLOCUTION (*Substantives*), address, apostrophe, interpellation, appeal, invocation, salutation, accost, greeting (894).

Feigned dialogue, imaginary conversation; inquiry, see 461.

(*Phrase*). A word in the ear.

(*Verbs*). To speak to, address, accost, apostrophise, appeal to, invoke, hail, make up to, call to, halloo (or hallo), salute.

587. RESPONSE (*Substantives*), answer, reply, etc., see 462.

(*Verbs*). To answer, respond, reply, etc.

(*Phrase*). To take up one's cue.

(*Adjectives*). Answering, responding, etc., responsive, respondent.

(*Phrases*). To talk with one in private; to break the ice.

(*Adjectives*). Accosting, etc., apostrophic.

(*Interjections*). Hallo! hullo! I say! what ho!

---

588. INTERLOCUTION (*Substantives*), collocution, colloquy, conversation, converse, confabulation, confab, talk, discourse, verbal intercourse, dialogue, duologue, logomachy, communication, intercommunication, commerce, debate.

589. SOLILOQUY (*Substantives*), monologue, apostrophe, aside.

(*Verbs*). To soliloquise; to say or talk to oneself; to say aside, to think aloud, to apostrophise.

(*Adjective*). Soliloquising, etc.

Chat, chit-chat, small talk, table-talk, tattle, gossip, tittle-tattle, babblement, clack, prittle-prattle, idle talk, town-talk, *on dit*, the talk of the town, *chronique scandaleuse*.

Conference, parley, interview, audience, reception, palaver, pow-wow, logomachy.

A talkèr, interlocutor, interviewer, gossip, tattler, chatterer, babbler (584), conversationalist, *causeur; dramatis personœ.*

(*Phrases*). "The feast of reason and the flow of soul"; *mollia tempora fandi;* a heart-to-heart talk.

(*Verbs*). To talk together, converse, collogue, commune, debate, discourse with, engage in conversation, interview; hold or carry on a conversation: chat, gossip, put in a word, chip in, tattle, babble, prate, clack, prattle.

To confer with, hold conference, etc., to parley, palaver, commerce, hold intercourse with, be closeted with, commune with, compare notes, intercommunicate.

(*Adjectives*). Conversing, etc., interlocutory, verbal, colloquial, chatty, gossiping, etc., conversable, conversational.

3. *Written Language*

590. WRITING (*Substantives*), chirography, pencraft, penmanship, calligraphy, quill-driving, pen-pushing, typewriting.

Scribble, scrawl, scratch, cacography, scribbling, etc., *griffonnage, barbouillage,* jotting, interlineation.

Uncial writing, cursive writing, cuneiform characters, demotic text, hieratic text, ogham, runes, a good running hand, current or flowing hand, a bad, cramped, crabbed, illegible hand or fist.

Pothooks and hangers.

(*Phrase*). A dash, stroke, or flourish of the pen.

Transcription, inscription, superscription, minute.

Shorthand, stenography, brachygraphy, tachygraphy, steganography.

Secret writing, writing in cipher, cryptography, polygraphy, stelography; cryptogram.

Automatic writing, planchette.

Composition, authorship, *cacoethes scribendi.*

Manuscript, MS., copy, transcript, rough copy, fair copy, flimsy, handwriting, script, autograph, signature, sign-manual, monograph, holograph, endorsement, paraph.

A scribe, amanuensis, scrivener, secretary, clerk, penman, calligraphist, copyist, transcriber, typist.

591. PRINTING (*Substantives*), print, letterpress, text, context, note, page, proof, etc.; press-work.

Typography, stereotypography, etc.; type, character, black-letter, fount (or font), pie, etc., capitals, majuscules, lower-case letters, minuscules, etc.; braille.

Folio, quarto, octavo, duodecimo, etc.

Printer, pressman, compositor, corrector of the press, proof-reader, etc.

Printing-press, linotype, monotype, etc.

(*Verbs*). To print, put to press, publish, edit, get out a work, etc.

(*Adjective*). Printed, etc.

Writer, author, scribbler, quill-driver, pamphleteer, essayist, critic, reviewer, novelist (*see* 593), journalist, editor, reporter, pressman, penny-a-liner, free-lance; Grub Street, Fleet Street.

Pen, quill, fountain-pen, stylograph, pencil, paper, parchment, vellum, tablet, slate, marble, pillar, table, etc.

Inscription on pillars, Stelography.

(*Verbs*). To write, pen, typewrite, write out, copy, engross, write out fair, transcribe, scribble, scrawl, scratch, interline; to sign, undersign, countersign, endorse, set one's hand to.

To compose, indite, draw up, minute, jot down, make or take a minute of, put or set down in writing; to inscribe, to dictate.

(*Phrases*). To take up the pen; to spill ink; to sling ink; set or put pen to paper; put on paper; commit to paper; dash off.

(*Adjectives*). Writing, etc., written, in writing, penned, etc., scriptorial; editorial, journalistic, reportorial.

(*Phrases*). Under one's hand; in black and white; off-hand; *currente calamo*.

592. CORRESPONDENCE (*Substantives*), letter, epistle, note, chit, billet, missive, circular, favour, *billet-doux*, dispatch, bulletin, presents, rescript, rescription.

Letter-bag, mail, post.

(*Verbs*). To correspond, write to, send a letter to.

(*Phrase*). To keep up a correspondence.

---

593. BOOK (*Substantives*), writing, work, volume, tome, library, opuscule, tract, manual, pamphlet, chap-book, brochure, enchiridion, circular, publication, part, number, journal, album, periodical, magazine, serial.

Writer, author, publicist, scribbler, pamphleteer, essayist, novelist, fabulist, editor (590).

Book-lover, bibliophile, bibliomaniac.

Bibliography, *incunabula*, Aldine, Elzevir, etc.

Publisher, bookseller, bibliopole, bibliopolist.
Paper, bill, sheet, leaf, fly-leaf, page, title-page.
Chapter, section, paragraph, passage, clause.
(*Adjectives*). Auctorial, bookish.

594. DESCRIPTION (*Substantives*), account, statement, report, return, delineation, sketch, representation, narration, narrative, yarn, relation, recital, rehearsal, annals, chronicle, saga, *adversaria*, journal (551), itinerary, log-book.

Historiography; historicity.

Story, history, memoir, tale, tradition, legend, folk-tale, folk-lore, anecdote, ana, analects (596), fable, fiction, novel, novelette, romance, short story, *conte*, *nouvelle*, apologue, parable; word-picture; local colour; historic muse, Clio.

Biography, necrology, obituary, life, personal narrative, adventures, autobiography, reminiscences.

A historian, historiographer, narrator, *raconteur*, annalist, biographer, fabulist, novelist, fictionist, story-teller.

(*Verbs*). To describe, state, set forth, sketch, delineate, represent, pourtray, depict, paint, shadow forth, adumbrate.

To relate, recite, recount, sum up, run over, recapitulate, narrate, chronicle, rehearse, tell, give or render an account of, report, draw up a statement, etc., spin a yarn, unfold a tale, novelise, actualise.

To take up or handle a subject; to enter into particulars, detail, etc., to particularise, detail, retail, elaborate, write up; to descend to particulars; to come to the point; to Boswellise.

(*Phrases*). To plunge *in medias res*; to fight one's battles over again.

(*Adjectives*). Descriptive, graphic, realistic, naturalistic, novelistic, historic, traditional, traditionary, legendary, romantic, anecdotic, Boswellian, described, etc.

595. DISSERTATION (*Substantives*), treatise, tract, tractate, thesis, monograph, essay, discourse, article, leading article, leader, leaderette, editorial, feuilleton, criticism, critique, review, memoir, prolusion, disquisition, exposition, exercitation, compilation, sermon, homily, pandect, *causerie*.

(*Verbs*). To dissert, descant, treat of, discuss, write, compile, touch upon, ventilate, handle a subject, do justice to a subject.

(*Adjectives*). Discursive, disquisitional, expository, compiled.

596. COMPENDIUM (*Substantives*), compend, summary, abstract, précis, epitome, *aperçu*, digest, sum and substance, *compte rendu*, *procès verbal*, draft, *exposé*, brief, recapitulation, résumé, conspectus, abridgment, *abrégé*, abbreviation, minute, note, synopsis, argument, plot, syllabus, *prodromus*, *spicilegium*, contents, heads, prospectus.

Scrap-book, album, note-book, commonplace-book, extracts, text-book, analects, *analecta*, excerpts, flowers, anthology, *collectanea*, memorabilia.

(*Verbs*). To abridge, abstract, excerpt, abbreviate, recapitulate, run over, make or prepare an abstract, etc. (*see* 201), sum up, summarise, boil down, anthologise.

(*Adjectives*). Compendious, etc., synoptic, abridged, etc., analectic, in short.

(*Phrase*). In a nut-shell.

597. POETRY (*Substantives*), poetics, poesy, the Muse, Calliope, Parnassus.

Verse, metre, measure, foot, numbers, strain, rhyme, heroic verse, alexandrine, octosyllables, *terza rima*, blank verse, *vers libre*, assonance, versification, macaronics, doggerel, jingle; prosody, scansion.

Poem, epic, epopee, epic poem, ode, idyll, lyric, eclogue, pastoral, bucolic, macaronic, dithyramb, anacreontic, sonnet,

598. PROSE (*Substantives*), proser, prosaist.

(*Verb*). To prose.

(*Adjectives*). Prosaic, prosing, prosy, rhymeless, unpoetical, commonplace, humdrum.

lay, roundelay, rondeau, rondel, ballade, villanelle, triolet, sestina, rhyme royal, madrigal, canzonet, libretto, posy, anthology, distich, stanza, stave, strophe, couplet, quatrain, cento, monody, elegy, *vers de société*.

A poet, bard, scald, poetess, rhymer, rhymist, versifier, rhymester, sonneteer, poetaster, minor poet, minnesinger, meistersinger, troubadour, *trouvère*.

(*Phrases*). *Genus irritabile vatum ; disjecta membra poetæ.*

(*Verbs*). To rhyme, versify, sing, make verses, scan, poetise.

(*Adjectives*). Poetical, poetic, Castalian, Parnassian, lyric, metrical, epic, heroic, etc., catalectic, dithyrambic, doggerel, macaronic, leonine, Pindaric, Hudibrastic, Whitmanesque.

599. THE DRAMA (*Substantives*), stage, theatre, the histrionic art, dramatic art, histrionics, acting, etc.; stage effect, *mise en scène*, stage production, setting, scenery; buskin, sock, cothurnus; Melpomene, Thalia; play-writing, dramaturgy.

Play, stage-play, piece, tragedy, comedy, tragi-comedy, morality, mystery, melodrama, farce, knock-about farce, comedietta, curtain-raiser, interlude, after-piece, vaudeville, extravaganza, *divertissement*, burletta, burlesque, variety show, revue; opera, grand opera, music-drama, comic opera, *opéra bouffe*, operetta, ballad opera, *singspiel*, musical comedy; ballet, pantomime, harlequinade, word-less play, dumb-show, by-play; monodrama, monologue, duologue; masque, pageant, show; scenario, libretto, book of words, part, role; matinée, benefit; motion picture, silent film, talkie.

Theatre, playhouse, cinema, music-hall, variety theatre; stage, scene, the boards, the footlights, green-room, foyer, proscenium, flies, wings, etc.

An actor, player, stage-player, performer, artiste, comedian, comedienne, tragedian, tragedienne, Thespian, clown, harlequin, pantaloon, *buffo*, buffoon, pierrot, pierrette, impersonator, entertainer, etc., strolling player; ballet-dancer, *ballerina*, figurant, mime; star, *prima donna, primo tenore*, etc., leading lady, heavy lead, juvenile lead, *ingénue*, soubrette, etc.; supernumerary, super, walking gentleman or lady, chorus-girl; *dramatis personæ*, cast, company, stock company, touring company, etc.; a star turn.

Mummer, guiser, masquer; dancer, nautch-girl, bayadère, geisha.

Stage-manager, impresario, producer, prompter, stage hands, etc.

Dramatic writer, mimographer, pantomimist, playwright, play-writer, dramatist, dramaturge, librettist, scenario-writer.

(*Phrase*). The profession.

(*Verbs*). To act, play, perform, personate (554), play or interpret a part, rehearse, spout, rant, gag, star, walk on.

(*Phrase*). To strut and fret one's hour on the stage.

To produce, present, stage, stage-manage, feature, screen.

(*Adjectives*). Dramatic, theatric, theatrical, scenic, histrionic, comic, tragic, buskined, farcical, knock-about, tragi-comic, melodramatic, transpontine, stagy, operatic.

CLASS V

WORDS RELATING TO THE VOLUNTARY POWERS

DIVISION I.—INDIVIDUAL VOLITION

SECTION I.—VOLITION IN GENERAL

1°. *Acts of Volition*

600. WILL (*Substantives*), volition, voluntariness, velleity, freewill, spontaneity, spontaneousness, freedom.

Pleasure, wish, mind, *animus*, breast, mood, bosom, *petto*, heart, discretion, accord.

Libertarianism.

Determination (*see* 604, 611), intention (*see* 620), choice (*see* 609).

(*Verbs*). To will, list, think fit, think proper, determine, etc. (604), settle (609), to take upon oneself, to have one's will, to do as one likes, wishes, or chooses; to use or exercise one's own discretion, *see* Freedom (748), to volunteer, lend oneself to.

(*Phrases*). To have a will of one's own; *hoc volo, sic jubeo*; *stet pro ratione voluntas*; to take the will for the deed; to know one's own mind; to know what one is about; to see one's way; to have one's will; to take upon oneself.

(*Adjectives*). Voluntary, volitional, willing, content, minded,

601. NECESSITY (*Substantives*), instinct, blind impulse, necessitation, fate, destiny, doom (152), foredoom, destination, election, predestination, preordination, compulsion (744), subjection (749), stern, hard, cruel, inexorable, iron necessity.

Determinism, Necessitarianism, Fatalism, Automatism.

The Fates, Parcæ, the stars, astral influence, spell, *see* 152.

(*Phrases*). Hobson's choice; a blind bargain; a *pis aller*.

(*Verbs*). To lie under a necessity, to be fated, doomed, destined, etc. (152), to need be, not to help, to leave to itself.

To necessitate, destine, doom, foredoom, predestine, preordain.

To compel, force, constrain, etc., cast a spell, etc. (992).

(*Phrases*). To make a virtue of necessity; to be pushed to the wall; to dree one's weird.

(*Adjectives*). Necessitated, fated, destined, doomed, elect, spell-bound.

Compelled, forced, etc., un-

spontaneous, free, left to oneself, unconstrained, unfettered, unbidden, unasked, unurged, uncompelled, of one's own accord, gratuitous, of one's own head, prepense, advised, express, designed, intended, calculated, premeditated, preconcerted, predetermined, deliberate.

(*Adverbs*). At will, at pleasure, *à volonté, ad libitum, ad arbitrium*, spontaneously, freely, of one's own accord, voluntarily, advisedly, designedly, intentionally, expressly, knowingly, determinately, deliberately, pointedly, in earnest, in good earnest, studiously, purposely, *proprio motu, suo motu, ex mero motu ; quo animo*.

(*Phrases*). With one's eyes open; in cold blood.

avoidable, inevitable, irresistible, irrevocable.

Compulsory, involuntary, unintentional, undesigned, unintended, instinctive, automatic, blind, mechanical, impulsive, unwitting, unaware; necessitarian.

(*Phrases*). Unable to help it; having no alternative.

(*Adverbs*). Necessarily, needs, of necessity, perforce, forcibly, compulsorily; on or by compulsion or force, involuntarily, etc., impulsively (612), unwittingly (491).

(*Phrases*). It must be; it needs must be; it cannot be helped; *che sarà sarà*; there is no help for it; there is no alternative; nothing for it but; necessity has no law; needs must when the devil drives; *dis aliter visum*.

602. WILLINGNESS (*Substantives*), voluntariness, disposition, inclination, leaning, *penchant*, humour, mood, vein, bent, bias, propensity, proclivity, aptitude, predisposition, predilection, proneness, docility, pliability (324), alacrity, earnestness, readiness, devices, assent (448).

(*Phrases*). A labour of love; *labor ipse voluptas*.

(*Verbs*). To be willing, etc., to incline to, lean to, mind, *see* Desire (865), to have lief, to propend.

(*Phrases*). To find in one's heart; to set one's heart upon; to make no bones of; have a mind to; have a great mind to.

(*Adjectives*). Willing, fain, disposed, inclined, minded, bent upon, set upon, forward, predisposed, hearty, ready, wholehearted, cordial, genial, keen, prepense, docile.

603. UNWILLINGNESS (*Substantives*), involuntariness, indisposition, indisposedness, backwardness, disinclination, averseness, aversion, reluctance, repugnance, demur, renitence, remissness, slackness, lukewarmness, indifference, nonchalance.

Hesitation, shrinking, recoil, suspense, dislike (867), scrupulousness, scrupulosity, delicacy, demur, scruple, qualm.

A recusant, *pococurante*.

(*Phrase*). Le médecin malgré lui.

(*Verbs*). To be unwilling, etc., to nill.

To demur, stick at, hesitate (605), waver, hang in suspense, scruple, stickle, boggle, falter, to hang back, hang fire, jib, grudge.

(*Phrase*). To stick in the throat.

To decline, reject, refuse (764), refrain, keep from, abstain, recoil, shrink, reluct.

Free, spontaneous, unforced, unasked, unsummoned, unbiased, unsolicited, unbesought, undriven, voluntary.

(*Adverbs*). Willingly, freely, readily, lief, heartily, with a good grace, without reluctance, etc., as soon, of one's own accord (600), certainly, be it so (488).

(*Phrases*). With all one's heart, *con amore*; with heart and soul; heart in hand; with a good grace; *à la bonne heure*; by all means; by all manner of means; nothing loth; *ex animo*; to one's heart's content.

(*Phrases*). To set one's face against; to draw the line at.

(*Adjectives*). Unwilling, unconsenting, disinclined, indisposed, averse, reluctant, not content, laggard, backward, remiss, slack, indifferent, lukewarm, frigid, scrupulous, repugnant, disliking (867).

Demurring, wavering, etc., refusing (764), grudging.

(*Adverbs*). Unwillingly, etc., perforce.

(*Phrases*). Against the grain; *invita Minerva*; *malgré soi*; *bon gré, mal gré*; *nolens volens*; with a bad grace; not for the world; willy-nilly.

---

604. RESOLUTION (*Substantives*), determination, decision, resolvedness, fixedness, steadiness, constancy, unchangeableness, inflexibility, decision, finality, firmness, doggedness, tenacity of purpose, perseverance, constancy, solidity, stability.

Energy, manliness, vigour, spirit, spiritedness, pluck, bottom, backbone, grit, an iron will; self-reliance; self-mastery; self-control.

A devotee, zealot, extremist, ultra, enthusiast, fanatic., fan.

(*Verbs*). To be resolved, etc., to have resolution, etc., to resolve, persevere, determine, conclude, make up one's mind, to stand, keep, or remain firm, etc., to come to a determination, to form a resolution, to take one's stand, to stand by, hold by, hold fast, stick to, abide by, adhere to, keep one's ground, persevere, keep one's course, hold on, hang on, not to fail.

To insist upon, to make a point of.

(*Phrases*). To determine once

605. IRRESOLUTION (*Substantives*), indecision, indetermination, demur, hesitation, suspense, hesitancy, vacillation, unsteadiness, inconstancy, wavering, fluctuation, flickering, changeableness, mutability, fickleness, levity, *légèreté*, trimming, softness, weakness, instability.

A weathercock, a shuttlecock, a butterfly, a harlequin, a chameleon.

(*Verbs*). To be irresolute, etc., to hesitate, hang in suspense, demur, waver, vacillate, quaver, fluctuate, shuffle, boggle, flicker, falter, palter, debate, dilly-dally, dally with, swerve, etc.

(*Phrases*). To hang fire; to hum and ha; not to know one's own mind; to leave "*ad referendum*"; letting "I dare not" wait upon "I would."

(*Adjectives*). Irresolute, undecided, unresolved, undetermined, vacillating, wavering, hesitating, faltering, shuffling, etc., double-minded, indecisive.

Unsteady, unsteadfast, fickle, flighty, changing, changeable,

for all; form a resolution; stand firm; remain firm; to pass the Rubicon; take a decisive step; to nail one's colours to the mast; to screw one's courage to the sticking-place; to take the bull by the horns; to mean business; to carry a stiff upper lip.

(*Adjectives*). Resolved, resolute, game, firm, steady, steadfast, staunch, constant; solid, manly, stout.

Decided, determinate, definitive, determined, uncompromising, purposive, fixed, unmoved, unshaken, unbending, unyielding, unflinching, inflexible, unwavering, unfaltering, unshrinking, undiverted, undeterred, immovable, not to be moved, unhesitating, unswerving.

versatile, variable, inconstant, mutable, protean, fluctuating, unstable, unsettled, unhinged, unfixed, shilly-shally.

(*Phrases*). Infirm of purpose; without ballast.

Weak, feeble-minded, frail, soft, pliant, giddy, volatile, fitful, frothy, freakish, lightsome, light-minded, invertebrate.

In suspense, in doubt, *see* 485.

Revocable, reversible.

(*Phrase*). Waiting to see which way the cat jumps, or the wind blows.

(*Adverb*). Off and on.

Peremptory, trenchant, inexorable, indomitable, strenuous, persevering, irrevocable, irreversible, reverseless, decisive, final.

Strenuous, bent upon, set upon, intent upon, proof against, master of oneself, steeled, staid, serious, stiff, stiff-necked; *see* Obstinate (606).

(*Phrases*). Firm as a rock; steady as time; true to oneself; master of oneself; *in utrumque paratus*.

(*Adverbs*). Resolutely, etc., without fail.

(*Phrases*). Through thick and thin; through fire and water; *per fas aut nefas*; *coûte que coûte*; *fortiter in re*; like grim death.

---

606. OBSTINACY (*Substantives*), obstinateness, wilfulness, self-will, pertinacity, pertinaciousness, pervicacity, pervicaciousness, tenacity, tenaciousness, inflexibility, doggedness, stubbornness, headiness, *see* Resolution (604), restiveness, contumacy, obduracy, obduration, unruliness.

Intolerance, dogmatism, bigotry, opinionatedness, opiniativeness, zealotry, infatuation, monomania, indocility, intractability, intractableness (481), pig-headedness.

An opinionist, *opiniâtre*, crank,

607. Change of mind, intention, purpose, etc.

TERGIVERSATION (*Substantives*), retractation, recantation, revocation, revokement, reversal, palinode, *volte-face*, renunciation, abjuration, abjurement, relinquishment (624), repentance (950), vacillation, etc. (605).

Going over, ratting, apostasy.

A turn-coat, rat, Janus, renegade, apostate, trimmer, time-server, opportunist, Vicar of Bray, deserter, weathercock, etc. (605), Proteus.

(*Verbs*). To change one's mind,

stickler, zealot, dogmatist, fanatic, mule.

A fixed idea, rooted prejudice, blind side, etc. (481).

(*Verbs*). To be obstinate, etc., to persist, stickle, opiniate.

(*Phrase*). To stick at nothing.

(*Adjectives*). Obstinate, opinionative, opinative, opinionated, opinioned, wedded to an opinion, self-opinioned, prejudiced (481), cranky, wilful, self-willed, positive, tenacious.

Stiff, stubborn, stark, rigid, stiff-necked, dogged, pertinacious, restive, pervicacious, dogmatic, unpersuadable, mulish, unmoved, uninfluenced, hard-mouthed, unyielding, pig-headed, wayward, intractable, haggard, headstrong, refractory, unruly, infatuated, heady, *entêté*, wrong-headed, cross-grained, obdurate, contumacious, fanatical, rabid, inexorable, impracticable.

(*Phrase*). Obstinate as a mule.

(*Adverbs*). Obstinately, etc., headlong, head-first, head-foremost, heels over head; at any rate, risk, price, cost, or sacrifice.

(*Phrases*). *Coûte que coûte; quand même*; through thick and thin; *per fas et nefas; à tort et à travers; vestigia nulla retrorsum*; at all risks or hazards.

etc., to retract, recant, revoke, unsay, take back, abjure, renounce, apostatise, relinquish, trim, straddle, veer round, change sides, rat; go over, pass, change, or skip from one side to another; back out, back down, swerve, flinch, balance.

(*Phrases*). To eat one's words; turn over a new leaf; think better of it; play fast and loose; blow hot and cold; sit on the fence; box the compass; swallow the leek; eat dirt.

(*Adverbs*). Changeful, changeable, mobile, unsteady (605), trimming, double-faced, ambidexter, fast and loose, time-serving, facing both ways.

Fugacious, *see* 111, revocatory.

(*Phrase*). A change coming over the spirit of one's dream.

608. CAPRICE (*Substantives*), fancy, fantasy, humour, whim, crotchet, fad, craze, *capriccio*, quirk, freak, maggot, vagary, whimsy, whim-wham, kink, prank, fit, flim-flam, escapade, *boutade*, wild-goose chase, freakishness, skittishness, volatility, fancifulness, whimsicality, giddiness, inconsistency, contrariety; a madcap.

(*Verb*). To be capricious, etc.

(*Phrases*). To strain at a gnat and swallow a camel; to take it into one's head; to let oneself go.

(*Adjectives*). Capricious, inconsistent, fanciful, fantastic, whimsical, full of whims, etc., erratic, crotchety, faddy, viewy, perverse, humoursome, wayward, captious, contrary, contrarious, skittish, fitful.

(*Phrases*). The head being turned; the deuce being in him; *nil fuit unquam sic impar sibi*.

609. CHOICE (*Substantives*), option, election, arbitrament, adoption, selection, excerption, co-optation, gleaning, eclecticism, lief, preference, predilection, pre-option, discretion, fancy.

610. Absence of Choice, *see* Necessity (601).

REJECTION (*Substantives*), refusal, *see* 764; declining, repudiation, exclusion.

Indifference, indecision (605).

Decision, determination, adjudication, award, vote, suffrage, ballot, referendum, verdict, voice, plumper.

Alternative, dilemma (704).

Persuasion, seduction, bringing over, *see* 615.

Chooser, elector, voter, constituent; constituency.

Thing chosen, choice, *élite* (650).

(*Verbs*). To choose, decide, determine, elect, list, think fit, use one's discretion, fancy, shape one's course, prefer, have rather, have as lief, take one's choice, adopt, select, fix upon, pitch upon, pick out, single out, vote for, plump for, co-opt, pick up, take up, catch at, jump at, cull, glean, pick, winnow.

(*Phrases*). To winnow the chaff from the wheat; to pick one's way; to indulge one's fancy; to pick and choose; to make no bones; to make or have no scruple; to take a decided step; to pass the Rubicon (604); to hold out; offer for choice; commend me to.

To be persuaded, etc.

(*Phrases*). To swallow the bait; to gorge the hook; to yield to temptation.

To persuade, overcome, seduce, entice, *see* 615.

(*Adjectives*). Optional, discretional, eclectic, choosing, etc., chosen, etc., decided, etc., preferential; left to oneself.

(*Adverbs*). Discretionally, at pleasure, *à plaisir*, *a piacere*, at discretion, at will, *ad libitum*.

Decidedly, etc., rather; once for all, either the one or the other, for one's money, for choice.

(*Verbs*). To reject, refuse, etc., decline, give up, repudiate, exclude, lay aside, to refrain, spare (678), abandon, turn down, black-ball.

(*Phrases*). To lay on the shelf; to throw overboard; to draw the line at.

(*Adjectives*). Rejecting, etc., rejected, etc., not chosen, etc.

Having no choice, indifferent, undecided (605).

(*Adverbs*). Neither; neither the one nor the other, nothing to choose between them.

---

611. PREDETERMINATION (*Substantives*), premeditation, predeliberation.

(*Verbs*). To predetermine, premeditate, resolve beforehand.

(*Adjectives*). Prepense, premeditated, predetermined, advised, predesigned, studied, designed (620).

(*Adverbs*). Advisedly, etc., with the eyes open.

---

612. IMPULSE (*Substantives*), sudden thought, inspiration, flash, spurt.

Improvisator, improvisatore, improvisatrice.

(*Verbs*). To flash on the mind; to improvise, improvisate, to extemporise, vamp.

(*Adjectives*). Extemporaneous, extemporary, impulsive, unrehearsed, unpremeditated (674), improvised, improvisatorial, improvisatory, unprompted, spontaneous, natural, unguarded, unreflecting.

(*Adverbs*). Extempore, offhand, impromptu, *à l'improviste*, out of hand.

(*Phrases*). On the spur of the moment, or of the occasion.

613. HABIT (*Substantives*), habitude, wont, rule, routine, jog-trot, groove, rut.

Custom, use, usage, practice, run, run of things, way, prevalence, observance, fashion (852), etiquette, convention, *convenances*, red-tape, red-tapery, red-tapism, routinism, vogue.

Seasoning, training, hardening, etc. (673), acclimatisation, acclimation, acclimatation.

A second nature, *cacoethes*, taking root, diathesis.

(*Verbs*). To be habitual, etc., to be in the habit of, be wont, be accustomed to, etc.

To follow, observe, conform to, obey, bend to, comply with, accommodate oneself to, adapt oneself to, fall into a habit, convention, custom, or usage, to addict oneself to, to get the hang of.

614. DESUETUDE (*Substantives*), disuse, want of habit or of practice, inusitation, newness to.

Non - observance, infraction, violation, infringement.

(*Verbs*). To be unaccustomed, etc., to be new to, to leave off, wean oneself of, break off, break through, infringe, violate, etc., a habit, usage, etc., to disuse, to wear off.

(*Adjectives*). Unaccustomed, unused, unusual, unwonted, unpractised, unprofessional, unfashionable, non-observant, disused, weaned.

Unseasoned, uninured, untrained.

Unhackneyed, unconventional, Bohemian (83).

(*Phrases*). To follow the multitude; *hurler avec les loups*; go with the current, stream, etc.; run on in a groove; *stare super antiquas vias*.

To become a habit, to take root, to gain or grow upon one, to run in the blood.

To habituate, inure, harden, season, form, train, accustom, naturalise, acclimatise, conventionalise.

To acquire a habit, to get into the way of, to learn, etc.

(*Adjectives*). Habitual, accustomed, habituated, etc.; in the habit, etc., of; used to, addicted to, attuned to, wedded to, at home in, usual, wonted, customary, hackneyed, groovy, fixed, rooted, permanent, inveterate, ingrained, running in the blood, hereditary, congenital, innate, inborn, natural, instinctive, etc. (5).

(*Phrases*). Bred in the bone, in the blood.

Fashionable, in fashion, in vogue, according to use, routine, conventional, etc.

(*Phrase*). *Naturam expellas furca, tamen usque recurret.*

(*Adverbs*). As the world goes, *more suo, pro more, pro forma*, according to custom, *de rigueur, more majorum*.

2°. *Causes of Volition*

615. MOTIVE (*Substantives*), reason, ground, principle, mainspring, *primum mobile*, account, score, sake, consideration, calculation, *raison d'être*.

(*Phrases*). The pros and cons; the why and wherefore.

Inducement, recommendation, encouragement, attraction, allectation, temptation, enticement, bait, allurement, charm, witchery, bewitchment.

Persuasibility, softness, susceptibility.

Influence, prompting, dictate, instance, impulse, impulsion, incitement, incitation, press, instigation, excitement, provocation, invitation, solicitation, suasion, persuasion, hortation, exhortation, seduction, cajolery, tantalisation, *agacerie*, seducement, bewitchment, inspiration, honeyed words.

Incentive, stimulus, spur, fillip, goad, rowel, provocative, whet, dram, cocktail, pick-me-up, appetiser.

Bribe, sop, lure, decoy, charm, spell, loadstone.

(*Phrases*). The golden apple; the voice of the tempter; the song of the sirens.

Prompter, tempter, seducer, seductor, siren, Circe, instigator, *agent provocateur*.

(*Verbs*). To induce, move, lead, draw, draw over, carry, bring, to influence, to weigh with, bias, to operate, work upon, engage, incline, dispose, predispose, prompt, whisper, call,

616. Absence of motive, *see* Caprice (608).

(*Phrase*). Without rhyme or reason.

DISSUASION (*Substantives*), dehortation, discouragement.

Inhibition, check, restraint, curb, bridle, rein, stay, damper, chill, remonstrance, expostulation.

Scruple, qualm, demur (867), reluctance, delicacy (868); counter-attraction.

(*Phrase*). A wet blanket.

(*Verbs*). To dissuade, dehort, discourage, disincline, indispose, dispirit, damp, choke off, dishearten, disenchant, disillusion, deter, keep back, put off, choke off, render averse, etc.

To withhold, restrain, hold, check, bridle, curb, rein in, keep in, inhibit, repel (751).

To cool, blunt, calm, quiet, quench, shake, stagger, remonstrate, expostulate, warn.

To scruple, refrain, abstain, etc. (603).

(*Phrases*). To throw cold water on; to turn a deaf ear to.

(*Adjectives*). Dissuading, etc., dissuasive, dehortatory.

Dissuaded, discouraged, etc., uninduced, unmoved, unactuated, uninfluenced, unbiased, unimpelled, unswayed, unprovoked, uninspired, untempted, unattracted.

Repugnant, averse, scrupulous, etc. (867), unpersuadable (606).

_____

call upon, recommend, encourage, entice, invite, solicit, press, enjoin, entreat (765), court, plead, advocate, exhort, enforce, dictate, tantalise, bait the hook, seduce, decoy, draw on, charm, bewitch, conciliate, wheedle, coax, speak fair, carny (or carney), cajole, pat on the back or shoulder, talk over, inveigle, persuade, prevail upon, get to do, bring over, procure, lead by the nose, sway, over-persuade, come over, get round, turn the head, enlist, retain, kidnap, bribe, suborn.

(*Phrases*). To grease the palm; to put a sop in the pan; a sop for Cerberus; to work the oracle.

To act upon, to impel, excite, suscitate, stimulate, key up, motivate, incite, animate, instigate, provoke, set on, urge, pique, spirit, inspirit, inspire, awaken, buck up, give a fillip, light up, kindle, enkindle, rekindle, quicken, goad, spur, prick, edge, egg on, hurry on, stir up, work up, fan, fire, inflame, set on fire, fan the flame, blow the coals, stir the embers, put on one's mettle, set on, force, rouse, arouse, lash into fury, get a rise out of.

(*Phrases*). To follow the bent of; to follow the dictates of; to make no scruple; to make no bones; to act on principle.

(*Adjectives*). Impulsive, motive, persuasive, hortatory, seductive, carnying, suasory, suasive, honey-tongued, tempting, alluring, piquant, exciting, inviting, tantalising, etc.

Persuadable, persuasible, suasible, soft, yielding, facile, easily persuaded, etc.

Induced, moved, disposed, led, persuaded, etc., spellbound, instinct with or by.

(*Adverbs*). Because, for, since, on account of, out of, from; by reason of, for the sake of, on the score of.

As, forasmuch as, therefore, hence, why, wherefore; for all the world.

(*Phrase*). *Hinc illæ lacrimæ.*

617. Ostensible motive, or reason assigned.

PLEA (*Substantives*), allegation, pretext, pretence, excuse, cue, colour, gloss, salvo, loophole, handle, shift, quirk, guise, stalking-horse, makeshift, special pleading, *cheval de bataille*, claptrap, advocation, soft sawder, a Canterbury tale, moonshine; a lame excuse or apology.

(*Phrase*). A hole to creep out of.

(*Verbs*). To make a pretext, etc., of; to use as a plea, etc.; to plead, allege, pretend, excuse, make a handle, etc. of, to gild the pill.

(*Adjectives*). Ostensible, colourable, pretended, alleged, etc.

(*Phrases*). *Ad captandum*; on the spur of the occasion; the grapes being sour; *qui s'excuse s'accuse*; playing to the gallery.

3°. *Objects of Volition*

618. GOOD (*Substantives*), benefit, advantage, service, interest, weal, boot, gain, profit, good turn, blessing, boon; behoof, behalf.

619. EVIL (*Substantives*), harm, injury, wrong, scathe, curse, detriment, hurt, damage, disservice, ill-turn, bale, grievance,

(Phrases). The main chance; *summum bonum.*

Luck, piece of luck, windfall, godsend, bonus; bonanza; prize.

Cause of good, *see* Utility (644), Goodness (648), and Remedy (662).

(Adverbs). Aright, well, favourably, to boot.

In behalf of, in favour of.

———

prejudice, loss, mischief, devilry (or deviltry), gravamen.

Disadvantage, drawback, trouble, annoyance, nuisance, molestation, oppression, persecution, plague, corruption (659).

Blow, bruise, scratch, wound, mutilation, outrage, spoliation, plunder, pillage, rapine, destruction, dilapidation, havoc, ravage, devastation, inroad, sweep, sack, foray (716), desolation, *razzia*, dragonnade.

Misfortune, mishap, woe, disaster, calamity, affliction, catastrophe, downfall, ruin, prostration, curse, wrack, blight, blast; Pandora's box; a plague-spot.

Cause of evil, *see* Bane (663).

Production of evil (649); Spoliation (791); Destruction (162).

(Adverbs). Amiss, wrong, evil, ill.

SECTION II.—PROSPECTIVE VOLITION [1]

1°. *Conceptional Volition*

620. INTENTION (*Substantives*), intent, purpose, design, purport, mind, meaning, animus, view, set purpose, point, bent, turn, proposal, study, scope, purview.

Final cause, object, aim, end, drift, destination, mark, point, butt, goal, target, prey, quarry, game, quintain, objective; the philosopher's stone.

Decision, determination, resolve, resolution (604), predetermination (611); set purpose.

A hobby, ambition, wish; *see* Desire (865).

Study of final causes, Teleology; of final issues, Eschatology.

(Verbs). To intend, purpose, design, destinate, mean, aim at, propose to oneself.

(Phrases). Have in view; have *in petto*; have in one's eye; have an eye to.

To be at, drive at, be after,

621. Absence of purpose in the succession of events.

CHANCE [2] (*Substantives*), fortune, accident, hazard, hap, haphazard (156), lot, chance-medley, hit, fluke, casualty, contingency, fate, adventure, random shot, off-chance.

(Phrases). A toss-up; a gamble; a turn of the dice or cards.

A godsend, luck, a run of luck, a windfall, etc. (618).

Drawing lots, sortilege.

Wager, bet, flutter, betting.

(Phrases). A blind bargain; a pig in a poke.

(Verbs). To chance, hap, turn up; to stand a chance.

(Phrases). To take one's chance; to chance it; try one's luck; shuffle the cards; put into a lottery, lay a wager; toss up, spin a coin, cast lots, draw lots; stand the hazard.

[1] That is, volition having reference to a future object.

[2] *See Note on* 156.

point at, level at, take aim, aspire at or after, endeavour after, destine.

To meditate, think of, dream of, premeditate (611), contemplate, compass.

To propose, project, devise, take into one's head.

(*Phrases*). Take upon oneself; to have to do; to see one's way; to find in one's heart.

(*Adjectives*). Intended, etc., intentional, minded, express, prepense, aforethought, set upon, bent upon, intent upon, in view, *in petto*, in prospect; teleological, eschatological.

(*Phrases*). In the wind; *sur le tapis*; in contemplation.

(*Adverbs*). Intentionally, etc., expressly, designedly, purposely, on purpose, with a view to, with an eye to, for the purpose of, with the view of, in order to, to the end that, on account of, in pursuance of, pursuant to, with the intent, etc.

(*Phrases*). In good earnest; with one's eyes open; to all intents and purposes.

To risk, venture, hazard, stake, incur, or run the risk; bet, wager, gamble, plunge, raffle.

(*Phrases*). To buy a pig in a poke; *alea jacta est*; the die being cast; to go nap on.

(*Adjectives*). Casual, fortuitous, accidental, fluky, contingent, random, adventitious, incidental.

Unintentional, aimless, driftless, undesigned, undirected; purposeless, causeless, without purpose, etc., unmeditated, unpurposed, indiscriminate, promiscuous.

On the cards, possible (470), at stake.

(*Adverbs*). Casually, etc., by chance, by accident, accidentally, etc., at haphazard; heads or tails.

(*Phrases*). As luck would have it; without rhyme or reason.

---

622. Purpose in action.

PURSUIT (*Substantives*), undertaking, enterprise, emprise, adventure, game, hobby, endeavour.

Prosecution, search, angling, chase, quest, hunt, shikar, race, battue, drive, course, direction, wild-goose chase, steeplechase.

Pursuer, huntsman, hunter, shikaree, hound, greyhound, bloodhound, sleuth - hound, beagle, harrier.

(*Verbs*). To pursue, undertake, engage in, take in hand, carry on, prosecute (461), endeavour.

To court, seek, angle, chase, give chase, course, dog, hunt, drive, follow, run after, hound, bid for, aim at, take aim, make a

623. Absence of pursuit.

AVOIDANCE (*Substantives*), forbearance, abstinence, sparing, refraining.

Flight, etc., evasion, elusion.

Motive for avoidance, counterattraction.

(*Verbs*). To avoid, refrain, abstain; to spare, hold, shun, fly, flee, eschew, run away from, shrink, hold back, draw back (see 287), recoil from, flinch, blench, shy, elude, evade, shirk, blink, parry, dodge, let alone.

(*Phrases*). To give the slip or go-by; to lead one a dance; to beat a retreat; get out of the way; steer clear of; fight shy of; to take to one's heels.

leap at, rush upon, jump at, quest, shadow.

(*Phrases*). Take or hold a course; tread a path; shape one's course; direct or bend one's steps or course; run a race; rush headlong; rush head-foremost; make a plunge; snatch at, etc.; start game; follow the scent; to run or ride full tilt at.

(*Adjective*). Pursuing, etc.

(*Adverbs*). In order to, in order that, for the purpose of, with a view to, etc. (620).

(*Phrases*). In full cry; after, on the scent of.

(*Adjectives*). Avoiding, etc., elusive, evasive, flying, unattempted, fugitive, etc., unsought.

(*Adverbs*). Lest, with a view to prevent.

(*Phrases*). *Sauve qui peut*; the devil take the hindmost.

624. RELINQUISHMENT (*Substantives*), dereliction, abandonment (782), renunciation, desertion (607), discontinuance (681).

Dispensation, riddance.

(*Verbs*). To relinquish, give up; lay, set, or put aside; drop, abandon, renounce, waive, desist from, desert, leave, leave off, back out of, quit, throw up, chuck up, give over, forsake, throw over, forswear, swerve from (279), put away, discontinue (681).

(*Phrases*). To drop all idea of; to think better of it; to wash one's hands of; to turn over a new leaf; to throw up the game or the cards; to have other fish to fry; to draw in one's horns; to lay on the shelf.

To give warning; to give notice.

(*Adjectives*). Relinquishing, etc., relinquished, etc., unpursued.

(*Interjections*). Hands off! keep off! forbear! avast!

625. BUSINESS (*Substantives*), affair, concern, task, work, job, stunt, errand, agenda, commission, office, charge, part, duty, rôle; a press of business.

Province, department, beat, mission, function, vocation, calling, avocation, profession, occupation, cloth, faculty, trade, industry, craft, mystery, walk, race, career, walk of life, *métier*.

Place, post, orb, sphere, capacity, employment, engagement, exercise, occupation; situation, undertaking (676).

(*Verbs*). To carry on or run a business, trade, etc.

(*Phrases*). To have to do with; have on one's hands; betake oneself to; occupy or concern oneself with; go in for; have on one's shoulders; make it one's business; go to do; act a part; perform the office of or functions of; to enter or take up a profession; drive a trade; spend time upon; busy oneself with, about, etc.

(*Adjectives*). Business-like, official, functional, professional, in hand.

(*Adverbs*). On hand, on foot, afoot, afloat, going.

(*Phrase*). In the swim.

626. PLAN (*Substantives*), scheme, device, design, project, proposal, proposition.

Line of conduct, game, card course, tactics, strategy, policy, polity (692), craft, practice, campaign, gambit.

Intrigue, cabal, plot, conspiracy, complot, machination, *coup d'état*.

Measure, step, precaution, proceeding, procedure, process, system, economy, organisation, expedient, resource, contrivance, artifice, shift, makeshift, gadget, stop-gap, manœuvre, stratagem, fetch, trick, dodge, machination, intrigue, stroke, stroke of policy, master-stroke, great gun, trump card.

Alternative, loophole, counterplot, counter-project, side-wind, last resort, *dernier ressort, pis-aller*.

Sketch, outline, programme, draught (or draft), scenario, *ébauche*, rough draught, skeleton, forecast, prospectus, *carte du pays*.

After-course, after-game, after-thought, *arrière-pensée*, under-plot.

A projector, designer, schemer, contriver, organiser, *entrepreneur*, artist, schematist, intriguant.

(*Verbs*). To plan, scheme, devise, imagine, design, frame, contrive, project, plot, conspire, cabal, think out, invent, forecast, strike out, chalk out, rough out, sketch, lay out, lay down, cut out, cast, recast, map out, countermine, hit upon, fall upon, arrange, mature, organise, concoct, digest, pack, prepare, hatch, elaborate, make shift, make do, wangle.

(*Phrases*). To have many irons in the fire; to dig a mine; to spring a project; to take or adopt a course; to make the best of a bad job; to work the oracle.

(*Adjectives*). Planned, etc., strategic; planning, scheming, etc.

Well-laid, deep-laid, cunning, well-devised, etc., maturely considered, well-weighed, prepared, organised, etc.

(*Adverbs*). In course of preparation, on the anvil, on the stocks, in the rough, *sur le tapis; faute de mieux*.

627. METHOD (*Substantives*), way, manner, wise, form, path, road, route, channel, walk, access, course, pass, ford, ferry, passage, line of way, trajectory, orbit, track, ride, avenue, approach, beaten track, pathway, highway, roadway, causeway, footway, pavement, foot-path, cinder-path, turnpike road, high road, railway, tramway, the King's highway, thoroughfare, gateway, street, lane, alley, gangway, hatchway, by-path, by-way, by-walk, cross-road, cross-way, by-road, cut, short cut, royal road, cross-cut, *carrefour*, promenade, subway.

Bridge, viaduct, stepping-stone, stair, corridor, staircase, escalator, companion-way, flight of stairs, ladder, step-ladder, scaffold, scaffolding, lift, elevator.

(*Phrase*). *Modus operandi.*

Indirect way: By-path, by-way, by-walk, by-road, back door, backstairs.

Inlet, gate, door, gateway, portal, porch, doorway, conduit, tunnel.

(*Adverbs*). How, in what way, in what manner, by what mode.

By the way, *en passant*, by the by, *in transitu, chemin faisant*.

One way or another, somehow, anyhow, by hook or crook, via. (*Phrases*). All roads lead to Rome; *hœ tibi erunt artes*; where there's a will there's a way.

628. MID - COURSE (*Substantives*), middle course, mean, *juste milieu, mezzo termine*; *see* Middle (68) and Mean (29).

Direct, straight, straightforward, course, path, etc.

(*Verb*). To keep in a middle course, etc.

(*Adjectives*). Undeviating, direct, straight, straightforward.

(*Phrases*). *In medio tutissimus ibis*; the golden mean; as the crow flies.

629. CIRCUIT (*Substantives*), roundabout way, zigzag, circuition, circumbendibus (311), wandering, deviation (279), divergence (291).

(*Verbs*). To perform a circuit, etc., to deviate, wander, go round about, meander, etc. (279).

(*Phrase*). To beat about the bush.

(*Adjectives*). Circuitous, indirect, roundabout, zigzag, etc.

(*Adverbs*). By a side wind, by an indirect course, etc.

630. REQUIREMENT (*Substantives*), requisition, need, occasion, lack, wants, requisites, necessities, desideratum, exigency, pinch, *sine qua non*, the very thing.

Needfulness, essentiality, necessity, indispensability, urgency, call for.

(*Verbs*). To require, need, want, have occasion for, stand in need of, lack, desire, be at a loss for, desiderate; not to be able to do without or dispense with; to want but little.

To render necessary, to necessitate, to create a necessity for, to call for.

(*Adjectives*). Requisite, required, etc., needful, necessary, exigent, essential, indispensable, irreplaceable, prerequisite, that cannot be spared or dispensed with, urgent.

2°. Subservience to Ends

1. Actual Subservience

631. INSTRUMENTALITY (*Substantives*), medium, intermedium, intervention, mediation, dint, *see* Agency (170), vehicle.

Midwife, *accoucheur*.

Key, master-key, passport, *passepartout*, "open sesame," a go-between (758), a cat's-paw, tool, mainstay, trump card.

(*Phrases*). Two strings to one's bow; *cheval de bataille*.

(*Adjectives*). Instrumental, intervening, intermediate, intermediary, subservient.

(*Adverbs*). Through, by, with, by means of, by dint of, *à force de*, along with, thereby, through the medium, etc., of, wherewith, wherewithal.

632. MEANS (*Substantives*), resources, appliances, ways and means, expedients, step, measure (626), aid (707), intermedium, medium.

Machinery, mechanism, mechanics, engineering, mechanical powers, scaffolding, ladder, mainstay.

(*Phrases*). Wheels within wheels; two strings to one's bow.

To beg, borrow, or steal.

(*Adjectives*). Instrumental, subservient, mechanical.

(*Adverbs*). How, by what means, by all means, by all manner of means, by the aid of, by dint of.

(*Phrases*). By hook or by crook; somehow or other; for love or money; by fair means or foul.

633. INSTRUMENT (*Substantives*), tool, implement, apparatus, utensil, gadget, craft, machine, engine, motor, lathe.

Weapon, arms, armoury, battery.

Equipment, gear, tackle, tackling, rigging, harness, paraphernalia, equipage, material, plant, appurtenances.

A wheel, jack, mill, clock-work, wheel-work, spring, screw, turbine, wedge, fly-wheel, lever, bascule, pinion, crank, winch, crane, capstan, windlass, pulley, monkey-engine, hammer, mallet, mattock, mall, bat, racket, sledge-hammer, mace, club, truncheon, pole, staff, bill, crow, crowbar, poleaxe, handspike, crutch, boom, bar, pitchfork, etc.

Organ, limb, arm, hand, finger, claw, paw, talons, tentacle, wing, oar, paddle, pincer, plier, forceps, thimble.

Handle, hilt, haft, shaft, shank, heft, blade, trigger, tiller, helm, treadle, pummel, peg (214, 215), key.

Edge-tool, hatchet, axe, pickaxe, etc. (253), axis (312).

634. SUBSTITUTE (*Substantives*), shift, makeshift, succedaneum, jury-mast, *pis-aller*, see Substitution (147) and Deputy (759).

635. MATERIALS (*Substantives*), materiel, stuff, pabulum, fuel, grist, provender, provisions, food, aliment, fodder, forage, prog, pasture, pasturage, see 298.

Supplies, munition, ammunition, reinforcement, relay, contingents.

Baggage, luggage, bag and baggage, effects, goods, chattels, household stuff, equipage, paraphernalia, impedimenta, stock-in-trade, pelf, cargo, lading, see 780.

Metal, ore, brick, clay, wood, etc.

(*Phrases*). A shot in the locker; a hand at cards.

636. STORE (*Substantives*), stock, fund, supply, reserve, relay, budget, quiver, *corps de réserve*, reserve fund, mine, quarry, vein, lode, fountain, milch-cow.

Collection, accumulation, heap (72), hoard, magazine, pile, rick, savings, bank (802), treasury, reservoir, repository, repertory, repertoire, depot, depository, treasure, thesaurus, museum, store-house, promptuary, reservatory, conservatory, menagerie, aviary, aquarium, receptacle, warehouse, entrepot, dock, larder, spence garner, granary, store-room, box-room, lumber-room, hanaper, silo, cistern, well, tank, mill-pond, armoury, arsenal, coffer, etc. (191), nest-egg.

(*Verbs*). To store, stock, treasure up, lay in, lay by, lay up, fund, garner, save, husband, hoard, deposit, accumulate (72).

To reserve, keep back, hold back.

(*Phrases*). To husband one's resources; to have two strings to one's bow; φειδέω τῶν κτεάνων.

(*Adjectives*). Stored, etc., in store, in reserve, spare.

637. PROVISION (*Substantives*), supply, providing, supplying, etc., purveyance, purveying, reinforcement, husbanding, commissariat, victualling.

Forage, pasture, food, etc. (298).

A purveyor, caterer, contractor, commissary, quartermaster, jackal, feeder, batman.

(*Verbs*). To provide, supply, furnish, purvey, suppeditate, replenish, fill up, feed, stock with, recruit, cater, find, fend, keep, lay in, lay in store, store, forage, husband (636), upholster.

(*Phrase*). To bring grist to the mill.

638. WASTE (*Substantives*), consumption, expenditure, exhaustion, drain, leakage, wear and tear, dispersion (73), ebb, prodigality (819), seepage.

(*Verbs*). To waste, spend, expend, use, consume, spill, leak, run out, run to waste, disperse (73), ebb, dry up, impoverish, drain, empty, exhaust; to fritter away, squander.

(*Phrases*). To cast pearls before swine; to burn the candle at both ends; to employ a steam-hammer to crack nuts; to break a butterfly on a wheel.

(*Adjectives*). Wasted, spent, profuse, lavish, etc., at a low ebb.

(*Phrase*). Penny-wise and pound-foolish.

639. SUFFICIENCY (*Substantives*), adequacy, competence; enough, satiety.

Fullness, plenitude, plenty, abundance, copiousness, amplitude, richness, fertility, luxuriance, uberty, lashings, foison.

(*Phrases*). The horn of plenty; the horn of Amalthea; cornucopia; the fat of the land.

Impletion, repletion, saturation.

Riches (803), mine, store, fund, (636); a bumper, a brimmer, a bellyful, a cartload, truck-load, ship-load; a plumper; a charge.

A flood, draught, shower, rain, (347), stream, tide, spring-tide, flush.

640. INSUFFICIENCY (*Substantives*), inadequacy, inadequateness, incompetence.

Deficiency, scantiness, scant, defect, defectiveness, default, defalcation, deficit, shortcoming, falling short (304), what will not do, scantiness, slenderness, a mouthful, etc. (32).

Scarcity, dearth, shortage, want, need, lack, exigency, inanition, indigence, poverty, penury (804), destitution, dole, pittance, short allowance, short commons, a banyan-day, a mouthful, starvation, malnutrition, famine, drought, emptiness, vacancy, flaccidity; ebb-tide, low water.

Moderation, *see* Mediocrity (651).

(*Verbs*). To be sufficient, etc., to suffice, to do, satisfy, satiate, sate, saturate, make up.

To abound, teem, stream, flow, rain, shower down, pour, swarm.

To render sufficient, etc., to make up, to fill, replenish, pour in, charge.

(*Adjectives*). Sufficient, enough, adequate, commensurate, *quantum sufficit*, what will just do.

Moderate, measured.

Full, ample, plenty, copious, plentiful, plenteous, plenary, wantless, abundant, abounding, flush, replete, laden, charged, fraught; well stocked or provided, liberal, lavish, unstinted, to spare, unsparing, unmeasured; *ad libitum*, wholesale.

Brim-full, to the brim, chokefull, saturated, crammed, up to the ears, fat, rich, full up, topfull, luxuriant, lush.

Unexhausted, unwasted, exhaustless, inexhaustible.

(*Phrases*). Having two strings to one's bow; enough and to spare; cut and come again; full as an egg; full as a vetch; ready to burst; plenty as blackberries; flowing with milk and honey; enough in all conscience; enough to go round.

(*Phrase*). A beggarly account of empty boxes.

(*Verbs*). To be insufficient, etc., not to suffice, etc., to come short of, to fall short of, fail, run out of, stop short, to want, lack, need, require (630); caret.

(*Phrase*). To be put upon one's shifts.

To render insufficient, etc., to stint, grudge, hold back, withhold, starve, pinch, skimp, scrimp, famish.

To empty, drain, etc., *see* 638.

(*Adjectives*). Insufficient, inadequate, incompetent, not enough, etc., scant, scanty, skimpy, scrimpy, deficient, defective, in default, scarce, empty, devoid, short of, out of, wanting, etc, hard-up for.

Destitute, dry, drained, unprovided, unsupplied, unfurnished, unreplenished, unfed, unstored, untreasured, bare, meagre, poor, thin, spare, skimpy, stinted, starved, famished, pinched, starveling, jejune, without resources (735), short-handed, undermanned, understaffed, etc.

(*Phrases*). Out at elbows; not having a leg to stand upon.

─────

641. REDUNDANCE (*Substantives*), superabundance, superfluity, superfluence, exuberance, profuseness, profusion, plethora, engorgement, congestion, glut, surfeit, gorge, load, turgidity, turgescence, dropsy, pleonasm.

Excess, an overdose, oversupply, overplus, surplusage, overflow, inundation, deluge, extravagance, prodigality (818), exorbitance, lavishness, immoderation.

An expletive, oath, swear-word, damn, dash, etc., *see* Malediction (908).

(*Phrases*). *Satis superque*; a drug in the market.

(*Verbs*). To superabound, overabound, run over, overflow, flow over, roll in, wallow in.

(*Phrase*). To go a-begging.

To overstock, overdose, overlay, gorge, engorge, glut, sate, satiate, surfeit, cloy, load, overload, surcharge, overrun, drench, inundate, whelm, deluge.

(*Phrases*). To put butter upon bacon; it never rains but it pours; to carry coals to Newcastle.

(*Adjectives*). Redundant, superfluous, exuberant, superabundant, immoderate, extravagant, excessive, in excess, overmuch, too much, *de trop*, needless, over and above (40), more than enough, *satis superque*, running to waste, overflowing, running over.

(*Phrase*). Enough and to spare.

Turgid, gorged, plethoric, dropsical, profuse, lavish, prodigal, supervacaneous, extra, supernumerary, expletive, surcharged, overcharged, sodden, overloaded, overladen, overburdened, overrun, overfed, overfull.

(*Adverbs*). Over, over and above, too much, overmuch, over and enough, too far, without measure, without stint.

(*Phrase*). Over head and ears.

2. *Degree of Subservience*

642. IMPORTANCE (*Substantives*), consequence, moment, weight, gravity, seriousness, consideration, concern, significance, import, influence (175), pressure, urgency, instancy, stress, emphasis, preponderance, prominence (250), greatness (31).

The substance, essence, quintessence, gist, pith, marrow, soul, gravamen.

The principal, prominent, or essential part.

A notability, somebody, personage (875), big-wig, toff, big pot.

(*Phrase*). *A sine qua non.*

(*Verbs*). To be important, or of importance, etc., to signify, import, matter, boot, weigh, count, to be prominent, etc., to take the lead.

(*Phrases*). To be somebody, or something; to fill the bill.

To attach, or ascribe importance to; to value, care for, etc. (897).

To over-estimate, etc. (482), to exaggerate (549).

643. UNIMPORTANCE (*Substantives*), indifference, insignificance, triflingness, triviality, triteness; paltriness, emptiness, nothingness, inanity, lightness, levity, frivolity, vanity, frivolousness, puerility, child's play.

Poverty, meagreness, meanness, shabbiness, etc. (804).

A trifle, small matter, *minutiæ*, bagatelle, cipher, moonshine, mole-hill, joke, jest, snap of the fingers, flea-bite, pinch of snuff, old song, *nugæ*, fiddlestick, fiddlestick end, bubble, bulrush, nonentity, lay figure, nobody.

A straw, pin, fig, button, rush, feather, farthing, brass farthing, doit, peppercorn, pebble, small fry.

Trumpery, trash, stuff, *fatras*, frippery, chaff, drug, froth, smoke, cobweb.

Toy, plaything, knick-knack, gimcrack, gewgaw, thingumbob, bauble, kickshaw, bric-à-brac, curio, *bibelot*.

Refuse, lumber, litter, orts,

(*Phrases*). To make much of; to make a stir, a fuss, a piece of work, or much ado about; set store upon; to lay stress upon; to take *au grand sérieux*.

To mark, underline, italicise, score, accentuate, emphasise, stress, rub in.

(*Adjectives*). Important, of importance, etc., grave, serious, material, weighty, influential, significant, emphatic, momentous, earnest, pressing, critical, preponderating, pregnant, urgent, paramount, essential, vital.

(*Phrase*). A matter of life and death.

Great, considerable, etc. (*see* 31), capital, leading, principal, superior, chief, main, prime, primary, cardinal, prominent, salient, outstanding.

Signal, notable, memorable, remarkable, etc., grand, solemn, eventful, stirring, impressive; not to be despised, or overlooked, etc., unforgettable, worth while.

(*Phrases*). Being no joke; not to be sneezed at; no laughing matter.

tares, weeds, sweepings, scourings, off-scourings; rubble, débris, dross, scoriæ, dregs, scum, flue, dust, *see* Dirt (653).

(*Phrases*). "Leather and prunella"; *peu de chose*; much ado about nothing; much cry and little wool; *nugæ canoræ*; a man of straw.

(*Verbs*). To be unimportant, to be of little or no importance, etc.; not to signify, not to deserve, merit, or be worthy of notice, regard, consideration, etc.

(*Phrases*). To catch at straws; to make much ado about nothing; to cut no ice; *le jeu ne vaut pas la chandelle*.

(*Adjectives*). Unimportant, secondary, inferior, immaterial, insignificant, unessential, nonessential, beneath notice, indifferent; of little or no account, importance, consequence, moment, interest, etc.; unimpressive, subordinate.

Trifling, trivial, trite, banal, slight, slender, flimsy, trumpery, foolish, idle, puerile, childish, infantile, frothy, trashy, catchpenny, fiddling, frivolous, commonplace, contemptible, cheap.

Vain, empty, inane, poor, sorry, mean, meagre, shabby, scrannel, vile, miserable, scrubby, weedy, niggling, beggarly, piddling, peddling, pitiful, pitiable, despicable, paltry, ridiculous, farcical, finical, finikin, fiddle-faddle, gimcrack, twopenny, twopenny-halfpenny, one-horse, piffling, jerry, jerry-built.

(*Phrases*). Not worth a straw; as light as air; not worth mentioning; not worth boasting about; neither here nor there.

(*Interjections*). No matter! pshaw! pooh! pooh-pooh! fudge! fiddle-de-dee! nonsense! stuff! *n'importe !*

(*Adverbs*). Meagrely, pitifully, vainly, etc.

---

644. UTILITY (*Substantives*), service, use, function, office, sphere, capacity, part, rôle, task, work.

Usefulness, worth, stead, avail,

645. INUTILITY (*Substantives*), uselessness, inefficacy, inefficiency, ineptness, ineptitude, inadequacy, inaptitude, fruitlessness, inanity, worthlessness, un-

advantageousness, profitableness, serviceableness, merit, *cui bono*, applicability, adequacy, subservience, subserviency, efficacy, efficiency, help, money's worth.

(*Verbs*). To be useful, etc., of use, of service.

To avail, serve, subserve, help, (707), conduce, serve one's turn, stand in stead, profit, advantage, accrue; bedstead.

To render useful, to use (677), to turn to account, to utilise, to make the most of.

To serve an office, act a part, perform a function, serve a purpose, serve a turn.

(*Adjectives*). Useful, beneficial, advantageous, serviceable, helpful, gainful, profitable.

Subservient, conducive, applicable, adequate, efficient, efficacious, effective, effectual, seaworthy.

Worth while.

(*Phrases*). *Valeat quantum valere potest*; take it for what it is worth.

(*Adverbs*). Usefully, etc.; *pro bono publico*.

productiveness, barrenness, sterility, vanity, futility, triviality, paltriness, unprofitableness, unfruitfulness, rustiness, obsoleteness, discommodity, supererogation, obsolescence.

(*Phrases*). The labour of Sisyphus; the work of Penelope; a slaying of the slain.

Litter, rubbish, lumber, trash, job lot, orts, weeds (643), hogwash.

A waste, desert, Sahara, wild, wilderness.

(*Verbs*). To be useless, etc., to be of no avail, use, etc. (644).

(*Phrases*). To use vain efforts; to beat the air; to fish in the air; to lash the waves; to plough the sands.

(*Adjectives*). Useless, inutile, inefficient, inefficacious, unavailing, inoperative, bootless, supervacaneous, unprofitable, unremunerative, unproductive, sterile, barren, unsubservient, supererogatory.

Worthless, valueless, at a discount, gainless, fruitless, profitless, unserviceable, rusty, effete, washy, wasted, nugatory, futile, inept, withered, good for nothing, wasteful, ill-spent, obsolete, obsolescent, stale, dud, dear-bought, rubbishy, rubbishing.

(*Phrases*). Not worth having; leading to no end; no good; not worth while; of no earthly use; a dead letter.

Unneeded, unnecessary, uncalled for, unwanted, incommodious, discommodious.

(*Phrases*). Much ado about nothing; much cry and little wool.

(*Adverbs*). Uselessly, etc.. to no purpose.

---

646. Specific subservience.

EXPEDIENCE (*Substantives*), expediency, fitness, suitableness, suitability, aptness, aptitude, appropriateness, pertinence, seasonableness (134), adaptation, congruity, consonance (23), con-

647. INEXPEDIENCE (*Substantives*), inexpediency, disadvantageousness, unserviceableness, disservice, unfitness, inaptitude, ineptitude, ineligibility, inappropriateness, impropriety, unseemliness, incongruity, impertinence,

venience, eligibility, applicability, seemliness, rightness.

(*Verbs*). To be expedient, etc.

To suit, fit, square with, adapt itself to, agree with, consort with, accord with, tally with, conform with, go with, do for.

(*Adjectives*). Expedient, fit, fitting, worth while, suitable, applicable, eligible, apt, appropriate, adapted, proper, advisable, desirable, pertinent, congruous, seemly, consonant, becoming, meet, due, consentaneous, congenial, well-timed, pat, seasonable, opportune, apropos, befitting, happy, felicitous, auspicious, acceptable, etc., convenient, commodious, right.

(*Phrases*). Being just the thing; being as well; *operæ pretium est.*

inopportuneness, unseasonableness.

Inconvenience, incommodiousness, incommodity, discommodity, disadvantage.

Inefficacy, inefficiency, inadequacy.

(*Verbs*). To be inexpedient, etc., to embarrass, cumber, lumber, handicap, etc.

(*Adjectives*). Inexpedient, disadvantageous, unprofitable, unfit, unfitting, unsuitable, amiss, improper, unapt, inept, unadvisable, ineligible, objectionable, inadmissible, unseemly, inopportune, unseasonable, inefficient, inefficacious, inadequate.

Inconvenient, incommodious, in the way, cumbrous, cumbersome, lumbering, unwieldy, unmanageable, awkward, clumsy.

---

648. Capability of producing good.

GOODNESS (*Substantives*), excellence, value, worth, price, preciousness, estimation, rareness, exquisiteness; masterpiece, chef-d'œuvre.

Superexcellence, superiority, supereminence, transcendence, perfection (650), élite.

Mediocrity (651), innocuousness, harmlessness, inoffensiveness.

(*Verbs*). To be good, etc.; to be superior, etc., to excel, transcend, top, vie, emulate (708).

To be middling, etc. (651); to pass, to do.

(*Phrases*). To challenge comparison; *probatum est*; to pass muster; to speak well for.

To produce good, benefit, etc., to benefit, to be beneficial, etc., to confer a benefit, etc., to improve (658).

(*Adjectives*). Harmless, in-

649. Capability of producing evil.

BADNESS (*Substantives*), hurtfulness, disserviceableness, injuriousness, banefulness, mischievousness, noxiousness, malignancy, venomousness, virulence, destructiveness, scathe, curse, bane (663), plague-spot.

Vileness, foulness, rankness, depravation, depravity; Deterioration, *see* 659.

(*Verbs*). To be bad, etc.

To cause, produce, or inflict evil; to harm, hurt, injure, mar, damage, damnify, endamage, scathe, prejudice, stand in the light of, worsen.

To wrong, molest, annoy, harass, infest, grieve, aggrieve, trouble, oppress, persecute, weigh down, run down, overlay.

To maltreat, abuse, ill-use, illtreat, bedevil, bruise, scratch, maul, mishandle, man-handle,

nocuous, innoxious, unoffending, inoffensive, unobjectionable.

Good, beneficial, valuable, estimable, serviceable, advantageous, precious, favourable, palmary, felicitous, propitious.

Sound, sterling, standard, true, genuine, household, fresh, in good condition, unfaded, unspoiled, unimpaired, uninjured, undemolished, undamaged, unravaged, undecayed, natural, unsophisticated, unadulterated, unpolluted, unvitiated.

Choice, select, picked, nice, fine, rare, felicitous, unexceptionable, excellent, admirable, first-rate, splendid, topping, top-hole, clipping, ripping, prime, tiptop, crack, cardinal, superlative, superfine, superexcellent, pucka, exquisite, high-wrought, inestimable, invaluable, incomparable, transcendent, matchless, priceless, peerless, inimitable, unrivalled, *nulli secundus*, second to none, *facile princeps*, spotless, immaculate, perfect (650), *récherché*, first-class, first chop.

Moderately good (651).

(*Phrases*). Of the first water; precious as the apple of the eye; worth a Jew's eye; *ne plus ultra; la crême de la crême;* sound as a roach; worth its weight in gold; right as a trivet; up to the mark; an easy winner.

strafe, knock about, strike, smite, scourge (972), wound, lame, maim, scotch, cripple, mutilate, hamstring, hough, stab, pierce, etc., crush, crumble, pulverise.

To corrupt, corrode, pollute, etc. (659).

To spoil, despoil, sweep, ravage, lay waste, devastate, dismantle, demolish, level, raze, consume, overrun, sack, plunder, destroy (162).

(*Phrases*). To play the deuce with; to break the back of; crush to pieces; crumble to dust; to grind to powder; to ravage with fire and sword; to knock the stuffing out of; to queer one's pitch; to let daylight into.

(*Adjectives*). Bad, evil, wrong, prejudicial, disadvantageous, unprofitable, unlucky, sinister, left-handed, obnoxious, untoward, unadvisable, inauspicious, ill-omened.

Hurtful, injurious, grievous, detrimental, noxious, pernicious, mischievous, baneful, baleful.

Morbific, rank, peccant, malignant, tabid, corroding, corrosive, virulent, cankering, mephitic, narcotic.

Deleterious, poisonous, venomous, envenomed, pestilent, pestilential, pestiferous, destructive, deadly, fatal, mortal, lethal, lethiferous, miasmal.

Vile, sad, wretched, sorry, shabby, scurvy, low-down (940), scrubby, shocking, horrid.

Hateful, abominable, loathsome, detestable, execrable, cursed, accursed, confounded, damnable, diabolic, devilish, demoniacal, infernal, hellish, Satanic, villainous, depraved, shocking (898).

(*Adverbs*). Wrong, wrongly, badly, to one's cost.

(*Phrase*). *Corruptio optimi pessima.*

---

650. PERFECTION (*Substantives*), perfectness, indefectibility,

651. IMPERFECTION (*Substantives*), imperfectness, unsound-

impeccability, unimpeachability, *beau idéal*, summit (210).

Masterpiece, *chef d' œuvre*, *magnum opus*, classic, model, pattern, mirror, phœnix, *rara avis*, paragon, cream, nonsuch, nonpareil, élite.

Gem, bijou, jewel, pearl, diamond, ruby, brilliant.

A Bayard, an Admirable Crichton.

(*Phrases*). The philosopher's stone; the flower of the flock; the cock of the roost; the pink or acme of perfection; *Natura il fece e poi roppe la stampa*; the *ne plus ultra*.

(*Verbs*). To be perfect, etc., to excel, transcend, overtop, etc.

To carry everything before it, to play first fiddle, bear away the bell.

To bring to perfection, to perfect, to ripen, mature, etc. (52, 729).

(*Adjectives*). Perfect, best, faultless, finished, indeficient, indefectible, immaculate, spotless, transcendent, matchless, peerless, unparagoned, etc. (648), inimitable, unimpeachable, superlative, superhuman, divine, classical.

(*Phrases*). *In seipso totus teres aque rotundus ; ad unguem ; sans peur et sans reproche.*

---

652. CLEANNESS (*Substantives*), cleanliness, purity (960), neatness, tidiness, spotlessness, immaculateness.

Cleaning, purification, mundification, lustration, abstersion, depuration, expurgation, purgation, castration.

Washing, ablution, lavation,

ness, faultiness, deficiency, drawback, inadequacy, inadequateness (645), handicap.

Fault, defect, flaw, lacuna (198), crack, twist, taint, peccancy, vice.

Mediocrity, mean (29), indifference, inferiority.

(*Verbs*). To be imperfect, middling, etc., to fail, lie under a disadvantage, be handicapped.

(*Phrases*). To play second fiddle; barely to pass muster; to muddle along; to have a screw loose; be out of order.

(*Adjectives*). Imperfect, deficient, defective, faulty, dud, inferior, inartistic, inadequate, unsound, vicious, cracked, warped, frail, flimsy, sketchy, botched, gimcrack, gingerbread, tottering, decrepit, rickety, ramshackle, rattletrap, battered, worn out, threadbare, seedy, worm-eaten, used up, decayed, mutilated, unrectified, uncorrected.

Indifferent, middling, mediocre, so - so, *couci - couci*, secondary, second-rate, second-best, secondhand, second fiddle.

Tolerable, passable, pretty well, well enough, rather good, decent, admissible, not bad, not amiss, not so dusty, unobjectionable, respectable, betwixt and between.

(*Phrases*). Having a screw loose; no great catch; milk and water; no great shakes; nothing to boast of; better than nothing; on its last legs; no class.

653. UNCLEANNESS (*Substantives*), immundicity, uncleanliness, soilure, sordidness, foulness, impurity (961), pollution, nastiness, offensiveness, beastliness, muckiness, defilement, contamination, abomination, taint, tainture, corruption, decomposition (49).

elutriation, lixiviation, clarification, defecation, edulcoration, filtration.

Fumigation, ventilation, disinfection; disinfectant.

Scavenger; brush, broom, besom, vacuum-cleaner, duster, mop, sieve, riddle, screen, filter.

(*Verbs*). To be clean, etc.

To render clean, etc., to clean, to mundify, cleanse, wipe, mop, sponge, scour, swab, scrub, brush, sweep, dust, brush up.

To wash, lave, sluice, buck, absterge, deterge, clear, purify, depurate, defecate, elutriate, lixiviate, edulcorate, clarify, rack, filter, filtrate, fine, fine down.

To disinfect, deodorise, fumigate, ventilate, purge, expurgate, bowdlerise, emasculate, castrate.

To sift, winnow, pick, weed.

(*Adjectives*). Clean, pure, spotless, unspotted, immaculate, unstained, stainless, unsoiled, unsullied, taintless, untainted, uninfected.

Cleansing, etc., detergent, detersive, abstersive, abstergent, purgatory, purificatory, etc., abluent, antiseptic.

Spruce, tidy, washed, swept, etc., cleaned, purified, etc.

(*Phrases*). Clean as a whistle; clean as a new penny; like a cat in pattens.

———

Slovenliness, slovenry, untidiness, sluttishness, coarseness, grossness, dregginess, squalor.

Dirt, filth, soil, slop, dust, cobweb, smoke, soot, smudge, smut, raff, *sordes*, mess, muck.

Dregs, grounds, sediment, lees, settlement, dross, drossiness, precipitate, scoriæ, slag, scum, sweepings, off-scourings, *caput mortuum*, residuum, draff, fur, scurf, scurfiness, furfur, dandruff, riff-raff, vermin.

Mud, mire, quagmire, slough, sludge, alluvium, silt, slime, spawn, offal, fæces, excrement, ordure, dung, guano, manure, compost, dunghill, midden, bog, laystall, sink, cesspool, sough, *cloaca*, latrine, privy, sewer; hogwash, bilge-water.

Sty, pigsty, dusthole, lair, den.

Rottenness, corruption, decomposition, decay, putrefaction, putrescence, putridity, purulence, feculence, rankness, rancidity, mouldiness, mustiness, mucidness, mould, mother, must, mildew, dry-rot, fetor (401).

Scatology, coprology.

(*Phrases*). A sink of corruption; an Augean stable.

(*Verbs*). To be unclean, dirty, etc., to rot, putrefy, corrupt, decompose, go bad, mould, moulder, fester, etc.

To render unclean, etc., to dirt, dirty, soil, begrime, smear, besmear, mess, smirch, besmirch, bemire, spatter, bespatter, splash, bedaggle, bedraggle, daub, bedaub, slobber, beslobber, beslime, to cover with dust, etc.

To foul, befoul, pollute, defile, debase, contaminate, taint, corrupt, deflower, rot, etc.

(*Adjectives*). Unclean, dirty, soiled, etc., dusty, dirtied, etc., sooty, smoky, reechy, thick, turbid, dreggy, slimy, filthy, mucky.

Slovenly, untidy, sluttish, blowzy, draggle-tailed, dowdy, slipshod, unkempt, unscoured, unswept, unwiped, unwashed, unstrained, unpurified, squalid.

Nasty, foul, impure, offensive, abominable, beastly, lousy·
Mouldy, musty, mildewed, rusty, mouldering, moth-
eaten, reasty, rotten, rotting, tainted, high, fly-blown,
maggoty, putrescent, putrid, putrefied, bad, festering, puru-
lent, feculent, fecal, stercoraceous, excrementitious.

(*Phrases*). Wallowing in the mire; rotten as a pear; rotten
as cheese.

654. HEALTH (*Substantives*),
sanity, soundness, heartiness,
haleness, vigour, freshness,
bloom, healthfulness, incorrup-
tion, incorruptibility.

(*Phrase*). *Mens sana in corpore
sano.*

(*Verbs*). To be in health, etc.,
to flourish, to bloom.

To return to health, to recover,
to get the better of.

To restore to health, to cure,
recall to life, bring to.

(*Phrases*). To keep on one's
legs; to take a new or fresh lease
of life; *non est vivere sed valere
vita.*

(*Adjectives*). Healthy, in
health, well, sound, healthful,
hearty, hale, fresh, whole, florid,
staunch, flush, hardy, vigorous,
blooming, weather-proof, fit.

Unscathed, uninjured, un-
maimed, unmarred, untainted.

(*Phrases*). Having a clean bill
of health; being on one's legs;
sound as a roach; fresh as a rose;
hearty as a buck; in fine feather;
in high feather; in good case;
sound as a bell; in the pink of
condition; in good form.

------

655. DISEASE (*Substantives*),
illness, sickness, ailment, ailing,
indisposition, complaint, disorder, malady, distemper.

Sickliness, sickishness, infirmity, diseasedness, tabescence,
invalidation, cachexy, withered-
ness, atrophy, *marasmus*, incurableness, incurability, palsy.

Taint, pollution, infection, sep-
ticity, epidemic, endemic, mur-
rain, plague, pestilence, virus, pox.

A sore, ulcer, abscess, fester,
rot, canker, cancer, carcinoma,
caries, gangrene, *sphacelus*,
leprosy.

A valetudinarian, an invalid,
a patient, a cripple.

Science of disease: Pathology,
Ætiology, Nosology.

(*Verbs*). To be ill, etc., to ail,
suffer, be affected with, etc., to
complain of, to droop, flag,
languish, halt, sicken, gasp.

(*Phrases*). To lay up; to keep
one's bed; to sham Abraham;
to malinger.

(*Adjectives*). Diseased, ill,
taken ill, seized, indisposed, un-
well, sick, sickish, seedy, queer,
ailing, suffering, laid up, confined,
bedridden, invalided.

Unsound, sickly, poorly,
weakly, cranky, healthless, infirm,
unbraced, drooping, flagging, withered, decayed, decrepit,
lame, crippled, battered, halting, worn out, used up, run
down, off colour, moth-eaten, worm-eaten.

Morbid, tainted, vitiated, peccant, contaminated, tabid,
tabescent, mangy, poisoned, immedicable, gasping, moribund (360).

(*Phrases*). Out of sorts; out of joint; out of heart; good

for nothing; on the sick-list; in a bad way; *hors de combat*; worn to the stump; on one's last legs; at the last gasp.

656. SALUBRITY (*Substantives*), healthiness, wholesomeness, innoxiousness.

Preservation of health, hygiene, sanitation.

(*Verbs*). To be salubrious, etc., to agree with.

(*Adjectives*). Salubrious, wholesome, healthy, sanitary, salutary, salutiferous, healthful, agreeing with, tonic, prophylactic, bracing, benign.

Innoxious, innocuous, harmless, uninjurious, innocent.

Remedial, restorative, sanatory, etc. (*see* 662), nutritious, hygienic.

658. IMPROVEMENT (*Substantives*), melioration, amelioration, betterment, mend, emendation, advance, advancement, progress, elevation, preferment, convalescence, recovery, recuperation, curability.

Repair, reparation, cicatrisation, correction, reform, reformation, epuration, purification, etc. (652), refinement, relief, redress, *limæ labor*.

New edition; *réchauffé, rifacimento*, revision, revise, recension, redaction.

Reformer, Radical, Liberal, Progressive.

(*Verbs*). To be, become, or get better, etc., to improve, mend, advance, progress (282), to get on, make progress, gain ground, make way, go ahead, pick up, rally, recover, get the better of, get well, get over it, pull through, convalesce, recuperate.

(*Phrases*). To be oneself again; to take a new lease; to turn over a new leaf; be all the better for.

To render better, improve,

657. INSALUBRITY (*Substantives*), unhealthiness, unwholesomeness, deadliness, fatality.

Malaria, etc. (663).

(*Adjectives*). Insalubrious, insanitary, unsanitary, unhealthy, ungenial, uncongenial, unwholesome, morbific, mephitic, septic, deleterious, pestilent, pestiferous, pestilential, virulent, poisonous, toxic, contagious, infectious, catching, epidemic, epizootic, endemic, pandemic, zymotic, deadly, innutritious (645).

(*Phrase*). "There is death in the pot."

659. DETERIORATION (*Substantives*), wane, ebb, debasement, degeneracy, degeneration, degradation, degenerateness.

Impairment, injury, outrage, havoc, devastation, inroad, vitiation, adulteration, sophistication, debasement, perversion, corruption, prostitution, pollution, alloy, venenation.

Decline, declension, declination, going down-hill, recession, retrogression, retrogradation (283), caducity, decrepitude, decadence, falling off, pejoration.

Decay, disorganisation, wear and tear, mouldiness, rottenness, moth and rust, dry-rot, blight, marasmus, falling to pieces, *délâbrement*.

Incurableness, incurability, remedilessness, *see* Hopelessness (859).

(*Verbs*). To be, or become deteriorated, to deteriorate, wane, ebb, degenerate, fall off, decline, go downhill, sink, go down, lapse, droop, be the worse for, recede, retrograde, revert (283),

mend, amend, better, meliorate, ameliorate, advance, push on, forward, enhance.

To relieve, refresh, restore, renew, redintegrate, heal, etc. (*see* 660); to palliate, mitigate.

To repair, refit, retouch, revise, botch, vamp, tinker, cobble, clout, patch up, touch up, cicatrise, heel-piece, darn, fine-draw, rub up, do up, furbish, refurbish, polish, bolster up, caulk, careen; to stop a gap, to stanch.

To purify, depurate (652), defecate, strain, filter, rack, refine, disinfect, chasten.

To correct, rectify, redress, reform, restore (660), mellow, cook, warm up, set to rights, put straight, straighten out, revise.

(*Adjectives*). Improving, etc., improved, etc., progressive, corrective, reparatory, emendatory, revisory, sanatory, advanced.

Curable, corrigible, capable of improvement.

fall into decay, fade, break, break down, fall to pieces, wither, moulder, rot, rust, crumble, totter, shake, tumble, fall, topple, perish, die (360).

(*Phrases*). To go to rack and ruin; to fall into the sere and yellow leaf; to go to the dogs; to go to pot; to go on from bad to worse; to go farther and fare worse; to run to seed.

To render less good; to deteriorate, impair, vitiate, debase, alloy, pervert.

To spoil, embase, defile, taint, infect, contaminate, sophisticate, poison, canker, corrupt, pollute, deprave, leaven, envenom, debauch, prostitute, defile, adulterate, stain, spatter, bespatter, soil, tarnish (653), addle.

To corrode, erode, wear away, wear out, gnaw, gnaw at the root of, sap, mine, undermine, shake, break up, disorganise, dismantle, dismast, lay waste, do for, ruin, confound.

To embitter, acerbate, aggravate.

To injure, harm, hurt, damage, endamage, damnify, etc. (649).

(*Phrases*). To play the deuce with; to sap the foundations of.

(*Adjectives*). Deteriorated, become worse, impaired, etc., degenerate, *passé*, on the decline, on the down-grade, deciduous, unimproved, unrecovered, unrestored.

Remediless, hopeless, past cure, past mending, irreparable, irremediable, cureless, incurable, irrecoverable, irretrievable, irreclaimable, irredeemable, irreversible, immitigable, helpless.

Decayed, etc., moth-eaten, worm-eaten, mildewed, rusty, time-worn, moss-grown, effete, wasted, worn, crumbling, tumble-down, dilapidated, overblown.

(*Phrases*). Out of the frying-pan into the fire; the worse for wear; worn to a thread; worn to a shadow; reduced to a skeleton; the ghost of oneself; a hopeless case; *ægrescit medendo*.

660. RESTORATION (*Substantives*), reinstatement, replacement, instauration, re-establishment, rectification, revendication,

661. RELAPSE (*Substantives*), lapse, falling back, retrogression, reaction, set-back, recidivism, retrogradation, etc. (659).

redintegration, refection, recon-
stitution, cure, sanation, refitting,
recruiting, redress, retrieval, etc.,
refreshment.

Renovation, reanimation, recovery, recure, resuscitation,
revivification, reviviscence, revival, renascence, renaissance,
rejuvenation, rejuvenescence,
regeneration, regeneracy, regenerateness, redemption; a
Phœnix.

Réchauffé, *rifacimento* (658), recast.

(*Phrases*). A new lease of life; "Richard's himself again."

(*Verbs*). To return to the original state, to right itself,
come to, rally, revive, recover.

To restore, replace, re-establish, reinstate, reseat, replant,
reconstitute, redintegrate, set right, set to rights, rectify,
redress, reclaim, redeem, recover, recoup, recure, retrieve,
cicatrise.

To refit, recruit, refresh, refocillate, rehabilitate, reconvert,
reconstitute, renovate, revive, regenerate, rejuvenesce,
rejuvenate, resuscitate, reanimate, recast, reconstruct, rebuild.

(*Phrases*). Recall to life; set on one's legs.

To cure, heal, cicatrise, remedy, doctor, physic, medicate.

(*Adjectives*). Restoring, etc., restored, etc.

(*Phrase*). Rising from its ashes.

Restorable, sanable, remediable, retrievable, recoverable.

(*Adverbs*). *In statu quo*; as you were; Phœnix-like.

Return to, or recurrence of a
bad state.

A recidivist, a throw-back.

(*Verbs*). To relapse, lapse, fall
back, slide back, sink back, go
back, return, retrograde, etc.

---

662. REMEDY (*Substantives*),
help, redress, cure, antidote,
counter - poison, vaccine, anti-
toxin, specific, prophylactic, corrective, restorative, sedative, anodyne, opiate, Nepenthe, Mith-
ridate.

Physic, medicine, drug, tonic,
medicament, nostrum, recipe,
prescription, catholicon.

Panacea, elixir, *elixir vitæ*,
balm, balsam, cordial, cardiac,
theriac, ptisan, carminative.

Pill, pilule, tablet, tabloid,
lozenge, powder, draught, etc.

Salve, ointment, plaster,
epithem, embrocation, liniment,
lotion, cataplasm, styptic, poultice, vulnerary, cosmetic, etc.;
sanativeness.

663. BANE (*Substantives*), rod,
scourge, curse, scathe, sting, gall
and wormwood.

Poison, leaven, virus, venom,
toxin, microbe, germ, bacillus,
miasma, mephitis, malaria, pest,
rust, canker, cancer, canker-
worm.

Hemlock, hellebore, night-
shade, henbane, aconite, upas-
tree.

Sirocco.

A viper, adder, serpent, cobra,
rattlesnake, cockatrice, scorpion,
wireworm, torpedo, hornet, vul-
ture, vampire, etc.; Demon, etc.
(980), Fury, Attila, *see* 913.

Science of poisons, Toxicology.

Treatment, diet, dieting, regimen; clinic.

Pharmacy, Pharmacology, Materia Medica, Therapeutics, Homœopathy, Allopathy, Radiotherapy, Hydropathy, Osteopathy, Dietetics, Dietary, Chirurgery, Surgery, Midwifery, Obstetrics; faith-healing.

A hospital, infirmary, pest-house, lazaretto, madhouse, asylum, lunatic asylum, *maison de santé*, ambulance, dispensary, sanatorium, nursing home.

(*Adjectives*). Remedial, medical, medicinal, therapeutic, surgical, chirurgical, sanatory, sanative, salutary, salutiferous, healing, paregoric, restorative, tonic, corroborant, analeptic, balsamic, anodyne, sedative, lenitive, demulcent, emollient, depuratory, detersive, detergent, abstersive, disinfectant, antiseptic, corrective, prophylactic, antitoxic, febrifuge, alterative, expectorant; veterinary.

Dietetic, alexipharmic, nutritious, nutritive, alimentary.

3. *Contingent Subservience*

664. SAFETY (*Substantives*), security, surety, impregnability, invulnerability, invulnerableness, escape (671).

Safeguard, guard, guardianship, chaperonage, protection, tutelage, wardship, wardenship, safe - conduct, escort, convoy, garrison.

Watch, watch and ward, sentinel, scout, watchman, patrol, vedette, picket, bivouac.

Watch-dog, bandog, Cerberus.

Protector, guardian, guard, defender, warden, warder, preserver, chaperon, tutelary saint, guardian angel; *see* Defence (717).

Custody, safe-keeping (751).

Precaution, quarantine; insurance, assurance; cover.

(*Verbs*). To be safe, etc.

(*Phrases*). To save one's bacon; to light upon one's feet; weather the storm; to make assurance doubly sure; to take no chances.

To render safe, etc., to protect, guard, shield, shelter, flank, cover, screen, shroud, ensconce,

665. DANGER (*Substantives*), peril, insecurity, jeopardy, risk, hazard, venture, precariousness, slipperiness.

(*Phrases*). The ground sliding from under one; breakers ahead; the sword of Damocles.

Liability, exposure (177), vulnerability, vulnerable point, the heel of Achilles.

Hopelessness (859), forlorn hope, alarm, *see* Fear (860), defencelessness.

(*Verbs*). To be in danger, etc., to be exposed to, to incur or encounter danger, run the danger of, run a risk.

(*Phrases*). To hang by a thread; to sit on a barrel of gunpowder; stand on a volcano.

To place or put in danger, etc., to endanger, expose to danger, imperil, jeopardise, compromise, adventure, risk, hazard, venture, stake.

(*Phrases*). To open the door to; to engage in a forlorn hope.

To ensnare, entrap, trap, entangle, illaqueate, noose.

ward, secure, fence, hedge in, entrench, house, nestle.

To defend, forfend, escort, convoy, garrison, mount guard, patrol, chaperon, picket.

(*Phrase*). To play gooseberry.

(*Adjectives*). Safe, in safety, in security, secure, sure, protected, guarded, etc., snug, scatheless, seaworthy.

Defensible, tenable; insurable.

Invulnerable, unassailable, unattackable, impregnable, inexpugnable.

Protecting, etc., guardian, tutelary.

Unthreatened, unmolested, unharmed, harmless, unhazarded.

(*Phrases*). Out of harm's way; under lock and key; on sure ground; under cover; under the shadow of one's wing; the coast being clear; the danger being past; out of the wood; proof against.

(*Interjections*). All's well! *salva est res !*

(*Phrase*). To lay or set a trap for.

(*Adjectives*). In danger, peril, jeopardy, etc., unsafe, insecure, unguarded, unscreened, unsheltered, unprotected, guardless, helpless, guideless, exposed, defenceless, vulnerable, at bay, on a lee-shore, on the rocks, waterlogged, *aux abois*, between two fires, in a tight place; at stake.

Unwarned, unadmonished, unadvised.

Dangerous, perilous, hazardous, parlous, risky, chancy, fraught with danger, adventurous, precarious, touch-and-go, breakneck, slippery, unsteady, shaky, tottering, top-heavy, harbourless, ticklish, dicky.

Threatening, ominous, alarming, minatory, minacious (909).

(*Phrases*). Not out of the wood; hanging by a thread; neck or nothing; out of the frying-pan into the fire; *cane pejus et angui*; between Scylla and Charybdis; breakers ahead; a snake in the grass; hard bested.

Nam tua res agitur paries dum proximus ardet ; incidit in Scyllam qui vult vitare Charybdim.

666. Means of safety.

REFUGE (*Substantives*), asylum, sanctuary, fastness, retreat, ark, hiding-place, dug-out, funk-hole, loophole, shelter.

Roadstead, anchorage, breakwater, mole, groyne, port, haven, harbour, harbour of refuge, pier.

Fort, citadel, fortification, etc., shield, etc., *see* Defence (717).

Screen, covert, wing, fence, rail, railing, wall, dike, ditch, etc. (232).

Anchor, kedge, grapnel, sheet-anchor, prop, stay, mainstay, jury-mast, life-boat, life-buoy, life-belt, plank, stepping-stone,

667. Source of danger.

PITFALL (*Substantives*), rocks, reefs, sunken rocks, snags, sands, quicksands, breakers, shoals, shallows, bank, shelf, flat, lee-shore, air-pocket.

Trap, snare, gin, springe, toils, noose, net, spring-net, spring-gun, masked battery, mine.

(*Phrases*). The sword of Damocles; a snake in the grass; trusting to a broken reed; a lion's den; *proximus ardet Ucalegon.*

umbrella, parachute, lightning-conductor, safety-valve, grappling-iron, safety-lamp.

668. WARNING (*Substantives*), caution, *caveat*, notice, premonition, premonishment, lesson, dehortation, admonition (864); alarm (669).

Beacon, light-house, pharos, watch-tower, signal-post, guide-post, etc., *see* 550.

Sentinel, sentry, watch, watchman, patrol, vedette, etc. (664).

(*Phrases*). The writing on the wall; the yellow flag; a red light.

(*Verbs*). To warn, caution, forewarn, premonish, give notice, give warning, admonish, dehort, threaten, menace (909).

(*Phrases*). To put on one's guard; to sound the alarm.

To take warning; to beware; to be on one's guard (864).

(*Adjectives*). Warning, etc., premonitory, dehortatory.

Warned, etc., careful, on one's guard (459).

(*Interjections*). Beware! mind what you are about! let sleeping dogs lie! *fœnum habet in cornu !* fore!

669. Indication of danger.

ALARM (*Substantives*), *alerte*, alarum, alarm-bell, tocsin, tattoo, signal of distress, blue lights, etc., warning voice; Cassandra.

False alarm, cry of wolf, bugbear, bugaboo, bogy.

(*Verbs*). To give, raise, or sound an alarm, to alarm, warn, ring the tocsin, *battre la générale*, to cry wolf.

(*Adjectives*). Alarming, etc., threatening.

670. PRESERVATION (*Substantives*), conservation, maintenance, support, upkeep, sustentation, deliverance, salvation, rescue, redemption, self-preservation, *see* Permanence (142), Continuance (143).

Means of preservation: prophylaxis, preservative, preserver, superstitious remedies, *see* 993.

(*Verbs*). To preserve, maintain, support, save, rescue, file (papers).

To embalm, mummify, dry, cure, kipper, salt, pickle, marinade, season, kyanise, bottle, pot, can, tin.

(*Phrases*). *Stare super antiquas vias ; nolumus leges Angliæ mutare.*

(*Adjectives*). Preserving, conservative, prophylactic, preservatory, hygienic.

Preserved, unimpaired, uninjured, unhurt, unsinged, unmarred.

671. ESCAPE (*Substantives*), scape, evasion, retreat, reprieve, reprieval, deliverance, redemption, rescue.

Narrow escape, hair's-breadth 'scape, close shave, *échappée belle*.

Means of escape: bridge, drawbridge, loophole, ladder, plank, stepping-stone, trap-door, etc. (666).

(*Verbs*). To escape, scape, elude, evade, wriggle out of, make or effect one's escape, make off, march off, pack off, skip, skip off, slip away, steal away, slink away, flit, decamp, run away, abscond, levant, skedaddle, fly, flee, bolt, bunk, vamose, elope, whip off, break loose, break away, get clear.

(*Phrases*). To take oneself off; play truant; to beat a retreat; to give one the slip; to slip the collar; to slip through the fingers; to make oneself scarce; to hop the twig; to take to one's heels; to show a clean pair of heels; to give leg-bail; to take French leave; to do a bunk; to cut one's lucky; to cut and run; *se tirer d'affaire*; to run for one's life; to make tracks.

(*Interjections*). *Sauve qui peut !* the devil take the hindmost!

(*Adjectives*). Escaping, etc., escaped, etc., fugitive, runaway, refugee.

(*Phrase*). The bird having flown.

672. DELIVERANCE (*Substantives*), extrication, rescue, redemption, salvation, riddance, redeemableness, redeemability.

(*Phrase*). A clean sweep.

(*Verbs*). To deliver, extricate, rescue, save, salvage, redeem, help out, bring off, *tirer d'affaire*, to get rid, to work off, to rid.

(*Phrases*). To save one's bacon; to find a hole to creep out of.

(*Adjectives*). Delivered, saved, etc., scot-free, scatheless. Extricable, redeemable, rescuable.

3°. Precursory Measures

673. PREPARATION (*Substantives*), making ready, providing, provision, providence, anticipation, preconcertation, precaution, laying foundations, ploughing, sowing, semination, cooking, brewing, digestion, gestation, hatching, incubation, concoction, maturation, elaboration, predisposition (611, 613).

Physical preparation: Training, drill, drilling, discipline, exercise, exercitation, gymnastics, callisthenics, eurhythmics, athletics, gymnasium, *palœstra*, prenticeship, apprenticeship, qualification, inurement, education, novitiate, *see* Teaching (537).

Putting or setting in order, putting to rights, clearance, arrangement, disposal, organisation, adjustment, adaptation, disposition, accommodation, putting in tune, tuning, putting in trim, dressing, putting in harness, outfit, equipment, accoutrement, etc.

674. NON-PREPARATION (*Substantives*), want or absence of preparation, inculture, inconcoction, improvidence.

Immaturity, crudeness, crudity, greenness, rawness, disqualification.

Absence of art, nature.

An embryo, skeleton, rough copy, draft, germ, etc., rudiment (153).

(*Verbs*). To be unprepared, etc., to want, or lack preparation.

(*P h r a s e*). *S'embarquer sans biscuits.*

To improvise, extemporise (612).

To render unprepared, etc., to dismantle, dismount, dismast, disqualify, disable, unrig, undress (226).

(*Phrases*). To put *hors de combat*; to put out of gear, to spike the guns; to remove the sparking-plug.

(*Adjectives*). Unprepared, rudimentary, immature, unripe,

(*Phrases*). A stitch in time; clearing decks; a note of preparation; a breather.

Groundwork, basis, foundation, pedestal, etc. (*see* 215), first stone, scaffold, scaffolding, cradle, sketch (626).

State of being prepared: preparedness, ripeness, maturity, readiness, mellowness.

Preparer, pioneer, avant-courier, sappers and miners, warming-pan.

(*Verbs*). To prepare, get ready, make ready, get up, anticipate, forecast, pre-establish, preconcert, settle preliminaries, to found.

To arrange, set or put in order, set or put to rights, organise, dispose, cast the parts, mount, adjust, adapt, accommodate, trim, tidy, fit, predispose, inure elaborate, mature, ripen, nurture, hatch, cook, concoct, brew, tune, put in tune, attune, set, temper, anneal, smelt, undermine, brush up, get up.

raw, green, crude, rough, rough-cast, rough-hewn, unhewn, unformed, unhatched, unfledged, unnurtured, uneducated, unlicked, untilled, natural, in a state of nature, *au naturel*, unwrought, unconcocted, undigested, indigested, unrevised, unblown, unfashioned, unlaboured, unleavened, fallow, uncultivated, untrained, undrilled, unexercised, unseasoned, disqualified, unqualified, out of order, unseaworthy.

Unbegun, unready, unarranged, unorganised, unsown, unfurnished, unprovided, unequipped, undressed, in dishabille, dismantled, untrimmed.

Shiftless, improvident, thoughtless, unthrifty.

Unpremeditated, off-hand (612), from hand to mouth, extempore (111).

————

(*Phrases*). To take steps; prepare the ground; lay or fix the foundations, the basis, groundwork, etc.; to clear the ground; clear the way, the course; clear decks; clear for action; close one's ranks; plough the ground; dress the ground; till the soil; sow the seed; open the way; pave the way; lay a train; dig a mine; prepare a charge; erect the scaffolding; *reculer pour mieux sauter.*

To provide, provide against, discount, make provision, keep on foot, take precautions, make sure, lie in wait for (507).

To equip, arm, man, fit out, fit up, furnish, rig, dress, dress up, furbish up, accoutre, array, fettle, vamp up, wind up.

(*Phrases*). Put in harness; sharpen one's tools; whet the knife; prime and load; shoulder arms; put the horses to; oil up.

To prepare oneself; lay oneself out for; get into harness; gird up one's loins; buckle on one's armour; serve one's time or apprenticeship; be at one's post; gather oneself together.

To set on foot, lay the first stone, break ground.

To train, drill, discipline, break in, cradle, inure, habituate, harden, case-harden, season, acclimatise, qualify, educate, teach, etc.

(*Phrases*). To erect the scaffold; to cut one's coat according to one's cloth; to keep one's powder dry; to beat up for recruits; *venienti occurrite morbo*; *principiis obsta*; to sound the note of preparation.

(*Adjectives*). Preparing, etc., in preparation, in course of preparation, in agitation, brewing, hatching, forthcoming, in embryo, afoot, afloat, on the anvil, on the carpet, on the stocks, *sur le tapis*, provisional, in the rough, rough-and-ready (111).

Prepared, trained, drilled, etc., forearmed, ready, in readiness, ripe, mature, mellow, fledged, ready to one's hand, on tap, cut and dried, annealed, concocted, laboured, elaborated, planned (626).

(*Phrases*). Armed to the teeth; armed cap-à-pie; the coast being clear; *in utrumque paratus*.

(*Adverbs*). In preparation, in anticipation of, etc., against.

675. ESSAY (*Substantives*), trial, experiment (463), probation, venture, adventure, tentative, *ballon d'essai*, *coup d'essai*, random shot, speculation.

(*Verbs*). To try, essay, make trial of, try on, experiment, make an experiment, grope, feel one's way, *tâtonner*; to venture, adventure, speculate, take upon oneself.

(*Phrases*). To put out or throw out a feeler; pick one's way; to send up a pilot balloon; to fish for information, compliments, etc.; to chance it; to risk it.

(*Adjectives*). Essaying, etc., experimental, tentative, empirical, on trial, probative, probatory, probationary, attempting, endeavouring.

(*Adverbs*). Experimentally, etc., *à tâtons*, at a venture.

676. UNDERTAKING (*Substantives*), enterprise, emprise, endeavour, attempt, move, first move, the initiative, first step, *see* Beginning (66), début, embarkation.

(*Verbs*). To undertake, take in hand, set about, go about, set to, fall to, set to work, engage in, launch into, embark in, plunge into, take on, set one's hand to, tackle, grapple with, volunteer, take steps, launch out.

To endeavour, strive, use one's endeavours; to attempt, make an attempt, tempt.

To begin, set on foot, set agoing, take the first step.

(*Phrases*). To break the neck of the business; take the initiative; to break ground; break the ice; break cover; to pass the Rubicon; to take upon oneself; to take on one's shoulders; *ce n'est que le premier pas qui coûte*; well begun is half done.

To take the bull by the horns; to rush *in medias res*; to have too many irons in the fire; to attempt impossibilities.

(*Adverbs*). Undertaking, attempting, etc.

677. USE (*Substantives*), employment, employ, application, appliance, adhibition, disposal, exercise.

678. DISUSE (*Substantives*), forbearance, abstinence, dispensation, desuetude.

(*Verbs*). To disuse, not to use,

Recourse, resort, avail, service, conversion to use, utilisation.

Agency (170); usefulness (644).

(*Verbs*). To use, make use of, utilise, exploit, employ (134), apply, adhibit, dispose of, work, wield, put to use; turn or convert to use; avail oneself of, resort to, recur to, take up with, betake oneself to.

(*Phrases*). To take advantage of; to turn to account; to make the most of; to make the best of; to bring to bear upon; to fall back upon; to press or enlist into the service; to make shift with; make a cat's-paw of; milk.

To render useful, serviceable, available, etc.; to utilise, draw, call forth, tax, task, try, exert, exercise, work up, consume, absorb, expend.

To practise, ply.

(*Phrases*). To pull the strings or wires; put in action; set to work; set in motion; put in practice.

To be useful, to serve one's turn, etc., *see* 644.

(*Adjectives*). Used, employed, etc., applied, exercised, tried, etc.

———

to do without, to dispense with, to let alone, to spare, waive.

To lay by; set, put, or lay aside; to discard, dismiss (756); cast off, throw off, turn off, turn out, turn away, throw away, shelve (133), shunt, side-track, get rid of, do away with; to keep back (636).

To dismantle, dismast, scrap.

(*Phrases*). To lay on the shelf; to lay up in ordinary; to lay up in a napkin; to consign to the scrap-heap; to cast, heave, or throw overboard; to cast to the winds; to turn out neck and heels; to send to the right-about; to send packing.

(*Adjectives*). Disused, etc., not used, unused, unutilised, unemployed, unapplied, unspent, unexercised, kept or held back.

Unessayed, untouched, uncalled for, ungathered, unculled, untrodden.

679. MISUSE (*Substantives*), misemployment, misapplication, misappropriation, abuse, profanation, prostitution, desecration.

Waste (818), wasting, spilling, exhaustion (638).

(*Verbs*). To misuse, misemploy, misapply, misappropriate, desecrate, abuse, profane, prostitute.

To waste, spill, fritter away, exhaust, throw or fling away, squander (818).

(*Phrases*). To waste powder and shot; cut blocks with a razor; cast pearls before swine; cast one's bread upon the waters.

(*Adjective*). Misused, etc.

SECTION III.—VOLUNTARY ACTION

1°. *Simple Voluntary Action*

680. ACTION (*Substantives*), performance, work. operation, proceeding, procedure, *démarche*, process, handiwork, handicraft, workmanship, manœuvre, transaction, bout, turn, job, doings, business, affair.

Deed, act, overt act, stitch, touch, move, strike, blow, *coup*, feat, stunt, exploit, passage, stroke of policy, *tour de force*, *coup de main, coup d'état*.

(*Verbs*). To act, do, work, operate, do or transact business, practise, perpetrate, perform (729), officiate, exercise, commit, inflict, strike a blow, handle, take in hand, put in hand, run.

To labour, drudge, toil, ply, set to work, pull the oar, serve, officiate, go about, turn one's hand to, dabble; to have in hand.

(*Phrases*). To have a finger in the pie; to take or play a part; to set to work; to pursue the even tenor of one's way; to put in execution; to carry into execution (729); to lay one's hand to the plough; to ply one's task; to get on with the job; to discharge an office; to go the whole hog.

(*Adjectives*). Acting, etc., in action, in operation, etc., operative, in harness, in play, on duty, on foot, at work.

(*Interjection*). Here goes!

681. INACTION (*Substantives*), abstinence from action, *see* Inactivity (683), non-intervention, non-interference, neutrality.

(*Verbs*). Not to do, to let be, abstain from doing; let or leave alone, refrain, desist, keep oneself from doing; let pass, lie by, let be, wait.

(*Phrases*). To bide one's time; to cool one's heels; to stay one's hand; to wash one's hands of; to leave in the lurch; to have other fish to fry; *stare super antiquas vias*; to sit on the fence.

To undo, take down, take or pull to pieces, do away with.

(*Phrases*). *Res infecta*; nothing doing.

(*Adjectives*). Not doing, not done, let alone, undone, etc.; neutral.

---

682. ACTIVITY (*Substantives*), briskness, quickness, promptness, readiness, alertness, smartness, sharpness, nimbleness, agility (274).

Spirit, vivacity, eagerness, *empressement, brio*, dash, *élan*, alacrity, zeal, push, energy (171), hustle, vigour, intentness.

Movement, bustle, commotion, stir, fuss, ado, fidget, restlessness, fidgetiness.

683. INACTIVITY (*Substantives*), inaction, idleness, sloth, laziness, indolence, inertness, lumpishness, supineness, sluggishness, languor, torpor, stagnation, lentor, limpness, listlessness, remissness, slackness.

Dilatoriness, cunctation, procrastination (133), relaxation, truancy, lagging, dawdling, rust, rustiness, want of occupation, resourcelessness.

Wakefulness, *pervigilium*, insomnia, sleeplessness.

Industry, assiduity, assiduousness, sedulity, sedulousness, diligence; perseverance, persistence, plodding, painstaking, drudgery, busyness, indefatigability, indefatigableness, patience, business habits, push.

Dabbling, meddling, interference, interposition, intermeddling, tampering with, intrigue, *tripotage*, supererogation.

A housewife, busybody, swot, mug, zealot, hustler.

Industrialism.

(*Phrases*). The thick of the action; *in medias res* ; too many cooks; new brooms; too many irons in the fire; a slaying of the slain.

(*Verbs*). To be active, busy, stirring, etc., to busy oneself in, stir, bestir oneself, bustle, fuss, make a fuss, speed, hasten, push, make a push, go ahead, hustle; to industrialise.

To plod, drudge, keep on, hold on, persist, fag at, hammer at, stick to, buckle to, stick to work, take pains; to take or spend time in; to make progress.

(*Phrases*). To look sharp; to lay about one; to have one's hands full; to kick up a dust; to stir one's stumps; to exert one's energies; to put one's best leg foremost; to do one's best; to do all one can; to leave no stone unturned; to have all one's eyes about one; make the best of one's time; to make short work of; to seize the opportunity; to come up to the scratch; to take time by the forelock; to make hay while the sun shines; to keep the pot boiling; to strike the iron while it is hot; to take advantage of; to kill two birds

Somnolence, drowsiness, doziness, nodding, oscitation, sleepiness, hypnosis.

Hypnology.

Sleep, nap, doze, slumber, snooze, dog-sleep, cat-nap, siesta, dream, trance, hypnotic state, snore, a wink of sleep, lethargy, hibernation, æstivation.

(*Phrases*). The Castle of Indolence; *dolce far niente* ; the Land of Nod; the Fabian policy; *laissez aller*; *laissez faire*; masterly inactivity; the thief of time.

An idler, laggard, truant, do-nothing, lubber, sluggard, slumberer, fainéant, flâneur, loafer, drone, dormouse, slow - coach, stick-in-the-mud, lounger, slug, lazy-bones, lotus-eater, slacker.

(*Phrases*). Sleeping partner; waiter on Providence; *fruges consumere nati.*

Cause of inactivity, *see* 174; hypnotism.

(*Verbs*). To be inactive, etc., to do nothing, let alone, lie by, lie idle, stagnate, lay to, keep quiet, hang fire, relax, slouch, loll, drawl, slug, dally, lag, dawdle, potter, lounge, loiter, laze, moon, moon about, loaf, hang about, mouch; to waste, lose, idle away, kill, trifle away, fritter away or fool away time; dabble, fribble, peddle, fiddle-faddle.

(*Phrases*). To fold one's arms; to let well alone; play truant; while away the time; to rest upon one's oars; to burn daylight; to take it easy; slack off.

To sleep, slumber, nod, close the eyes, close the eyelids, doze, drowse, fall asleep, take a nap, go off to sleep, hibernate, æstivate, yawn.

(*Phrases*). To sleep like a top; to sleep as sound as a top; to

with one stone; to move heaven
and earth; to go through fire and
water; to do wonders; to go all
lengths; to stick at nothing; to
go the whole hog; to keep the
ball rolling; to put one's back
into it; to make things hum,
see 684.

To meddle, moil, intermeddle,
interfere, interpose, tamper with,
fool with, get at, nobble, agitate,
intrigue.

To overact, overdo, overlay,
outdo, ride to death.

(*Phrases*). To have a hand in;
to thrust one's nose in; to put
in one's oar; to put one's foot in
it; to mix oneself up with;
steal a march upon.

(*Adjectives*). Active, brisk,
quick, prompt, alert, on the
alert, stirring, spry, sharp, smart,
quick, nimble, agile, light-footed,
tripping, ready, awake, broad
awake, wide awake, alive, at call,
lively, live, vivacious, frisky, forward, eager, strenuous, zealous,
enterprising, pushing, pushful,
spirited, in earnest, up in arms,
go-ahead.

Working, on duty, at work,
hard at work, intent, industrious,
assiduous, diligent, sedulous,
notable, painstaking, business-
like, practical, in harness, operose,

sleep like a log; to sleep like a
dormouse; to eat the bread of
idleness; to loll in the lap of
indolence.

To render idle, etc., to slug-
gardise.

(*Adjectives*). Inactive, unoccupied, unemployed, unbusied,
doing nothing (685), resourceless.

Indolent, easy-going, lazy,
slothful, idle, lusk, slack, inert,
torpid, sluggish, languid, supine,
heavy, dull, stagnant, lumpish,
soulless, listless, moony, limp,
languorous, exanimate.

Dilatory, laggard, lagging,
tardigrade, drawling, creeping,
dawdling, faddling, rusty, lacka-
daisical, fiddle-faddle, shilly-
shally, unpractical, unbusiness-
like.

(*Phrases*). With folded arms;
les bras croisés; with the hands
in the pockets; at a loose end.

Sleepy, dozy, drowsy, somno-
lent, dormant, asleep, lethargic,
napping, slubbering, somniferous,
soporific, soporous, soporose,
somnific, hypnotic, narcotic, un-
awakened, unwakened.

(*Phrase*). In the arms or lap
of Morpheus.

———

plodding, toiling, hard-working, fagging, busy, bustling,
restless, fussy, fidgety, pottering, dabbling; industrial.

Persevering, indefatigable, untiring, unflagging, unremitting, unwearied, never-tiring, undrooping, unintermitting,
unintermittent, unflinching, unsleeping, unslumbering, sleep-
less, persistent.

Meddling, meddlesome, peddling, pushing, intermeddling,
tampering, etc., officious, over-officious, intriguing, managing.

(*Phrases*). Up and doing; up and stirring; busy as a bee;
brisk as a bee; on the qui vive; nimble as a squirrel; the
fingers itching; *nulla dies sine linea*; a rolling stone gathers
no moss; the used key is always bright; *nec mora nec requies*.

(*Adverbs*). Actively, etc., see 684.

(*Interjections*). Look alive! get a move on!

684. HASTE (*Substantives*), dispatch, precipitancy, precipitation, precipitousness, impetuosity, post-haste, acceleration, *see* 274.

Hurry, flurry, bustle, fuss, splutter, scramble, brusquerie, fidget, fidgetiness (682).

(*Verbs*). To haste, hasten, urge, press on, push on, bustle, hurry, buck up, precipitate, accelerate ; to bustle, scramble, scuttle, scurry, scoot, plunge, dash on, press on.

(*Phrases*). To make the most of one's time; to lose not a moment; *festina lente* ; *nec mora nec requies* ; *veni, vidi, vici*.

685. LEISURE (*Substantives*), leisureliness, spare time, breathing-time, off-time, slack time, holiday, bank-holiday, vacation, recess, red-letter day, repose.

(*Phrases*). *Otium cum dignitate*; time to spare; time on one's hands.

(*Verbs*). To have leisure, take one's leisure, repose (687), pause.

(*Phrase*). To shut up shop.

(*Adjectives*). Leisurely, undisturbed, quiet, deliberate, calm, reposing, etc.

(*Adverbs*). Leisurely, etc., at leisure.

(*Adjectives*). Hasty, hurried, precipitate, scrambling, etc., headlong, boisterous, impetuous, brusque, slapdash, cursory.

(*Adverbs*). Hastily, etc., headlong, in haste, slapdash, amain, hurry-skurry, helter-skelter, head and shoulders, head over heels, by fits and starts, by spurts.

(*Phrase*). No sooner said than done.

---

686. EXERTION (*Substantives*), labour, work, toil, fag, exercise, travail, sweat, exercitation, duty, trouble, pains, ado, drudgery, fagging, slavery, operoseness.

Effort, strain, grind, tug, stress, tension, throw, stretch, struggle, spell, etc.

(*Phrases*). A stitch of work; the sweat of one's brow.

(*Verbs*). To labour, work, exert oneself, toil, strive, use exertion, fag, strain, drudge, take pains, take trouble, trouble oneself, slave, pull, tug, ply the oar, rough it, sweat, bestir oneself, get up steam, get a move on, fall to work, buckle to, stick to.

(*Phrases*). To set one's shoulder to the wheel; to strain every nerve; to do as much as in one lies; to work day and night; to do double duty; to work double tides; to put forth one's strength, etc.; to work like a galley-slave (*see* 682); to go

687. REPOSE (*Substantives*), rest, halt, pause, relaxation, breathing-time, respite, *see* Leisure (685).

Day of rest Sabbath, holiday.

(*Verbs*). To repose, rest, relax, take rest, breathe, take breath, take one's ease, gather breath, recover one's breath, respire, pause, halt, stay one's hand, lay to, lie by, lie fallow, recline, lie down, go to rest, go to bed, go to sleep, etc., unbend, slacken.

(*Phrases*). To rest upon one's oars; to take a holiday; to shut up shop.

(*Adjectives*). Reposing, resting, etc., restful, unstrained.

through fire and water; to put one's best leg forward; to do one's level best; to grub along; to lay oneself out.

(*Adjectives*). Labouring, etc., laborious, toilsome, troublesome, operose, herculean, gymnastic, palæstric.

Hard-working, painstaking, strenuous (682).

(*Adverb*). Laboriously, etc.

(*Phrases*). By the sweat of the brow; *suo marte*; with all one's might; *totis viribus*; with might and main; *vi et armis*; with tooth and nail; *unguibus et rostro*; hammer and tongs; through thick and thin; heart and soul.

688. FATIGUE (*Substantives*), assitude, weariness, tiredness, exhaustion, sweat, collapse, prostration, swoon, faintness, faint, *deliquium*, syncope, yawning, anhelation; overstrain.

(*Verbs*). To be fatigued, etc., to droop, sink, flag, wilt, lose breath, lose wind, gasp, pant, puff, blow, yawn, drop, swoon, faint, succumb.

To fatigue, tire, weary, fag, jade, harass, exhaust, knock up, wear out, strain, overtask, overwork, overburden, overtax, overstrain, drive, sweat.

689. REFRESHMENT (*Substantives*), recovery of strength, recruiting, repair, refection, refocillation, relief, bracing, regalement, restoration, revival.

(*Phrase*). A giant refreshed.

(*Verbs*). To refresh, recruit, repair, refocillate, give tone, restore, recover.

To recover, regain, renew, etc., one's strength.

(*Adjectives*). Refreshing, etc., refreshed, etc., untired, unwearied, etc. (682).

(*Adjectives*). Fatigued, tired, unrefreshed, weary, wearied, jaded, wayworn; overworked, hard-driven; done up.

Breathless, out of breath, windless, out of wind, blown, winded, broken-winded.

Drooping, flagging, faint, fainting, done up, knocked up, exhausted, sinking, prostrate, spent, overspent, dead-beat, fagged out.

Worn out, played out, battered, shattered, seedy, weatherbeaten, footsore, *hors de combat*, done for.

(*Phrases*). Ready to drop; dog-tired; tired to death; on one's last legs; off one's legs; having too many irons in the fire.

Fatiguing, etc., tiresome, irksome, wearisome, trying.

690. AGENT (*Substantives*), doer, performer, operator, hand, employee, commissionaire, executor, maker, effector, consignee, midwife, middleman, jobber.

Artist, workman, workwoman, charwoman, worker, artisan, artificer, architect, handicraftsman, mechanic, machinist, manufacturer, practitioner, operative, journeyman, labourer, navvy, stevedore, docker, smith, wright, day-labourer, co-worker; *dramatis personæ*.

Bee, ant, worker-bee, drudge, fag, man or maid of all work, factotum, handy-man.

(*Phrase*). "*Quorum pars magna fui.*"

691. WORKSHOP (*Substantives*), laboratory, manufactory, mill, works, factory, mint, forge, stithy, loom, cabinet, office, bureau, studio, atelier, hive, hive of industry, workhouse, nursery, hot-house, hotbed, kitchen, dock, slip, yard, foundry, furnace.

Crucible, alembic, cauldron, matrix.

2°. *Complex Voluntary Action*

692. CONDUCT (*Substantives*), course of action, practice, procedure, transaction, dealing, ways, tactics, policy, polity, generalship, statesmanship, economy, strategy, husbandry, seamanship, house-keeping, housewifery, ménage, régime, *modus operandi*, economy.

Execution, manipulation, handling, treatment, process, working-out, course, campaign, career, walk.

Behaviour, deportment, comportment, carriage, *maintien*, de-meanour, bearing, manner, observance.

(*Verbs*). To conduct, carry on, run, transact, execute, carry out, work out, get through, carry through, go through, dispatch, treat, deal with, proceed with, officiate, discharge, do duty, play a part or game, run a race.

To behave, comport, acquit oneself, demean oneself, carry oneself, hold oneself.

(*Phrases*). To turn over a new leaf; to lead the way.

(*Adjectives*). Conducting, etc., strategical, businesslike, practical, executive.

693. DIRECTION (*Substantives*), management, government, bureau-cracy, statesmanship, conduct (692), regulation, charge, agency, senatorship, ministry, ministration, managery, directorate, director-ship, chairmanship, guidance, steerage, pilotage, superintendence, stewardship, supervision, surveillance, proctorship, state-craft, politics, *haute politique*, king-craft.

Committee, sub-committee, council, cabinet, staff, board (696).

(*Verbs*). To direct, manage, govern, guide, conduct, regulate, steer, con, pilot, have or take the direction, take the helm, have the charge of, superintend, overlook, supervise, control, boss, run, preside, hold office, hold the portfolio.

To head, lead, show the way, etc.

(*Phrase*). To pull the wires.

(*Adjective*). Directing, etc.; dirigible, etc.

694. DIRECTOR (*Substantives*), manager, master (745), prime minister, premier, governor, comptroller, superintendent, matron, supervisor, president, chairman, headman, supercargo, inspector, visitor, monitor, overseer, overlooker, shop-walker, taskmaster,

Reis Effendi, official, jack-in-office, bureaucrat, red-tapist, officer (726).

Conductor, steersman, pilot, coxswain, guide, *cicerone*, guard, driver, whip, charioteer, coachman, chauffeur, postilion, *vetturino*.

Steward, factor, factotum, bailiff, landreeve, foreman, forewoman, whipper-in, shepherd, proctor, procurator, housekeeper, major-domo, *chef*.

695. ADVICE (*Substantives*), counsel, suggestion, recommendation, hortation, exhortation. dehortation, instruction, charge, monition, admonition, admonishment, caution, warning, expostulation, obtestation, injunction, persuasion.

Guidance, helm, cynosure, rudder, lodestar, pole-star, guide, handbook, chart, compass, manual, itinerary, road-book, reference.

An adviser, senator, counsellor, counsel, consultant, specialist, monitor, mentor, Nestor, guide, teacher (540), physician, leech, doctor.

Referee, arbiter, arbitrator, referendary, assessor.

(*Verbs*). To advise, counsel, give advice, admonish, submonish, caution, warn, forewarn.

To persuade, dehort, exhort, enjoin, expostulate, charge, instruct.

To deliberate, consult together, hold a council, etc., confer, call in, refer to, take advice, be closeted with.

(*Phrases*). To lay one's heads together; to take counsel of one's pillow.

(*Adjectives*). Monitory, monitive, admonitory, recommendatory, hortatory, dehortatory, exhortatory, exhortative, warning, etc.

(*Interjection*). Go to!

696. COUNCIL (*Substantives*), conclave, court, chamber, cabinet, cabinet council, cockpit, house, committee, sub-committee, board, meeting, sitting, *comitia*, staff.

Senate, *senatus*, parliament, synod, soviet, convocation, congress, consistory, witenagemot, junta, states-general, diet, Cortes, Riksdag, Storthing, Reichsrat, Reichstag, Duma, Sobranje, Skupshtina, Tynewald, divan, musnud, Areopagus, sanhedrim, directory, etc.

A meeting, assembly, sitting, session, séance, sederunt.

697. PRECEPT (*Substantives*), direction, instruction, prescript, prescription, recipe, receipt, order (741).

Rule, *lex scripta*, canon, code, formula, formulary, rubric, maxim, apophthegm, etc. (496).

698. SKILL (*Substantives*), skilfulness, cleverness, ability, talent, genius, ingenuity, calibre, capacity, shrewdness, sagacity, parts, faculty, gift, forte, strong point, turn, invention, headpiece. Address, dexterity, adroitness,	**699. UNSKILFULNESS** (*Substantives*), inability, incompetence, incompetency, infelicity, inexpertness, indexterity, unaptness, ineptitude, lefthandedness, awkwardness, maladroitness, clumsiness, gaucherie, rawness, slovenli-

felicity, knack, expertness, quickness, sharpness, resourcefulness, smartness, readiness, excellence, habilitation, technique, virtuosity, artistry, ambidexterity, ambidextrousness, sleight of hand (545), knowingness.

Qualification, proficiency, panurgy, accomplishment, acquirement, craft, mastership, seamanship, rope-dancing.

Tact, knowledge of the world, *savoir faire*, discretion, finesse, worldly wisdom.

Prudence, *see* Caution (864).

Art, science, management, tactics, manœuvreing, sleight, policy, strategy, jobbery, temporisation, technology.

A master-stroke, *chef-d'œuvre*, a masterpiece, *tour de force*, a bold stroke, *coup de maître*, a good hit (650).

(*Verbs*). To be skilful, skilled, etc., to excel in, to specialise in, be master of; to temporise, manœuvre.

(*Phrases*). To play one's cards well; to stoop to conquer; *reculer pour mieux sauter*; to keep one's hand in; to keep one's balance; to cut one's coat according to one's cloth; to know what one is about; to know the ropes.

(*Adjectives*). Skilled, skilful, etc., clever, able, accomplished, talented, versatile, many-sided, resourceful, ingenious, inventive, shrewd, gifted, hard-headed, sagacious, sharp-witted.

Expert, dexterous, scientific, adroit, apt, sharp, handy, deft, ready, quick, smart, slick, spry, yare, nimble, ambidextrous, fine-fingered.

Conversant, versed, proficient, competent, qualified, good at, a dab at, up to, master of, cut out for, at home in, knowing.

ness, greenness, inexperience, disqualification.

Bungling, blundering, fumbling, floundering, stumbling, muddling, unteachableness, dullness, stupidity (499).

Indiscretion, imprudence (863), thoughtlessness, giddiness, wildness, mismanagement, misconduct, maladministration, misrule, misgovernment, misapplication, misdirection.

(*Phrase*). A blazing indiscretion.

Absence of rule, the rule of thumb.

(*Verbs*). To be unskilled, unskilful, etc.

To mismanage, bungle, blunder, botch, boggle, fumble, muff, foozle, miscue, muddle, murder, mistake, misapply, missend.

(*Phrases*). To make a mess or hash of; to begin at the wrong end; to make sad work or a bad job of; to put one's foot in it; to lose or miss one's way; to lose one's balance; to stand in one's own light; to quarrel with one's bread and butter; to have too many irons in the fire; to have too many eggs in one basket; to kill the goose which lays the golden eggs; to lock the stable when the horse is stolen; to make two bites at a cherry.

(*Adjectives*). Unskilled, etc., unskilful, bungling, etc., awkward, clumsy, unhandy, unworkmanlike, unscientific, shiftless, lubberly, *gauche*, maladroit, left-handed, hobbling, slovenly, sloppy, slatternly, giddy, gawky, dull, unteachable, at fault.

Unapt, unqualified, inhabile, incompetent, disqualified, untalented, ill-qualified, inapt, inept, inexpert, inartistic, raw, green, rusty.

Experienced, practised, hackneyed, trained, initiated, prepared, primed, finished, schooled, thoroughbred, masterly, consummate.

Technical, artistic, workmanlike, dædalian, masterly, statesmanlike.

Discreet, politic, tactful, diplomatic, sure-footed, felicitous, strategic.

(*Phrases*). A nice hand, etc., *see* 700.

(*Adverbs*). Skilfully, etc., aright.

(*Phrases*). *Suo marte*; to the best of one's abilities; *secundum artem*.

Unaccustomed, unused, unhackneyed, unexercised, untrained, unpractised, undisciplined, uneducated, undrilled, uninitiated, unschooled, unconversant, unversed, inexperienced, unstatesmanlike, non-professional.

Unadvised, misadvised, ill-judged, ill-advised, unguided, misguided, foolish, wild, ill-devised, misconducted.

(*Phrases*). *Ne sutor ultra crepidam*; *il se noyerait dans une goutte d'eau*; penny-wise and pound-foolish.

---

700. Proficient (*Substantives*), adept, expert, specialist, genius, dab, crack, master, master-hand, virtuoso, champion, ace, artist, tactician, politician, marksman, sharp blade, acrobat, gymnast, rope-dancer, funambulist, old stager, veteran, top-sawyer, picked man, cunning man, conjuror, wizard, etc. (994); a prodigy (872), an Admirable Crichton.

Connoisseur (850).

(*Phrases*). A man of business; a nice hand; good hand; swell hand; dead shot; crack shot; jack of all trades; smart customer; old file; deep file; sharp as a needle; an all-round man.

701. Bungler (*Substantives*), marplot, greenhorn, lubber, landlubber, fumbler, muddler, duffer, butter-fingers, novice, sloven, slattern, no conjuror, flat, muff, babe.

(*Phrases*). A bad hand at; no good at; one's fingers all thumbs; a fresh-water sailor; the awkward squad; not likely to set the Thames on fire.

---

702. Cunning (*Substantives*), craft, artfulness, subtlety, shrewdness, smartness, archness, insidiousness, slyness, opportunism, artificialness, artificiality.

Artifice, stratagem, wile, dodge, finesse, ruse, diplomacy, politics, *ruse de guerre*.

Duplicity, guile, circumvention, chicane, chicanery, sharp practice, Machiavellism, legerdemain, trickery, etc. (545).

Net, toils, trap, etc. (667).

703. Artlessness (*Substantives*), nature, naturalness, simplicity, ingenuousness, *bonhomie*, frankness, naïveté, openness, *abandon*, candour, outspokenness, sincerity, straightforwardness, honesty (939); innocence (946).

(*Phrases*). *Enfant terrible*; a mere babe.

(*Verb*). To be artless, etc.

(*Adjectives*). Artless, natural, native, plain, simple-minded, in-

A slyboots, Ulysses, Machiavel, opportunist, time-server.

(*Verbs*). To be cunning, etc., to contrive, design, manœuvre, wriggle, wangle, intrigue, temporise, circumvent, get round, nobble, undermine.

(*Phrases*). To stoop to conquer; to steal a march on; *reculer pour mieux sauter*; to know on which side one's bread is buttered.

(*Adjectives*). Cunning, crafty, artful, knowing, wily, sly, sharp, smart, slim, feline, subtle, arch, designing, intriguing, contriving, insidious, canny, downy, deceitful (545), artificial, deep, profound, diplomatic, vulpine, Machiavellian, time-serving.

(*Phrase*). Cunning as a fox; sharp as a needle; not to be caught with chaff.

genuous, candid, naïve, sincere, frank (543), open, frank-hearted, open-hearted, above-board, downright, guileless, inartificial, undesigning, single-minded, honest, straightforward, outspoken.

Section IV.—Antagonism

1°. *Conditional Antagonism*

704. Difficulty (*Substantives*), delicacy, hardness, hard work, hard task, troublesomeness, laboriousness.

Impracticability, infeasibility, intractability, toughness, perverseness, *see* Impossibility (471).

Embarrassment, awkwardness, perplexity, intricacy, intricateness, entanglement, knot, Gordian knot, labyrinth, net, meshes, maze, etc. (248).

Dilemma, nice point, delicate point, knotty point, stumbling-block, vexed question, crux; *pons asinorum*, poser, puzzle, floorer, nonplus, quandary, strait, pass, critical situation, crisis, trial, emergency, exigency, scramble.

Scrape, hobble, fix, hole, lurch, contretemps, hitch, how-d'ye-do, slough, quagmire, hot water, stew, imbroglio, mess, ado, false position, stand, deadlock, encumbrance, cul-de-sac, impasse.

705. Facility (*Substantives*), practicability, feasibility, practicableness, *see* Possibility (470).

Ease, easiness, child's play, smoothness, tractability, tractableness, ductility, flexibility, malleability, capability, disentanglement, freedom, advantage, vantage-ground.

(*Phrases*). Plain sailing; smooth water; smooth sailing; fair wind; full play or swing; a clear coast; a holiday task; a royal road; a walk-over; a soft job.

(*Verbs*). To be easy, etc., to flow, swim, or drift with the tide or stream; to do with ease, to throw off.

(*Phrases*). To have it all one's own way; to walk over the course; to go with the stream.

To render easy, etc., to facilitate, popularise, smooth, ease, lighten, free, clear, disencumber, deobstruct, disembarrass, clear

(*Phrases*). A screw loose; a ticklish card to play; a sea of troubles; horns of a dilemma; a peck of troubles; a kettle of fish; a handful; "Ay, there's the rub."

(*Verbs*). To be difficult, etc.

To meet with, experience, labour under, get into, plunge into, be surrounded by, be encompassed with, be entangled by, to struggle, contend against or grapple with difficulties.

To come to a stand, to stick fast, to be set fast, to boggle, flounder, get left.

(*Phrases*). To stand in one's own light; come to a deadlock; to get into hot water; to put one's foot in it; to get into a mess; to be bunkered; to fish in troubled waters; to buffet the waves; to be put to one's shifts; not to know whether one stands on one's head or one's heels; *perdre son Latin*; to skate over thin ice.

To render difficult, etc., to embarrass, perplex, put one out, bother, pose, puzzle, floor, nonplus, ravel, entangle, gravel, flummox, run hard.

(*Phrases*). To lead a pretty dance; to put to one's shifts; to put a spoke in one's wheel; leave in the lurch; bring to a deadlock.

the way, smooth the way, disentangle, unclog, disengage, extricate, unravel, disburden, exonerate, emancipate, free from; to lubricate, etc. (332).

(*Phrases*). To leave a hole to creep out of; to bridge over; to grease the wheels.

(*Adjectives*). Easy, facile, attainable, handy, practicable, feasible, achievable, performable, possible (470), superable, surmountable, accessible, comeatable, get-at-able.

(*Phrases*). The coast being clear; as easy as lying.

Easily managed or accomplished, etc., tractable, manageable, smooth, glib, pliant, yielding, malleable, ductile, flexible, plastic, submissive.

At ease, free, light, easy, unburdened, unencumbered, unloaded, disburdened, disencumbered, disembarrassed, exonerated, unrestrained, unobstructed, unimpeded, untrammelled, at home.

(*Phrases*). Quite at home; in one's element; in smooth water; on velvet.

(*Adverb*). Easily, etc.

———

(*Adjectives*). Difficult, not easy, hard, stiff, troublesome, laborious, onerous, operose, awkward, unwieldy, beset with or full of difficulties, uphill work, Herculean, Sisyphean.

Unmanageable, tough, stubborn, hard to deal with, *difficile*, ill-conditioned, refractory, perverse, crabbed, intractable, against the grain.

Embarrassing, perplexing, delicate, ticklish, pernickety, intricate, thorny, spiny, knotty, tricky, pathless, trackless, labyrinthine.

Impracticable, not possible, impossible (471), not practicable, not feasible, infeasible, unachievable, uncomeatable, inextricable, impassable, innavigable, desperate, insuperable, insurmountable, unplayable.

In difficulty, perplexed, etc., beset, waterlogged, put to it, hard put to it, run hard, hard pressed, thrown out, adrift, at fault, abroad, pushed.

Stranded, aground, stuck fast, at bay.

(*Phrases*). At a stand-still; at a stand; surrounded with shoals and breakers; thrown on one's beam-ends; out of one's depth; at the end of one's resources; put to one's shifts; in a cleft stick; on a wrong scent; driven from pillar to post; things being come to a pretty pass; at a pinch; between two stools; in the wrong box; in a fix; in a hole.

(*Adverbs*). With difficulty, hardly, etc., against the stream, against the grain, uphill.

2°. *Active Antagonism*

706. HINDRANCE (*Substantives*), prevention, preclusion, impedance, retardment, retardation.

Obstruction, stoppage, interruption, interclusion, oppilation, restraint, inhibition, embargo, blockade, embarrassment.

Interference, interposition, obtrusion, discouragement, chill.

An impediment, hindrance, obstacle, obstruction, bunker, hazard, let, stumbling-block, check, impasse, countercheck, set-back, hitch, bar, barrier, barrage, barricade, turnpike, wall, dead wall, bulkhead, portcullis, etc. (717), dam, weir, boom, turnstile, tourniquet.

Drawback, objection.

An encumbrance, impedimenta, onus, clog, drag, weight, dead weight, lumber, top-hamper, pack, millstone, incubus, nightmare, Ephialtes; trammel, etc. (752), set-back.

(*Phrases*). A spoke in the wheel; a wet blanket; the old man of the sea; *damnosa hereditas*.

A hinderer, a marplot; a killjoy, an interloper; an opponent (710).

(*Verbs*). To hinder, impede,

707. AID (*Substantives*), assistance, help, succour, support, relief, advance, furtherance, promotion.

Coadjuvancy, patronage, auspices, championship, countenance, favour, helpfulness.

Sustentation, alimentation, nutrition, nourishment; ministration, ministry, accommodation.

Supplies, reinforcements, succours, contingents, recruits; physical support, *see* 215.

(*Verbs*). To aid, assist, help, succour, support, subscribe to, finance, promote, further, abet, advance, foster; to give, bring, furnish, afford or supply support, etc., to reinforce, nourish, nurture, suckle, dry-nurse.

To favour, countenance, befriend, smile upon, encourage, patronise, make interest for.

To second, stand by, back, back up, take part in, side with, to come or pass over to, to join, to rally round, play up to.

(*Phrases*). To take the part of; consult the wishes of; to take up the cause of; to espouse the cause of; to enlist under the banners of; to join hand in hand; to lend or bear a hand; to hold

prevent, preclude, retard, slacken, obviate, forefend, avert, turn aside, ward off, draw off, cut off, counteract, undermine.

To obstruct, stop, stay, let, make against, bar, debar, inhibit, cramp, restrain, check, set back, discourage, discountenance, foreclose.

(*Phrases*). To lay under restraint; to tie the hands; to keep in swaddling-bands.

To thwart, traverse, contravene, interrupt, intercept, interclude, frustrate, defeat, disconcert, baffle, undo, intercept; to balk, cushion, stymie, spoil, mar.

To interpose, interfere, intermeddle, obtrude (682).

(*Phrases*). To stand in the way of; to break in upon; to run or fall foul of.

To hamper, clog, cumber, encumber, saddle with, load with, overload, overlay, lumber, block up, incommode, hustle; to curb, shackle, fetter; to embog.

out a helping hand; to give one a lift; to do one a good turn; to see one through; to take in tow; to beat up for recruits; pay the piper; help a lame dog over the stile; give a leg-up.

To serve, do service, minister to, oblige, accommodate, work for, administer to, pander to; to tend, attend, take care of, wait on, nurse, dry-nurse, entertain.

To speed, expedite, forward, quicken, hasten, set forward.

(*Adjectives*). Aiding, helping, assisting, etc., auxiliary, adjuvant, ancillary, accessory, subsidiary, helpful.

Friendly, amicable, favourable, propitious.

(*Adverbs*). On or in behalf of; in the service of; under the auspices of; hand in hand.

(*Interjections*). Help! save us!

(*Phrases*). To put a spoke in the wheel; to clog the wheel; to throw cold water on; to nip in the bud; to apply the closure.

(*Adjectives*). Hindering, etc., in the way of, impedimental, inimical, unfavourable, onerous, burdensome, cumbrous, obstructive.

Hindered, etc., wind-bound, water-logged, heavy-laden.

Unassisted, unaided, unhelped, unsupported, single-handed, unbefriended.

(*Phrase*). Prevention being better than cure.

708. Opposition (*Substantives*), antagonism, counteraction (179), contravention, control, clashing, collision, competition, rivalry, emulation.

Absence of aid, etc., counterplot (718).

(*Phrase*). A head-wind.

(*Verbs*). To oppose, antagonise, cross, counteract, control, contravene, countervail, counter-

709. Co-operation (*Substantives*), coadjuvancy, collaboration, concert, collusion, complicity, co-efficiency, *see* Concurrence (178).

Alliance, colleagueship, joint-stock, co-partnership, coalition, amalgamation, federation, confederation (712).

(*Phrases*). A helping hand; a long pull.

work, stultify, thwart, counter, countermine, run counter, go against, collide with, clash, rival, emulate, put against, militate against, beat against, stem, breast, encounter, compete with, withstand, to face, face down.

(*Phrases*). To set one's face against; to make a stand against; to stand out against; to fly in the face of; to fall foul of; to come into collision with; to be or to play at cross-purposes; to kick against the pricks; to buffet the waves; to cut one another's throats; to join issue.

(*Adjectives*). Opposing, etc., adverse, antagonistic, opposed, conflicting, contrary, unfavourable, cross; up in arms.

Unaided, unassisted, unhelped, unsustained, unseconded, etc., unsupported, unbefriended.

(*Verbs*). To co-operate, concur, conspire, concert, collaborate, draw or pull together, to join with, collude, unite one's efforts, club together, fraternise, be in league, etc., with, be a party to, to side with.

(*Phrases*). To understand one another; to be in the same boat; to play into the hands of; to hunt in couples; to hit it off together, to play booty.

(*Adjectives*). Co-operating, etc., co-operative, co-operant, in co-operation, etc., in concert, allied, etc.

(*Phrase*). Wind and weather permitting.

Unopposed, unobstructed, unimpeded.

(*Adverbs*). As one man, *see* Unanimity (488).

(*Adverbs*). Against, *versus*, counter to, against the stream, tide, wind, etc., in the way of, in spite of, in despite of, in the teeth of, in the face of, *per contra*; single-handed.

Across, athwart, overthwart.

Though, although (179), even, *quand même*, all the same.

(*Phrases*). In spite of one's teeth; with the wind in one's teeth; off one's own bat; on one's lonesome.

---

710. OPPONENT (*Substantives*), antagonist, adversary, adverse party, rival, competitor, backfriend, enemy, foe (891), assailant; malcontent.

711. AUXILIARY (*Substantives*), assistant, adjuvant, adjunct, adjutant, help, helper, helpmate, colleague, partner, confrère, coadjutor, co-operator, collaborator, ally, aide-de-camp, accomplice, accessory; votary; midwife.

Friend (890), confidant, champion, partisan, right hand, stand-by; adherent, *particeps criminis*, confederate, bottleholder, second, candle-holder, servant (*see* 746); *fidus Achates*.

(*Phrase*). *Deus ex machina.*

712. PARTY (*Substantives*), partnership, fraternity, sodality, company, society, firm, house, body, corporation, corporate body, union, association, syndicate, guild, joint concern, faction.

Fellowship, brotherhood, sisterhood, communion, community, clan, clanship, club, friendly society, clique, junto, coterie, faction, gang, *camarilla*, cabal, league, confederacy, confederation, federation; side, *esprit de corps*; alliance, partisanship.

Band, staff, crew, set, posse, phalanx, *dramatis personæ*.

(*Verbs*). To unite, join, club together, join forces, federate, cooperate, befriend, aid, etc. (707), cement, form a party, league, etc., to be in the same boat.

(*Adjectives*). In partnership, alliance, etc., federal, federated, bonded, banded, linked, cemented, etc., together, embattled.

---

713. DISCORD (*Substantives*), disagreement (24), variance, difference, dissent, dissension, misunderstanding, jar, jarring, clashing, friction, odds, disaccord.

Disunion, schism, breach, falling out, rupture, disruption, open rupture, *brouillerie*, feud, vendetta, contentiousness, litigiousness, strife, contention (720); enmity (889).

Dispute, controversy, polemics, quarrel, tiff, *tracasserie*, altercation, *imbroglio*, bickering, snip-snap, chicanery, squabble, row, brawl, debate (476).

Litigation, words, war of words, logomachy, wrangling, wrangle, jangle, declaration of war, *see* Warfare (722).

Subject of dispute, ground of quarrel, disputed point, a bone to pick, the bone of contention, the apple of discord, *casus belli*.

(*Verbs*). To be discordant, etc., to differ, dissent, disagree, clash, jar, to misunderstand one another.

714. CONCORD (*Substantives*), accord, agreement (23), unison, unity, union, good understanding, quiet, peace, unanimity (488), harmony, amity, *entente cordiale, rapprochement*, alliance.

(*Phrases*). The bonds of harmony; a happy family; a happy band of brothers.

(*Verbs*). To agree, accord, be in unison, etc., to harmonise with, fraternise, stand in with.

(*Phrases*). To understand one another; to see eye to eye with; to hit it off together; to remain at peace; to keep the peace; to sing in chorus; to pull together.

(*Adjectives*). Concordant, agreeing, etc., united, in unison, etc., harmonious, allied, cemented, friendly, amicable, fraternal, at peace, peaceful, pacific, tranquil.

(*Phrases*). In still water; at one with; with one voice.

To fall out, dispute, controvert, litigate; to quarrel, wrangle, squabble, bicker, spar, jangle, brangle, brawl; to break with; to declare war.

(*Phrases*). To be at odds with; to fall foul of; to have words with; to have a bone to pick with; to be at variance with; to join issue; to pick a quarrel with; to live like cat and dog.

To embroil, entangle, disunite, set against, pit against; to sow dissension, disunion, discord, etc., among.

(*Phrases*). To set together by the ears; sow or stir up contention.

(*Adjectives*). Discordant, disagreeing, differing, disunited, clashing, jarring, dissentient, sectarian, at variance, controversial.

Quarrelsome, disputatious, litigious, litigant, factious, pettifogging, polemic, schismatic; unpacified, unreconciled.

(*Phrases*). At odds; in hot water; at daggers drawn; up in arms; at sixes and sevens; at loggerheads; together by the ears; a house divided against itself.

715. DEFIANCE (*Substantives*), challenge, cartel, daring, war-whoop.

(*Verbs*). To defy, challenge, dare, brave, beard, bluster, look big.

(*Phrases*). To set at naught; snap the fingers at; to bid defiance to; to set at defiance; to hurl defiance at; to double the fist; to stand akimbo; to show a bold front; to brave it out; to show fight; to throw down the gauntlet or glove; to call out.

(*Adjective*). Defying, etc.

(*Adverbs*). In defiance of; with arms akimbo.

(*Interjections*). Come on! marry come up!

(*Phrase*). *Nemo me impune lacessit.*

716. ATTACK (*Substantives*), aggression, offence, assault, charge, onset, onslaught, assault, brunt, thrust, pass, passado, cut, sally, inroad, invasion, irruption, sortie, *camisade*, storm, storming, boarding, escalade, foray, raid, *Jacquerie*, *razzia*, dragonnade (*see* 619); siege, investment.

Fire, volley, cannonade, barrage, broadside, bombardment, raking fire, platoon-fire, fusillade.

Kick, buffet, etc. (276), a run at, a dead set at, carte and tierce, a backhander.

An assailant, aggressor.

(*Verbs*). To attack, assault, assail, go for, fall upon, close with, charge, bear down upon, set on, have at, strike at, run at, make a run at, butt, tilt at, poke at, make a pass at, thrust at, cut and thrust, pitch into, kick, buffet, bonnet, beat (*see* 972), lay about one, lift a hand against, come on, have a fling at, slap on the face, pelt, throw stones, etc., to round on.

(*Phrases*). To shoot at; fire at; fire upon; pop at; let off a gun; shoot; let fly at; open

717. DEFENCE (*Substantives*), self-defence, self-preservation, protection, ward, guard, guardianship, shielding, etc., *see* Resistance (718), and Safety (664).

Fence, wall, parapet, dike, etc. (232), boom, picket, mound, mole, outwork, trench, entrenchment, fortification, embankment, bulwark, barbican, battlement, stockade, laager, zareba, abattis, casemate, muniment, vallum, circumvallation, contravallation, sunk fence, ha-ha, buttress, abutment, breastwork, hornwork, portcullis, glacis, bastion, redoubt, rampart.

Hold, stronghold, keep, donjon, palladium, fort, fortress, blockhouse, sconce, citadel, tower, castle, capitol, fastness, barracoon, asylum (666).

Anchor, sheet-anchor.

Shield, buckler, ægis, breastplate, coat of mail, cuirass, hauberk, habergeon, *chevaux de frise*, screen, etc. (666); helmet, casque, shako, bearskin, gas-mask, panoply; fender, cow-catcher, buffer.

Defender, protector, guardian

fire; pepper; bombard; pour a broadside into; fire a volley.

To beset, besiege, lay siege to, invest, beleaguer, open the trenches, invade, raid, storm, board, scale the walls.

To press one hard, be hard upon, drive one hard.

(*Phrases*). To take the bull by the horns; to run amuck; take the offensive; assume the aggressive; make a dead set at.

(*Adjectives*). Attacking, etc., aggressive, offensive, up in arms.

(*see* 664), champion, protagonist, knight-errant.

(*Verbs*). To defend, shield, fend, fence, entrench, guard (664), keep off, keep at bay, ward off, beat off, parry, repel, bear the brunt of, put to flight.

(*Phrases*). To fall back upon; to act on the defensive; to maintain one's ground; to stand in the gap; to put on the gloves.

(*Adjectives*). Defending, etc., defensive, defended, etc., armed.

(*Phrases*). Armed cap-à-pie; armed to the teeth.

(*Adverbs*). Defensively, on the defence, on the defensive, at bay.

(*Phrase*). Pro aris et focis.

---

718. RETALIATION (*Substantives*), reprisal, retort, counter-stroke, reciprocation, *tu quoque*, recrimination, retribution, counterplot, counterproject, counterblast, *lex talionis*, *see* Revenge (919) and Compensation (30).

(*Phrases*). Tit for tat; a Roland for an Oliver; diamond cut diamond; the biter bit; catching a Tartar; *suo sibi gladio jugulo*; hoist with his own petard.

(*Verbs*). To retaliate, retort, recriminate, counter, be even with one, pay off.

(*Phrases*). To turn the tables; to return the compliment; to pay in one's own coin; to give a *quid pro quo*; to give a Roland for an Oliver.

(*Adjectives*). Retaliating, retaliatory, retaliative, recriminatory, recriminative.

(*Adverbs*). In retaliation, *en revanche*; *tu quoque*; *mutato nomine, de te fabula narratur*; *par pari refero*.

---

719. RESISTANCE (*Substantives*), stand, oppugnation, reluctation, front, repulse, rebuff, kicking, etc., *see* Disobedience (742), recalcitration.

Strike, meeting, tumult, riot, *pronunciamento*, *émeute*, mutiny.

Revolt, rising, insurrection, rebellion, *levée en masse*, *Jacquerie*.

(*Verbs*). To resist, not to submit, etc., to withstand, stand against, stand firm, make a stand, repugn, confront, face down.

(*Phrases*). To present a front; to show a bold front; to make head against; to stand one's ground; to stand the brunt of; to keep at bay; to stem the torrent; to champ the bit; to sell one's life dearly.

To kick, kick against, recalcitrate, lift the hand against, *see* Attack (716), repel, repulse, to rise, revolt, mutiny.

(*Phrases*). To fly in the face of; to kick against the pricks; to take the bit between one's teeth.

(*Adjectives*). Resisting, etc., resistive, resistant, refractory, mutinous, recalcitrant, up in arms, *see* Disobedient (742).

Unyielding, unconquered, indomitable.

(*Interjections*). Hands off! keep off!

---

720. Contention (*Substantives*), contest, struggle, contestation, debate (476), logomachy, high words, rivalry, corrivalry, corrivalship, competition, *concours*, gymkhana, race, heat, steeplechase, bickering, strife (713).

Wrestling, jiu-jitsu, pugilism, boxing, fisticuffs, spar, prize-fighting, set-to, round, fracas, row, shindy, scrap, dust, rumpus, outbreak, clash, collision, shock, breach of the peace, brawl.

721. Peace (*Substantives*), amity, truce, harmony. *see* Concord (714), tranquillity.

(*Phrase*). Piping time of peace.

(*Verbs*). To be at peace, etc., to keep the peace, etc. (714).

(*Adjectives*). Pacific, peaceable, peaceful, tranquil, untroubled, halcyon.

(*Phrase*). Hors concours.

(*Phrases*). A stand-up fight; hand-to-hand fight.

Conflict, skirmish, rencounter, scuffle, encounter, rencontre, velitation, tussle, scrimmage, scrummage, broil, fray, affray, mêlée, affair, brush, bout, fight, battle, combat, action, engagement, battle-royal, running fight, free fight, joust, tournament, tourney, pitched battle, death-struggle, Armageddon.

Naval engagement, *naumachia*, naumachy, sea-fight.

Duel, satisfaction, monomachy, single combat, passage of arms, a triangular duel.

(*Verbs*). To contend, contest, struggle, vie with, race, race with, outvie, battle with, cope with, compete, join issue, bandy, try conclusions with, close with, square, buckle with, wrestle, joust, enter the lists, take up arms, take the field, encounter, struggle with, grapple with, tackle, engage with, strive with, fall to, encounter, collide with.

(*Phrases*). Join battle; fall foul of; have a brush with; break the peace; take up the cudgels; unsheath the sword; couch one's lance; to run a tilt at; give satisfaction; measure swords; lay about one; cut and thrust; fight without the gloves; go on the warpath.

(*Adjectives*). Contending, etc., *see* 722; pugilistic, agonistic, competitive, rival, polemical (476), rough-and-tumble.

(*Adverbial Phrases*). *A verbis ad verbera*; *à outrance*; pull devil, pull baker.

---

722. Warfare (*Substantives*), war, hostilities, fighting, etc., open war, *ultima ratio*, war to the knife, internecine war, *guerre à mort* ; *guerre à outrance*.

723. Pacification (*Substantives*), reconciliation, accommodation, arrangement, *modus vivendi*, adjustment, terms.

Peace - offering, olive -branch,

Battle array, campaign, crusade, war-path.

Warlike spirit, military spirit, militarism, bellicosity.

(*Phrase*). The mailed fist.

The art of war, tactics, strategy, military evolutions, arms, service, etc., Mars, Bellona.

War-cry, fiery cross, trumpet, clarion, bugle, pibroch, war-whoop, beat of drum, *rappel*; mobilisation.

(*Verbs*). To fight, set to, spar, scrap, tussle, joust, tilt, box, skirmish, fight hand to hand, fence, measure swords, engage, combat, give battle, go to battle, join battle, engage in battle, wage war, go to war, come to blows, break a lance with, couch the lance, appeal to arms, appeal to the sword, give satisfaction, take the field, keep the field, fight it out, fight to a finish, spill blood, carry on war, carry on hostilities, to fight one's way, to serve, to see service, to fight like devils, to sell one's life dearly.

calumet or pipe of peace, preliminaries of peace.

Pacifism, pacificism.

Truce, armistice, suspension of arms, of hostilities, etc., convention, *détente.*

(*Phrases*). Hollow truce; *pax in bello.*

Flag of truce, white flag, cartel.

(*Verbs*). To make peace, pacify, make it up, settle, arrange, accommodate matters, tranquillise, compose, hush up, settle differences, restore harmony, heal the breach.

(*Phrases*). To put up the sword; to sheathe the sword; *tantas componere lites* ; to bury the hatchet; to smoke the calumet of peace; to close the temple of Janus; to cry quits.

(*Adjective*). Pacified, etc.

(*Phrase*). *Requiescat in pace.*

(*Adjectives*). Contending, etc., unpeaceful, contentious, belligerent, bellicose, jingo, chauvinistic, martial, warlike, military, militant, gladiatorial, chivalrous, in arms, embattled.

(*Phrases*). Together by the ears; sword in hand.

(*Adverbs*). *Pendente lite*, the battle raging, *flagrante bello*, in the thick of the fray.

(*Interjections*). *Væ victis !* to arms! to your tents, O Israel!

724. MEDIATION (*Substantives*), intervention, interposition, interference, intermeddling, intercession, parley, negotiation, arbitration, mediatorship, good offices, diplomacy, peace-offering, eirenicon.

A mediator, intermediary, go-between, intercessor, peacemaker, makepeace, negotiator.

(*Verbs*). To mediate, intermediate, intercede, interpose, interfere, intervene, negotiate, arbitrate, compromise.

(*Phrase*). *Magnas componere lites.*

725. SUBMISSION (*Substantives*), surrender, non-resistance, yielding, capitulation, cession.

(*Verbs*). To surrender, succumb, submit, yield, give in, bend, truckle to, knuckle down or under, knock under, capitulate, lay down or deliver up one's arms, retreat, give way, cave in.

(*Phrases*). Beat a retreat; strike one's flag or colours; surrender at discretion; make a virtue of necessity; to come to terms.

(*Adjectives*). Surrendering, etc., non-resisting, unresisting, submissive, crouching.

Undefended, untenable, indefensible.

726. COMBATANT (*Substantives*), belligerent, champion, disputant, litigant, competitor, rival, corrival, assailant, bully, bruiser, fighter, duellist, fighting-man, pugilist, boxer, the fancy, prizefighter, fighting-cock, gladiator, fire-eater, berserker; swordsman, wrestler, Amazon, Paladin, son of Mars; staff, *état major*, brass hats; militarist; effective.

726A. NON-COMBATANT (*Substantives*), civilian; passive resister, conscientious objector, pacifist, pacificist; non-effective. Quaker, Dukhobor.

(*Adjective*). Non-effective.

Warrior, soldier, man-at-arms, red-coat, man in khaki, Tommy Atkins, tommy, trooper, dragoon, *voltigeur*, light horseman (or hussar), grenadier, fusilier, guardsman, lifeguard, lancer, cuirassier, spearman, musketeer, carabineer, rifleman, sharpshooter, *bersagliere*; ensign, standard-bearer, halberdier; private, subaltern, conscript, rank and file.

Engineer, artilleryman, gunner, cannoneer, bombardier, sapper, miner, archer, bowman.

Marine, jolly; seaman, bluejacket, tar, A.B.

Guerrilla, cossack, sepoy, gurkha, spahee, janizary, zouave, bashi-bazouk.

Armed force, the army, the military, soldiery, infantry, fencibles, volunteers, territorials, *Landwehr*, *Landsturm*, yeomanry, cavalry, horse artillery, horse, light horse, horse and foot, commando.

Militia, train-band, legion, phalanx, myrmidons, squadron, troop, cohort, regiment, corps, platoon, battalion, company (72), column, detachment, brigade, garrison, battle-array, order of battle.

727. ARMS (*Substantives*), weapons, armament, armour, armoury, quiver, arsenal, magazine, armature.

Mail, chain-mail, lorication; ammunition, powder, gunpowder, cartridge, cartouche (635).

Artillery, park, ordnance-piece, gun, cannon, swivel, howitzer, carronade, culverin, field-piece, machine-gun, mitrailleuse, basilisk, mortar, grenade, petronel, petard, falconet.

Fire-arms, side-arms, stand of arms, musketry, musket, fusil, musketoon, caliver, firelock, match-lock, flint-lock, fowling-piece, rifle, revolver, carbine, blunderbuss, pistol, derringer, Winchester, Lee-Metford, Mauser, Maxim, etc.

Bow, harquebus (or arquebus), cross-bow, ballista, sling, catapult, catamaran.

Missile, projectile, shot, ball, grape, grape-shot, chain-shot, bullet, stone, shell, gas-shell, bomb, torpedo, rocket, congreve, shrapnel; Ballistics.

Pike, lance, spear, spontoon, javelin, dart, arrow, reed, shaft, bolt, boomerang, harpoon.

Bayonet, sword, sabre, broadsword, cutlass, falchion, scimetar, rapier, skean, toledo, tuck, claymore, creese (or kris), dagger, dirk, hanger, poniard, stiletto, stylet, dudgeon, axe, bill, poleaxe, battle-axe, halberd, tomahawk, bowie-knife, snickersnee, yataghan, kukri, assagai (or assegai).

Club, mace, truncheon, staff, bludgeon, cudgel, knobkerrie, life-preserver, knuckle-duster, shillelagh, bat.

Catapult, battering-ram; tank.

728. ARENA (*Substantives*), field, walk, battle-field, field of battle, lists, palæstra, course, cinder-track, stage, boards, race-course, *corso*, circus, ring, cock-pit, bear-garden, scene of action, theatre of war, the enemy's camp, amphitheatre, hippodrome, aerodrome, coliseum (or colosseum), proscenium; playground, Aceldama.

SECTION V.—RESULTS OF VOLUNTARY ACTION

729. COMPLETION (*Substantives*), accomplishment, performance, fulfilment, fruition, execution, achievement, dispatch, work done, superstructure, finish, termination, dénouement, consummation, *fait accompli*, winding up, the last stroke, finishing stroke, *coup de grâce*, last finish, final touch, crowning touch, *see* End (67), Arrival (292), and Completeness (52).

(*Verbs*). To complete, effect, perform, do, execute, go through, accomplish, fulfil, discharge, achieve, compass, effectuate, dispatch, knock off, close, terminate, conclude, finish, end (67), consummate, bring about, bring to bear, bring to pass, get through, carry through, bring through, work out, make good, carry out, wind up, dispose of, bring to a close, termination, conclusion, etc., shut up shop, bring off.

To perfect, bring to perfection, stamp, put the seal to, polish off, crown.

730. NON-COMPLETION (*Substantives*), inexecution, short-coming (304), non-performance, neglect; incompleteness (53); a drawn battle or game, a draw, a stalemate.

(*Phrase*). The work of Penelope.

(*Verbs*). Not to complete, perform, etc., to fall short of, leave unfinished, etc., neglect, leave undone, etc., draw.

(*Phrases*). To scotch the snake, not kill it; hang fire; do by halves.

(*Adjectives*). Not completed, etc., uncompleted, incomplete, unfinished, left undone (53), short, unaccomplished, unperformed, unexecuted.

In progress, in hand, proceeding, going on, on the stocks.

(*Adverb*). *Re infecta.*

To reach, arrive (292), touch, reach, attain the goal; to run one's race.

(*Phrases*). To give the last finish, or finishing touch; to put the last, or finishing hand to; to get in the harvest; to carry into execution; to be through with; to get it over; to deliver the goods.

(*Adjectives*). Completing, final, terminal, concluding, conclusive, crowning, etc., done, completed, wrought, high-wrought.

(*Phrases*). The race being run; *finis coronat opus*; *actum est*.

(*Adverbs*). Completely, etc. (52), out of hand, effectually, with a vengeance, with a witness.

---

731. SUCCESS (*Substantives*), successfulness, speed, thrift, advance, luck, good fortune (734), godsend, prize, trump-card, hit, stroke; lucky or fortunate hit; bold stroke, master-stroke, *coup de maître*, knock-out blow, checkmate, *see* Skill (698), time well spent.

Continued success, run of luck, tide, flood, high tide, heyday.

(*Phrase*). The course running smooth.

Advantage over, the upper hand, the whip-hand, ascendancy, mastery, conquest, subdual, victory, subjugation, triumph, exultation, etc. (884).

A conqueror, victor.

(*Verbs*). To succeed, to be successful, to come off successful, to be crowned with success, to come or go off well, catch on, to thrive, speed, prosper, bloom, blossom, flourish, go on well, be well off.

To gain, attain, carry, secure, or win a point or object; to triumph, be triumphant, etc.; to surmount, overcome, conquer, master, or get over a difficulty or obstacle; to score, make a hit.

To advance (282), come on, get on, gain ground, make one's way, make progress, progress, worry along.

(*Phrases*). To strive to some purpose; to gain an advantage.

732. FAILURE (*Substantives*), unsuccess, non-success, disappointment, blow, frustration, discomfiture, abortion, miscarriage, lost trouble; vain, ineffectual, or abortive attempt or effort.

A mistake, error, blunder, fault, miss, oversight, blot, slip, trip, stumble, claudication, breakdown, false step, wrong step, *faux pas*, titubation, scrape, *balourdise*, *bévue*, botch, bungle, foozle, mess, lurch, stalemate, botchery, fiasco, sad work, bad job, want of skill.

Mischance, mishap, misfortune, misadventure, disaster.

Repulse, rebuff, set-down, defeat, fall, downfall, rout, discomfiture, collapse, wreck, perdition, shipwreck, ruin, subjugation, overthrow, death-blow, knock-out, destruction, etc.

A victim, bankrupt, insolvent (808).

(*Phrases*). A losing game; a flash in the pan; *une affaire flambée*; a wild-goose chase; a mare's nest; a sleeveless errand; the mountain bringing forth a mouse; *parturiunt montes*, etc.

(*Verbs*). To fail, to be unsuccessful, etc., to come off badly, go badly, go amiss, go wrong, fall flat, fall through, fizzle out, turn out ill, work ill,

To bring to bear, to bring about, to effect, accomplish, complete (729), make sure; to reap, gather, etc., the benefit of.

To master, get the better of, to get the upper hand, conquer, subdue, subjugate, reduce, overthrow, overpower, vanquish, get under; get or gain the ascendancy, obtain a victory; to worst, beat, lick, floor, knock out, put down, trip up, beat hollow, checkmate, nonsuit, trip up the heels of, capsize, shipwreck, ruin, do for, victimise, put to flight, drown, etc.; to roll in the dust, to trample under foot, to mop the floor with.

To baffle, disconcert, frustrate, discomfit, dish, foil, outgeneral, outmanœuvre, outflank, outwit, overreach, balk, outvote, circumvent, score off, catch napping.

To answer, succeed, work well, turn out well.

(*Phrases*). To sail before the wind; to swim with the tide; to stem the torrent; to turn a corner; to weather a point; to fall on one's legs or feet; *se tirer d'affaire*; to take a favourable turn; to turn up trumps; to have the ball at one's feet; to come off with flying colours; to win or gain the day; to win the palm; to breast the tape; to bear away the bell; to get the upper hand; to get the whip-hand of; to have on the hip; to get the start of; to have a run of luck; to make a hit; to score a success; to reap or gather the harvest; to give a good account of oneself; to carry all before one; to put to rout; to settle one's hash.

(*Adjectives*). Succeeding, etc., successful, prosperous, felicitous, blooming, etc., set up, triumphant, victorious, cock-a-hoop.

lose ground, recede (283), fall short of (304).

To miss, miss one's aim; to labour, toil, etc., in vain; to lose one's labour, flounder, limp, miss one's footing, miscarry, abort; to make vain, ineffectual, or abortive efforts; to make a slip; to make or commit a mistake, commit a fault, make a mess of; to botch, make a botch of, bungle, foozle.

To be defeated, overthrown, foiled, worsted, let down, etc.; to break down, sink, drown, founder, go to ruin, etc., fall, slip, tumble, stumble, falter, be capsized, etc., run aground, crock up, collapse.

(*Phrases*). To come to nothing; to end in smoke; to slip through one's fingers; to take an ugly turn; to hang fire; to miss fire; to miss stays; to flash in the pan; to split upon a rock; to be thrown on one's back; to bite the dust; to be thrown on one's beam-ends; to go to the wall; to take a back seat; to get the worst of it; to go to the dogs; to go to pot; to break one's back; to be all up with; to be in the wrong box; to stand in one's own light; to catch a Tartar; to get hold of the wrong sow by the ear; to burn one's fingers; to shoot at a pigeon and kill a crow; to beat the air; to skin a flint; to wash a blackamoor white; to fight against windmills; to roll the stone of Sisyphus; to fall between two stools; to come a cropper, or mucker.

(*Adjectives*). Unsuccessful, failing, etc., unfortunate, in a bad way, unlucky, luckless, out of luck, ill-fated, ill-starred, disastrous.

Unavailing, abortive, addle,

Unfoiled, unbeaten, unsubdued, etc.

(*Phrases*). Flushed with success; the spoilt child of fortune.

(*Adverbs*). Successfully, etc., triumphantly, with flying colours, in triumph, *à merveille*, to good purpose.

(*Phrase*). *Veni, vidi, vici.*

---

still-born, fruitless, bootless, ineffectual, unattained, lame, hobbling, *décousu*, futile.

Aground, grounded, swamped, stranded, cast away, wrecked, on the rocks, foundered, capsized, shipwrecked, etc. (731).

Defeated, overcome, overthrown, overpowered, mastered, worsted, vanquished, conquered, etc. (*see* 731), subjugated, routed, silenced, distanced, foiled, unhorsed, baffled, *flambé*, dished, tossed about, stultified, undone, done for, down and out, ruined, circumvented, planet-struck, being all up with.

(*Phrases*). *Allant à tort et à travers;* wide of the mark; not having a leg to stand upon; ruined root and branch; the sport of fortune; the mountain bringing forth a mouse; hoist by one's own petard; left in the lurch; out of the running.

(*Adverbs*). Unsuccessfully, etc., in vain, to no purpose, all up with.

(*Phrases*). Out of the frying-pan into the fire; *sic transit gloria mundi.*

---

733. TROPHY (*Substantives*), laurel, palm, crown, bays, wreath, chaplet, civic crown, medal, cup, scalp, prize, triumphal arch, ovation, triumph (883), flourish of trumpets, flying colours.

(*Phrase*). A feather in one's cap.

---

734. PROSPERITY (*Substantives*), see Success (731), thrift, good fortune, welfare, well-being, luck, good luck, a run of luck, fair weather, sunshine, fair wind, palmy days, the smiles of fortune, halcyon days, *Saturnia regna*, Saturnian age.

An upstart, *parvenu, nouveau riche*, skipjack, mushroom, self-made man.

A made man, a lucky dog.

(*Verbs*). To prosper, thrive, flourish, be well off; to flower, blow, blossom, bloom, fructify; to bask in the sunshine; to rise in the world; to make one's way; to have a run; to light on one's feet.

(*Phrase*). To feather one's nest.

735. ADVERSITY (*Substantives*), bad, ill, evil, adverse, etc., fortune, hap, or luck, tough luck, reverse, broken fortunes, falling or going down in the world, hard times.

Fall, ruin, ruination, ruinousness, undoing, disaster, calamity, catastrophe (619); a hard life; evil star, evil genius.

(*Phrases*). The frowns of fortune; the ups and downs of life; the times being out of joint.

(*Verbs*). To be ill off; to decay, sink, go under, fall, decline, go down in the world, lose caste; to go hard with.

(*Adjectives*). Unfortunate, unlucky, luckless, untoward, ill off, badly off, decayed, ill-fated, ill-

(*Adjectives*). Prosperous, fortunate, lucky, well off, well-to-do, solvent (803), thriving, set up, prospering, etc., blooming, palmy, halcyon.

Auspicious, propitious, in a fair way.

(*Phrases*). Born with a silver spoon in one's mouth; the spoilt child of fortune; *enfant gâté*; in luck's way.

starred, devoted, bankrupt (808), unprosperous, adverse, untoward.

Disastrous, calamitous, ruinous, dire, deplorable, etc.

(*Phrases*). Down on one's luck; having seen better days; born with a wooden ladle in one's mouth; one's star on the wane; down and out.

---

736. MEDIOCRITY (*Substantives*), the golden mean, *aurea mediocritas*, moderate circumstances; the middle classes, *bourgeoisie*.

(*Adjectives*). Tolerable, fair, middling, mediocre; middle-class, *bourgeois*.

(*Phrase*). *Medio tutissimus ibis*.

DIVISION II.—INTERSOCIAL VOLITION[1]

SECTION I.—GENERAL INTERSOCIAL VOLITION

737. AUTHORITY (*Substantives*), influence, credit, power, prerogative, control, censorship, authoritativeness, absoluteness, despotism, absolutism, tyranny.

Command, empire, sway, rule, dominion, domination, supremacy, suzerainty, lordship, seigniory, seigniorship, mastery, mastership, office, government, administration, gubernation, empire, body politic, accession.

Hold, grasp, gripe, grip, reach, fang, clutches, talons, helm, reins.

Reign, régime, directorship, proconsulship, prefecture, caliphate, seneschalship, magistrature, magistracy, presidency, presidentship, premiership.

Empire, monarchy, dynasty, kinghood, kingship, royalty, regality, kingcraft, aristocracy, oligarchy, democracy, demagogy,

738. Absence of authority.

LAXITY (*Substantives*), laxness, licence, licentiousness, relaxation, looseness, loosening, slackness, toleration, remission.

Misrule, anarchy, interregnum. Deprivation of power, dethronement.

Denial of authority: anarchism, nihilism.

Anarchist, nihilist.

(*Phrases*). A dead letter; *brutum fulmen*.

(*Verbs*). To be lax, etc., to hold a loose rein, tolerate, to relax, to misrule.

(*Phrase*). To give a loose to.

To dethrone.

(*Adjectives*). Lax, loose, slack, remiss, relaxed, licensed, reinless, unbridled, anarchic, anarchical, nihilistic.

Unauthorised (925).

---

[1] Implying the action of the will of one mind over the will of another.

ochlocracy, mobocracy, mob-rule, dictatorship of the proletariat, Bolshevism, militarism, stratocracy, *imperium in
imperio*, dictatorship, protectorate, protectorship, directorate,
directory, executive, raj, patriarchy, patriarchism.

Vicarious authority, *see* 755 and 759.

Gynarchy, gynæcocracy, petticoat government, matriarchy.

(*Verbs*). To have, hold, possess, or exercise authority, etc.

To be master, etc.; to have the control, etc.; to overrule,
overawe, dominate.

To rule, govern, sway, command, control, direct, administer, lead, preside over, boss; to dictate, reign, hold the reins;
to possess or be seated on the throne; to ascend or mount the
throne; to sway or wield the sceptre.

(*Phrases*). To have the upper hand; to have the whip-hand;
to have one's own way; to rule the roast; to be cock of the
roost; to have under the thumb; to keep under; to lead by the
nose; to wear the breeches; to have the ball at one's feet; to
play first fiddle.

(*Adjectives*). Ruling, etc., regnant, dominant, authoritative,
executive, administrative, official, *ex officio*.

Imperial, regal, sovereign, royal, monarchical, imperatorial,
princely, baronial, feudal, seigneurial, seigniorial, aristocratic,
etc.; ultramontane, absolutist.

Imperative, peremptory, overruling.

(*Adverbs*). In the name of, by the authority of, in virtue of,
de par le roi, at one's command, under the auspices of.

---

739. SEVERITY (*Substantives*),
strictness, rigour, rigidity, rigid-
ness, sternness, stringency, aus-
terity, harshness, acerbity, stiffness, rigorousness, inexorability.

Arbitrary power, absolutism,
despotism, dictatorship, auto-
cracy, domineering, tyranny;
Moloch.

(*Phrases*). Iron rule; reign of
terror; blood and iron.

Assumption, usurpation, arro-
gance, *see* 885.

740. LENITY (*Substantives*),
mildness, lenience, gentleness,
indulgence, clemency.

(*Verbs*). To be lenient, etc., to
tolerate, indulge, to allow to
have one's own way, to let down
gently.

(*Adjectives*). Lenient, mild,
gentle, soft, indulgent, tolerant,
clement.

(*Phrase*). Live and let live.

A tyrant, disciplinarian, martinet, bashaw; a strong hand,
a tight hand; King Stork.

(*Verbs*). To be severe, etc.; to assume, usurp, arrogate,
take liberties; to hold or keep a tight hand; to bear or lay
a heavy hand on; to be down on; to dictate; to domineer,
tyrannise, inflict, wreak; to keep one's nose to the grindstone.

(*Phrases*). To lord it over; to carry matters with a high
hand; to ride rough-shod over; to rule with a rod of iron; to
deal faithfully with.

(*Adjectives*). Severe, strict, rigid, stern, stiff, dour, strait-laced, rigorous, stringent, hard-and-fast, peremptory, absolute, positive, uncompromising, harsh, austere, haughty, arrogant, dictatorial, imperious, domineering, tyrannical, masterful, inflexible, inexorable, exigent, inclement, Rhadamanthine, Draconian, overbearing.

(*Adverbs*). Severely, etc., with a high hand, with a strong, tight, or heavy hand.

741. COMMAND (*Substantives*), order, fiat, bidding, dictum, hest, behest, call, beck, nod, message, direction, injunction, charge, demand, exaction, imposition, requisition, requirement, claim, reclamation, revendication.

Dictation, dictate, mandate, caveat, decree, decretal, enactment, precept, prescript, writ, rescript, law, ordinance, ordination, bull, regulation, prescription, brevet, placet, ukase, firman, warrant, passport, mittimus, mandamus, summons, subpœna, interpellation, word of command.

(*Verbs*). To command, to issue a command, order, give order, bid, require, enjoin, charge, claim, call for, demand, exact, insist on, make a point of, impose, entail, set, tax, prescribe, direct, dictate, ordain, decree, enact; to issue or promulgate a decree, etc.

To cite, summon, call for, call up, send for, requisition, subpœna; to set or prescribe a task, to set to work, to give the word of command, to call to order.

(*Phrase*). The decree is gone forth.

(*Adjectives*). Commanding, etc., authoritative, peremptory, decretive, decretory, etc., *see* 737.

(*Adverbs*). On the first summons, with a dash of the pen.

(*Phrase*). Le roy le veult.

---

742. DISOBEDIENCE (*Substantives*), non-compliance, insubordination, contumacy, defection, infringement, infraction, violation.

See Defiance (715), Resistance (719), and Non-observance (773).

Rising, insurrection, revolt, rebellion, turn-out, strike, riot, riotousness, mutinousness, mutiny, tumult, sedition, treason, lèse-majesté.

An insurgent, mutineer, rebel, rioter, traitor; *carbonaro, sansculotte, frondeur*; agitator, demagogue, Jack Cade, Wat Tyler, etc.; ringleader.

(*Verbs*). To disobey, resist

---

743. OBEDIENCE (*Substantives*), submission, non-resistance, passiveness, resignation, cession, compliance, surrender (725), subordination, deference, allegiance, obeisance, homage, fealty, prostration, kneeling, genuflexion, curtsy, kotow, salaam, submissiveness, obsequiousness (*see* 886), servitorship, subjection (749).

(*Verbs*). To be obedient, etc.; to obey, submit, succumb, give in, knock under, cringe, yield (725), comply, surrender, follow, give up, give way, resign, bend to, bear obedience to.

To kneel, fall on one's knees,

(719), defy (715), turn restive, shirk, kick, strike, mutiny, rise, rebel, lift the hand against, turn out, come out, go on strike.

(*Phrases*). To champ the bit; to unfurl the red flag.

(*Adjectives*). Disobedient, resisting, unruly, unsubmissive, uncomplying, uncompliant, restive, insubordinate, contumacious, mutinous, riotous, seditious, refractory, naughty.

Unbidden, unobeyed, a dead letter.

(*Phrase*). The grey mare being the better horse.

bend the knee, curtsy, kotow, salaam, bow, pay homage to.

(*Phrases*). To kiss the rod; to do one's bidding; to lick the dust; to eat humble - pie; to play second fiddle; draw in one's horns; to take it lying down.

To attend upon, tend; to be under the orders of, to serve.

(*Phrase*). To dance attendance on.

(*Adjectives*). Obedient, submissive, resigned, passive, complying, compliant, yielding, biddable, unresisting, henpecked; restrainable, unresisted.

---

744. COMPULSION (*Substantives*), coercion, coaction, force, constraint, enforcement, press, *corvée*, conscription, levy, brute force, main force, the sword, *ultimo ratio*, *argumentum baculinum*.

(*Verbs*). To compel, force, drive, coerce, constrain, enforce, put in force, oblige, force upon, press, conscribe, extort, put down, bind, pin down, bind over, impress, commandeer.

(*Phrases*). To cram down the throat; to say it must be done; to make a point of.

(*Adjectives*). Compelling, etc., compulsory, compulsatory, forcible, coercive, coactive, peremptory, rigorous, stringent, inexorable, etc. (*see* 739); being fain to do, having to do.

(*Adverbs*). By force, perforce, under compulsion, etc., *vi et armis*, by main force, by brute force, in spite of one's teeth, *bon gré, mal gré*; willy-nilly; *nolens volens*; *de rigueur*.

---

745. MASTER (*Substantives*), lord, laird, chief, leader, captain, protagonist, coryphæus, head, chieftain, commander, commandant, director (694), ruler, potentate, dictator, liege, sovereign, monarch, autocrat, despot, tyrant, demagogue, ringleader, boss, fugleman.

Crowned head: emperor, king, majesty, tetrarch, *imperator*, protector, president, stadtholder, gubernator; empress, queen.

Cæsar, czar, sultan, soldan, caliph, sophi, khan, cacique, shah, Khedive, pasha (or bashaw), dey, cham, judge, aga, voivode, hospodar, mikado, exarch.

746. SERVANT (*Substantives*), servitor, employé (or employee), attaché, secretary, subordinate, subaltern, retainer, vassal, *protégé*, dependent, hanger-on, pensioner, client, emissary.

Retinue, cortège, staff, court, entourage, clientele, suite.

An attendant, squire, henchman, led captain, chamberlain, follower, usher, page, donzel, train-bearer, domestic, butler, footman, lackey, flunkey, valet, waiter, *garçon*, equerry, groom, jockey, tiger, buttons, livery servant, hireling, mercenary, underling, menial, under-strapper, journeyman, whipper-in,

Prince, seignior, highness, archduke, duke, margrave, landgrave, elector, doge, satrap, rajah, maharajah, emir, bey, effendi, nizam, nawaub, mandarin, beglerbeg, sirdar, ameer, sachem, sagamore.

Princess, duchess, infanta, margravine, etc.

Nobility, see 875.

Military authorities, marshal, field-marshal, *maréchal*, generalissimo, commander - in - chief, admiral, commodore, general, colonel, lieutenant-colonel, officer, captain, major, lieutenant, adjutant, aide-de-camp, ensign, cornet, cadet, subaltern, non-commissioned officer, serjeant, corporal, centurion, seraskier, hetman, subahdar, condottiere.

Civil authorities, mayor, prefect, chancellor, provost, magistrate, palatine, syndic, alcade (or alcayde), burgomaster, *corregidor*, sheik, seneschal, burgrave, alderman, warden, constable (965), beadle, alguazil, kavass, tribune, consul, ædile.

Statesman, politician, statist, legislator, lawgiver.

President, chairman, speaker, moderator, vice-president, comptroller, director (694).

bailiff, castellan, seneschal, major-domo, cup-bearer, bottle-washer.

Serf, slave, galley-slave, thrall, helot, bondsman, *âme damnée*, *adscriptus glebæ*, wage-slave.

A maid, handmaid, abigail, chamber-maid, lady's maid, *fille de chambre*, parlour-maid, house-maid, nurse, *bonne*, scullion, etc.

Badge of slavery, bonds, chains, etc., see 752.

(*Verbs*). To serve, attend upon, dance attendance, wait upon, squire, valet.

(*Adverbs*). In one's pay or employ, in the train of.

---

747. Ensign, or badge of authority.

Sceptre (*Substantives*), regalia, crown, coronet, rod of empire, mace, *fasces*, wand, baton, truncheon, staff, key, portfolio.

Helm, bit, curb, reins, leading-strings, bridle.

A throne, chair, divan, dais, woolsack.

Diadem, tiara, ermine, signet, seals, talisman, cap of maintenance, toga, robes of state.

---

748. Freedom (*Substantives*), independence, liberty, self-government, autonomy, scope, range, latitude, play, swing, free play, full play, elbow-room, margin.

Franchise, immunity, exemption, emancipation (750), naturalisation, denizenship.

Free land, allodium, see 780.

A freeman, freedman, denizen.

(*Phrase*). A place in the sun.

(*Verbs*). To be free, to have scope, etc.

(*Phrases*). To have the run of;

749. Subjection (*Substantives*), dependence, thrall, thraldom, subjugation, bondage, serfdom, servitude, slavery, vassalage, villainage, service, clientship, liability (177), enslavement, "involuntary servitude."

Yoke, harness, collar (751).

(*Verbs*). To be subject, dependent, etc., to fall under, obey, serve (743).

(*Phrases*). To drag a chain; to be led by the nose; to be or lie at the mercy of.

to have one's own way; to stand on one's legs; to stand on one's rights; to have a will of one's own; to play a lone hand.

To take a liberty; to make free with; to take the bit between one's teeth.

To render free, etc., to free, to emancipate, etc. (750), naturalise.

(*Adjectives*). Free, independent, loose, unconstrained, unrestrained, unchecked, unobstructed, unconfined, unsubdued, unsubjugated, self-governed, autonomous, self-supporting, unbound, uncontrolled, unchained, unshackled, unfettered, uncurbed, unbridled, unrestricted, unmuzzled, unbuttoned, unforced, uncompelled, unhindered, unthwarted, heart-whole, uncaught, unenslaved, unclaimed, ungoverned, resting.

To subject, enthral, enslave, keep under, control, etc. (751), to reduce to slavery, mediatise, break in.

(*Phrase*). To have one on the hip.

(*Adjectives*). Subject, dependent, subjected, in subjection to, in thrall to, feudatory, feudal, a slave to, at the mercy of, stipendiary, in leading-strings, enthralled, controlled, constrained, etc. (*see* 751), the puppet, sport, plaything of, etc.

(*Phrases*). Under the thumb of; on the hip; under the lash; at the mercy of; at the feet of; tied to the apron-strings of.

(*Phrases*). Free as air; one's own master; *sui juris*; on one's own bottom; on one's own.

Free and easy, at ease, *dégagé*, wanton, rampant, irrepressible, unprevented, unvanquished, exempt, enfranchised, emancipated, released, disengaged, etc., *see* 750, out of hand.

(*Phrase*). A cat may look at a king.

750. LIBERATION (*Substantives*), disengagement, release, enlargement, emancipation, mancipation, affranchisement, enfranchisement, manumission, discharge, dismissal.

Escape (671), deliverance (672), redemption, extrication, absolution (970).

Licence, toleration; parole, ticket of leave.

(*Verbs*). To gain, obtain, acquire, etc., one's liberty, freedom, etc., to get off, get clear, to deliver oneself from, to cast off trammels.

To break loose, escape, slip away, make one's escape, cut and run, slip the collar, bolt, etc. (671).

751. RESTRAINT (*Substantives*), constraint, coercion, discipline.

Confinement, durance, duress, detention, imprisonment, incarceration, prisonment, internment, quarantine, coarctation, entombment, "durance vile," limbo, captivity, penal servitude.

Arrest, arrestation, custody, keep, care, charge, ward.

Curb, etc. (752); *lettre de cachet*.

(*Verbs*). To be under restraint or arrest, to be coerced, etc.

To restrain, constrain, coerce, curb, cramp, keep under, enthral, put under restraint, detain, debar; to chain, enchain, fasten, tie up (43), picket, fetter, shackle,

(*Phrases*). To shake off the yoke; tear asunder one's bonds; break prison.

To liberate, free, set free, set at liberty, release, loose, let loose, loosen, relax, unloose, untie, unbind, unhand, unchain, unshackle, unfetter, unclog, disengage, unharness, etc., *see* 44.

To enlarge, set clear, let go, let out, disenchain, disimprison, unbar, unbolt, uncage, unclose, uncork, discharge, disenthral, dismiss, deliver, extricate, let slip, enfranchise, affranchise, manumit, denizen, emancipate, assoil (748).

To clear, acquit, redeem, ransom, get off.

(*Phrases*). To give one one's head; to let one paddle one's own canoe; to send to the right-about.

(*Adjectives*). Liberated, freed, etc.

———

trammel, bridle, muzzle, gag, pinion, pin down, tether.

To confine, shut up, shut in, clap up, lock up, cage, encage, impound, pen, coop, hem in, jam in, enclose, mew, wall in, rail in, cloister, bolt in, close the door upon, imprison, incarcerate, immure, entomb, seclude, corral.

(*Phrases*). To put in irons; to put in a strait-waistcoat; to put into bilboes.

To take charge of, lead captive, send or commit to prison, give in charge, or in custody, arrest, commit, run in, lag; re-commit, remand.

(*Adjectives*). Restrained, coerced, etc., buttoned up, pent up.

Coactive, stiff, restringent, strait-laced.

(*Phrases*). In limbo; in Lob's pound; laid by the heels; "cabined, cribbed, confined"; in quod; in durance vile; bound hand and foot.

752. Means of restraint.

PRISON (*Substantives*), jail, gaol, prison-house, house of detention, lock-up, the cells, clink, coop, den, cell, stronghold, fortress, keep, dungeon, bastille, *oubliette*, Bridewell, toll-booth, panopticon, penitentiary, guardroom, hold, roundhouse, black-hole, station, enclosure, pen, fold, pound, paddock, stocks, bilboes.

Newgate, King's Bench, Fleet, Marshalsea, Pentonville, Holloway, Dartmoor, etc., Sing-Sing.

Fetter, shackle, trammel, bond, chain, iron, collar, cangue, pinion, gyve, fetlock, fetterlock, manacle, handcuff, darbies, strait-waistcoat; muzzle, gag, bridle, curb, bit, snaffle, rein, martingale, leading-strings, swaddling-bands, tether, picket, band, brake.

Bolt, bar, lock, padlock, rail, wall, paling, palisade (232), fence, corral, barrier, barricade.

753. KEEPER (*Substantives*), custodian, *custos*, warder, jailer (or gaoler), castellan, guard, watch, watchman, watch and ward, sentry, sentinel, escort, watch-dog.

Concierge, duenna, chaperon.

754. PRISONER (*Substantives*), captive, *détenu*, convict, lag.

(*Adjectives*). In custody, in charge, imprisoned, locked up, incarcerated.

———

755. Vicarious authority.

COMMISSION (*Substantives*), delegation, consignment, assignment, devolution, procuration, deputation, legation, mission, agency, clerkship, agentship; errand, embassy, charge, brevet, diploma, exequatur, committal, commitment.

Appointment, nomination, ordination, installation, inauguration.

Investiture, coronation.

Vicegerency, regency, regentship.

(*Verbs*). To commission, delegate, depute, devolve, send out, consign, charge, entrust with, commit to, enlist.

To appoint, name, nominate, ordain, install, induct, inaugurate, invest, crown, return.

Employ, empower, set over.

To be commissioned, to represent.

---

756. ABROGATION (*Substantives*), annulment, cancel, cancellation, revocation, repeal, rescission, rescinding, deposal, defeasance, dismissal, *congé*, demission.

Abolition, abolishment, counter-order, countermand, repudiation, nullification, recantation, palinode, retractation, *see* 607.

(*Verbs*). To abrogate, annul, cancel, revoke, repeal, rescind, over-rule, abolish, disannul, dissolve, quash, repudiate, nullify, retract, recant, recall, countermand, counter-order, break off, disclaim, declare null and void, set aside, do away with; to be off.

To dismiss, send off, send away, discard, turn off, turn away, cashier, sack, oust, unseat, unthrone, dethrone, depose, uncrown, send back.

(*Phrases*). Send about one's business; put one's nose out of joint; give one the mitten, the chuck, the sack, the boot.

(*Adjectives*). Abrogated, etc.; *functus officio*.

(*Interjections*). Get along with you! begone! go about your business!

---

757. RESIGNATION (*Substantives*), retirement, abdication, renunciation, abjuration.

(*Verbs*). To resign, give up, throw up, retire, abdicate, lay down, abjure, renounce, forgo, disclaim, retract, etc. (*see* 756); to tender one's resignation, abandon (oneself), send in one's papers.

(*Adjective*). Emeritus.

Phrase). "Othello's occupation's gone."

---

758. CONSIGNEE (*Substantives*), delegate, commissary, commissioner, vicegerent, legate, representative, secondary, nominee, surrogate, functionary, trustee, assignee.

Corps diplomatique, plenipotentiary, emissary, nuncio, internuncio.

Agent, factor, attorney, broker, factotum, bailiff, man of business, go-between, intermediary, middleman, commission agent, commercial traveller, bagman, colporteur, commissionaire, employé, attaché, curator, clerk, placeman.

759. DEPUTY (*Substantives*), substitute, vice, proxy, locum-tenens, chargé d'affaires, delegate, representative, surrogate, understudy.

Regent, viceroy, vicegerent, satrap, exarch, vizier, minister, premier, commissioner, chancellor, prefect, warden, lieutenant, archon, consul, Reis Effendi, legate.

(*Verbs*). To deputise; to be deputy, etc., for; to appear for; to understudy; to take duty for.

(*Phrase*). To stand or walk in the shoes of.

(*Adverbs*). In place of, *vice*.

SECTION II.—SPECIAL INTERSOCIAL VOLITION

760. PERMISSION (*Substantives*), leave, allowance, sufferance, tolerance, toleration, liberty, law, licence, concession, grant, vouchsafement, authorisation, accordance, admission, favour, dispensation, exemption, connivance.

A permit, warrant, brevet, precept, authority, firman, pass, passport, furlough, ticket, licence, *congé d'élire*, carte-blanche, exeat.

(*Verbs*). To permit; give leave or permission; to let, allow, admit, suffer, tolerate, concede, accord, vouchsafe, humour, indulge, to leave it to one; to leave alone; to grant, empower, authorise, warrant, license; to give licence; to give a loose to.

(*Phrases*). To give carte-blanche; to give one rope; to give a horse his head; to stretch a point; leave the door open; to let one have a chance; to give one a fair show.

761. PROHIBITION (*Substantives*), inhibition, veto, disallowance, interdiction, hindrance (706), restriction, restraints (751), embargo, an interdict, ban, taboo, proscription; *index librorum prohibitorum*.

(*Verbs*). To prohibit, forbid, inhibit, disallow, bar, debar, interdict, veto, keep in, hinder, restrain (751), restrict, withhold, limit, circumscribe, keep within bounds.

To exclude, shut out, proscribe.

(*Phrase*). To clip the wings of.

(*Adjectives*). Prohibitive, restrictive, exclusive, prohibitory, forbidding, etc.

Not permitted, prohibited, etc., unlicensed, etc.

(*Phrases*). Under the ban of; on the Index.

(*Interjections*). Hands off! keep off!

To let off, absolve, dispense with, favour, wink, connive at.

To take a liberty; to use a freedom; to beg leave.

(*Adjectives*). Permitting, etc., permissive, conceding, etc. Unforbid, unforbidden, unconditional.

762. CONSENT (*Substantives*), compliance, acquiescence, assent (488), agreement, concession, yieldingness, acknowledgment, acceptance.

Settlement, ratification, confirmation.

(*Verbs*). To consent, give consent, assent, comply with, acquiesce, agree to, accede, accept.

(*Phrase*). To take at one's word.

To concede, yield, satisfy, grant, settle, acknowledge, confirm, homologate, ratify, deign, vouchsafe.

(*Adjectives*). Consenting, etc., having no objection, unconditional, *see* Assent (488).

(*Adverbs*). Yes (488); if you please, as you please, by all means, by all manner of means, so be it, of course, certainly, etc.

763. OFFER (*Substantives*), proffer, tender, present, overture, proposition, motion, proposal, invitation, presentation, offering, oblation, bid, bribe.

Sacrifice, immolation.

(*Verbs*). To offer, proffer, tender, present, invite, volunteer, propose, move, make a motion, start, press, bid, hold out, hawk about.

(*Phrase*). To grease the palm. To sacrifice, immolate.

(*Adjective*). Offering, etc.

———

764. REFUSAL (*Substantives*), rejection, declining, non-compliance, declension, dissent, denial, repulse, rebuff, discountenance, *see* 489.

Disclaimer, recusancy, abnegation, protest.

Revocation, violation, abrogation (756), flat refusal, peremptory denial.

(*Verbs*). To refuse, reject, deny, decline, disclaim, protest, resist, repel, refuse or withhold one's assent; to excuse oneself, to negative, turn down, grudge, begrudge.

To discard, set aside, rescind, declare off, revoke, discountenance, forswear.

(*Phrases*). To turn a deaf ear to; to shake the head; not to hear of; to send to the right-about; to hang fire; to wash one's hands of, to declare off.

(*Adjectives*). Refusing, etc., recusant, uncomplying, unconsenting.

(*Adverbs*). No, by no means, etc. (489).

(*Phrases*). Your humble servant (ironically); *bien obligé*; excuse me; by no means; nothing doing.

765. REQUEST (*Substantives*), asking, petition, demand, suit, solicitation, craving, entreaty, begging, postulation, adjuration, canvass, candidature, prayer, supplication, impetration, imploration, instance, obsecration, obtestation, importunity, application, address, appeal, motion, overture, invocation, interpellation, apostrophe, orison, incantation, imprecation, conjuration.

Mendicancy, begging letter, grace, *brigue*.

Claim, reclamation, revendication.

766. Negative request.

DEPRECATION (*Substantives*), expostulation, intercession.

(*Verbs*). To deprecate, protest, expostulate; to enter a protest; to intercede for.

(*Adjectives*). Deprecating, etc., deprecatory, expostulatory, deprecated, protested.

Unsought, unbesought.

(*Adverbs*). By no means; on no account; not for the world; cry you mercy.

(*Interjections*). God forbid! forbid it heaven! *absit omen !*

———

(*Verbs*). To request, ask, beg, cadge, crave, pray, petition, solicit, beg a boon, demand, prefer a request or petition, ply, apply to, make application, put to, make bold to ask, invite, beg leave, put up a prayer, pop the question.

To beg hard, entreat, beseech, supplicate, implore, conjure, adjure, invoke, evoke, kneel to, fall on one's knees, impetrate, imprecate, appeal to, apply to, put to, address, call for, press, urge, beset, importune, dun, tax, besiege, cry to, call on, throw oneself at the feet of.

Prithee, do, please, be good enough, pray, be so good as, have the goodness, vouchsafe.

To bespeak, canvass, tout, make interest, court.

To claim, reclaim, sue.

(*Adjectives*). Requesting, asking, beseeching, etc., precatory, suppliant, supplicatory, importunate, bowing, etc.,

(*Phrases*). Cap in hand; on one's knees.

(*Adverbs*). For heaven's sake, for goodness' sake, for God's sake.

767. PETITIONER (*Substantives*), solicitor, applicant, suppliant, supplicant, mendicant, beggar, mumper, suitor, candidate, postulant, canvasser, tout, cadger.

SECTION III.—CONDITIONAL INTERSOCIAL VOLITION

768. PROMISE (*Substantives*), word, troth, plight, parole, word of honour, assurance, vow, oath.

Engagement, insurance, contract (769), obligation; affiance, betrothal, betrothment.

(*Verbs*). To promise, give a promise, assure; to give, pass, pledge or plight one's word, honour credit, faith, etc.; to warrant, guarantee (467); to swear, vow, be sworn; take oath, make oath, kiss the book; to attest, adjure.

(*Phrases*). To call heaven to witness; swear by bell, book, and candle.

To engage; to enter on, make or form an engagement, take upon oneself; to bind, tie, or pledge oneself; to be in for it; to contract an obligation; to be bound; to undertake; to hold out an expectation.

To answer for, be answerable for, secure, give security (771).

(*Adjectives*). Promising, etc., promised, pledged, sworn, etc.; votive.

(*Phrases*). Under one's hand and seal; as one's head shall answer for.

(*Interjection*). So help me, God!

768A. Release from engagement, *see* Liberation (750).

(*Adjectives*). Absolute, unconditional; uncovenanted, unsecured.

769. COMPACT (*Substantives*), contract, agreement, bargain, deal, pact, paction, stipulation, covenant, settlement, convention, *nudum pactum*, charter, treaty, indenture, *concordat*, *Zollverein*, Pragmatic Sanction, *Sonderbund*.

Negotiation, transaction, bargaining, haggling, chaffering, bargain by inch of candle; diplomacy.

Ratification, settlement, signature, endorsement, seal, signet, bond.

A negotiator, diplomatist, diplomat, agent, contractor, underwriter, attorney, broker, etc. (759).

(*Verbs*). To contract, covenant, bargain, agree for, strike a bargain, engage, etc., *see* Promise (768); to underwrite.

To treat, negotiate, bargain, stipulate, haggle (or higgle), chaffer, stickle for, insist upon, make a point of, compound for.

To conclude, close, confirm, ratify, endorse, clench, come to an understanding, take one at one's word, come to terms; to bargain by inch of candle.

To subscribe, sign, seal, indent, put the seal to, sign and seal.

770. CONDITIONS (*Substantives*), terms, articles, articles of agreement, clauses, proviso, provisions, salvo, covenant, stipulation, ultimatum, *sine qua non, casus fœderis*.

(*Verbs*). To make it a condition, make terms, etc., to stipulate, insist upon, etc.

(*Adjectives*). Conditional, provisional, guarded, fenced, hedged in, etc.

(*Adverbs*). Conditionally, with the understanding; provided, unless, *see* 469.

(*Phrases*). Wind and weather permitting; God willing; D.V.; *Deo volente.*

771. SECURITY (*Substantives*), surety, guaranty, guarantee, mortgage, warranty, bond, debenture, pledge, tie, plight, caution, sponsion, hostage, sponsor, bail, parole.

Deed, instrument, deed-poll, indenture, warrant, charter, cartel, protocol, recognisance; verification, acceptance, endorsement, signature, execution, I O U.

Stake, deposit, pool, earnest, handsel.

(*Verbs*). To give security, assure, pawn (787), accept, endorse, stamp.

To hold in pledge.

772. OBSERVANCE (*Substantives*), performance, fulfilment, satisfaction, discharge, compliance, acquittance, quittance, acquittal, adhesion, acknowledgment, fidelity (939).

(*Verbs*). To observe, perform,

773. NON-OBSERVANCE (*Substantives*), failure, neglect, laches, laxity, infringement, infraction, violation, forfeiture, transgression.

Retractation, repudiation, nullification, protest, forfeiture.

keep, fulfil, discharge, comply
with, meet, satisfy, adhere to, be
faithful to, stand to one's engagement, acquit oneself.

(*Phrase*). To redeem one's
pledge.

(*Adjectives*). Observant, faithful, true, honourable, etc. (939),
strict, rigid, punctilious.

(*Adverb*). Faithfully, etc., to
the letter.

(*Phrase*). As good as one's
word.

Informality, lawlessness, disobedience, bad faith (742).

(*Verbs*). To break, violate, fail,
neglect, omit, forfeit, infringe,
transgress.

To retract, discard, protest, go
back upon or from one's word,
repudiate, nullify, ignore, wipe
off, cancel, etc. (552), to fob off,
palter, elude, evade.

(*Phrases*). To apply the sponge;
to stretch a point.

(*Adjectives*). Violating, etc.,
elusive, evasive, transgressive,
unfulfilled; etc.; compensatory
(30).

---

774. COMPROMISE (*Substantives*), composition, middle term, *mezzo
termine, modus vivendi*; bribe, hush-money.

(*Verbs*). To compromise, compound, take the mean, split the
difference, come to terms, come to an understanding, to meet one
half-way.

SECTION IV.—POSSESSIVE RELATIONS [1]

1°. *Property in general*

775. ACQUISITION (*Substantives*), obtainment, gaining, earn-
ing, procuration, procuring,
gathering, gleaning, picking, col-
lecting, recovery, *trouvaille*, find.

Book-collecting, book-hunting,
etc., philately.

Gain, profit, benefit, emolu-
ment, the main chance, pelf,
lucre, loaves and fishes, produce,
proceeds, return, fruit, crop,
harvest, scoop, winnings.

Inheritance, bequest, legacy.

Fraudulent acquisition, subreption, stealing (791).

Profiteering, pot-hunting.

A collector, book - collector,
etc., china-maniac, philatelist;
a profiteer, pot-hunter.

776. LOSS (*Substantives*), perdition, forfeiture, lapse.

Privation, bereavement, deprivation (789), dispossession,
riddance.

(*Verbs*). To lose; incur, experience, or meet with a loss;
to miss, mislay, throw away,
forfeit, let slip, allow to slip
through the fingers; to get rid of
(782), to waste (638, 679).

(*Adjectives*). Losing, etc., lost,
etc.

Devoid of, not having, un-
obtained, unpossessed, unblest
with.

Shorn of, deprived of, bereaved of, dispossessed, out of
pocket, *minus*, cut off.

[1] That is, relations which concern property.

(*Verbs*). To acquire, get, gain, win, earn, realise, regain, receive (785), take (789), obtain, procure, derive, secure, collect, reap, come in for, step into, inherit, come by, scrape together, get hold of, scoop.

To profit, make profit, turn to profit, make money by, obtain a return, make a fortune, coin money, profiteer.

(*Phrases*). To turn a penny; to bring grist to the mill; to feather one's nest; to reap or gain an advantage; to keep the wolf from the door.

To be profitable, to pay, to answer.

To fall to, come to, accrue.

(*Adjectives*). Acquisitive, acquiring, acquired, etc., profitable, remunerative, paying.

(*Phrase*). On the make.

Irrecoverable, irretrievable, irremediable, irreparable.

(*Interjections*). Farewell to! adieu to!

---

777. POSSESSION (*Substantives*), ownership, proprietorship, occupancy, hold, holding, preoccupancy.

Exclusive possession, impropriation, monopoly, inalienability.

Future possession, heritage, inheritance.

(*Phrases*). A bird in the hand; *uti possidetis*; *beati possidentes*; the haves and the have-nots.

(*Verbs*). To possess, have, hold, own, be master of, be in possession of, enjoy, occupy, be seised of, be worth, to have in hand or on hand; to inherit (775).

To engross, monopolise, corner, preoccupy.

To be the property of, belong to, appertain to, pertain to, be in the hands of, be in the possession of.

(*Adjectives*). Possessing, etc., possessed of, worth, endowed with, instinct with, fraught, laden with, charged with.

Possessed, etc., proprietary, proprietorial; on hand, in hand, unsold, unshared; inalienable.

778. Joint possession.

PARTICIPATION (*Substantives*), joint stock, common stock, partnership, copartnership, communism, possession in common, communion, community of possessions or goods, socialism, collectivism, St.-Simonianism, Fourierism, syndicalism, etc.

Snacks, share-out, picnic.

A syndicate, ring, corner, combine, trust, knock-out.

A partner, copartner, shareholder, *actionnaire*; a communist, socialist, etc.

(*Verbs*). To participate, partake, share, communicate, go snacks, go halves, share and share alike; to have or possess, etc., in common; to come in for a share; to stand in with; to socialise; to pool.

(*Adjectives*). Partaking, etc.; socialist, socialistic, communistic, etc.

(*Adverb*). Share and share alike, fifty-fifty.

---

779. POSSESSOR (*Substantives*), owner, holder, proprietor, proprietress, proprietary, master, mistress, heritor, occupier, occupant, landlord, tenant; occupant, lodger.

Future possessor, heir, heiress, inheritor.

780. PROPERTY (*Substantives*), possession, ownership, seisin, tenancy, tenure, lordship, legal and equitable estate, *meum et tuum*, occupancy.

Estate, effects, assets, stock, goods, chattels, fixtures, movables, furniture, things, traps, trappings, paraphernalia, luggage, baggage, bag and baggage, cargo, lading; patrimony, heirloom.

Real property, land, landed estate, manor, demesne, domain, tenement, holding, hereditament, household, freehold, farm, ranch, *hacienda, estancia*, fief, feoff, apanage, seigniority, allodium.

Ground, acres, field, close.

State, realm, empire, kingdom, principality.

(*Adjectives*). Predial, manorial, freehold, etc., copyhold, leasehold.

781. RETENTION (*Substantives*), keep, holding, keeping, retaining, detention, custody, grasp, gripe, grip, tenacity. Fangs, teeth, clutches, claws, talons, nails. Incommunicableness, incommunicability. (*Phrase*). A bird in the hand. (*Verbs*). To retain, keep, keep in hand, detain, hold fast, grasp, clutch, clench, cinch, gripe, grip, hug, withhold, keep back. (*Adjectives*). Retaining, etc., retentive, tenacious. Unforfeited, undeprived, undisposed, uncommunicated, incommunicable.	**782. RELINQUISHMENT** (*Substantives*), cession, abandonment (624), renunciation, surrender, rendition, riddance (776), resignation (758). (*Verbs*). To relinquish, give up, let go, lay aside, resign, forgo, waive, renounce, surrender, part with, get rid of, lay down, abandon, cede, yield, dispose of, divest oneself of, spare, give away, throw away, cast away, fling away, fling up, chuck up, let slip, make away with, make way for. (*Phrase*). To lay on the shelf. (*Adjectives*). Relinquished, etc., left, residuary (40), unculled.

2°. *Transfer of Property*

783. TRANSFER (*Substantives*), interchange, exchange, transmission, barter (794), abalienation, demise; metastasis.

(*Verbs*). To transfer, consign, make over, pass, transmit, interchange, exchange (148).

To change hands, change from one to another, alienate, devolve.

To dispossess, abalienate, disinherit.

(*Adjective*). Alienable.

784. GIVING (*Substantives*), bestowal, donation, accordance to, presentation, oblation, presentment, delivery, granting.	**785. RECEIVING** (*Substantives*), reception, acceptance, admission. A recipient, stipendiary, beneficiary, almsman.

Cession, concession, consignment, dispensation, benefaction, charity, almsgiving.

Gift, donation, bonus, boon, present, testimonial, presentation, fairing, benefaction, grant, offering, contribution, subscription, whip-round, donative, meed, tribute, gratuity, tip, *douceur*, *pourboire*, backsheesh, bribe, free gift, favour, bounty, largess, subsidy, allowance, endowment, charity, alms, dole, peace-offering, *see* Payment (807).

Bequest, legacy, demise, dotation.

(*Phrase*). *Panem et circenses.*

(*Verbs*). To give, bestow, accord, confer, grant, concede, present, give away, deliver, deliver over, make over, consign, entrust, hand, tip, render, impart, hand over, part with, yield, dispose of, put into the hands of, vest in, assign, put in possession, settle upon, endow, subsidise.

To bequeath, leave, demise, devise.

To give out, dispense, deal, deal out, dole out, mete out.

To contribute, subscribe, put up a purse, send round the hat, pay (807), spend (809).

To furnish, supply, administer, afford, spare, accommodate with, indulge with.

To bribe, suborn, grease the palm.

(*Adjectives*). Giving, etc., given, etc., charitable, eleemosynary, tributary.

(*Phrase*). *Bis dat qui cito dat.*

(*Verbs*). To receive, take (789), accept, admit, catch, catch at, jump at, take in.

(*Adjectives*). Receiving, etc., recipient.

Not given, unbestowed.

———

786. APPORTIONMENT (*Substantives*), distribution, allotment, partition, division, deal, share-out.

Dividend, portion, contingent, share, allotment, lot, measure, dole, pittance, quantum, ration, quota, modicum, allowance, appropriation.

(*Verbs*). To apportion, divide, distribute, billet, allot, cast, share, mete, parcel out, serve out, deal, partition, appropriate, assign.

(*Adjective*). Apportioning, etc.

787. LENDING (*Substantives*), loan, advance, mortgage, accommodation, pawn, pignoration, hypothecation, investment; pawnshop, *mont de piété*.

Lender, pawnbroker, uncle.

(*Verbs*). To lend, advance, mortgage, invest, pawn, impawn, hypothecate, impignorate, place

788. BORROWING (*Substantives*), pledging, replevin, borrowed plumes, plagiarism, plagiary.

(*Verbs*). To borrow, raise money, raise the wind; to plagiarise.

(*Adjectives*). Borrowing, etc., borrowed, second-hand.

or put out to interest, accommodate with.

(*Adjectives*). Lending, etc., unborrowed.

(*Adverb*). In advance.

(*Phrases*). To borrow of Peter to pay Paul; to run into debt; to put up the spout.

---

789. TAKING (*Substantives*), appropriation, prehension, capture, seizure, abduction, ablation, catching, seizing, etc., kidnapping, round-up.

Abstraction, subtraction, deduction, subduction.

Dispossession, deprivation, deprival, bereavement, divestment, sequestration, confiscation, disendowment.

Resumption, reprise, reprisal. Clutch, swoop, wrench.

(*Verbs*). To take, capture, lay one's hands on; lay, take, or get hold of; to help oneself to; to possess oneself of, take possession of, make sure of, make free with.

790. RESTITUTION (*Substantives*), return, reddition, rendition, restoration, rehabilitation, reinvestment, reparation, atonement.

Redemption, recovery, recuperation, release, replevin.

(*Verbs*). To return, restore, give back, bring back, render, refund, reimburse, rehabilitate, repair, reinvest.

To let go, disgorge, regorge, regurgitate.

(*Adjective*). Restoring, etc., reparative.

(*Phrase*). *Suum cuique.*

To appropriate, impropriate, pocket, put into one's pocket, bag, sack; to ease one of.

To pick up, gather, collect, round up, net, absorb (296), reap, glean, crop, get in the harvest, intercept, tap.

To take away, carry away, carry off, bear off, hurry off with, abduct, kidnap, crimp.

To lay violent hands on, fasten upon, pounce upon, catch, seize, snatch, nip up, whip up, jump at, snap at, hook, claw, clinch, grasp, gripe, grip, grab, clutch, wring, wrest, wrench, pluck, tear away, catch, nab, capture, collar, throttle.

To take from, deduct, subduct (38), subtract, curtail, retrench, abridge of, dispossess, expropriate, take away from, abstract, deprive of, bereave, divest, disendow, despoil, strip, fleece, levy, distrain, confiscate, sequester, sequestrate, oust, extort, usurp, suck, squeeze, drain, bleed, milk, gut, dry, exhaust.

(*Phrases*). To suck like a leech; to be given an inch and take a mile; to sweep the board.

(*Adjectives*). Taking, etc., privative, prehensile, predatory, rapacious, raptorial, predial, ravenous.

---

791. STEALING (*Substantives*), theft, thieving, thievery, appropriation, plagiarism, depredation, pilfering, rape, larceny, robbery, shop-lifting, burglary, house-breaking, abaction (of cattle), kidnapping.

Spoliation, plunder, pillage, sack, rapine, brigandage, foray, dragonnade, marauding.

Peculation, embezzlement, swindling (545), blackmail, *chantage*, smuggling; thievishness, rapacity, kleptomania; the den of Cacus, Alsatia.

Licence to plunder, letters of marque.

(*Verbs*). To steal, rob, abstract, appropriate, filch, pilfer, purloin, nab, nim, prig, grab, bag, lift, pick, pinch.

To convey away, carry off, make off with, run or walk off with, abduct, kidnap, crimp, seize, lay violent hands on, etc. (789), **abact** (of cattle), shanghai.

To cabbage, crib, sponge, swindle (545), peculate, embezzle, poach, run, smuggle.

To plunder, pillage, rifle, sack, ransack, burgle, spoil, spoliate, despoil, hold up, strip, fleece, gut, loot, forage, levy blackmail, pickeer, pirate, plagiarise.

(*Phrases*). To live by one's wits; to rob Peter to pay Paul; to set a thief to catch a thief.

(*Adjectives*). Stealing, etc., thievish, light-fingered, larcenous, stolen, furtive, etc.

792. THIEF (*Substantives*), robber, spoiler, pickpocket, cutpurse, depredator, footpad, highwayman, burglar, house-breaker, shop-lifter; swell mob; the light-fingered gentry; kleptomaniac.

Swindler, smuggler, bootlegger, cracksman, sharper, blackleg, shark, trickster, harpy, *chevalier d'industrie*, peculator, plagiarist, blackmailer, long firm; reciever., fence.

Brigand, freebooter, bandit, pirate, viking, corsair, buccaneer, thug, dacoit, picaroon, moss-trooper, rapparee, marauder, filibuster, bushranger; Autolycus, Turpin, Macheath, Bill Sikes.

(*Phrase*). *Homo triarum literarum.*

793. BOOTY (*Substantives*), spoil, plunder, swag, loot, prey, pickings, grab, forage, blackmail, graft, prize

3°. *Interchange of Property*

794. BARTER (*Substantives*), exchange, truck, interchange, commutation.

Traffic, trade, commerce, dealing, business, custom, negotiation, jobbing, agiotage, bargain, deal, commercial enterprise, speculation, brokery.

(*Phrases*). A Roland for an Oliver; a *quid pro quo*; robbing Peter to pay Paul; a blind bargain; a pig in a poke; taking for better, for worse.

(*Verbs*). To barter, exchange, truck, interchange, commute, scorse, traffic, trade, speculate, transact or do business with, deal with, have dealings with; open, or keep an account with; to carry on a trade; to rig the market.

To bargain; **drive, make, or strike a bargain**; negotiate, bid for, haggle (or higgle), chaffer, dicker, stickle, cheapen, compound for, beat down, outbid, outbargain, come to terms, do a deal, quote, underquote.

(*Phrase*). To give a sprat to catch a herring.

(*Adjectives*). Commercial, mercantile, interchangeable, negotiable; wholesale, retail.

795. PURCHASE (*Substantives*), emption, buying, purchasing, shopping; pre-emption, bribery, co-emption.

A buyer, purchaser, customer, emptor.

(*Verbs*). To buy, purchase, procure, hire, rent, farm, pay, fee, repurchase, keep in one's pay; pre-empt, bribe, suborn, square, buy over.

(*Adjective*). Purchased, etc.

(*Phrase*). *Caveat emptor.*

796. SALE (*Substantives*), vent, disposal, custom.

Auction, Dutch auction, roup, Lease, mortgage.

Vendibility, salability.

Dead stock.

A vendor, seller, etc. (797).

To sell, vend, dispose of, retail, dispense, auction, auctioneer, hawk, peddle, undersell.

(*Phrases*). Put up to sale or auction; bring to the hammer.

To let, sublet, lease, set, mortgage.

(*Adjectives*). Vendible, salable; unpurchased, unbought, on one's hands, unsalable.

797. MERCHANT (*Substantives*), trader, dealer, tradesman, buyer and seller, vendor, monger, shopkeeper, shopman, salesman, saleswoman, changer.

Retailer, chapman, hawker, huckster, regrater, higgler, pedlar, cadger, sutler, Autolycus, middleman, coster, costermonger; auctioneer, broker, money-broker, bill-broker, jobber, factor, go-between, money-lender.

House, firm, concern, partnership, company, guild, syndicate.

Buyer, customer, purchaser.

798. MERCHANDISE (*Substantives*), ware, mercery, commodity, effects, goods, article, stock, stock-in-trade, cargo, produce, freight, lading, ship-load, staple commodity.

799. MART (*Substantives*), market, change, exchange, market-place, fair, hall, staple, bazaar, guild-hall, tollbooth (or tolbooth), custom-house.

Office, shop, counting-house, bureau, counter, stall, chambers.

Warehouse, depôt, store (636), entrepôt, emporium.

4°. *Monetary Relations*

800. MONEY (*Substantives*), funds, treasure, capital, stock, proceeds, assets, cash, bullion, ingot, nugget; sum, amount, balance.

Currency, circulating medium, specie, coin, hard cash; pounds, shillings and pence.

Ready, rhino, blunt, dust, mopus, tin, ducats, the needful.

Gold, silver, copper, nickel, *rouleau*, dollar, etc.

Currency, finance; gold standard, monometallism, bimetallism.

Pocket-money, change, small coin; doit, farthing, penny, shilling, etc., rap, mite, *sou*.

Sum, amount, balance.

Paper-money, note, bank-note, Treasury note, greenback, note of hand, promissory note, I O U.

Bill, draught (or draft), check (or cheque), order, remittance, postal order, money order, warrant, coupon, debenture, bill of exchange, exchequer bill, Treasury bill, assignat.

A drawer, a drawee.

False money, base coin, flash note, kite.

Science of coins, Numismatics.

(*Phrase*). The sinews of war.

(*Verbs*). To draw, draw upon, endorse.

(*Adjectives*). Monetary, pecuniary, fiscal, financial, sumptuary; monometallic, bimetallic; numismatical.

(*Phrases*). To touch the pocket; *argumentum ad crumenam*.

801. TREASURER (*Substantives*), purse-bearer, purser, questor, bursar, banker, moneyer, paymaster, cashier, teller, cash-keeper.

Chancellor of the exchequer, minister of finance, financier.

802. TREASURY (*Substantives*), bank, savings-bank, exchequer, coffer, chest, stocks, money-box, money-bag, strong-box, strong-room, safe, bursary, stronghold, till, purse, *porte-monnaie*, purse-strings, pocket, breeches-pocket, fisc.

803. WEALTH (*Substantives*), fortune, riches, opulence, affluence, independence, solvency, competence, easy circumstances, command of money, El Dorado, plutocracy.

(*Phrases*). A well-lined purse; the purse of Fortunatus; a mint or pot of money; a pile; a plum.

Means, provision, substance, revenue, income, alimony, livelihood, subsistence, loaves and fishes, pelf, mammon, lucre, dower (810), pension, superannuation, annuity, unearned increment, pin-money.

A rich man, capitalist, plutocrat, financier, money-bags, millionaire, a Nabob, Dives, Crœsus, Midas; rentier.

(*Verbs*). To be rich, etc., to afford.

804. POVERTY (*Substantives*), indigence, penury, pauperism, destitution, want, need, lack, necessity, privation, distress, an empty purse; bad, reduced, or straitened circumstances; narrow means, straits, insolvency, beggary, mendicancy, mendicity.

(*Phrases*). *Res angusta domi*; the wolf at the door.

A poor man, pauper, mendicant, beggar, tramp, starveling; the proletariat; *un pauvre diable*; *qui n'a pas le sou*.

Poorhouse, workhouse.

(*Verbs*). To be poor, etc., to want, lack, starve.

(*Phrases*). To live from hand to mouth; come upon the parish; not to have a penny; *cantabit vacuus coram latrone viator*.

To render poor, etc., to reduce.

(Phrases). To roll in riches; to wallow in wealth; to hold one's head above water.

To enrich, fill one's coffers, etc.; to capitalise.

(Adjectives). Wealthy, rich, affluent, opulent, flush, solvent (734), moneyed, plutocratic.

(Phrases). Made of money; rich as Crœsus; rich as a Jew; rolling in riches, etc.

One's ship come home.

---

to impoverish, reduce to poverty, depauperate, ruin; to pauperise.

(Adjectives). Poor, indigent, penniless, moneyless, short of money, out of money, out of cash, out of pocket, needy, destitute, necessitous, seedy, distressed, hard-up, in need, in want, poverty-stricken, badly off, in distress, pinched, dowerless, fortuneless, reduced, insolvent *(see* 806), bereft, bereaved, fleeced, stripped, stony-broke, stony.

(Phrases). Unable to make both ends meet; out at elbows; under hatches; not having a penny; not worth a *sou*; poor as a rat; poor as Job; poor as a church mouse; down or out at heels; on one's uppers.

(Adverb). In forma pauperis.

805. Credit *(Substantives),* trust, tick, score, account.

Letter of credit, duplicate.

A creditor, lessor, mortgagee, debenture-holder; a dun, usurer, gombeen-man, Shylock.

(Verbs). To keep an account with, to credit, accredit.

(Adjective). Crediting.

(Adverbs). On credit, on tick, on account, to pay, unpaid for.

---

806. Debt *(Substantives),* obligation, liability, debit, indebtment, arrears, deficit, default, insolvency.

Interest, usance, usury.

Floating debt, bad debt, floating capital, debentures; deferred payment, hire system.

A debtor, debitor, lessee, mortgagor; a defaulter (808).

(Verbs). To be in debt, to owe, to answer for, to incur a debt, *see* Borrow (788).

(Phrases). To run up a hill; to go on tick.

(Adjectives). In debt, indebted, owing, due, unpaid, outstanding, in arrear, being minus, liable, answerable for, insolvent.

Unrequited, unrewarded.

807. Payment *(Substantives),* discharge, quittance, acquittance, settlement, clearance, liquidation, satisfaction, remittance, reckoning, arrangement, composition, acknowledgment, release.

Repayment, reimbursement, retribution, reward, *see* 973.

(Phrase). A quid pro quo.

Bill, cheque, cash, ready money, etc. (800).

(Verbs). To pay, defray, dis-

---

808. Non-payment *(Substantives),* default, defalcation, protest.

Insolvency, bankruptcy, repudiation, application of the sponge.

Waste papers, dishonoured bills, etc.

A defaulter, a bankrupt, an insolvent debtor, a lame duck.

(Verbs). Not to pay, to fail, to break, to become insolvent or bankrupt, to default.

charge, settle, quit, acquit one-self of, account or reckon with, remit, clear, liquidate, release.

(*Phrases*). To fork out money; to pay on the nail; to honour a bill; to strike a balance; to settle, balance, or square accounts with; to be even with; to wipe off old scores; to satisfy all demands; to pay in full of all demands; to grease the palm.

To repay, refund, retribute, reimburse.

(*Adjectives*). Paying, etc., paid, owing nothing, out of debt.

809. EXPENDITURE (*Substantives*), money going out; outgoings, expenses, disbursement, outlay.

Money paid: Pay, payment, fee, hire, wages, perquisites, vails, allowance, stipend, salary, screw, appointments, subsidy, batta, bat-money, shot, scot.

Remuneration, recompense, reward (*see* 973), drink-money, *pourboire*, largess, honorarium, refresher, bribe, *douceur*, hush-money, extras, commission.

Pay in advance: Earnest, handsel, deposit, prepayment, entrance-fee, entrance.

Contribution, donation, sub-scription, deposit, contingent, dole, quota.

Investment, purchase, etc. (*see* 795), alms (*see* 748).

(*Verbs*). To expend, spend, pay, disburse, lay out, lay or pay down, to cash, to come down with, to fork out, bleed, make up a sum, to invest, sink money, prepay, to tip.

(*Phrases*). To unloose the purse-strings; fork out the money; to pay the piper; to pay through the nose.

(*Adjectives*). Expending, etc., expended, etc., sumptuary.

To protest, dishonour, re-pudiate, nullify.

(*Phrases*). To apply the sponge; to pay over the left shoulder.

(*Adjectives*). Not paying, in debt, insolvent, bankrupt, ga-zetted, ruined.

(*Phrases*). Being *minus*, or worse than nothing; deep in debt; plunged, or over head and ears in debt; in the gazette; in Queer Street.

---

810. RECEIPT (*Substantives*), money coming in, incomings.

Income, revenue, rent, rental, rent-roll, rentage, return, pro-ceeds, premium, bonus, gate-money, royalty.

Pension, annuity, jointure, dower, dowry, *dot*, alimony.

Emoluments, perquisites, re-compense, etc. (*see* 809), sinecure.

(*Verbs*). To receive, pocket, bag, etc.; *see* Take (785 and 789), to draw from, derive from.

To bring in, yield, return, afford, pay, accrue.

(*Phrases*). To get what will make the pot boil; keep the wolf from the door; bring grist to the mill.

(*Adjectives*). Receiving, etc., received, etc.

Gainful, profitable, remunera-tive, lucrative, advantageous, etc. (775).

---

811. ACCOUNTS (*Substantives*), money matters, bills, score: balance-sheet, books, account-books, ledger, debtor and creditor accounts, cash-book, cash account, running account.

Book-keeping, audit, double entry, reckoning.

An accountant, auditor, actuary, book-keeper.

(*Verbs*). To keep accounts, enter, post, credit, debit, carry over; balance, make up accounts, take stock, audit.

To falsify, garble, cook, or doctor accounts.

812. PRICE (*Substantives*), cost, expense, charge, demand, run upon, damage, fare.

Dues, duty, toll, tax, supertax, rate, cess, levy, gabelle, octroi, assessment, benevolence, custom, exactment, ransom, salvage, excise, tariff, brokerage.

Bill, account, score, reckoning.

Worth, rate, value, valuation, evaluation, appraisement, market price; money's worth, pennyworth; price-current, price list.

(*Verbs*). To set or fix a price, appraise, assess, value, evaluate, price, charge, demand, ask, require, exact.

(*Phrases*). To run up a bill; to amount to.

To fetch, sell for, cost, bring in, yield, make, change hands for, go for, realise, run into, stand one in; afford.

(*Adjectives*). Priced, charged, etc., to the tune of, *ad valorem*.

(*Phrases*). No penny, no paternoster; *point d'argent, point de Suisse*; no longer pipe, no longer dance.

813. DISCOUNT (*Substantives*), abatement, reduction, deduction, allowance, drawback, poundage, *agio*, percentage, rebate, set-off, salvage.

(*Verbs*). To discount, bate, abate, rebate, reduce, take off, allow, give, discount, tax.

(*Adjective*). Discounting, etc.

(*Adverb*). At a discount.

---

814. DEARNESS (*Substantives*), costliness, high price, expensiveness, rise in price, overcharge, surcharge, extravagance, exorbitance.

(*Verbs*). To be dear, etc., to cost much, to come expensive; to overcharge, surcharge, fleece (791).

To pay too much, to pay through the nose.

(*Adjectives*). Dear, high, high-priced, expensive, costly, dear-bought, precious, unreasonable, extravagant, exorbitant, steep, stiff.

(*Adverbs*). Dear, at great cost, *à grands frais*.

815. CHEAPNESS (*Substantives*), low price, bargain, absence of charge, gratuity, etc., peppercorn rent, a dead head.

(*Verbs*). To be cheap, etc., to cost little, to come down or fall in price, to cut prices.

(*Phrase*). To have one's money's worth.

(*Adjectives*). Cheap, low, moderate, reasonable, inexpensive, unexpensive, low-priced, worth the money, half-price.

Gratuitous, gratis, free, for nothing, given away, free of cost, without charge, not charged, untaxed, scot-free, shot-free, expenseless, free of expense, free of all demands, honorary.

(*Phrases*). Cheap as dirt; dirt-cheap; dog-cheap; for a mere song; a drug in the market; at cost price; at a reduction.

816. LIBERALITY (*Substantives*), generosity (942), bounty, munificence, bounteousness, bountifulness, charity, hospitality.

(*Verbs*). To be liberal, etc., spend freely.

(*Phrases*). To loosen one's purse - strings; to give *carte blanche*; to bleed freely.

(*Adjectives*). Liberal, free, generous, charitable, hospitable, bountiful, bounteous, handsome, ungrudging, free-handed, open-handed, open - hearted, free-hearted, munificent, princely. Overpaid.

818. PRODIGALITY (*Substantives*), unthriftiness, thriftlessness, waste, profusion, profuseness, extravagance, dissipation, squandering, malversation.

A prodigal, spendthrift, squanderer, waster.

(*Verbs*). To be prodigal, etc., to squander, lavish, waste, dissipate, exhaust, run through, spill, misspend, throw away money, drain.

(*Phrases*). To burn the candle at both ends; to make ducks and drakes of one's money; *manger son blé en herbe*; to outrun the constable; to fool away, potter, muddle away, fritter away, etc., one's money; to pour water into a sieve; to go the pace.

(*Adjectives*). Prodigal, profuse, thriftless, unthrifty, wasteful, extravagant, lavish, dissipated.

(*Phrases*). Penny - wise and pound-foolish; money burning in one's pocket.

817. ECONOMY (*Substantives*), frugality, thrift, thriftiness, care, husbandry, good housewifery, retrenchment; savings; a save-all.

(*Phrase*). Cheese-parings and candle-ends.

(*Verbs*). To be economical, etc., to save, economise, meet one's expenses, retrench; to lay by, put by, save up, invest, bank, hoard, accumulate.

(*Phrases*). To cut one's coat according to one's cloth; to make both ends meet; to provide for a rainy day.

(*Adjectives*). *Economical*, frugal, thrifty, canny, careful, saving, chary, spare, sparing, cheese-paring.

(*Phrases*). *Ne quid nimis*; penny-wise.

819. PARSIMONY (*Substantives*), stint, stinginess, niggardliness, cheese-paring, illiberality, closeness, penuriousness, avarice, tenacity, covetousness, greediness, avidity, rapacity, venality, mercenariness, cupidity.

(*Phrase*). *Auri sacra fames*.

A miser, niggard, churl, screw, skin-flint, money-grubber, codger, muck-worm, hunks, curmudgeon, harpy, Harpagon, Jew.

(*Verbs*). To be parsimonious, etc., to grudge, stint, pinch, screw.

(*Phrases*). To skin a flint; to drive a hard bargain; to tighten one's purse-strings.

(*Adjectives*). Parsimonious, stingy, miserly, mean, shabby, near, niggardly, cheese-paring, close, close-fisted, close-handed, chary, illiberal, ungenerous, churlish, hide-bound, sordid, mercenary, venal, covetous, avaricious, greedy, griping, pinching, rapacious.

(*Phrases*). Having an itching palm; with a sparing hand.

CLASS VI

WORDS RELATING TO THE SENTIENT AND MORAL POWERS

SECTION I.—AFFECTIONS IN GENERAL

820. AFFECTIONS (*Substantives*), character, qualities, disposition, nature, spirit, temper, temperament; cast, or frame of mind, or soul; turn, bent, idiosyncrasy, bias, turn of mind, predisposition, proneness, proclivity, vein, humour, grain, mettle.

Soul, heart, breast, bosom, the inner man, inmost heart, heart's core, heart-strings, heart's-blood, heart of hearts, *penetralia mentis; ab imo pectore.*

Passion, pervading spirit, ruling passion, master-passion.

(*Phrases*). Flow of soul; fullness of the heart; hey-day in the blood; flesh and blood.

(*Verbs*). To have or possess affections, etc.; be of a character, etc.; to breathe.

(*Adjectives*). Affected, characterised, formed, moulded, cast, tempered, attempered, framed, disposed, predisposed, prone, inclined, having a bias, etc., inbred, inborn, engrained.

821. FEELING (*Substantives*), endurance, experience, suffering, tolerance, sufferance, patience, content (831).

Non-endurance, *see* 825.

Impression, sensation, affection, response, emotion, pathos, warmth, glow, fervour, fervency, heartiness, effusiveness, effusion, gush, cordiality, ardour, exuberance, zeal, eagerness, passion, *empressement, élan*, enthusiasm, verve, inspiration.

(*Phrase*). The fullness of the heart.

Blush, suffusion, flush, hectic, tingling, thrill, turn, shock, agitation (315), heaving, flutter, flurry, fluster, twitter, tremor, throb, throbbing, panting, palpitation, trepidation, perturbation, ruffle, hurry of spirits, the heart swelling, throbbing, thumping, pulsating, melting, bursting, etc.

Passion, *see* 825; transport, rapture, ecstasy, ravishment, *see* 827.

(*Verbs*). To feel, receive an impression, etc.; to be impressed with, affected with, moved with, touched with, keen on, etc.

To bear, bear with, suffer, endure, brook, tolerate, **stomach**, stand, experience, taste, meet with, go through, put up with, prove; to harbour, cherish, support, abide, undergo.

(*Phrase*). To swallow the pill; to pocket the affront (826).

To blush, tingle, twitter, throb, heave, pant, palpitate, go pit-a-pat, agitate, thrill, tremble, shake, quiver, wince, simmer, burble.

To swell, glow, warm, flush, catch the flame, catch the infection, respond, enthuse.

To possess, pervade, penetrate, imbue, absorb, etc., the soul.

(*Phrase*). To come home to one's feelings, or bosom.

(*Adjectives*). Feeling, suffering, enduring, etc.

Impressed, moved, touched, affected with, etc., penetrated, *pétri*.

Warm, quick, lively, smart, strong, sharp, keen, acute, cutting, piercing, pungent, racy, piquant, poignant.

Deep, profound, indelible, ineffaceable, impressive, effective, deep-felt, home-felt, heart-felt, warm-hearted, hearty, cordial, swelling, thrilling, soul-stirring, deep-mouthed, heart-expanding, electric.

Earnest, hearty, eager, exuberant, gushing, effusive, breathless, glowing, fervent, fervid, ardent, soulful, burning, red-hot, fiery, flaming, boiling, boiling over, zealous, pervading, penetrating, absorbing, over head and ears; the heart being big, full, swelling, overflowing, bursting.

Wrought up, excited, passionate, enthusiastic, *see* 825.

(*Phrases*). From the bottom of one's heart; *de profundis*; heart and soul.

822. SENSIBILITY (*Substantives*), impressibility, sensibleness, sensitiveness, responsiveness, affectibility, susceptibleness, susceptibility, susceptivity, excitability, mobility, vivacity, vivaciousness, tenderness, softness; intolerance.

Physical sensibility, *see* 375.

(*Verbs*). To be sensible, etc., shrink, etc., to be without skin.

(*Phrases*). "To die of a rose in aromatic pain"; to feel where the shoe pinches; to take it hard; to take to heart.

(*Adjectives*). Sensible, sensitive, impressible, impressionable, susceptive, susceptible, responsive, excitable, mobile, thin-skinned, tremblingly alive, vivacious, lively, mettlesome, high-strung, intense, emotional, tender,

823. INSENSIBILITY (*Substantives*), inertness, insensitivity, impassibility, impassibleness, apathy, phlegm, dullness, hebetude, coolness, coldness, supineness, stoicism, insouciance, nonchalance, indifference, lukewarmness, frigidity, cold blood, sang-froid, dry eyes, cold heart, deadness, torpor, torpidity, ataraxia, pococurantism.

Lethargy, coma, trance, stupor, stupefaction, paralysis, palsy, hebetation, anæsthesia (381), stock and stone, neutrality.

Physical insensibility, *see* 376.

(*Verbs*). To disregard, be insensible, not to be affected by, not to mind, to vegetate, *laisser aller*, not to care; to take it easy.

To render insensible, (376), numb, benumb, paralyse, deaden,

soft, sentimental, romantic, enthusiastic, neurotic.

(*Adverbs*). Sensibly, etc., to the quick.

———

render callous, sear, inure, harden, steel, case-harden, stun, daze, stupefy, brutalise, hebetate.

(*Adjectives*). Insensible, unconscious, impassive, unsusceptible, insusceptible, impassible, unimpressionable, unresponsive, unfeeling, dead to, passionless, spiritless, soulless, apathetic, phlegmatic, callous, thick-skinned, pachydermatous, obtuse, proof against, case-hardened, inured, steeled against, stoical, dull, frigid, cold, cold-blooded, cold-hearted, flat, maudlin, sloppy, inert, bovine, supine, sluggish, torpid, languid, tame, tepid, numb, numbed, sleepy, yawning, comatose, anæsthetic.

Indifferent, insouciant, lukewarm, careless, mindless, regardless, disregarding, unconcerned, uninterested, *pococurante*; taking no interest in.

Unfelt, unaffected, unruffled, unimpressed, unmoved, unperturbed, uninspired, untouched, etc.; with withers unwrung, unshocked, with dry eyes, platonic, imperturbable, vegetative, automatic.

(*Adverbs*). Insensibly, etc., *æquo animo*.

(*Phrases*). No matter; never mind; *n'importe*; it matters not; it does not signify; it is of no consequence or importance (643); it cannot be helped; nothing coming amiss; being all the same, or all one to; what's the odds?

824. EXCITATION (*Substantives*) of feeling, excitement, galvanism, stimulation, provocation, calling forth, infection, animation, agitation, perturbation, subjugation, fascination, intoxication, enravishment, unction; a scene, a sensation, a tableau, a shocker.

Repression of feeling, *see* 826.

(*Verbs*). To excite, affect, touch, move, stir, wake, awaken, raise, raise up, evoke, call up, summon up, rake up, rip up.

To impress, strike, quicken, swell, work upon.

To warm, kindle, stimulate, whet, animate, hearten, inspire, impassion, inspirit, spirit, provoke, irritate, sting, rouse, work up, hurry on, ginger up, commove.

To agitate, ruffle, flutter, fluster, flush, shake, thrill, penetrate, pierce, cut; to work oneself up, to simmer, bubble, burble.

To soften, subdue, overcome, master, overpower, overwhelm, bring under.

To shock, stagger, stun, astound, electrify, galvanise, give one a shock, petrify.

To madden, intoxicate, fascinate, transport, ravish, enrapture, enravish, entrance.

(*Phrases*). To come home to one's feelings; to make a sensation; to prey on the mind; to give one a turn; to cut to the quick; to go through one; to strike one all of a heap; to make one's blood boil; to lash to a fury; to make one sit up.

(*Adjectives*). Excited, affected, etc. (*see* 825), wrought up, worked up, strung up, *bouleversé*, lost, *éperdu*, wild, haggard, feverish, febrile.

Exciting, etc., impressive, pathetic, sensational, dramatic, warm, glowing, fervid, swelling.

(*Phrases*). Being all of a twitter; all of a flutter; ready to sink; the head being turned.

825. Excess of sensitiveness.

EXCITABILITY (*Substantives*), intolerance, impatience, wincing, disquiet, disquietude, restlessness, fidgets, fidgetiness, fuss, hurry, agitation, flurry, fluster, flutter, irritability (901), hypersensitiveness, hyperæsthesia.

(*Phrase*). *Noli me tangere.*

Passion, excitement, vehemence, impetuosity, flush, heat, fever, fire, flame, fume, wildness, turbulence, boisterousness, tumult, effervescence, ebullition, boiling, boiling over, whiff, gust, storm, tempest, outbreak, outburst, burst, fit, paroxysm, the blood boiling.

Fierceness, rage, fury, *furor*, furore, hysteria, raving, delirium, frenzy, intoxication, fascination, infection, infatuation, fanaticism, Quixotism, *la tête montée*.

(*Verbs*). To be intolerant, etc., not to bear, to bear ill, wince, chafe, fidget, fuss, not to be able to bear, stand, tolerate, etc.

To break out, fly out, burst out, explode, run riot, boil, boil over, fly off, flare up, fire, take fire, fume, rage, rampage, rave, run mad, run amuck.

(*Phrases*). To fly off at a tangent; to be out of all patience; *faire le diable à quatre*; to get the wind up; to make a scene.

(*Adjectives*). Excitable, etc., excited, etc.

Intolerant, impatient, unquiet, restless, restive, fidgety, irritable, mettlesome, chafing, wincing, etc.

826. Absence of excitability.

INEXCITABILITY (*Substantives*), hebetude, tolerance, patience.

Coolness, composure, calmness, imperturbability, sang-froid, collectedness, tranquillity, quiet, quietude, quietness, sedateness, soberness, composure, staidness, gravity, placidity, sobriety, philosophy, stoicism, demureness, meekness, gentleness, mildness.

Submission, resignation, sufferance, endurance, longanimity, long-sufferance, forbearance, fortitude, equanimity.

Repression, restraint, etc. (174), hebetation, tranquillisation.

(*Phrases*). Patience of Job; Spartan endurance; a sober-sides.

(*Verbs*). To be composed, etc., to bear, to bear well, tolerate, put up with, bear with, stand, bide, abide, aby, take easily, rub on, rub along, make the best of, acquiesce, submit, yield, bow to, resign oneself, suffer, endure, support, go through, reconcile oneself to, bend under; subside, calm down.

To brook, digest, eat, swallow, pocket, stomach, brave, make light of.

(*Phrases*). To pocket the affront; to swallow the pill; to eat the leek; to shrug the shoulders; *æquam servare mentem.*

To be borne, endured, etc., to go down.

To allay, compose, calm, still, lull, pacify, placate, quiet, tranquillise, hush, smooth, appease,

Vehement, boisterous, impetuous, demonstrative, fierce, fiery, flaming, boiling, ebullient, over-zealous, passionate, impassioned, enthusiastic, rampant, mercurial, high-strung, high-wrought, overwrought, overstrung, hysterical, hot-headed, hurried, turbulent, furious, fuming, boiling, raging, raving, frantic, phrenetic, rampageous, wild, heady, delirious, intoxicated, demoniacal; hypersensitive.

Overpowering, overwhelming, uncontrolled, stanchless, irrepressible, ungovernable, uncontrollable.

(*Phrases*). More than flesh and blood can stand; stung to the quick.

(*Interjections*). Pish! pshaw! botheration!

assuage, mitigate, soothe, soften, temper, chasten, alleviate, moderate, sober down, mollify, lenify, tame, blunt, obtund, dull, deaden, slacken, damp, repress, restrain, check, curb, bridle, rein in, smother, quell, lay, *see* 174, 823.

(*Phrase*). To set one's heart at rest or at ease.

(*Adjectives*). Inexcitable, unexcited, calm, cool, temperate, composed, collected, placid, quiet, tranquil, unstirred, undisturbed, unruffled, serene, demure, sedate, staid, sober, dispassionate, unimpassioned, passionless, platonic, philosophic, stoical, imperturbable, cold-blooded, insensible (823).

Meek, tolerant, patient, submissive, unoffended, unresenting, content, resigned, subdued, bearing with, long-suffering, gentle, mild, sober-minded, cool-headed.

(*Phrases*). Gentle or meek as a lamb; patient as Job; armed with patience; cool as a cucumber.

END OF VOL. I

EVERYMAN'S LIBRARY

By ERNEST RHYS

VICTOR HUGO said a Library was 'an act of faith,' and another writer spoke of one so beautiful, so perfect, so harmonious in all its parts, that he who made it was smitten with a passion. In that faith Everyman's Library was planned out originally on a large scale; and the idea was to make it conform as far as possible to a perfect scheme. However, perfection is a thing to be aimed at and not to be achieved in this difficult world; and since the first volumes appeared there have been many interruptions, chief among them Wars, during which even the City of Books feels the great commotion. But the series always gets back into its old stride.

One of the practical expedients in the original plan was to divide the volumes into separate sections, as Biography, Fiction, History, Belles-lettres, Poetry, Philosophy, Romance, and so forth; with a shelf for Young People. The largest slice of this huge provision of nearly a thousand volumes is, as a matter of course, given to the tyrranous demands of fiction. But in carrying out the scheme, publishers and editors contrived to keep in mind that books, like men and women, have their elective affinities. The present volume, for instance, will be found to have its companion books, both in the same class and not less significantly in other sections. With that idea too, novels like Walter Scott's *Ivanhoe* and *Fortunes of Nigel*, Lytton's *Harold*, and Dickens's *Tale of Two Cities*, have been used as pioneers of history and treated as a sort of holiday history books. For in our day history is tending to grow more documentary and less literary; and 'the historian who is a stylist,' as one of our contributors, the late Thomas Seccombe, said, 'will soon be regarded as a kind of Phoenix.'

As for history, Everyman's Library has been eclectic enough to choose its historians from every school in turn, including Gibbon, Grote, Finlay, Macaulay, Motley, and Prescott, while among earlier books may be found the Venerable Bede and the Anglo-Saxon Chronicle. On the classic shelf too, there is a Livy in an admirable translation by Canon Roberts, and Caesar, Tacitus, Thucydides, and Herodotus are not forgotten.

'You only, O Books,' said Richard de Bury, 'are liberal and independent; you give to all who ask.' The variety of authors old and new, the wisdom and the wit at the disposal of Everyman in his own Library, may even, at times, seem all but embarrassing. In the Essays, for instance, he may turn to Dick Steele in *The Spectator* and learn how Cleomira dances, when the elegance of her motion is unimaginable and 'her eyes are chastised with the simplicity and innocence of her thoughts.' Or he may take *A Century of Essays*, as a key to a whole roomful of the English Essayists, from Bacon to Addison, Elia to Augustine Birrell. These are the golden gossips of literature, the writers who learnt the delightful art of talking on paper. Or again, the reader who has the right spirit and looks on all literature as a great adventure may dive back into the classics, and in Plato's *Phaedrus* read how every soul is divided into three parts (like Caesar's Gaul). The poets next, and he may turn to the finest critic of Victorian times, Matthew Arnold, as their showman, and find in his essay on Maurice de Guerin a clue to the 'magical power of poetry,' as in Shakespeare, with his

daffodils
That come before the swallow dares, and take
The winds of March with beauty.

Hazlitt's *Table Talk* may help us again to discover the relationship of author to author, which is another form of the Friendship of Books. His incomparable essay, 'On Going a Journey,' is a capital prelude to Coleridge's *Biographia Literaria*; and so throughout the long labyrinth of the Library shelves one can follow the magic clue in prose or verse that leads to the hidden treasury. In that way a reader becomes his own critic and Doctor of Letters, and may turn to the Byron review in Macaulay's *Essays* as a prelude to the three volumes of Byron's own poems, remembering that the poet whom Europe loved more than England did was, as Macaulay said, 'the beginning, the middle and the end of all his own poetry.' This brings us to the provoking reflection that it is the obvious authors and the books most easy to reprint which have been the signal successes out of the many hundreds in the series, for Everyman is distinctly proverbial in his tastes. He likes best of all an old author who has worn well or a comparatively new author who has gained something like newspaper notoriety. In attempting to lead him on from the good books that are known to those that are less known, the publishers may have at times been even too adventurous. But the elect reader is or ought to be a party to this conspiracy of books and book-men. He can make it possible, by his help and his co-operative zest, to add still more authors, old and new. 'Infinite riches in a little room,' as the saying is, will be the reward of every citizen who helps year by year to build the City of Books. With such a belief in its possibilities the old Chief (J. M. Dent) threw himself into the enterprise. With the zeal of a true book-lover, he thought that books might be alive and productive as dragons' teeth, which, being 'sown up and down the land, might chance to spring up armed men.' That is a great idea, and it means a fighting campaign in which every new reader who buys a volume, counts as a recruit.

> To him all books which lay
> Their sure foundation in the heart of man . . .
> From Homer the great Thunderer, to the voice
> That roars along the bed of Jewish song . . .
> Shall speak as Powers for ever to be hallowed!